MEDITATIONS

ON THE

MYSTERIES OF OUR HOLY FAITH.

VOCABITVR QVI FECERIT, ET DOCVERIT HIC MAGNVS
Venerabilis P. Ludovicus de Ponte
Soc. Iesu Vallisoletanus, obijt magna cũ
opinione Sanctitatis Vallisoleti in Collegio
S. Ambrosij decimo sexto Februarij Anno M.DC.
XXIV. Ætatis suæ Septuagesimo.

MEDITATIONS

ON THE

MYSTERIES OF OUR HOLY FAITH:

TOGETHER WITH

A TREATISE ON MENTAL PRAYER.

BY THE VEN. FATHER LOUIS DE PONTE, S. J.

BEING THE

TRANSLATION FROM THE ORIGINAL SPANISH BY JOHN HEIGHAM.

REVISED AND CORRECTED.

TO WHICH ARE ADDED

THE REV. F. C. BORGO'S

MEDITATIONS ON THE SACRED HEART.

TRANSLATED FROM THE ITALIAN.

IN SIX VOLS.—VOL. III.

Permissu Superiorum.

SAINT LOUIS

LIBRI SANCTI PRESS

MMXXIII

NIHIL OBSTAT
GEORGE PORTER, *SJ.*

IMPRIMATUR
✠ HENRY EDWARD,
Archbishop of Westminster

*Originally published by
Richardson & Son, 1852*

SECOND PRINTING

ISBN 979-8-8689-8506-5

TABLE OF CONTENTS OF VOL. III.

CONTENTS.

III.—FOR PROFICIENTS IN THE ILLUMINATIVE WAY.

B.—THE INTRODUCTION AND FUNDAMENTAL MEDITATION.

ON THE TWO LIVES, ACTIVE AND CONTEMPLATIVE, FIGURED BY THE TWO SISTERS MARTHA AND MARY;—AND ON THE LIFE CALLED MIXED, OR COMPOSED OF BOTH, PRACTISED BY CHRIST OUR LORD IN THE TIME OF HIS PREACHING.

1. It is the common opinion of the holy Fathers and spiritual masters, that the spiritual life comprehends *two sorts* of works and exercises, which they call the *active* and *contemplative* life.

i. The *active* is a manner of life *dedicated* principally to *exterior works* for our own spiritual profit, or for the profit of our neighbours, exercising towards them the works of charity, and of mercy, either the corporal, with which beginners are to commence, or the spiritual, to teach and to preach, which are more proper to the perfect.

ii. The *contemplative* life is a manner of life *dedicated* principally to the *interior works* of the *knowledge* and *love* of Almighty God, ascending by the degrees and exercises of reading, meditation, prayer, and contemplation, of which we have treated at the beginning of this book, in the abridgment of mental prayer ; which brief abridgment comprehends them all.

2. These two ways are wont to go together, and wonderfully to aid one another with the intermixture of their

actions, whence results the life that is called *mixed*, composed of both, (1) comprising that which is more perfect, both in the one and in the other.

Hence it is that as Christ our Lord came into the world as a master and universal pattern of all perfection, in all sorts of lives, and for all sorts of persons, after, in the first thirty years of His age, He had exercised humility, obedience, and silence, with other exterior works of the active life, for our example and utility, He would, towards the latter end of this life, leave us an heroic model of the most excellent works of the *active* life, conjoining them with the life contemplative, by a most excellent perfection, more divine than human, as we shall see in the ensuing meditations of this third part.

3. For the foundation of which I suppose it necessary, first to declare the *functions* of these two lives, their *actions* and *properties*, in the same manner that our Lord Jesus Christ exercised them, grounding the whole upon the history which the evangelist St. Luke recounts of the two sisters ; Martha who harboured Jesus Christ in her house, and Mary who sat at His feet to hear His doctrine. According to the common opinion of the holy Fathers, in whose writings we find the most sublime and profitable lessons that can be wished, both of the one and of the other, these are lively figures of these two lives. Wherefore, to fulfil at once two commandments, and to accomplish my own intention, I am desirous to make a meditation upon it.

CHAP. I.   ON THE PRINCIPAL ACTIONS OF THE ACTIVE
LIFE.

The principal actions and functions of the active life, are mystically declared by the evangelist St. Luke, saying,

(1) S. Th. 3. p. q. lx. art. 51 ad. 2 et 3.

Jesus " entered into a certain town; and a certain woman named Martha received Him into her house."(2)   In which discourse, He touches upon three functions belonging to this manner of life.

I. The first is, *to prepare the house of our soul*, spiritually to harbour therein Christ Jesus our Lord : which we do by the following exercises.—i. By cleansing it from all sin with *the works of penance :* because the wisdom Incarnate " will not enter into a soul defiled, nor dwell in a body subject to sin." (3)—ii. By quieting and appeasing the storms and tumults of disordered passions, with the practice of *mortification :* because no guest takes delight long to lodge in a house which is full of noise and disturbance. —iii. In *adorning* it with *moral virtues*, in practising the works of piety with great fervour and perfection : because our Lord Jesus Christ delights to dwell in a house decked with this so precious tapestry, and is well pleased and contented to remain in it, uniting Himself with His host by the singular union of grace and charity.

2. The second function of this active life is, to *harbour* with us in our house, Christ our Lord, *in His poor members* as Martha harboured Him with His poor apostles, serving them, and exercising towards them, the seven corporal works of mercy, of whom our Lord Himself said, " As long as you did to one of these my least brethren, you did it to me." (4)   " I was a stranger " in them, and you have harboured me.   " I was hungry " and " thirsty " in them, and you have given me to eat and drink ; I therefore hold myself indebted to you, for all the good which you have done to my poor and needy members, for I and they are but one, and I am in them.

3. The third function which appertains to the active

<hr>

(2) Luc. x. 38.   (3) Sap. i. 4.   (4) Matt. xxv. 40.

life more sublime, and much more perfect when it is joined with the contemplative, (5) is, to *procure a lodging for Christ our Lord in the souls of our neighbours*, inciting them to harbour Him, and to dispose and render them fit for this reception : because Christ our Lord much delights to be lodged in them. This is performed by means of the spiritual works of mercy ;—such are, to instruct, counsel, correct, preach, confess, administer sacraments, and the like : wherein greatly shine the works of charity, love of our neighbour, and our burning zeal of their salvation. This was the office of the disciples whom Christ our Lord sent before Him into all the cities and places into which IIe Himself intended to enter ; that they might prepare Him a lodging in the souls of men.

Chap. II. On the actions and works of tiie contemplative life.

The principal actions of the contemplative life are declared by St. Luke the evangelist, where he says : Martha "had a sister called Mary, who sitting also at the Lord's feet, heard His word." (6) In which words IIe represents to us, what the principal office, and occupation of the contemplative life is, viz. : (7) to enjoy that divine guest, whom her sister, the active life, had lodged in the soul, and prostrate in spirit at His feet, to *hearken* to IIis *heavenly doctrine;* for as they are both sisters, and daughters of the self-same Father, Almighty God, engendered for one and the self-same end of our perfection, and of His glory; thence it is that the Holy Ghost begets first the active life, which is the elder sister, and lesser in perfection, and by the help of her, adorns the house in which He Himself will lodge, and the bed in which IIe

(5) S. Th. a. 3. q. clxxxii. art. 2, ad. 3.
(6) Luc. x. 38. (7) S. Th. 2. 2. q. clxxxii. a. 4.

proposes to repose.—Then He produces the contemplative life; because He desires that His host should hear His doctrine, and receive the sweet embrace of divine love. (8) The properties of this contemplative life, of which we shall presently treat, are these that follow.

1. The first is, to *approach and draw near to our Lord* Jesus Christ: because Martha, being busied in the work of the house, was the more remote from Jesus Christ: but Mary fixedly sat at His feet. Even so, those who give themselves to contemplation, approach much more near to God in spirit, and remain more assiduously in His presence by knowledge and love, to receive from Him the light and splendour of divine virtues, according to that which David says:—"Come ye to" God, "and be enlightened." (9)

2. The second property is, to *sit in quiet near to Christ;* for ceasing then from those exterior works, which are wont to disquiet us, we manage to recollect all our powers, and to appease all our imaginations, thoughts, and affections, and endeavour only to know and love Almighty God, and to hear what He speaks within our heart, conformably to that which He said by David:—" Be still and see that I am God," (10) and to that which David himself says, "I will hear what our Lord God will speak in me." (11)

3. The third property is, to *sit at the feet* of our Lord Jesus Christ, protesting as it were by this action various holy and devout *affections.*—i. Of *humility,* choosing the lowest place in the presence of this our Lord.—ii. Of *reverence,* acknowledging the greatness of the majesty of this master.—iii. Of *subjection,* offering to obey Him in all He shall command us.—iv. Of *imitation,* truly resolving to follow His steps :—and all this with love, humility, re-

(8) Cant. i.　(9) Ps. xxxiii. 6.　(10) Ps. xlv. 11.　(11) Ps. xlviii.

verence, subjection, and imitation, desiring from the bottom of our hearts, to embrace the feet of our Lord Jesus. For all those who come in this manner to contemplation, obtain that which the Scripture says:—"They that approach to His feet, shall receive of His doctrine."(12)

4. The fourth property, and particular work of the contemplative life is, *attentively to hearken to the word of God:* (13) which is practised in several ways, one of them disposing to the other.—i. To hear the word of God, by reading it in *devout and sacred books:* by means of which God speaks to us, teaching us the doctrine which we read. (14)—ii. To hear the word of Almighty God, by the mouth of the *preachers, teachers,* and *masters* of it: by whom Christ speaks as well as by His own mouth.— iii. To hear the same from *God Himself* in devout *meditation,* discoursing with Him interiorly within our hearts by divers affections, searching out divine truths, and receiving from this divine master, the understanding of them.—iv. And lastly, to hear the same in *contemplation,* which is a simple and affectionate view of those truths which we consider as being in God; the highest act of which the holy Scripture declares by His word, to "*hear*" as St. Paul says, that he "*heard*" in his ecstasy the "secret words" of Almighty God: (15) and our Lord Jesus Christ said to His disciples, that He had taught them all that which He had heard of His heavenly Father. (16) For even as he that hearkens and listens attentively, using nothing of his own discourse, receives purely and truly the doctrine which the master teaches; so the soul in contemplation with little labour, and with much delight, receives interiorly, profound inspirations,

(12) Deut. xxxiii. 3.
(13) S. Th. 2. 2. q. xxxii. art. 3. ad arg.
(14) 2 Cor. xiii. 11. (15) 2 Cor. xii. 4. (16) Joan. xv. 15.

illustrations, and marvellous sentiments of Almighty God; with which He instructs, illustrates, feeds, and inflames her in the affections of love, even to a receiving within her by the self-same word, the Word incarnate, which is God Himself, with whom she unites herself to the perfect union of grace and charity. (17)

CHAP. III.   OF THE NECESSITY WHICH THE ACTIVE LIFE HAS OF THE CONTEMPLATIVE ; AND ON THE COMPLAINTS MADE AGAINST THE CONTEMPLATIVE.

Martha overburdened with the anxiety which she had about the household affairs, went to Christ, and said: "Lord, hast Thou no care that my sister hath left me alone to serve? speak to her therefore, that she help me." (18)

1. In this complaint is represented, in a lively manner, the *necessity* which the *active life has of the contemplative* : for first, after the example of Martha, she freely confesses that she is not of herself sufficient to serve Jesus Christ as He desires, although she performs all the functions properly belonging to her state, unless she be assisted by her sister, contemplation; to whom it appertains to procure devotion and sweetness in the practice of many exterior works : without which, the active life remains dry, disgusted, replete with complaints, and many repugnances. For which reason St. Bernard says, (19) "that consideration ought to precede, and go before action : for although without perfect contemplation a man may enter into heaven, yet, that without some manner of contemplation, we cannot walk with gust, nor support with sweetness, the burden and yoke of the law of God."

2. Hence it is, that her own very necessity constrains

(17) Jac. i. 17.   (18) Luc. x. 40.
(19) Lib. i. de. Consid. ad Eugenium.

the active life to repose with Martha, "who *stood*," and addressed herself to Jesus Christ by prayers and petitions, craving of Him the spirit of contemplation, in such degree as was most fitting and meet to help her. And so she says with an affectionate complaint :—" Lord, Thou art forgetful of me, and leavest me destitute and alone, without the company of my sister contemplation, speak to her therefore that she help me. And since Thy saying is doing, and Thy will working, give me the spirit of contemplation, 'send' 'out of Thy holy heaven, and from the throne of Thy majesty,' the spirit of wisdom, together with the gifts which proceed from the same spirit, ' that' ' He may be with me, and may labour with me, that I may know what is acceptable with Thee.' " (20)

3. But here we must beware of *certain complaints* which some imperfect persons are wont to make, who wholly exercise themselves in the active life; for which notwithstanding they are well rewarded.

i. For some by a secret pride, complain and bewail to Christ our Lord, that labouring much in His holy service with exterior works, He *leaves them alone* without the tenderness and gust of contemplation, as if He had no care of them, nor rewarded their labours with the same reward as others, as the elder brother of the prodigal child complained to his father, that he did not treat him so well as he did the younger; (21)—an egregious mistake, for this sovereign Father of all forgets not any, but is fully as careful, even of the least labourer, as of the highest contemplator, favouring all according to their function. Therefore to tax Almighty God with carelessness on this point, is an argument that he neither knows Him, nor yet himself, for lack of humility; for whoever knows Him, and knows himself, holds himself exceedingly

<hr>

(20) Sap. ix. 10.　　　　(21) Luc. xv. 29 & 30.

happy only to serve Him, contenting himself without other recompence, or other reward than God Himself: and until he thus humbles himself, he cannot attain to contemplation, which, as the Scripture says, "is denied to the proud and lofty, and is bestowed on the humble and lowly."

ii. Others complain silently of the contemplative, as Martha of Mary, *reputing them as idle and of little profit to the Church*, advising their neighbours to counsel them to give over and relinquish contemplation, and to come to assist them in those exterior works which they have undertaken: and, in disgust, ask of Christ to speak to them and command them, to get up on their feet, and come to help them;—a complaint palpably erroneous, and proceeding from persons of very shallow experience, who will needs direct all the world, by the same way in which they themselves walk: for the contemplatives are not idle, but very well employed in the work of their Lord, as in a thing in which he takes singular delight, and ex-ceedingly assist and aid the Church and all her workmen, entreating for them grace and favour from God our Lord, both to labour, and to reap the fruits of their holy labours: so that even God Himself becomes the patron of the contemplatives, as on this occasion is manifest in Mary, and as we shall forthwith further see.

4. It is therefore of great importance to me, that *I re-sign myself* into the hands of my heavenly Father, who gives His gifts and graces to whom He pleases, and how He pleases, imparting to every one that which is most meet and convenient for him: (22) and with this as-surance I will accept and follow that kind of life which He has allotted me, rendering Him humble thanks also, for that which He has given to others, and rejoice to see

(22) 1 Cor. xii.

them so exalted, since their greatness helps my littleness, and by the means of charity, I will appropriate to myself the gifts of others.

Colloquy.—O God of my heart, chase far away from me such sorts of complaints, and let it suffice to appease me, that it is Thy pleasure so to dispose: for whatever proceeds from Thee, will ever be good and profitable for me.

Chap. IV. On other imperfections of the active life; and on Christ our Lord's method of correcting it.

Our Lord replied, "Martha, Martha, thou art careful, and art troubled about many things." (23) In which answer, Christ our Lord, repeating twice the name of Martha, *discovered* the love which He bore her, but withal blamed her for her too great care and anxiety about things, even though they were good : thereby declaring to us, the abuses which commonly accompany the imperfect in the active life, although He does not on that account cease to love them; because, as David said:—"Thy eyes did see my imperfect being, O Lord, and in Thy book all shall be written." (24)

The *roots* of this anxious and troublesome solicitude, are usually these three.

1. The first is, the *natural character of the party:* (25) because, as St. Gregory remarks, (26) some are by nature turbulent, and wholly unapt for the quiet of contemplation; so that the more they retire themselves, the more is their imagination troubled. On the contrary, others there are who of their own natural character are quiet, peaceable, and altogether addicted to retirement, and in

(23) Luc. x. 41.   (24) Ps. cxxxviii. 16.
(25) S. Tho. q. clxxxiii. art. 4. ad. 3.
(26) Moral, lib. viii. cap. 1.

a manner wholly unfit for exterior works. For this reason as the love of God is wont to cause the one to issue forth from their retirement; even so the fear of God causes the others to taste of contemplation, which, as an anchor, retains firm and stable the ship of their soul, amidst the waves and tempests which toss her; for that is possible to grace which seems impossible to nature: so that, such as feel themselves desirous of prayer and contemplation ought not to be dismayed, but to fix and fasten their heart upon Almighty God, with these two anchors of fear and confidence, dreading the loss they may sustain, if they do not apply themselves to prayer, hoping with the help and assistance of God, to attain to it.

2. The second root is, *inexperience, dismayed zeal,* or *lack* of *knowledge* and *discretion* in this important affair. Hence it proceeds, that with a false apprehension of necessity or piety, one seeks to embrace many things, and to charge himself with a multitude of affairs, above his forces; and to this is annexed trouble, and interior anxiety to comply with the whole. And with this it was, that Christ our Lord taxed Martha, who under the pretext of assisting and serving Him, and preparing His dinner, busied herself therein with too great trouble and anxiety. The remedy for this is, to correct the errors of the judgment, and to undertake only moderate occupations, in such a manner that the spirit be not choked or stifled, and that we come not to lose the quiet convenient for contemplation, remembering what the Wise man says, (27)—"My son, meddle not with many matters," and learn wisdom by little and little, for "he that is less in action" (28) shall receive wisdom.

3. The third root is, a certain sort of *propriety*, which proceeds from self-love, which intrudes and intermingles

(27) Ecclus. xi. 10.   (28) Ecclus. xxxviii. 25.

itself amongst good things: and although they be but little, yet pursuing them so passionately, they procure us trouble: and particularly happen to three sorts of persons.—i. To those who are very *sensitive*, and of a violent complexion, though their intention be very good.—ii. To the *vain-glorious*, who possessed with this vice strive and struggle, and will perforce bring all things to pass.—iii. To the *indiscreet* and *ignorant*, who presuppose for expedient, all that appears to be lawful, and by the abuse of their affections, render themselves subject to their own passions. Against these persons the apostle says,—"All things are lawful to me, but all things are not expedient," "but I will not be brought under the power of any:" (29) I will make myself the slave of none, nor will I possess them with a servile passion, but with freedom of reason, and with the pure love of Almighty God as one that is free.

From these roots it may proceed, that the active life may come to hinder the contemplative. (30) But by duly mortifying them, they may both live united together as loving sisters, the one not hindering the principal exercises of the other, in the times assigned to the one, and the other.

CHAP. V. ON THE "ONE THING NECESSARY;" WHICH IS THE DIRECTING END OF THE CONTEMPLATIVE LIFE.

Our Lord Jesus Christ continuing to reprehend Martha, said to her,—"Porro unum est necessarium."—"*But one thing is necessary.*" (31) In which words He laid the foundation, both of the defence and praise of Mary, and consequently of the contemplative life, the end of which is, to *reduce all things to unity*, rejecting, multiplicity and diver-

(29) 1 Cor. vi. 12.   (30) S. Th. 2. 2. cxxxii. art. 1 et 2.
(31) Luc. x. 41.

sity, as much as may be. To this it aspires by the following steps and degrees.

1. The *first unity* is, in the *use* of *temporal* things, reducing them to that " one " " necessary," that is, to that which suffices to sustain our life. (32) Hence Christ our Lord admonished Martha, saying,—" I would not have thee so solicitous in providing such a diversity of things for me and my disciples, because 'one thing' alone will suffice us to sustain nature, and with that we will content ourselves."

This unity, so abridged and restrained in the use of temporal things, greatly disposes to quietness of heart and contemplation, because with it one cuts off all desires and anxious cares. For thus, the great and contemplative saints took little care for temporal things, contenting themselves with that which is necessary for their life and clothing, as the apostle says. Wherefore if I deserve to serve Almighty God, and to taste the sweetness of contemplation, I must avoid that multiplicity, which is contrary to this unity, or " one thing necessary :" because he that contents himself with little of temporal things, amasses much of spiritual; and he who enjoys but scantily the recreations of the earth, will receive in great abundance the delights of heaven.

2. The *second unity* is in the *end* and *intention* of *all our works*, reducing them to *one* only and necessary *end*, which is the *glory of God*, the accomplishment of His will, and our own salvation ; mortifying and cutting off the multitude, or variety, of all intentions, or aims contrary to this one thing, or which do not directly lead or conduce to it. And for this reason Christ our Lord said to Martha, that " *one* " only thing was " necessary ;" which thing Mary had in view in " hearing " this doctrine to sustain her

(32) Theoph.

soul, and to obtain the end of it : for nothing will it profit me to "gain the whole" multitude of things that are in this world, if I "lose" this "one necessary," which is, the salvation of my soul, with the grace and favour of Almighty God. So that I ought, with great fervour, to procure what holy David says :—"One thing I have asked of the Lord, this will I seek after, that I may dwell in the house of the Lord all the days of my life:" (33) to see by contemplation the excellency of His glory, of IIis divine will, and of His delights, loving what I see, and pursuing what I love.

Particularizing this, I *will reduce all my affairs to this one necessary*, which the apostle from point to point explains, saying : (34) "one body and one Spirit," "one hope of your calling," "one Lord, one faith, and one baptism," one mediator, "one God and Father of all ;" so that I must detest and renounce every desire or pursuit of things contrary to the unity of the mystical "body" of the Church, of the Holy "Spirit" who governs the same, of the "hope" of my salvation, of the vocation that calls me, of the faith of which I make profession, of the "baptism" I have received, of the Mediator Jesus Christ who has redeemed me, of God our "Lord" who has created me, of the "Father" who regards me as His son, and will make me inheritor of His celestial Kingdom.

3. The *third unity* proper to the contemplative (35) life, is, in the *right use* of the *senses* and *interior powers* of the *soul*, reducing them all to union, wholly attending to the knowledge and actual love of Almighty God : and for this reason Christ our Lord said to Martha,—"Thou art troubled and perplexed with many thoughts, affections, and cares, but the most necessary point is, that thy soul

---

(33) Ps. xxvi. 4.

(34) Ephes. iv. 4.; 1 Tim. ii. 5.   (35) S. Aug. ib.

be one, that is to say, united and recollected within itself; one in her sensual *affections*, reducing them to union with the spirit, and mortifying the rebellions of the flesh ; *one* in her *will*, referring her whole will entirely to the will of Almighty God, renouncing all will or contentment to be taken in creatures; *one* in her *cares*, abridging them all in one, to become agreeable to the divine bounty, leaving the rest to His providence; *one* in her *thoughts*, gathering them all together, nor to think of any other thing but only of God, resisting distractions and wanderings as much as is possible, considering the frailty of our present condition; one finally in love, placing it wholly in one only infinite good, who shall satisfy and satiate it, saying with David,—" What have I in heaven, and besides Thee what do I desire upon earth?" (36)

CHAP. VI. ON THE EXCELLENCIES OF THE CONTEMPLATIVE LIFE.

Our Lord Jesus Christ concludes His intention, saying, " *Mary has chosen the best part which shall not be taken away from her.*"

1. In which words it is first to be marked, (37) that although our Saviour said that Mary had chosen the better part, viz., *contemplation*, because she liberally applied herself to this sort of life, yet the *spring* and *root* of this *election* was, the *grace* and inspiration of Almighty God, which moved her will to make this choice : for in the manner of living is verified that which our Lord said to His apostles, —" You have not chosen me: but I have chosen you."(38) For it appertains to the Holy Ghost, who imparts other graces, to impart also this, inspiring it to whom He pleases,

(36) Ps. lxxii. 25.   (37) S. Th. 2. 2. q. clxxxii. art. 1 et 2. (38) Joan. xv. 16.

and to whom it is convenient for His salvation and perfection.

2. But that none may excuse themselves from applying, as much as they can, to obtain this grace, Jesus Christ said, that Mary had chosen this "best part" of the contemplative life, which in the judgment of the same Lord, is better than the part of Martha, which is the active life, because *it is more united with the sovereign good,* whence "every best and every perfect gift" proceeds. For it makes a man more like Almighty God and His angels ;— it perfects the two most noble powers of the soul, which are the understanding and the will;—illustrating the understanding with the most excellent act of wisdom, which is the knowledge of God, and inflaming the will with the most heroic act of charity, which is the love of the same God;—and as from this the love of our neighbour proceeds, even so from contemplation proceeds the perfection of exterior works, producing fervour of spirit, sweetness, and integrity.

3. To these excellencies Christ our Lord has added another, saying, *that it should "not be taken away from her."* As if He had said,—" Not for all thy reasons, Martha, nor for thy complaints, will I take from Mary that part which she has chosen, to make her take thine, although it be good, because hers is better :" this our Lord accomplishes in three ways:—

i. First, whomever He has, by special vocation, called to this sort of life, *He, on His part, never takes it from them,* nor desires that others should take it from them, nor that they should suffer themselves to be withdrawn by any persuasions, or human apparent reasons, but wills that they should persevere in their vocation to death.

ii. Secondly, those whom once He has drawn by His inspiration and motion to this sovereign exercise, according to the times and hours designed, *He never withdraws* them *from it*, nor desires that others withdraw them, or divert them from it under any pretended titles of virtue; but, on the contrary, He defends them as He defended Mary, and says in their favour that of the Canticles, (39) "I adjure you, O ye daughters of Jerusalem, that you make not the beloved to awake till she please," that is to say, that you disquiet not the sweet sleep of her contemplation, nor disturb the discourse she hold with me, until she has satisfied her longing and necessity, because her will being conformable with mine, she will leave her sleep when I wish her to do so; (40) as also, when either charity towards her neighbour, or obedience to her superior, requires otherwise, promptly and readily she will assent to them.

iii. Lastly, never will Almighty God take contemplation from His elect here beneath, but *will perfect it.* For although death causes the exercises of the active life to cease, yet neither ceases, nor ever shall cease, the contemplation of God, in which consists felicity and life eternal: and as St. Augustine says, (41) "in heaven we shall behold and see, we shall see and love, we shall love and praise; we shall see without end, love without loathing, and praise without weariness;" this function, this affection, and this exercise will be common to all, in it we shall continue for ever and ever. Amen.

CHAP. VII. ON THE EXCELLENCY OF THE MIXED LIFE, OR LIFE COMPOSED OF BOTH, COMPREHENDING THE ACTIVE AND CONTEMPLATIVE.

(42) With great mystery does Christ our Lord call the

(39) Cant. ii. 7.
(40) S. Th. 2, 2. clxxx. art. 4. et clxxxi. art. 4.
(41) Lib. Ult. de Civitat. Dei ad fin.
(42) S. Th. 2. 2. q. clxxix. a. 2. ad 2.   S. Aug. lib. 19. de Civit. Dei.

life of Mary *a part*, being compared with that of Martha, to give us to understand that there is *another most excellent life*, which is composed of these two parts *as a whole*, and comprehends the exercises of both, the contemplative and active life, especially the most noble of them, which tends to the profit and good of souls.

1. This life, as St. Thomas says, (43) *Christ Himself* chose as the more perfect, at such time as He was to preach: and at the same time, it was likewise practised by His precursor, St. *John*, and in him was imitated by His *apostles*, and since by the sacred *doctors*, and other illuminated *saints* of the Catholic Church, who, like the angels, mounted up even to the last degree of the ladder on which Almighty God leaned, uniting themselves with Him by contemplation, and then descended down to the foot of the same ladder, (44) at which Jacob lay asleep, to waken and encourage men to the service of their Creator.

2. And although this perfection is very rare, as Cassian says, (45) and granted to few, notwithstanding *all* spiritual persons ought to aspire to it, according to their vocation; inasmuch as the contemplative life, when it is perfect with the love of God, presently engenders a great love of our neighbour, and zeal for His salvation, which, as the holy Fathers say, (46) is the most precious gift we can offer to Jesus Christ, becoming His co-adjutors in the conquest of souls: in such a manner that the self-same contemplation, to accomplish the will of Almighty God, interrupts her own works, to gain souls which love and glorify the same God. (47)

3. And even as Martha beholding the quietude of her

<hr>

(43) S. Th. 3. p. q. xl. art. 1. ad 2 et 3.
(44) Gen. xxviii. 12.   (45) Collat. xix. cap. 9.
(46) Richard de S. Vict. lib. i. de cont. cap. 40 et 44.   S. Greg. hom. 12 & 15, in Ezech.   S. Dion. lib. de celest. Hier. cap. 3.
(47) S. Th. 2. 2. q. clxxxii. art. 2.   Gen. xxx. 1.

sister Mary, complained of her to Christ our Lord, the master of both, praying Him to command her to help her;—even so by another extremity, Rachael, who is a figure of the contemplative life, seeing the fecundity, and great number of children which her sister Lia had, who represents the active life, complained to Jacob the husband of both, and said to him—"Give, me" as many "children" as my sister, or else I die from sorrow; for whoever attains to perfect contemplation and the love of God, *desires with St. Paul, to engender spiritual children to Christ*, (48) —and this zeal burns his bowels, and he dies with sorrow when these die, and lives with joy when these live.

4. This is the sum of those things which the active and contemplative comprehend, and of that which is composed of them both, which I am to procure to the utmost of my power, craving them of our Lord Jesus Christ, with these or the like colloquies.

Colloquies.—O most sweet Jesus, who lodgedst in the house of Martha, where her sister Mary so fortunately found Thee; vouchsafe to lodge in my soul, cleansing it, and adorning it, with the exercises of the active life like to Martha; yet in such manner, that jointly it hear and contemplate Thy holy doctrine with Blessed Mary.   Amen.

O most compassionate Saviour, who reprehendedst the indiscreet solicitude and trouble of Martha, and approvedst the quietude and tranquillity of Mary, permit, I beseech Thee, that I may so exercise myself in the works of the active life in Thy holy service, that I be not molested with its cares, calming them with the peace and tranquillity of the contemplative life. Amen.

O lover of souls, for whose sake Thou art come into

(48) Gal. iv. 19.

the little dwelling of this 'world, desiring to lodge with them, grant that, with Mary, I so choose the better "part," that I forget not that good part allotted to Martha, labouring for the good of souls, to the end that both they and I may devoutly lodge Thee as Thou desirest, that so Thou mayest hereafter lodge us in Thy heaven as we desire.   Amen.

O my good, and my glory, suffer not that I be so solicitous for the good of others, that I be forgetful of myself, or become negligent in contemplating Thy divine doctrine.   Bridle, (49) O Lord, the pride of Martha, that she intrude not upon the place and time appertaining to Mary ; and so dispose of Mary, that she leave not her sister Martha all alone.   Amen.

O Redeemer of sinners, who at the prayers of Mary and Martha, didst raise again their brother Lazarus, grant to all the faithful of Thy Church, that we may join together in prayer for our sinful brethren, that Thou mayest vouchsafe to raise them again to the life of grace ; by which we may begin to exercise the works of these two lives, active and contemplative, with such perseverance, that we may all obtain the life eternal.   Amen.

CHAP. VIII. ON THE EXCELLENT MANNER IN WHICH OUR LORD JESUS CHRIST HAS JOINED THE CONTEMPLATIVE LIFE WITH THE ACTIVE.

It remains that we declare that most excellent *manner* in which Christ our Lord, in the time of His *preaching,* *united* these two sorts of lives for our example;—which He did in two ways.

1. First, by dividing the time in *two parts,* giving *the day to his neighbour,* and reserving *the night for prayer,* (50) according as St. Luke recounts :—"He went out into a mountain to pray, and He passed the whole night in the

<hr>

(49) Luc. x. 41.   (50) S. Greg. lib. vi. mor. c. 24.

prayer of God." (51) In which words are remarked the *preparation* which Christ our Lord made for His prayer, the *time* He continued it, and the *fervour* with which He performed it, not for any necessity of His own, but for our example.

i. His *preparation* was, in choosing all that might assist recollection, as, the *place*, the *time*, and *company:* for He chose a solitary place, the season of the night, which is most silent, and was *alone*, without any other witness of His prayer, than His eternal Father, to whom He prayed in the hidden secret of His heart. (52)—ii. The *time* His prayer lasted was *long*, passing all the night in this holy exercise.—iii. And He persevered in it, until the *morning*, because ordinarily, one attains not to the height of contemplation, without most strict recollection, and long wrestling like another Jacob, from the evening "till morning," (53) to obtain the benediction of Almighty God.

For this cause the Wise man says, that "better is the end of prayer, than the beginning," (54) presupposing, that there ought to be some distance between the beginning and ending, and consequently, that it ought to be *long*, obtaining much more perfection in the ending than in the beginning. The excellency of the prayer of our Lord, the Evangelist describes with those phrases with which the holy Scripture ordinarily declares very high things, calling it, "the prayer of God," that is to say, a high and elevated prayer, a prayer worthy of Almighty God, whereby, as Jeremiah says, the man that is "solitary," does silently raise himself above himself, (55) and ascends even to the uniting of himself with Almighty God.

2. The reason why this prayer is called "the prayer of

(51) Luc. vi. 12.　　(52) Marc. vi. 46.　　(53) Gen. xxxii. 29.
(54) Eccles. vii. 9.　　(55) Thren. iii. 28.

God," is, because all that is in it is from God, containing *four most excellent properties all from God:—*

i. The first property is, that it *proceeds from* the self-same *God*, and from the inspiration of His divine Spirit, who, as St. Paul says, "Himself asketh for us, with unspeakable groanings," (56) inspiring us with the meditations and affections of the things we ought to ask, and the fervour with which we ask (57) them; for otherwise that prayer will prove very dry, which does not proceed from His inspiration.

ii. The second property is, that it is made in the *presence of Almighty God*, exercising the memory and the understanding only in God, conversing with Him, without diverting itself to any other thing not directed to God, conformable to what David says,— "I will enter into the powers of the Lord; O Lord, I will be mindful of Thy justice alone," (58) that is to say, of Thy only bounty and felicity, and other perfections which I meditate.

iii. The third property is, that the matter or subject of all the affections, desires and petitions "be *of God*," or what God wills and requires, and be only for *the glory of Almighty God:* in such a manner that one neither desire nor ask for aught, which is not first identified with the will and glory of Almighty God;—above all that he ask or demand God Himself, contenting himself with nothing less than Him, saying with holy Moses, Lord, "show me Thy face" (59) that I may know Thee, for Thou alone wilt suffice me, and in Thee alone all good whatsoever is contained.

iv. Finally, this prayer is called "the prayer of God," the end and fruit of which is, *union and transformation into the same God* by perfect *love*, which renders us wholly

(56) Rom. viii. 26.   (57) S. Bon. opusc: de Itinerit. ætern. ii. dist. 5.
(58) Ps. lxx. 16.   (59) Exod. xxxiii. 13.

like Him, as children who resemble their father. Hence it is, that the works which proceed from the same prayer, participate of the same excellency; and when the prayer is the prayer of God, the justice will likewise be like "the mountains of God," (60) and the mercy will be the virtues of God: and they likewise who practise them, will be, as the prophet David says, "gods" (61) by participation.

This is that excellent prayer which Christ our Lord exercised, whose wonderful effects He discovered in the prayer which He made at His holy baptism, and Transfiguration, as we shall further see in its place, to which we all of us ought to aspire: for notwithstanding it be high and difficult, yet with the inspiration and help of heaven, it will be made most easy to us.

3. Out of this so divine recollection, Christ our Lord issued to exercise the works of *the active life*, joining also with them prayer, by another second means;—for commonly He began first by brief prayer, as He prayed when He wrought the miracles of the five loaves, healed certain sick and possessed with devils, and when He raised up Lazarus. And the like He did in His other works, though secretly: teaching us by this example, that the contemplative and active life, ought to fraternise together, not only on the same day, and at different times, but even at the same hour, accompanying the works of the active life with some short prayer, and lifting up, as Jeremiah says, "our hearts with our hands to the Lord in the heavens;" (62)—the hands to work, and the heart to pray, (63) as has been said in the introduction of this book.

4. Lastly, the works of the active life, which Christ our Lord exercised at this time, were most *glorious to God,*

(60) Ps. xxxv. 7; 2 Reg. ix.   (61) Ps. lxxxi. 6.
(62) Thren. iii. 41.   (63) S. Greg. lib. xviii. c. 5.

and most profitable to men, for after His baptism He began to publish His law of grace, and to teach the doctrine of evangelical perfection, which He explicated by admirable sermons, elucidated by heroic examples, and confirmed by evident miracles. The sermons being mingled with most high reasons, and with words breathing peace. The examples were eminent in all kinds of virtues, performing first by work, what He taught by word. The miracles were wonderful in all sorts of things, and profitable to all sorts of persons, in their bodies and in their souls, intermingled with admirable virtues, manifesting His almighty power, and the divinity of His Person.

This in short was the life of our Lord Jesus Christ in the time of His preaching;—whence we may gather, that the four things which shone forth in Him, viz., prayer, preaching, examples and miracles, may serve for ample matter of meditation in this third part, and shew the excellence of the contemplative life, though my intention be not to meditate them all, but only the more important of them. Nor will I tie myself to the order in which they succeeded each other, that I may gather together such meditations as have a relation to each other, and are directed to the same end ; so that persons desirous of some particular virtue, find joined together, sundry meditations which may further their object.

5. And as these meditations are proper for those who pass from the state of beginners, to the state of proficients in virtues, it seems good to admonish them of that which St. Augustine says in these memorable words :—" Many there are, who in the beginning of their conversion pray very fervently, and with great attention and devotion; but a little after they languish, and pray loosely with distractions and remiss affections; afterwards they pray coldly with aridity and dryness of heart; lastly, they pray negligently

with great interruptions and losses." (64)   And the worst is, that with all this they hold themselves as secure, not dreaming that "whilst they sleep," their "enemy watches," and stand in great danger of dying by his hand; for which reason Christ our Saviour said, "that we ought always to pray," (65) without intermission; that is to say, to pray with such fervour and perseverance, that we cease not, nor give not over the exercise of prayer, preparing ourselves to it with such diligence, that being favoured of His divine Spirit, it may merit the name of " the prayer of God."

(64) In Ps. lxv. in fine.   (65) Luc. xviii. 1.

MEDITATIONS

ON THE

CHIEF MYSTERIES OF OUR LORD'S LIFE, TEACHING AND MIRACLES,

FROM HIS BAPTISM UP TO THE END OF HIS PREACHING.

1.—MEDITATIONS ON THE LIFE OF OUR LORD'S PRECURSOR, ST. JOHN.

MEDITATION I.

ON THE MARVELLOUS LIFE AND PREACHING OF ST. JOHN THE BAPTIST, UNTIL THE BAPTISM OF CHRIST OUR LORD.

Before the meditation of the baptism (1) of Christ our Lord, let us make one concerning the Baptist, as well because the order of the history requires it, as also because there are to be seen practised in them, the fundamental virtues of evangelical perfection.

POINT I.

The glorious Baptist, even from his very infancy, *remained in the desert for many years*, until the time when he began to preach, leading there a miraculous life: in which he made himself very renowned, especially in *those four virtues* which are the four pillars, or bases, on which evangelical perfection is built and founded.

1. First he excelled in *penance* and *corporal austerity*, which he exercised in all things with the greatest rigour.

i. His food was "locusts and wild honey," which he found in the open fields ; his apparel, a garment of camel's

(1) Luc. iii. 3 ; Matt. iii. 1 ; Marc. i. 4.

hair, girt with a girdle rough and painful. His chamber and lodging a cave, or pent of some ruinous rock ; and his bed, the bare ground, enduring with unspeakable patience, the colds, heats, and common injury of the air.

ii. All this he endured, not in punishment of his sins past, being sanctified from his mother's womb, so as never to have committed any grievous sin ; but to *preserve himself the better even from the least offences*, to subdue his flesh, to render it subject to the spirit, and to dispose himself to receive the gifts of heaven, which are not obtained ordinarily, but by such hard and painful asperities.

Hence will I draw internal desires to imitate this saint wherein he is imitable, conformably to my feebleness, *embracing corporal austerity* as much as I may, chastising my flesh, and offering it up as "a living sacrifice wholly pleasing unto God :" (2) not only for the ends before mentioned, but also in satisfaction for many sins, which I have committed by means of it.

And because this is the proper livery of all the servants of the celestial king, since, as Christ our Lord says, those who walk a contrary way, "are in the houses of earthly kings," (3) and glory to serve them,—I, O eternal king, will rejoice to be Thy servant, and henceforth will clothe myself with this selfsame livery, wearing upon my flesh Thy mortification, as this Thy holy forerunner did.

2. Secondly, he employed himself in *prayer*, perpetual and very sublime contemplation, having by a singular privilege, the Holy Ghost Himself for master, who led him "into the wilderness, and spoke to his heart," (4) teaching him and comforting him with marvellous illustrations and consolations, far more abundant than those of

(2) Rom xii. 1.   (3) Mat. xi. 8.

(4) Ose. ii. 14.

Moses, Elias, David, and all the prophets that went before him. (5)

i. And amongst other reasons I will consider this; that as it is impossible to live without some delight, so the more one deprives himself, for the love of God, of the delights of the flesh, with so much greater abundance *will he receive the delights of the spirit.* For even so, St. John, wholly renouncing the riches, honours, dignities, and delights, of his father's house, and afflicting so rudely his own flesh, God rewarded him a hundred fold, imparting to him ineffable celestial joys, in such a manner that the desert was his house of recreation, his cavern or hole was to him a heaven, and his solitude procured him the company of angels, and of God Himself. (6)

ii. Hence will I derive great willingness to *endure hardships* and subjection of the body, since God rewards them with the delights of heaven : as also to addict *myself to prayer*, and to conversing with God our Lord, from whom such consolation and comfort is received: endeavouring to climb " the mountain of myrrh," and "the hill of frankincense," (7) because the one helps the other. And to this effect I will beseech the Holy Ghost to be my tutor interiorly, not leaving for this those spiritual tutors whom God has appointed here on earth, for I will not aspire to enjoy the privilege granted by our Lord to this blessed Baptist.

3. Thirdly, he excelled in great *fortitude* and *constancy*, persevering so many years in these two kinds of painful exercises. And it is very probable that during this time, he suffered several great temptations and attacks of the Devil. For if our Lord Jesus Christ endured them in the forty days He withdrew Himself into the desert; how

(5) S. Greg. lib. xviii. mor. c. 8.
(6) S. Greg. lib. i. dial. c. 1.   (7) Cant. iv. 6.

many more did St. John endure in the course of so many years, leading there so admirable a life? At which the Devil was mad with anger, desiring to supplant him, greedy as he always is to swallow down the sweetest morsels, (8) and persuaded himself that he should soon drink up the "river Jordan," (9) that is to say, this most perfect and penitent saint.

He also represented to him the delights which he might have in his father's house, and amongst his kindred ; the dignity of priesthood which fell to him by inheritance; the horrors of the life he had undertaken, and assailed him with other similar invisible and visible attacks; all which were permitted by our Lord for the exercise of this saint, to cause him to increase in all sorts of virtue and fortitude, since he resisted valiantly, and ever triumphed over his enemy.

4. Fourthly, he made himself admirable for *purity of heart,* avoiding even the least offences, with fervour increasing in all these virtues ; and on this account St. Luke says, that he grew and was strengthened in spirit: (10) that is, that he grew both corporally and spiritually : because the Holy Ghost comforted and assisted him, accomplishing in him that which David said:—" Blessed is the man whose help is from Thee," (11) because by Thine aid, " in his heart he hath disposed to ascend by steps," and he shall " go from virtue to virtue, until he shall see the vision of the God of gods in Sion."

These four virtues in which St. John made himself so remarkable, are the most efficacious of all others to attain to the summit of perfection, and to become great in the sight of God, which I will beseech Him, by the merits of this saint, to grant me according to my state and condition of life.

(8) Habac. i. 16.

(9) Job xl. 18.

(10) Luc. i. 80.

(11) Ps. lxxxiii. 6, 8.

Colloquy.—O Holy Spirit, fortify my feeble spirit, to the end that, after the example of this valorous precursor, I may with rigour chastise my flesh, courageously resist the malignant spirits, and make daily progress in contemplation, and in celestial virtues, increasing like the light of the morning, until the height of the perfect day.   Amen.

POINT II.

Having attained man's estate, (12) he walked upon the bank of the river Jordan, *to preach baptism and penance* for the remission of sins, saying,—" Do penance : for the kingdom of heaven is at hand," (13) and many from Jerusalem and all Judea went forth to him, and were baptized by him, confessing their sins.

Here we are to consider, i. *what moved* St. John to these exercises of preaching and baptizing:—ii. *with what spirit* he performed them:—iii. *what things* he preached:—iv· and the *fruit and profit* of his preaching.

i. First, He *that moved him* was the *Holy Ghost,*—even He who had drawn him into the desert : for it is the property of this divine Spirit, after He has made His elect most perfect, to move them to procure the perfection of others.   This was the reason which moved St. John, with which he issued forth to preach and prepare unto Christ our "Lord a perfect people." (14)   Moreover, having dwelt so many years within the most secret cellar of the wines of God,(15) inebriated with the most strong wine of charity, she herself forced him to issue forth of his retirement, to invite men to the service of her beloved; for thus the love of God and our neighbour, and obedience to the inspiration of the Holy Spirit, draw men forth in public, and make them manifest themselves to Israel.   Whence

(12) S. Th. 3, 2. q. xxxviii.   (13) Matt. iii. 2; Luc. iii. 3.
(14) Luc. i. 17.   (15) Cant. ii. 4.

I will draw motives that I ought to imitate the like exercises, if I would not err in discharging my duty.

ii.   Secondly, the *spirit* with which he preached, was on the one part *zealous* and terrible, as that of Elias, and on the other part *merciful* and compassionate, as of another Moses; for treating with the Pharisees and Sadducees, most obdurate people, he used great zeal, with terrible words, and fearful threatenings, saying unto them :—" Ye brood of vipers, who hath shewed you to flee from the wrath threatened against you?   Think not to say within yourselves, We have Abraham for our father," for that will avail you little, yourselves being evil: " for God is able of these stones to raise up children to Abraham, (16) in whom He will fulfil His promise."   Furthermore, he received a great number of people, of publicans and soldiers, with great mercy and benignity, without excluding any one, giving them wholesome counsel to accomplish their charge, to hurt none, to do good to all, and to give alms according to their means.

iii. Thirdly, the *matter or subject* of his sermons was an *exhortation to penance,* to " bring forth fruits worthy of" it, to which he induced them, with the hope of an eternal recompence, because the kingdom of heaven was at hand, as also by the threats of eternal punishment, for that " the axe was laid to the root of the tree, and that every unfruitful tree should be cut down, and cast into the fire :" and that God held " His fan in His hand, to cleanse the floor " of the world, and to " gather the good wheat into " His celestial granaries; and " the chaff," which are the wicked, He will burn with unquenchable fire.

All this will I apply to myself, exhorting myself to do penance for these two reasons;—*hope of reward,* and *fear*

(16) Matt. iii. 7.

of punishment; imagining that perhaps "the axe" is already "laid to the root of the tree" of my life to cut it down, and that unless I amend, I shall become "the chaff," which shall be cast into everlasting fire.

iv. Fourthly, the *fruit* of his preaching was most *abundant*, inasmuch as an innumerable multitude of people of all conditions ran to him and obeyed him, suffering themselves to be baptized by him, with such great signs of humility and repentance, that they confessed and declared their sins to him. (17) And that which is most admirable, is, that he persuaded them without working any miracles; though indeed his whole life was nothing else, but a most continual and remarkable miracle. Hence is to be seen, the efficacy of the exemplary life of him that preaches, to persuade that which he preaches, although the thing be very difficult, and the auditors of an obdurate heart.

Colloquy.—O eternal Father, raise up in Thy Church many imitators of this great precursor to Thy Son, preparing Him a perfect people, preaching His holy law with zeal and mercy, confirming by their life, that which they teach by word, that they may gather a rich harvest of many souls into life eternal. Amen.

POINT III.

The authority of St. John increased so greatly with the people, that they supposed, as St. Luke says, that he was the Christ and Messiah promised to them; and some of them indeed held him to be so. But the holy precursor understanding this, whether by revelation from God, or by their words and their behaviour toward him, presently contradicted them, saying, "I indeed baptize you in water unto penance, but He that shall come after me, is mightier

(17) Matt. iii. 6. Marc. i. 5.

than I, *whose shoes I am not worthy* to bear; He shall baptize you in the Holy Ghost and fire." (18)

1. Here weigh the rare humility of John the Baptist, which he discovered in *three heroic acts*, in the very midst of this his greatness.

i. The first act was, *not to become proud* by reason of that austere life which he had led, nor of those excellent gifts and favours which he had received from God in contemplation, nor of the applause of the people, nor of the good opinion they had of Him, nor the great honour which every one paid him. A very rare thing, as St. Bernard says, (19) and found in very few eminent saints, to join humility, with innocency and much honoured sanctity. And in this St. John, although a Nazarite, differed from others, inasmuch as he nourished not in himself, one hair of high thoughts, (20) but always cast deep roots in the abyss of his own nothing.

ii. The second act was, *publicly to confess his own baseness*, and the greatness of Christ our Lord, saying :—" although you esteem me to be so great, know that there is another greater than I, and much more powerful in word and work, who surpasses me, not merely in some one thing, but is so great, that I am not worthy to be the least of His slaves, nor to have the basest office in His service, which is to untie the latchet of His shoes." Hence we see, that the perfectly humble, the more holy he is, so much the more vile and base does he hold himself in the sight of God our Lord, considering himself unworthy, even to be His slave; and not content to have this opinion of himself, desires that every one esteem him so.

(18) Matt. iii. 11.
(19) Ser. 8. in Cant. & 42, & ep. 42.   S. Greg. lib. i. mor. cap. 26.
(20) Num. vi 18, & seq.

iii. The third act was, *the contempt of his own baptism,* to countenance and aggrandise that of Christ's, saying that his was of water only, without power to pardon sins, or to cleanse the soul : but that another would come, who would baptize them with a baptism, which should give to them "the Holy Ghost," together with the "fire" of divine love. In this is discovered how the perfectly humble man undervalues and depreciates his own works, inasmuch as they are his, desiring that men should make no more account of them than they deserve, so that the works of Almighty God may be magnified by every one as reason requires.

2. Weighing *these three acts of humility,* I will excite myself to a great confusion to see myself destitute of them, and following pride, which conducts me the contrary way : and I will conceive very great purposes, to imitate them according to my state and condition ; for without this humility, there is no true sanctity, nor assured greatness, nor can I accomplish my charge, so as to make myself acceptable to God and His angels, and edifying to my neighbour.

Colloquy.—O glorious precursor, my soul rejoices to see thee so humble amidst so many honours which thou receivest from God and men. Beseech our Lord, who gave thee this rare humility, to impart to me some part of it, for fear lest I lose by my pride, the good which God has given me by His grace. O my soul, since thou hast such great occasion to humble thyself, because of the great spiritual poverty and misery, confess what thou art, and despise thyself as thou deservest : for, as much as the humble rich man is agreeable to God, so much the " poor man that is proud " (21) is displeasing to Him.

(21) Ecclus. xxv. 4.

MEDITATION II.

The rumour increasing amongst the people, that St.
John was the Messiah whom they expected, the Jews sent
certain priests and Levites from Jerusalem, making some
particular *demands* to know who He was: in his answers
to which St. John displayed *four most excellent acts of
humility*, which are the foundation of spiritual life in the
highest degree; and with which many others go in company, as well as of virtue, as of others.

POINT I.

The first was—"Who art thou?" Art thou the Christ
expected to come? "And he confessed, and did not deny :
and he confessed," saying, "I am not the Christ." (1)

1. In which answer shone forth that *most heroic act of
humility* of this saint, in which he was so firmly founded,
—in no wise to usurp the honour of Jesus Christ, but *to
render all to Him whose it was*, and to whom it belonged;
for he instantly affirmed the truth with strong asservera-
tion, and without denying that he was not Christ; which
he would have ratified and repeated a thousand times if
his questioners had persevered in asking. For even as
pride greatly affects the excellency of Jesus Christ, and
to be as God; (2) even so humility extremely detests so
devilish a presumption. And as this pride expelled Lucifer and his angels out of heaven, and Adam and Eve
of Paradise; and has cast headlong into the depths of
hell, many princes and mighty monarchs of the world,
and is a sign of the reprobate sons of Satan, who is king
of the proud : even so the contrary,—humility, has pre-

(1) Joan. i. 20.   (2) Is. xiv. 12; Ezech. xxviii. 2; Job x. 6.

served the angels of heaven in their excellency; and the holy precursor, and the apostles of Christ, (3) with great constancy refused all sort of adoration and divine honour offered to them; this being a true mark of the elect, who in all, and through all, seek to subject themselves to Almighty God, desiring that all honour be given to Him alone, and that He may be glorified by all, as is His due. (4)

2. I will likewise consider *the subtilty of Satan*, who envious of the sanctity of St. John, seeing that he could not supplant him by different temptations which he had contrived, devised this by which there was offered to him divine honour, imagining that with this he would be overcome, as he himself had been overcome by it. In the same manner he tempts the saints, making them offers of greater honours and dignities than they deserve, thereby to cause them to stumble : but the elect, founded in true humility, knowing themselves, detest all manner of dignity or pre-eminence whatever, of name, title or place which surpasses their merits, contenting themselves with that which belongs to them, for fear of losing both the one and the other, and rather on the contrary, the more they see themselves esteemed and honoured, the more do they humble themselves, as the Wise man says, (5) to honour God.

Colloquy.—O most mighty God, who truly art honoured by the humble : give me true humility by which I may yield unto Thee the honour which Thou deservest, and utterly detest that which I myself deserve not. Amen.

POINT II.

The second demand was,—"*Art thou Elias?* And he said I am not." "Art thou a prophet? And he answered, No."

(3) Act. xiv. 13.　　　　　(4) S. Greg. l. xxxiv. moral. c. 18.
(5) Ecclus. iii. 20.

1. In which answers, the *second act of heroic humility* shone in St. John, which he added to the former, for he might have affirmed that he was Elias, in the manner that our Lord had named him, that is, "in spirit," (6) but he would not, answering to the sense in which he was asked, to which he replied with great resolution, that he was not He : for the truly humble man does not only refuse the honour which he does not deserve, but *flies by all the means* he may, that very honour which he might accept. Moreover, the truly humble, loves the truth that is pure and simple, without duplicity or disguise, especially in things which serve for his humiliation : and for this reason he simply confessed that he was not Elias.

2. He might more truly have said that he was a "prophet," although he answered "no," in that sense in which we ordinarily call them prophets who foretell future things; for the truly humble man invents devices in which to conceal his own greatness, and to avoid the honour which he deserves for them. On the contrary, the proud man devises means to discover himself for more than indeed he is, and to attribute to himself that honour which is not due to him, although it be with lies and exaggerations.

3. Lastly, to all this he answered with brief words, and very dry, and so briefly and drily, as to use a flat denial, or " No." For the truly humble are so far off from kissing the hands of those that show them honour, or applaud them with praises and flatteries, that they treat them coldly and harshly : they seek not to be repaid with honour and fame, and take no delight, as Job says, (7) in admiring " the sun" of worldly glory when he shines, nor " the moon" of fame when she is at the full, and feels not

(6) Matt. xi. 14.　　　　　(7) Job xxxi. 26.

what they are in themselves, nor what others say of them.

Colloquy.—O sun of justice, from whom Thy fore-runner received so great a light, as to despise the splendour of the world: vouchsafe to illuminate me with the like light, which may so shut my eyes, that they delight not to behold that which may blind me with vanity. Amen.

POINT III.

The third demand was, " *Who*," *then*, "*art thou*, that we may give an answer to them that sent us? What sayest thou of thyself?"(8) He answered, "I am the voice of one crying in the wilderness : prepare ye the way cf the Lord, as said the prophet Isaiah."(9)

In this answer was displayed *the third act* of heroic humility in St. John, in which he so manifested the office charged to him on God's behalf, as to discover at the same time, that *he reputed himself as nothing* of himself : saying, that his office was only to serve as the voice of the herald of Jesus Christ, admonishing men to make them-selves ready to receive Him.

1. He styled himself a "*voice*," because, as the voice has not any being or substance of itself, but is dependant on him that pronounces it;—even so he considered himself to have no other being or title in this office, but that which he received from Almighty God, who spoke by him, and whose voice he was : in which it is to be observed how quick and sharpsighted humility is, to acknowledge the gifts which she holds from God, and how eloquent to manifest them when occasion is afforded; not-withstanding, he published them with words of humility, manifesting his dependence on Almighty God, and his

(8) Joan. i. 22.　　　　　(9) Isai. xl. 3.

own nullity, to give the whole glory to Him to whom it belongs.

2. Moreover, as St. John answered not that he was the son of Zachary, and of the priestly tribe of Levi, but that he was "*the voice*" *of Christ*, glorifying himself in that alone; even so he that is truly humble never makes mention of his honourable lineage, nor of his relationships according to the flesh, nor of the offices which he enjoys by inheritance, but only of his being a servant of Christ, consecrated to accomplish His holy will; and this he says he is, and nothing else conformably to the saying of Solomon : (10)—"Fear God and keep His commandments : for this is all man :" that is to say, the true honour of every man consists in this, and in this he ought to glory above all things, contrary to the proud man, who boasts of the glory which proceeds from his ancestors, and the like.

3. I will further consider how St. John called himself "the voice that cried, Prepare ye the way of the Lord :" because his life, his doctrine, his examples, and his words, were nothing else but voices, which exhorted to sanctity and perfection;—yes, the voice of God, whereby the greatness and majesty of Almighty God was made known, even as a man is known by his voice. In imitation of which I ought to endeavour to become the voice of Jesus Christ in all my words, and in all my works.

Colloquy.—O eternal God, make me the voice of Thine Only-begotten Son Jesus Christ, granting me grace to lead a life so perfect, that it may be a voice to publish His glory, attributing it not to myself, but to Thee, from whom all good proceeds; to whom be all honour and glory, for ever and ever. Amen.

POINT IV.

The last demand was,   *why then dost thou baptize*

if thou be not Christ, nor Elias, nor the prophet ?" St. John answered :—" I baptize with water, but there hath stood one in the midst of you, whom you know not, who is the Messiah that is to come, who is greater than I, the latchet of whose shoes I am not worthy to loose." (11)

In this answer shone *the fourth degree* of heroic humility, which this holy precursor St. John possessed.

1. First, finding himself reprehended for usurping the office of baptizing, whereas he was not a prophet, he neither *excused himself nor defended his mission* for that purpose. And although he might with truth have answered, that he baptized because God had commanded him, yet he refrained from justifying himself for fear of gaining honour and authority to himself: for the humble man rejoices in being reprehended even when he is faultless, not seeking to discover the secret of his honour, except when it is to the honour of God, which he endeavours to promote on all occasions.

2. St. John advanced yet further, for in the presence of those priests and Levites, he confirmed the testimony which before he had given of Jesus Christ and of himself, before all the people, *depreciating his own person and his Baptism, to exalt the person and Baptism of Christ* our Lord, as we have pondered at the end of the preceding meditation. For this embassage being so remarkable, and his answer having to be related to the whole senate of Jerusalem, he would discover who he himself was, and who Christ was, that he might make Him known to all the world, that all might reverence Him for the Messiah; that he himself might be esteemed only as a simple voice; and the Baptism of Christ be of much greater estimation than his, that so it might the better be received and embraced by all.

(11) Joan. i. 25.

3. Hence we are to understand with how great reason Christ our Lord said of St. John, that *he was not "a reed shaken* or moved *with every wind,"* (12) but firm and stable like the earth, because he was founded on his own nothing; it being generally the property of the humble, to show themselves constant in their purposes, as well in humbling themselves, as in exalting Almighty God, taking pleasure in doing so before all the world, namely, in propagating the knowledge of their own baseness, and the greatness of Almighty God.

Colloquy.—O eternal God, who hast elaborated with Thine own hand this pattern of humility, sending him before Thy Son, who came to be his Lord and master, help me that I may learn by these examples to be truly humble, and by humility to dispose my heart to receive the gifts of Thy holy grace which Thou deniest to the proud, (13) and grantest to the humble, elevating them from their own baseness, to the height of Thy glory, world without end. Amen.

2.—MEDITATIONS ON OUR LORD'S PUBLIC LIFE.

MEDITATION III.

ON THE BAPTISM OF OUR LORD JESUS CHRIST.

POINT I.

Christ our Lord having completed the age of thirty years, took leave of His holy mother, telling her that the time was now come in which *He was to manifest Himself to the world,* and to perform the office of a Redeemer and master amongst men : at which she rejoiced greatly from the desire which she had of our redemption ; and although

(12) Matt. xi. 7.   (13) Jac. iv. 6.

she felt it some pain and loneliness that He should absent Himself from her for some days, yet she supported it with singular patience, making more account of the will of God than of her own, and of our profit than her own comfort.

Then our Lord Jesus Christ *went directly to the river Jordan*, where St. John preached and baptized all such publicans and sinners as sought to receive his Baptism:(1) and hearing in their company St. John's sermon, He presented Himself to be baptized. In which history are to be considered the *causes* which moved Christ our Lord to act thus.

1. The first was, to *enter into his office of a preacher* and master, giving us an example of rare humility, the master humbling himself to His disciple, and the Redeemer to His redeemed, the Son of the living God to His precursor, and the author of sanctity taking upon Him the form of a sinner; for Jesus Christ, the infinite wisdom and master of all, sat down amongst the soldiers and publicans to hear the sermon of St. John; and whereas He was most pure and without all spot, would yet receive the Baptism of sinners, as if He had been a sinner, not being obliged to it by any other law than His own good will, which made Him so humble Himself like other sinners : even as in His infancy He received circumcision, like other infants which were conceived in original sin.

Colloquy.—O most innocent Lamb, " that takest away the sins of the world," what need hast Thou to be baptized? Why dost Thou wash Thyself amongst a people bespotted with sin? Thou, O Lord, will be held for a sinner, although Thou art not, and I am sad and pensive that I am not esteemed just, being yet a sinner. O that my pride might be annihilated by this singular act of humility.

(1) Matt. iii.; Luc. iii.; Joan. i.; S. Tho. 3, p. q. xxxvi.

i. Hence *I* may learn, that *every good beginning of great things* ought to be *grounded in the exercises of humility*, by which we dispose ourselves to be employed by Almighty God, who will work in us things altogether for His glory. And for this reason Isaiah says, that those who are ordained to be saved, " shall take root downward, and shall bear fruit upward :" (2) as much as to say, that first, by humility, they are to hide themselves underneath the earth like the roots of trees, and afterwards to manifest themselves by most glorious actions, as the tree manifests itself by its fruits. Wherefore, O my soul, if thou desirest that the tower of perfection which thou intendest to build, should mount up to heaven, humble thyself to the bottom of the earth : for the higher thou wilt raise thy building, so much lower oughtest thou to dig and hollow the foundations. (3)

ii. I will remark that humility is a great disposition for baptism and penance, and for obtaining that purity which is conferred on the soul by these holy sacraments, confessing myself a sinner, and that I stand in need of being washed and cleansed of my faults, saying to our Lord with David:—" Thou shalt sprinkle me with hyssop, and I shall be cleansed : Thou shalt wash me, and I shall be made whiter than snow." (4)

Colloquy.—O sweet Jesus, who for humility's sake wouldst be washed by St. John, with his Baptism of mere water, wash me with the water of Thy grace, in virtue of Thy precious blood, mingled with the hyssop of Thy humility. O my soul, embrace this sovereign virtue which, like hyssop, gathers up the living water of grace, and in virtue of the blood of my Saviour,

(2) Isai. xxxvii. 31.   (3) S. Aug. ser. 10, de verbis Dom.
(4) Ps. l. 9. S. Greg. in psalm. l. penit.

sacrificed on the tree of the cross by many torments, to cleanse me from the leprosy of my sins.   Amen.

2. The *second cause* of this fact was *to work before teaching;* and before the preaching of a new Baptism of water and of the Holy Ghost, to receive that of water only, lest any should disdain to receive His Baptism, which was so precious. So that by the way He honoured the Baptism of His precursor, and approved it also by effect as He received circumcision, giving to understand that He approved that law, and reverenced the same as given by God.

Hence I will gather the obligation we have of keeping the precepts and counsels of the holy Gospel, which is to approve them by work, and highly to reverence them; as to violate the law is to infringe it in effect, despising as the apostle says, (5) Him that gave it. And if our Lord Jesus Christ would receive the Baptism of St. John, it not being of precept, to keep the counsel of His precursor; how much more reasonable is it that I should keep His precepts and counsels, doing more things than I am bound to do, especially in the way of humility.

POINT II.

Immediately that Christ our Lord demanded baptism of St. John, and that he was upon the point to baptize Him, the *Holy Ghost revealed to him interiorly*, that this same man was the Messiah, for he had never as yet seen Him, in flesh, upon which he refused to baptise Him, saying :—"I ought to be baptized of Thee, and comest Thou to me?" Christ our Lord answered him:—"Suffer it to be so now, for so it becometh us to fulfil all justice."(6)

1. Here I will meditate, first, *on the unspeakable joy* which St. John felt in his soul, as soon as he knew Christ

(5) Rom. ii. 4.   (6) Mat. iii. 14.

Jesus our Lord, renewing the former exultation which he had, when he knew Him in His mother's womb. This joy he accompanied with singular *reverence and humility*, confessing of himself that he was a sinner, and stood in need that Christ our Lord should wash and purify him with the Baptism of the Holy Ghost: and wholly astonished with *admiration* to behold Him so greatly humbled, he exclaimed with these words:—" Tu ventis ad me?" " How comest Thou to me to be baptized ! Thou, infinite God ! Thou Saviour of the world, and forgiver of sinners ! Thou, who sanctifiedst me in my mother's womb, comest Thou to me? To me, Thy creature? To me, Thy servant? To me, a worm of the earth? And wilt Thou that I baptize Thee with my Baptism of water only, Thou who art the author of the Baptism of grace? O most profound humility of my Lord !"

The like affections will I endeavour to excite within myself, especially when I am to communicate, and will jointly exercise myself in these two notions, of God our Lord, and of myself, and in the affections which proceed from both, which always go together, the one of them aiding and assisting the other.

2. Secondly, I will greatly consider *the answer of Jesus Christ our Lord*, which was wonderful. " So it becometh" thee and me " to fulfil all justice," that is to say, the whole work of sanctity. I, by humbling myself to be baptized, and thou by obeying my command to baptize me. Giving us this to understand, that all our sanctity consists in *humility and obedience;* humbling ourselves before God and men, and in obeying God and His lawful ministers : embracing the three degrees contained in those two virtues. i. First to *subject myself to those who are greater than myself,* in respect of some pre-eminence they have above me, either in dignity, office, age or understanding.—ii. The

second, more perfect, to subject myself to *my equals*, endeavouring to give them the greater honour, and the better place, and to obey them in what they desire, it being good, as if they were my superiors that did command me.—iii. The third most perfect, is, to subject myself to myself, *even to my inferiors*, and that with such resignation and promptitude, as if they were " better than" myself. (7)

By these degrees Christ our Lord walked, and practised the sum of all justice and sanctity : which we ought to imitate, submitting ourselves, as St. Peter says,—" to every human creature for God's sake," (8) in such things as are conformable to His holy will, maintaining exteriorly, as St. Gregory says, the authority and decency which is belonging to the state of every one, according to the rules of prudence. Moreover, with these two virtues, we shall perform all that justice which belongs to God, to ourselves, and to our neighbour; inasmuch as they move us to respect and obey God, to mortify ourselves, and to give good example to our neighbour, winning their loves, and living in peace and amity with them.

All this Christ our Lord comprehended in His answer. And with this spirit will I encourage myself to the practice of these two virtues, saying to myself : " Thus does it" become thee " to fulfil all justice," not a part, but all; not with a half, but with a whole and perfect heart : and though thou be great in the world, and holdest some dignity in the Church, it imports thee to accomplish all His justice, obeying and humbling thyself as Jesus Christ did to His precursor."

3. *St. John immediately obeyed*, with the three degrees or marks of perfect obedience,—in the manner of obeying, by a *punctual execution ;*—in the *promptitude of his will ;*

(7) Phil. ii. 3.   (8) 1 Pet. ii. 13.

—in the *submission of his judgment* to the judgment of Christ, obeying His word and baptizing Him with very great reverence; for our Lord delights to see His servants submit to His divine judgment, and not dispute His commands, as St. Peter did, being yet imperfect, not permitting him to "wash" his "feet;" (9) who thereby put himself in danger of losing the friendship of Christ if he had persevered in his refusal, as we will show in its proper place.

POINT III.

The eternal Father beholding His only Son so greatly humbled, *repvted himself obliged to honour and authorize him*, to fulfil the truth of what he had said :—"He that humbles himself shall be exalted :" (10) for even in those things in which a man humbles himself, in the same is God accustomed to exalt him; and therefore if he humble himself to be held for an idiot, or a sinner, he exalts him in wisdom and sanctity.

The *means* which the eternal Father used to honour His Son in this occasion, were *three*, and those most excellent; which we will examine in the very words reported by the Evangelist.

"THE HEAVENS OPENED." (11)

1. The first means was, *that the heavens opened* with marvellous splendour and division, which was formed in the air.

i. And St. Matthew says, that "the heavens were opened to Him," (12) that is, for His respect and for His honour; showing that Jesus Christ our Lord was a man, but not "earthly," and made of earth as the first man Adam was, but a man "heavenly" (13) and descended

(9) Joan. xiii. 6.   (10) Luc. xiv. 11.   (11) Marc. i. 10.
        (12) Mat. iii. 16.   (13) 1 Cor. xv. 48.

from heaven : and by consequence, that His life and doctrine, His laws and His works were all celestial. Also, to signify, that by His means the gates of heaven open to all those who imitate Him, because in imitation of Him they should become men celestial; and by this means did He verify the theme, which St. John took in his preaching, saying,—"Do penance, for the kingdom of heaven is at hand :" (14) which being opened to Christ our Lord, gave us to understand, that they would be open to all those who should do penance, and follow His doctrine.

ii. St. Mark says that He "saw the heavens opened :" signifying, that our Lord Jesus Christ, by His infinite wisdom, penetrated all the celestial secrets, so that He might report to us as an eye-witness, all that which passed above in heaven, and that by His means the heavens should likewise be "opened" to us, so that being here beneath in earth, as was St. Stephen, (15) we might see and contemplate the secrets of heaven, and "have our conversation" there. (16)

Colloquy.—O sweet Jesus, our heavenly Adam, rightly did the heavens open to honour Thee, since with Thy humility, Thou hast merited the same and conquered them ; it is but reasonable that they open themselves to invite Thee to mount to them, since they are Thine. Sweet Lord, so open them to me, that they be never shut against me : and for this effect, blot out of my soul " the image of the earthly" Adam, and imprint in it the image of the heavenly. (17)   Amen.

" AND HE SAW THE SPIRIT OF GOD DESCENDING AS A DOVE, AND COMING UPON HIM." (18)

2. The second means which the Father used to honour His Son was *to send down upon Him the Holy Ghost in form*

(14) Mat. iii. 2.   (15) Act. vii. 55.   (16) Phil. iii 20.
(17) Cor. xv. 49.   (18) Joan. i. 32 ; Matt. iii. 17.

of a dove, which reposed upon His head; declaring by this exterior sign, the plenitude of the divine Spirit which dwelt within Him from the first instant of His conception, reposing upon this rod and root of Jesse, (19) with the immensity of His seven celestial gifts.

i. He descended in the form of a dove,—to signify;

(a) The *innocence, purity, and meekness* of Christ, that all men might understand, that although He was baptized with the Baptism of penance, yet that He was no sinner, nor had anything common with sinners, (20) but that He was just, pure, simple, and like a dove, without the gall of sin, anger, duplicity, or any guile.

(b) That He was not only pure from sin, but also that He was "*the Lamb of God that taketh away the sins of the world.*" For as the dove in the time of Noah brought the sign of the ceasing of the waters of the deluge;—so this day the presence of Jesus Christ is a sign, that by His merits He would cause to cease the deluge of sins which drowned the world.

(c) That this our Lord should neither be solitary nor unfruitful, but *should engender and bring forth many children*, imitators of His innocence, of which He would make one Church, united in one faith and one charity, whereof He would say, "one is my dove." (21)

Colloquy.—O holy Spirit, I render Thee thanks for the glorious testimony which Thou hast given of the innocence and sanctity of our Saviour; descend upon me like a dove, replenishing my soul with purity and sanctity. O that Thou wouldst "give me the wings of a dove," (22) to fly into the holes of this living rock, upon whom this day Thou didst repose, to the end that my heart may repose interiorly with His, uniting it with His by perfect love. Amen.

(19) Is. xi. 1.   (20) 1 Pet. ii. 23.
(21) Cant. viii. 8.   (22) Ps. liv. 7.

ii. I may likewise dwell in thought on the great gladness which the Baptist felt when he saw the Holy Ghost come down upon Christ in the form of a dove, and the joy with which he published the same to all those that had not seen it: beseeching the divine Spirit to illuminate the eyes of my soul, that she may see with the light of faith, the gifts and inestimable riches which are contained in Christ our Lord, that I may love and esteem Him as I ought.

"AND, BEHOLD, A VOICE FROM HEAVEN, SAYING, THIS IS MY BELOVED SON, IN WHOM I AM WELL PLEASED." (23)

3. The third means which the Father took to honour His Son, was, *to speak with a voice formed in the air*, not terrible and frightful, but most sweet and amiable, saying, —" This is my well-beloved Son, in whom I am well pleased :" every word of which has its particular mystery.

i. The word " this," is as if He had said, " this " which appears a pure man, mortal and passible,—" this," who humbles himself to appear a sinner, in being baptized with the Baptism of sinners,—" this," upon whom this dove reposes,—" this is my Son;" not my adopted son, like other just sons who had gone before Him, but my natural and Only-begotten Son at this present time by means of baptism, but engendered and begotten from all eternity, (24) as ancient as I, as wise and as holy as I because He is God as well as I : and by excellence is my well-beloved, whom I cherish and love above all things created or to be created; whom I love as myself with an infinite love.—ii. In Him " I am well-pleased," (25) and I delight in Him, esteeming myself happy in having such a Son, because He is always agreeable to me, doing all those things which delight me.   He had no need of this baptism

(23) Mat. iii. 17.   (24) Ps. cix. 3.   (25) Joan. viii. 29.

to make Himself more agreeable to me, being ever before so agreeable to me, that none without Him could be agreeable to me, and for His sake also all those who imitate Him shall be right pleasing and agreeable to me.

Colloquy.—O eternal Father, I give Thee thanks for the honour which Thou then didst to Thy Blessed Son, when He so humbled Himself for the love of Thee, rejoicing in the love and the good pleasure which Thou tookest in Him: in respect of which I beseech Thee to assist me, that, after His example, I may always accomplish that which is agreeable to Thee, that so Thou mayest likewise take pleasure in me. O my Saviour, I congratulate Thee with the honour which Thy Father and the Holy Ghost did Thee this day, approving Thee by such singular testimonies to be our master and our Redeemer, render me, O Lord, agreeable to Thy celestial Father, and worthy to be received as His son. Amen.

2. Lastly, consider that by the merits of Jesus Christ our Lord, this day the mystery of the most Holy Trinity began to manifest itself in the voice of the eternal Father, and in the dove which figured and represented the Holy Ghost. At this time the Father did not call Christ our Lord His servant, as He called Him by the prophet Isaiah, when He said,—"Behold my servant in whom my soul delighteth," (26) but He called Him His Son; thus discovering the divinity of Him who, as man, was but His servant. With this consideration I will render thanks to our Lord for having manifested to us this divine mystery, beseeching Him to enlighten my soul to understand and reverence it.

POINT IV.

1. Christ our Lord, as St. Thomas says, (27) *instituted*

(26) Is. xlii. 1.   (27) 3. p. q. lxvi. art. 2.

at that time His own Baptism, very different from that of St. John, giving to it the virtue and efficacy represented to us by these three miraculous signs: namely, to open to us the gates of heaven;—to give to us the gifts and graces of the Holy Ghost;—and to make us the adopted sons of Almighty God, acceptable in His sight, by the faith and acknowledgment of the most Holy Trinity, in whose virtue and name it is conferred upon us with such singular plenitude, that whosoever dies immediately after he has been baptized, will go to heaven directly without delay, and possess the inheritance of the Son of God, clearly seeing the most Holy Trinity; the only sight of whom makes the beholder perfectly blessed.

Colloquy.—O Saviour of the world, I give Thee as many thanks as I am able, that Thou hast instituted for the beginning of Thy Evangelical law, so sweet and profitable a sacrament, with so many prerogatives and spiritual gifts as are granted to us in virtue of it. I thank Thee also with all my heart, for the grace which Thou hast done me in admitting me, so unworthy a servant, to this Baptism, of which so many persons are deprived, and in having received me into the ark of Thy Catholic Church that I might be saved, permitting others to perish in the deluge.   I beseech Thee, O Lord, that the gates of heaven, which then were opened unto me, may never be shut against me; that the Holy Ghost, who then was given me, never abandon me, and that I never lose the dignity of the son of God, to which Thou then didst elevate me; but always be so agreeable to Thee, that finally I may come to enjoy Thee in Thy glory.   Amen.

2. Christ our Lord on that day, not only instituted the sacrament of Baptism, but also with the same highly *honoured His precursor,* (28) accomplishing the desire

(28) S. Th. 3. p. q. xxxviii. a. 6, ad 3.

which he discovered to Him, when he said, "I ought to be baptized by Thee." (29) For it is the property of Christ our Lord, to accomplish the desires of those that love Him. And since St. John obeyed Him in baptizing Him with his Baptism of water, it was most fitting that Christ should baptize him with His Baptism of the Holy Ghost and of fire, heaping upon him anew, most high graces and celestial gifts. O how great was the joy of the holy precursor, and how well did he deem the labours of his office to have been employed, receiving, as he did from Christ on this day, so copious a retribution for them? O how well might he say to Almighty God, that which Simeon said,—"Now Thou dost dismiss Thy servant, O Lord, according to Thy word in peace," (30) because my eyes have seen my Saviour. But as he was fervent and grateful, so he resolved to manifest his gratitude in giving public testimony of the excellencies of his Lord, so long as life should last him, as afterwards he did. And I, after his example, will make the like purposes, in acknowledgment of the favours which I have received from my Saviour.

POINT V.

Lastly, all these wonderful effects took place, as St. Luke says, *whilst Christ our Lord was in prayer*, for as soon as He was baptized He set Himself to prayer : this being the first time that the Gospel mentions that Christ prayed.

1. Which sundry *excellencies of prayer* are discovered to us, showing of what necessity it is, and that we should often frequent the same.

i. The first excellency is, that prayer in itself is a very *efficacious means* to obtain of Almighty God the three before recited wonderful effects; for first,—it *opens to us the*

(29) Matt. iii. 14.   (30) Luc. ii. 29.

gates of the kingdom of heaven, and discovers to us celestial secrets; as it is said of the apostle St. Peter; that praying, "the heavens opened"(31) to him.—Secondly It *procures* for us *the plenitude of the Holy Ghost* and of His gifts: as the apostles praying were often replenished with the Holy Ghost; as we shall see in the fifth part. Thirdly, In prayer, *we hear the voice of our heavenly Father*, in His divine inspirations; we labour to attain the dignity of the sons of God; and practise the means to make ourselves agreeable and pleasing to Him—and when this prayer is joined with the humiliation of ourselves, as Christ our Lord joined it in this instance, it is then of more importance than all the rest : for, as the Wise man says :—" The prayer of him that humbles himself shall pierce the clouds," (32) and even to the opening of the heavens, and bring down the presents and gifts, which the Father of lights is wont to give.

ii. The second excellency is, that Christ *our Lord joined prayer with baptism:* to signify, that prayer, devotion, and frequenting the sacraments, ought to accompany all our works, to the end that they may be received and used by us in a proper manner; beseeching our Lord, to remove the impediments which the devils use to hinder the fruits of them, and to assist us with His holy favour, to bring them to a happy and prosperous end.

iii. Moreover, Christ our Lord being baptized, set Himself to prayer, to declare to us the *necessity* which the *baptized* and the faithful have *to apply themselves to prayer*, and that prayer ought to be their principal exercise, frequenting it often to prevent the temptations which assail them, and to begin with fervour the new life of

---

(31) Acts x. 10.   (32) Ecclus. xxxv. 21.

which they have made profession, as also to preserve the graces and gifts which they have received in holy Baptism.

2. It is likewise credible that Christ our Lord prayed, not only in the manner in which one asks something for his own necessity, but also with the other parts of prayer mentioned by St. Paul, (33) *giving thanks* to His Father for the favours which He had done Him, as also for those others which He hoped to receive; as He prayed when He raised Lazarus.(34) He further prayed *for all those* who were there expecting to be baptized; and for all those who should hereafter receive His Baptism, in order that they might receive the same unfeignedly. And generally He prayed for all men, because, as much as was requisite on His part, He instituted this sacrament for the good of all, and His desire was that all should receive and enjoy the graces and gifts which were figured and signified by these exterior signs.

3. From all these considerations I am to draw a great esteem and affection to prayer, and great purposes to exercise myself in it, according to the example of Christ our Lord : for whose holy merit's sake, I will crave of the most Blessed Trinity, to grant to me this spirit of prayer, with the graces and effects which follow it.

MEDITATION IV.

ON CHRIST OUR LORD'S ABODE, AFTER HIS BAPTISM, IN THE DESERT, FASTING FORTY DAYS AND FORTY NIGHTS.

POINT I.

First, consider how Christ our Lord being baptized, and as St. Luke says, "full of" and replenished with " the Holy Ghost, *returned from the Jordan,*" (1) leaving the

(33) Phil. iv. 6 ; 1 Tim. ii.   (34) Joan. xi. 41.
(1) Matt. iv. 1; Marc. ii. 12; Luc. iv. 1.

company of St. John, and of such others as were there, pondering the *cause* which moved Him to it; which was, to practise some certain virtues proper to those who are filled with the Holy Ghost.

1. The first was, His desired *humility*, presently flying all human praises, worldly honours and promotions; for as the whole multitude of people, who had both seen and heard the wonders which occurred at His baptism, would never have ceased to extol and honour Him, this caused Him to fly and to hide Himself;—not that He was in any danger of falling into vain-glory, but to instruct us by this example, to avoid places and occasions of our own praise, especially at the first when virtue is yet but green, and in danger to wither and die in the flower, with the wind of vain-glory, as it is written in Job, (2) saying, that the virtue of hypocrites does easily perish.

2. Secondly, He retired from the Jordan; to signify, that men replenished with the Holy Ghost, ought *not to despise exterior ceremonies*, such as Baptism was, of only water, but in complying with them, presently to *refer them to the interior*, and more elevated exercises of spiritual virtues, for fear lest that be said of them, which the same Lord said of the Pharisees, that they made over great account of exterior washings, and added :—"This people honoureth me only with their lips," and with exterior ceremonies, "but their heart is far from me :" (3) there are amongst you many hypocrites, who make clean the outside of the vessel and platter, but leave the inside full of foulness and uncleanness.

3. Thirdly, He retired from the Jordan : to show, that when any one replenished with the Holy Ghost, has the secrets of the Kingdom of heaven, and has tasted in prayer the sweetness of God, he forthwith desires to fly

(2) Job xv. 34.   (3) Matt. xv. 8; Marc. vii. 6.

from the press and tumult of the people, to meditate in secret on what he has seen, and immediately to employ himself in the contemplation of that which has been revealed to him.

Colloquy.—O most sweet Jesus, replenish me, I beseech Thee, with the same Holy Spirit with which Thou wast filled, that I may begin to imitate the example which Thou hast given me, retiring at certain times to pray to Thee, as Thou retiredst to pray for me.   Amen.

POINT II.

"And immediately the Spirit drove Him out into the desert.   And He was in the desert forty days and forty nights;   and was tempted by Satan, and He was with beasts." (4)

1. In this I am to reflect *what spirit* it was which impelled Him—in *what manner*—into *what place*—for *what causes*—and *in what He exercised Himself* during His abode and residence there.

i. Christ our Lord was not induced by the spirit of vanity, nor by impetuosity of passion, nor only by the spirit of man, but by *the Spirit of Almighty God* with which He was filled.   In this we are taught the difference that there is between the sons of God, and of the celestial Adam, and the sons of this world and of the earthly Adam : for these in all their actions are moved by the impulse of the evil spirit, which is the spirit of the Devil, of the world, of the flesh, or of their own *perverse* spirit, wholly inclined to its own opinion, and to its own will : on the contrary, the others are moved by the good Spirit, following His inspirations and divine impulses, according as St. Paul says :—"whosoever are led by the Spirit of

(4) Marc. i. 12.

God, they are the sons of God;"(5) and if I suppose my-self to be the son of God, I ought in all my works to follow the impulse of the Spirit of God, and not of my own private spirit, which is contrary to that of God.

ii. The *manner* how this Spirit impelled and induced Jesus Christ, was, as the Evangelists say, with *promptitude, efficacy,* and wonderful *sweetness:* for being baptized, "*Statim,*" forthwith; "*expulit,*" He drove and im-pelled Him efficaciously, but sweetly, as one who guided and led Him by the hand. In this we discern the pro-perties of the Holy Spirit in His inspirations, who is an enemy of delays, of slackness, tepidity, and of slothfulness in our actions, as likewise of violence and repugnance in them, *disposing* "*all things,*" "*fortiter et suaviter,*"(6) and "sweetly." Those therefore who are the sons of Almighty God, ought to obey with the like promptitude, efficacy, delight and suavity, rejoicing to follow His di-rection, without diverting themselves to other things : as the four holy beasts went whither they were driven by "the impulse of the spirit" that conducted them, "and they turned not as they went."(7)

iii. The *place* to which the Spirit impelled and conducted Him, was "*the desert.*" So that He moved Him not to go to Jerusalem, or to populous cities, there to converse and to treat with men; but for that time He inspired Him to go into the desert and into solitude, and to dwell and abide amongst "the beasts," (8) that before He manifested Him-self to the world, He should first *exercise some works of remarkable virtue* for our example and instruction.

iv. And this to no other end than He should practice *true humility:* therefore as, when He was born He was laid in a manger amidst brute beasts, to enter into the world

(5) Rom. viii. 14.   (6) Sap. viii. 1.
(7) Ezech. i. 12.   (8) Mar. i. 13.

with humiliation; so before He would manifest Himself to the same world, He would converse forty days in the company of beasts, He who was the Lord of angels, to humble Himself for man, who by his sin was become a beast. (9)

v. That He should employ all that time in the exercise of *penance and prayer;* solitude and the desert greatly conducing to this purpose, which Christ our Lord exercised with great contentment, saying that of the Canticles :—"*I will go to the mountain of myrrh, and to the hill of frankincense:*" (10) viz : to the practice of penance and prayer, of mortification and contemplation, and all this with singular highness and sublimity. He gave Himself to the works of penance, watching much, lying upon the bare ground, suffering the injury of the air without any shelter, and fasting a fast, very rigorous and miraculous. He continually frequented prayer and contemplation : in such a manner, that although His body was in the company of beasts, yet His spirit conversed with the angels in heaven, so that He always ascended from this desert like the "smoke of myrrh and incense," (11) giving sweet odour to the eternal Father.

2. Hence I will gather, that it is the property of the Holy Spirit, to inspire these two sorts of exercises; and likewise the property of those who wish to imitate Jesus Christ to spend much time in them, especially such as are novices in virtue; as also those who are to issue out in public to perform great things in the service of Almighty God : For to enterprise this business happily, they ought first to sequester and withdraw themselves for some days into "solitude," (12) disposing themselves to hear what Almighty God will speak to their heart, suggesting to

(9) Ps. xlviii.	(10) Cant. iv. 6.
(11) Cant. iii. 6.	(12) Ose. ii. 14.

them what they are to do, and giving them force to accomplish it : for it is very meet, as Job says, that those which are the "kings and consuls of the earth," governing souls and guiding them as is convenient, that first they should "build themselves solitudes," (13) to learn the manner how to govern, and how they are to direct others.

Colloquy.—O most sacred Spirit, inspire me and guide me effectually to the "mountain of myrrh, and to the hill of frankincense" that I may follow my Saviour. O my Saviour, since, for my example, Thou goest to the desert, vouchsafe to conduct and lead me in Thy company, instructing me to seek within myself this "solitude," to exercise prayer and penance in it. Amen.

POINT III.

Thirdly, consider *how Christ our Lord fasted forty days, and forty nights :* meditating on all the *causes* and *circumstances* of this fast.

1. The chief and principal causes were only *two.*

i. The first was, to *satisfy* for the *gluttony* of our first parents, who, contrary to the commandment of Almighty God, eat of the fruit of the forbidden tree; and likewise, to satisfy for all the gluttonies and excesses of the whole world; for in the very matter in which men had transgressed, in the self-same Christ our Lord would suffer pain, for satisfaction of their offences : (14) which ought to teach me to chastise my excesses and surfeits with fastings, since Christ our Lord has fasted for them.

ii. The other cause was, *to instruct us* how the baptized who desire to serve Almighty God our sovereign Lord, are to endeavour to subdue by fastings the flames of their flesh, to render it subject to the spirit. Their first combat ought to be against gluttony, endeavouring to

(13) Job iii. 14.   (14) S. Tho. 3. p. q. xl. a. 2, ad. 3. et. q. xli. a._3.

overcome their domestic enemy, which is their flesh, of which the Devil makes use for his temptations. (15) In this manner also ought the ministers of the Gospel to fight and combat, chastising, as the Apostle St. Paul says, their bodies, and bringing them into due subjection, for fear lest it befal them, that preaching to others, themselves become reprobate. (16) Wherefore, if thou desirest that the heavens be not shut against thee, which holy Baptism opened to thee, bridle thy appetite by fasting, for gluttony cast our first parents out of paradise, and abstinence will aid thee to be again admitted into it.

2. The *circumstances* were—

i. That this fast was *very rigorous*, although miraculous, without eating or drinking of anything, either day, or night; to teach us, that our fast ought to be the most rigorous possible, without asking any miracle, yet so that we destroy not nature, nor lose the forces necessary for the service of Almighty God, contenting ourselves as the Apostle St. Paul says, with that which is necessary, and offering up our bodies to God our Lord a living sacrifice : yet in such manner, that the rigour of our fast be measured with reason. (17)

ii. This fast was *long* and continuing, namely, for the space of *forty days and forty nights:* to denote the constancy which we ought to hold in the works of penance, and in the castigation of the flesh, persevering even until we arrive at perfection; for, although Christ our Lord prolonged not His fast more than "forty days," yet was He prepared to continue the same for a longer time, if it had been necessary : by which He authorized the forty days of the Lenten fast, which the Church observes so

(15) Cassian, lib. v. c. 3; S. Greg. lib. xxx. Mor. c. 26.
(16) 1 Cor. ix. 27.
(17) Rom. xii. 1; 1 Tim. vi; Cas. col. xxi. c. xxii.

exactly. By His example I will encourage myself to observe the same with all perfection and exactness, ordaining the four decades of this number, to four ends :—The first, in satisfaction for my sins.—The second, in thankfulness for the benefits I have received.—The third, to obtain the virtues which are wanting to me.—The fourth, to dispose myself for the glory of the resurrection, which I expect in recompence of my labours.

iii. His fast, although on the one side severe and rigorous, yet on the other it was exceeding *sweet*, for as is collected out of the Evangelists, all this time He felt no hunger, because the virtue of the divinity, and the sweetness of divine contemplation, caused His sacred flesh to suffer no hunger nor pain in this His fasting, from which Moses and Elias were likewise exempt: (18)—the one being in the mountain and conversing with God;—and the other, walking towards the mountain to converse with God, being fortified with the bread which the angel brought him; which teaches us, that prayer and devotion make fasting sweet, recompencing the assistance which they receive from it, with the relish which they give it. (19)

Colloquy.—O most sweet Jesus, I render Thee thanks for that so rigorous a fast which Thou sufferedst in satisfaction for my sins, by which I beseech Thee to forgive them : and so assist me that for the time to come, my body may fast by forbearing from meats, and my spirit may fast by refraining from vices. Amen.

(18) Exod. xxxiv.; 3 Reg. xix.
(19) S. Ber. ser. iv. quadrag.

MEDITATION V.

ON THE TEMPTATIONS ENDURED BY CHRIST OUR LORD IN THE DESERT.

POINT I.

The first shall be to consider how Christ our Lord, "was led by the Spirit into the desert :" amongst other ends, as St. Matthew says, "to be tempted by the Devil." (2)

1. It is the *property of the Holy Spirit* to put such as are *perfect* men, in *places* and *occasions* where they may be *tempted*, to manifest in them the force and vigour of His grace; giving them glorious victories, and trophies or tokens of great virtues and merits. So that, although I may not rashly expose myself to such occasions, yet if I meet them, I may presume that they come by the providence and permisson of the Holy Ghost, that with IIis assistance I may combat against them : since, as the apostle teaches, this appertains to IIis care and fidelity.(3)

Colloquy.—O sacred Sprit, I wholly resign myself to Thy providence, that Thou conduct me whither it pleases Thee, that I may be tried and tempted, so that Thou be my second and assistant in all my combats and temptations : for with Thine assistance, if I suffer not myself to be vanquished, I shall be certain of the victory.

2. The Holy Spirit conducted Christ our Lord "*into the desert*," rather than into any other place, there "to be *tempted;*" the desert being a place occasioning the temptations of the Devil, by reason of its solitude; for the Devil seeing a man to be all alone and having none to help him with his counsel and direction, and with such other means

(1) S. Tho. 3. p. q. xiv.

(2) Matt. iv. 1.   (3) 1 Cor. x. 13.

as spiritual Fathers are wont to give to such as are tempted, hoping easily to overcome him, and setting upon him with great activity as he set upon Eve seeing her alone and sequestered, apart from Adam her husband, whom he vanquished and gained with great facility : for which cause as the holy Fathers say, none who are imperfect, ought to enter into the deserts, there to lead or undertake a solitary life. (4)

i. Hence I will gather, that although I live amidst a multitude, and converse with many, if I seek not to give an account of my temptations to my confessor or ghostly Father, that I am indeed alone, and live in the desert, and in evident danger of being easily tempted and vanquished by the Devil, because, as Ecclesiastes says :—" If the serpent bites in silence," (5) and without hissing, the enchanter cannot take him : which is to say, when the Devil tempts and bites, by the means of sin, and he that is bitten is hushed or holds his peace, although he have a skilful physician to cure him, yet he shall not be cured, because he is as it were alone, and being alone, if he chance to fall, he has not any to help him up.

ii. Moreover, as the life of the solitaries or hermits, spent in asperity and prayer, is exceedingly perfect, so Satan seeing any to undertake it, he repairs to tempt him, to cut off his passage. And although he abhor and tempt all men in general, yet much more the fervent, who begin to serve Almighty God with perfection wheresoever it be. Yet must not any for this lose courage, because the Holy Ghost who inspired this sort of life, will likewise inspire with efficacy, the means to vanquish the temptations which the Devil contrives against them. And as

(4) Bazil. Reg. viii. ex. Cas. lib. 3. fusis. viii. c. 17; Clim. c. iv. C. x. juxta. Septuag: Cas. col. 1. c. 11.

(5) Eccles. iv. 10, 11.

the fervent with their fervour "raise up a Leviathan" (6) against themselves, which is the malignant spirit by which he tempts them; even so do they awaken and provoke the Holy Ghost to succour and assist them.

3. The third shall be to consider the *causes* for which Christ our Lord would be tempted immediately after His Baptism and fasting, to the end I may make my profit of it.—i. First, although He was not a beginner in the practice of virtue, yet would He pass by the ordinary law of those who begin to serve Almighty God, who, as the Wise man says, "prepare" their "soul for temptation." (7) As also to make Himself like other men, in all sorts of miseries excepting sin, or the appearance of sin : so that knowing by experience what it is to be "tempted," He might "have compassion, " as St. Paul says, (8) on those that are tempted, and so by the victory over His temptations, He might teach us how to vanquish ours, and give us force and courage to overcome them.

Hence it was, that although He was tempted with divers temptations during the space of "forty days," as St. Luke and St. Mark give us to understand, yet at the end of those days, He was tempted with three visible temptations, in which, as in the root or seed all the others are contained, because by them we learn the manner how to combat against them. (9)

4. Hence I may gather three very important lessons against the time when I shall be tempted.—i. First, not to afflict or discomfort myself, as if I had received some disgrace before Almighty God; for since my Saviour was tempted being the Son of God, it is no wonder that I should be tempted; the spiritual joy amidst temptations,

<hr>

(6) Job iii. 8.   (7) Ecclus. ii. 1.   (8) Heb. iv. 15.
(9) S. Tho. q. i. a. 3. ad. 2.

being an excellent armour, offensive and defensive, to come off victoriously from them.

ii. Secondly, to have recourse to our Lord, with great confidence for a remedy and help in my temptations, saying :—

Colloquy.—O my King, since Thou knowest so well, and hast Thyself tried what it is to be tempted, " have compassion " upon me, taking from me the temptation, or giving me force to overcome it. Amen.

iii. The third is, *to arm myself with prayer and fasting* before the temptation, as our Lord and Saviour did: for, as He said to His Apostles, there are certain kinds of devils, who cannot be expelled from the bodies they possess, but by "prayer and fasting."(10) There is also a kind of devils which can be overcome only with the same weapons; and in preparing myself, I will see in what manner Christ our Lord overcame His temptations, that I may combat against mine in the same manner.

POINT II.

Consider the *three temptations* with which the Devil assailed Christ our Saviour, and the *manner how He surmounted them;* the first was in the sin of *gluttony*, the second in *vain-glory*, the third in *ambition* or *avarice*, nevertheless, they were all mixed with *pride*, and a desire of excellency: for, as the Devil is proud, and fell by his pride, and by the same overcame the first man, so knowing full well the force of this temptation, he intermixed the same amongst the others, to overthrow men with the more facility. And on the other hand, Christ our Saviour repelled all these temptations by *humility*, which is a most powerful armour to let us free from the snares of Satan.

(10) Mat. xvii.

THE FIRST TEMPTATION.

1. The first temptation was that of *gluttony*, by the desire and means of eating ; for the forty days of fast being expired, Christ our Lord, as man, became hungry; and the Devil, who watched and pried into His actions, let not slip the occasion seeing Him in necessity and hunger, and with the show of pity, said to Him:—"If Thou be the Son of God, command that these stones be made bread;"(11) as if he had said, "Make use of the power which Thou hast to work miracles, to relieve Thy necessity and Thy hunger;" provoking Him hereby to an inordinate appetite of eating, even to the working of a miracle to obtain food.

i. In this point we are to ponder the *different ways* which the Devil uses to tempt us with gluttony. He tempts those that are *dainty*, setting before them the *desire of exquisite meats*, making them to tread under foot the law of Almighty God to enjoy their sweetness, as Eve did. He tempts the *needy*, provoking them to *remedy their necessities* by unlawful means: sometimes openly, inciting them to stealing; at other times insinuating false dispensations, and feigning revelations, as he deceived a holy prophet;(12) sometimes under pretext or *colour of* piety, suggesting vain and presumptuous means, and in this manner he tempted Christ our Lord; and by one way or another, he greatly labours to vanquish those who are spiritual, by the vice of gluttony; for, being overcome by a vice so base, he knows they will become more cowardly in other combats of greater importance.

ii. Christ our Lord, with great *humility*, answered with a text of holy Scripture:—"Not in bread alone doth man live, but in every word that proceedeth from the mouth

(11) Mat. iv. 4.   (12) 3 Reg. xiii. 15,

of God,"(13) as much as to say, "I will not work miracles at thy persuasion, nor yet for daintiness sake, since God can sustain me by other means, and with what else it may please Him, without the use of any bread. I believe whatsoever is written in holy Scripture concerning the same, and I trust in His fatherly providence, which will never fail me." In this He teaches us the manner how to overcome temptations arising from temporal necessities, and from the want of sustenance or other commodities, namely, by humility and faith in the word of God, and a firm confidence in His fatherly providence: for if Almighty God "giveth to beasts this food and to the young ravens,"(14) shall our heavenly Father deny the same to His own sons, when they ask the same of Him confidently?

THE SECOND TEMPTATION.

2. After this victory, the Devil took occasion to tempt Christ our Lord with *vanity, presumption*, and *unlimited confidence*, and setting Him upon the pinnacle of the Temple of Jerusalem, he said to Him:—" If thou be the Son of God, cast Thyself down, for it is written, that He hath given His angels charge over Thee, and in their hands they shall bear Thee up, less perhaps Thou dash Thy foot against a stone;"(15) as if he had said:—" if Thou dost this, those who shall behold this sight will believe in Thee, and will glorify Thy Father who is in heaven."

i. Here we are to ponder, first, the *property* of the Devil in his temptations, that we suffer not ourselves to be deceived by his subtleties; who always in the first temptation labours to know the inclinations and affections of every one, and from them takes occasion to invent and adapt new snares and temptations, more subtle and forcible than the former. In such a manner, that he takes occa-

(13) Deut. viii. 3.   (14) Ps. cxlvi. 9.   (15) Mat. iv. 5.

sion to tempt us not only with the wants which we suffer, or the evil inclinations which are in us, but even with our best qualities, inciting us to use them with indiscretion, sinister intention, or other evil circumstances, exceeding the limits of reason.—Those who trust in Almighty God, he induces to confide in Him immeasurably, that so they may then become presumptuous. The zealous of the glory of God, he endeavours to make choleric; and if he see that they are learned, and that they ground their virtue upon the sayings of sacred Scripture, even these will serve his turn to disguise his temptation, and to seduce them.

Hence I will learn, not to assure myself over-much of that which seems good, but first examining well the end, the intention, and the particular circumstances, proving and examining, as S. John says, " the spirits if they be of God,"(16) before I fully assent to them.

ii. I will examine the *difference* betwixt the *evil spirit* and the *good*, which is discovered in this present point : for the good Spirit led Christ our Lord "into the desert," to fly from the vain commendations of men, and from the vain-glory which proceeds from them; on the other hand, the evil spirit drew Him out of the desert, and set Him upon the pinnacle of the Temple in the presence of many people, persuading Him to seek these praises under the feigned and disguised title of the glory of God; for seeing that Christ our Lord refused in the desert to convert miraculous stones into bread, he imagined that perhaps He would rather work some other miracle in public, because vain-glory is of much more force before many persons, who may applaud and praise our work, than when alone.

(16) 1 Joan. iv. 1.

iii. I will meditate *on the part of Christ our Lord*, His admirable *meekness*, to suffer Himself to be taken up by the Devil, and to be carried from the desert, till he had set Him upon the pinnacle of the Temple of Jerusalem, without resisting or contradicting him, which He could have done with such facility, hiding for that present His omnipotence, so that the tempter did not know Him to be the Son of God, thus giving us an example of true humility.

Colloquy.—O most meek and gentle Lamb, how goest Thou in the hands of that ravenous wolf! Deliver me from them, for Thy mercies sake, that he cast me not down from the pinnacle of Thy grace, into the abyss and depth of deadly sins.   Amen.

iv. After this, I will consider the *manner* how He *overcame* this temptation, answering the Devil:—" It is written, Thou shalt not tempt the Lord thy God;" (17) as much as to say, that miracles were not to be wrought for vanity, for every slight occasion, and without necessity, and that confidence in God ought not to be either rash or presumptuous, for since I may descend by the steps of a ladder, why should I tempt Almighty God, by casting myself headlong from on high?   By this it may be seen, that humility and discretion, with tranquillity and meekness, avail very much to vanquish the temptations of vanity, coloured with the counterfeit show and appearance of virtue; humility even disposes us to acquire this light and discretion, for as the wise man says, " Where humility is, there also is wisdom." (18)   Therefore we must crave the same of God, to whose almighty power, as Himself said to holy Job, (19) it belongs to unmask the Devil, and the shadow of virtue with which he disguises himself to deceive our souls.

(17) Deut. vi. 16.   (18) Prov. xi.   ⁷   (19) Job xli.

Colloquy.—O powerful and most skilful warrior, Christ Jesus, open the eyes of my soul with Thy celestial light, to know the subtilty of the Devil when he transforms himself "into an angel of light" to deceive me : and so assist me with Thine omnipotence, that neither the fierceness of this lion affright me, nor the subtilty of this dragon deceive me. Amen.

THE THIRD TEMPTATION.

3. The third temptation was, of *avarice and ambition.* "Again the Devil took Him up into a very high mountain, and showed Him all the kingdoms of the world, and the glory of them, and said unto Him, 'To Thee will I give all this power, and the glory of them, for to me they are delivered, and to whom I will, I give them. If Thou wilt therefore adore before me, all shall be Thine.' "

i. Here first I reflect on that *enraged thirst* which the *Devil* has of my *damnation*, since he would give me the whole world, if it were his, so that I would commit one mortal sin against Almighty God. Whence I will conceive a very great esteem of my own salvation, and a very firm and effectual purpose not to do aught against the good of my soul for all the wealth that the earth contains, learning of my enemy highly to esteem eternal felicity, and despise all that is temporal and transitory. Therefore against this temptation Christ our Lord directly said:—" What doth it profit a man if he gain the whole world,' by becoming its sole lord and master, "and suffer the loss of his own soul?" (20) And those in hell confessed, though sore against their wills, saying:—" What hath our pride profited us, or what advantage hath the boasting of riches brought us?" (21)

ii. *It is the proper character of the Devil,* the father of

(20) Mat. xvi. 26.   (21) Sap. v. 8.

lies, to *cozen men* with the false and deceitful promises of that which neither is his, nor yet can be disposed of by him at his pleasure. This he sometimes does by the means of our own imagination, building castles in the air, and a hope of great good, if we will condescend to commit but a mortal sin. Other times he uses some worldly, flattering, and deceitful friends, who plausibly persuade us under seeming pretences, with deceitful hope to escape with them; whence may be seen what madness it is to give credit to him, who neither by himself, nor by the mouth of another, can speak the truth, but always lies and deceives, to procure my damnation.

iii. How *monstrous an evil mortal sin is*, especially *avarice* and *ambition*, since it is no other thing but to fall on the ground and to adore the Devil, for which reason S. Paul says, that avarice "is the service of idols;" (22) because money is an idol, within which the Devil dwells, whom the avaricious adores. And for this reason Christ our Lord said, that it was impossible to "serve two masters," "God and mammon," (23) whence I will conceive great compassion for those who prostrate on the ground adore the Devil, not because he gives them the whole world, but even for a little part of it, that is to say, for a little fortune and a little honour.

iv. Consider the *manner how Christ our Lord surmounted* this temptation, saying to the Devil imperiously:—"Begone, Satan, for it is written, The Lord thy God shalt thou adore, and Him only shalt thou serve." (24) In this answer Christ our Lord showed the great zeal which He had for the honour of God, for seeing the impudence of the Devil, full of wrath against him, He drove him from Him, and forced him to fly, vanquished, affrighted, and confounded. And with this example He instructs me how

(22) Colos. iii.   (23) Mat. vi.   (24) Deut. vi. 13,

much I ought to be armed with holy zeal against those tempters which rise up against the honour of Almighty God, chasing them from me with a valorous courage, vaunting myself that I bow not my knee, nor subject myself to any other but to God alone, and for His sake to all those whom He shall please to place over me, but to none at all against Him, for this holy liberty affrights the devils, quite confounds them, and forces them to fly.

Colloquy.—O God of armies, who, armed with Thy zeal, didst valorously fight against the prince of the world, and by Thy virtue didst force him to fly, assist my feebleness, I beseech Thee, that I may vanquish and chase him from me by the help of Thy grace. Give me temperance against " concupiscence of the flesh," poverty of spirit against " concupiscence of the eyes," and humility of heart against " pride of life :" (25) that having vanquished these three vices, I may likewise vanquish the world which is built upon them, as Thou didst vanquish and " overcome it," to whom be all honour and glory for this worthy victory, world without end. Amen.

POINT III.

" Then the *Devil left Him*, and the *angels* came and *ministered* to Him."

1. Here will I ponder—*who sent* these angels, *how many came*,—to what end,—and *what they did*.

i. It was the *eternal Father* who sent them to *honour His Son*, to solemnise His victory, and to show thereby the care He had of Him, and has of all those that are tempted ;—ii. and although one angel might have been sufficient to have served Him in this necessity, yet He caused *many* to come,—iii. to congratulate Him on His victory, and to rejoice with Him, for having vanquished the

(25) 1 John ii. 16.

Devil.—iv. Then with great reverence they *dressed a table in the desert*, and besought Him to eat to satisfy His hunger, *serving* Him and waiting upon Him as dutiful creatures upon their Lord and their Creator.

2. Whence I will gather,

i. First, great *confidence* in the Divine Providence, since He has so great a care of His children, and of those who fight and combat for Him in the desert of this life.

Colloquy.—Blessed be, O heavenly Father, Thy divine providence; I thank Thee for the care which Thou hadst of Thine Only-begotten Son, and for the honour which Thou didst Him in this victory.   I beseech Thee, for the love of Him, that Thou wouldst likewise take care of me, and vouchsafe to help me, according as my hope is in Thee.   Amen.

ii. Hence I will collect, that the *holy angels invisible, assist all such as fight and combat*, to help them to vanquish, and when they get the upper hand, rejoice with them, and solemnize their victories, (as shall be shown in the sixth part,) serving as instruments of the divine Providence, to redress our necessities, and therefore I am bound to love, reverence, and invoke them to my assistance, and not to yield or consent to temptations, if I desire not to deprive them of this joy.   This truth is so certain, that Satan himself tempting our Saviour, confessed the same, and called to memory the Psalm of David, (26) which he himself cited, the divine Providence permiting the same to fortify us; for the Devil knows full well that there is another angel far stronger than himself who contradicts him, has as great a care in defending us, as he has in tempting us, and curbs his pride that he cannot do us all the mischief which he desires.

iii. I will learn to have *patience* and endurance in *tem-*

(26) Ps. xc.

poral necessities, seeing that God in His good time will send a remedy for them, and to have a steadfast confidence in my temptations, although they should be multiplied and prolonged, because God in due season will cause them to cease, driving far from me the wicked Devil. But yet I must not assure myself from them during this life, for not without cause does the Evangelist say, that the Devil departed from Him " for a time," to signify, that though he retires for the present, yet he returns afterward to prove and provoke me again with new temptations, more strong and more forcible than the former; (27) but He who helps me to overcome one, will likewise help me to overcome the other.

MEDITATION VI.

ON THE VOCATION AND ELECTION OF THE APOSTLES.

POINT I.

Consider, the *quality* (1) of those apostles which Christ our Lord chose, in regard of their *condition*, comparing them with the greatness of the *end* for which He chose them, and pondering the *reasons* and causes of them.

1. For first, Christ our Lord, intending to chose twelve men, to be the twelve foundations of His Church, through His pure mercy called and chose them, casting His eyes, not upon the noble, rich, and powerful of Judea and Galilee, nor yet upon the learned and sages of the law, nor yet upon the Pharisees, who were the religious people of that time, but upon some *poor men, humble, ignorant, and engaged in very low and contemptible offices:* and these He elected, leaving others.

(27) Luc. iv. 13.
(1) Mat. iv.; Marc. i. 3; Luc. v.; Joan. i.; Apoc. **xxi**; Joan. **xv.**

2. The *causes* which moved Him to this choice were these.

i. First, because, although it be true, as is testified in Job, that "God doth not cast away the mighty, because He Himself also is mighty," (2) nor despise the wise, because He Himself is wise, notwithstanding abasing Himself so far as to become man, and making Himself for our sakes, poor, humble and despised, He thus *came to be the master of all humility*, which He sought to exercise on all occasions, choosing poor and humble men for His disciples, with whom He conversed familiarly : for God always takes delight in conversing with the simple and humble of heart; contrary to the proud masters of the world, who boast and glory in having disciples of noble birth, and qualified with some notable natural talents.

ii. The second cause was, that Christ our Lord *desired that His disciples should be most humble in spirit*, and that they should not attribute to themselves those excellent gifts He was to impart to them, nor those glorious works He intended to do by the means of their ministry. For which cause the apostle St. Paul says, that He chose "not many wise according to the flesh, not many mighty, not many noble,"(3) who are wont to be exceeding proud; but illiterate, and ordinary men, and such as were well grounded in the knowledge of their own weakness, by the experience of that little esteem which they had of themselves. "Ne glorietur omnis caro in conspectu ejus." (4) That no man, remembering what he is of his own frail flesh, should vainly glory in the presence of God, attributing to himself that which is none of his. Whence I may see, how much it imports me, to ground myself in profound humility, if I desire that Almighty God should make choice of me for great things in His service, remem-

(2) Job xxxvi. 5.   (3) 1 Cor. i. 27.   (4) 1 Cor. i. 29.

bering that which Christ our Lord said to His eternal Father, thanking Him that He had "hid" the mysteries of our redemption from the "wise and prudent" of the world, and had "revealed them to little ones." (5)

Colloquy.—O sovereign Father, Lord both of heaven and earth, I praise and glorify Thee for the choice which Thou hast made of the low and humble, to make them partakers of Thy mysteries; make me, O Lord, little and low in mine own eyes, that so I may be great in Thine, taking me for an instrument of Thine omnipotence, to work things worthy of Thy greatness. Amen.

iii. Hence proceeds the third cause, which was, that the miraculous *conversion of the world*, should not be attributed to the *force* of *man*, but to the *power and goodness of Almighty God:* for it was impossible, that men so poor and so despised, should persuade a world so proud and covetous, to embrace a faith so new, a doctrine so sublime, a law so pure, and a life so rigorous as is the law of the Gospel, if the omnipotence of God had not wrought this work, and "the right hand of the Most High" made this "change;" for which I should render many thanks, acknowledging that the self-same was effected in the conversion of that abridgment of a world,—my sinful soul,— because no human force could ever convert me, if the virtue of the omnipotent did not assist me, nor could I say with holy David:—"Now have I begun" a new life, "this is the change of the right hand of the most high."(6)

POINT II.

Consider the *quality* of these persons whom Christ our Lord chose, in regard to their *manners*, that is, the virtues or vices, the good or evil customs to which they were

(5) Matt. xi. 25.   (6) Ps. lxxvi. 11.

habituated, considering the *state whence He drew them*, and the *motives* which incited Him to do so.

1. The divine vocation has only *two causes*, viz. : the infinite *goodness of Almighty God* and the *merits of Jesus Christ our Lord*, by which, as St. Paul says, "God hath chosen us, and called us by His holy calling, not according to our works, but according to His own purpose and grace." (7) Here we see that, sometimes God our Lord has regard in these vocations, to some qualities and dispositions of the persons ordained for the end to which He called them, the better to encourage us to procure the like. Sometimes He calls such as are disqualified that we may understand that the vocation is entirely of grace, and that we must not puff up ourselves that we have these good parts, nor yet despair if we be without them : and for this cause the Evangelist, recounting these vocations, attributes their original to the loving look of Jesus Christ, who cast His merciful eyes on those whom He called, rather than on others, whom He could have called if He had pleased.

2. All this is to be considered in the vocation of the apostles, applying to myself that part which touches me.

i. First, our Lord drew some disciples from the *school of John the Baptist*, in which they had been bred up and nurtured in virtue, to honour herein the school of His precursor, and to give us to understand that He desired to meet with such men, for great things appertaining to His service. Of this number was the first of the disciples who followed Him, namely, St. Andrew,(8) in whom were found two remarkable dispositions recounted by the Evangelist; the one, a great *desire of his own perfection*, and to follow that which was the best; for having studied in the school St. John, and hearing him say, that Christ was " the

<hr>

(7) 2 Tim. i.   (8) Joan. i.

Lamb of God," he forthwith left his master, and ran after Christ, making choice of a better master, by whom he might be taught greater perfection;—the other, a great *zeal that his brethren should also gain the same good* which he had gained, calling them and inviting them, that they should likewise follow Him whom he followed, and so coming to his brother St. Peter, he brought him to Christ. These two properties disposed him in some manner, that Jesus Christ our Lord vouchsafed to call him, because they were qualifications most fit and proper for the office of an Apostle, whose end is, both to attend to his own salvation, and also to the salvation of his neighbours.

ii. Secondly—Christ our Lord called others *who were virtuous,* and well inclined, and exercised in good works, to honour virtue, and to quicken and allure us to its laudable exercises : such were the four fishers, who fished in the sea of Galilee, Peter and Andrew, James and John, sons of Zebedee, (9) in whom other admirable qualities were conspicuous. One was, their *application* to their laborious and humble art to avoid idleness, getting their bread in the sweat of their brows, and mending their nets with their own hands. The other was the *brotherly love* which they bore towards each other: for they were not only brethren according to the flesh, but also according to the spirit, with great conformity of wills aiding and assisting one another, desiring to each other, the good which he wished to himself. These two properties were very convenient for the office of an apostle, which is chiefly grounded on the union of charity, with a will to labour for the good of many. In *these four* I ought to endeavour to excel, if I desire that Christ our Lord should make choice of me for His disciple, and employ me in the great affairs of His service.

(9) Marc. i.

iii. Thirdly—He called *others who were great sinners,* evil inclined, and much addicted to the things of this life, drawing them from the world, and out of the abyss of their own sins; as first Matthew, (10) and afterwards Saul, to manifest in them the efficacy of His grace, and the greatness of His mercy, to the end, that no sort of sinner might despair, or distrust the mercy of God, or hold himself excluded from Him, since He embraces all, and ever desires to do good to all.

Colloquy.—O sovereign master, infinitely merciful, let all the angels praise Thee for so great mercies, since Thou disdainest not to elect for Thy disciples men so abject, nor to choose for apostles such abominable sinners : Thou bringest up clouds from the end of the earth,(11) making of men wholly terrestrial, men celestial, and of hearts cold and dry, preachers fervent and devout, who, like clouds, fly round about the world to dew and water it with their doctrine, and the admirable example of their life. Look upon me, O Lord, with the eyes of Thy mercy, and quite dry up in me, by Thy divine countenance, my earthly affections, lifting me up to the desire of heavenly things, to manifest thereby the greatness of Thy mercy, in a man replete with such great misery. O my soul, glorify thy God, who without thy merit has vouchsafed to call thee to His school, leaving others in the abyss and sink of errors and sin : sit down with humility in the lowest place of the earth, that the sun of justice may look upon thee, and may lift thee up as a cloud to the height of heaven. Amen.

POINT III.

I. Consider the wonderful *manner* in which Christ our Lord called and elected His apostles, admiring the

(10) Mat. ix. 9; Luc. v. 27.
(11) Ps. cxxxiv ; Jerem. li.

sweetness, the efficacy, and the words of this vocation, which were very different;—i. for some He called, *disposing them by little and little :*—ii. others, at once : others with *words accommodated to their art :*—iii. others with *one only word,* and with *divine and irresistible power.*

i. First, He disposed *S. Andrew and S. Peter by little and little,* calling them, as S. Augustin and other doctors say,(12) three times.—(a) The first was, that they might *know Him,* admitting them to the place where He reposed for two or three hours towards the evening, conversing with them as He did with many others.—(b) The second was, that they might *hear His doctrine,* and that He might make Himself more familiar to them, as He admitted His other disciples.—(c) That third time He called them, that they might *abandon all things and follow Him* through life. (13) This did Christ our Lord do, to teach us that men ordinarily mount by degrees to perfection, passing by the three states of beginners, proficients, and perfect; because the seed of divine inspiration, as the same Lord says, first shoots forth young blades, then grows up into ear, and after is filled with full corn in the ear; (14) that is to say, He first moves us to mean and interior works, and if we obey Him in them, then He moves us to grow up, and to execute greater; and, persevering in obeying Him, He fills us with perfect works. Hence I will gather how much it imports me to obey every inspiration and interior vocation, although it be in mean matters, and ordinary prayer; because by this obedience I dispose myself that His Divine Majesty vouchsafe to call me to greater things, and to other more elevated prayer.

ii. Christ our Lord called *others all at once* and at the

(12) Lib. ii. 2 de Consensu Evangel. 17, and S. Ignat.
(13) Joan. i.; Luc. v.
(14) Marc. iv. 28; S. Greg. lib. xxii. mor. c. 14.

first sight, to show the omnipotence of His will to call such as He pleased, drawing them in an instant out of the mud wherein before they stuck fast, changing their hearts in a moment. In this manner He called *the sons of Zebedee,* when they were fishing with their father and mending their nets. And *S. Matthew,* when he was sitting at the custom house, busily trafficking and negotiating with others; and he was bound with a " threefold " cord " not easily broken;"(15) that is to say, his evil inclination, the possession of much wealth, and the public office of collecting tolls, together with the company which he kept with other publicans; yet from all this He unloosed him with one only word, saying to him: " *Follow me,*" tearing from him all at once the evil habit and inclination which withheld him, and causing him to leave in an instant the riches, the office, and the company which he frequented, showing herein the efficacy of His grace, and the power which He holds over nature.

In the company of these men will I consider myself, hampered and entangled in the nets and snares of my own passions and inordinate affections, and with the cares and embarrassments of this world, and so feeble that I cannot with my own strength defend myself, and so beaten down that I neither will nor desire to be freed from them; but, on the contrary, am content to see myself so entangled, and, as a certain prophet says, I " sacrifice to my own " nets,"(16) adoring as idols these affections, these earthly and pleasing things, which enslave me together with them; but the mercy of our Lord Jesus Christ is so great and so powerful, that with one only word He can cause me to forsake them, and give me force also to free myself from them.

Colloquy.—O Almighty God, break asunder in-

(15) Eccles. iv. 12.   (16) Habac. i. 16.

stantly my cords, so that I may never more " sacrifice to these nets," but only to Thee with " sacrifice of praise " (17) and invocation of Thy holy name. O my soul, doubt not one day to see Thyself delivered and changed, for " it is easy before God " suddenly to enrich the poor, and to repair with one only look all Thy losses.

iii. How *imperiously* Christ our Lord called *Matthew and others*, commanding them to follow Him, without giving them any reason of this His commandment, only that He discovered them interiorly how much it imported them to follow Him, and yet how sweetly He said to the four fishermen, " Come after me, and I will make you to become fishers of men," alluring them with His amiable promise to follow Him; as if He had said, " I will not that you abandon your inclination, nor quite give over your occupation, but will better it, by changing it into another much more perfect; for I will make you fishers, not of fishes, but of souls, which you shall fish to heaven by the net of your doctrine." By this I see that our Lord desired to accommodate His grace according to that good, which nature already possessed, to perfect it, so that the one and the other proceeding in accordance together, obtain their end more agreeably.

2. Thus the grace and proper vocation of a Christian or Religious, helps to cut off the evil natural inclinations, as they did those of S. Matthew, and to perfect the good as they did those of these fishermen, whose vocation I will apply to myself, imagining that Christ our Lord says to my heart, " Forsake the nets with which thou fishest for the delights and pleasures of this life, and " come after me," following my counsels, and I will make thee a fisher of other delights and celestial enjoyments; and " I will " also

(17) Ps. cxv.

"make thee to become a fisher of men," whom thou shalt gain to heaven by thy preaching and example.

3. Hence I will conclude from all that has been said, that the apostolic vocation embraces two parts:—First, to follow Jesus Christ, imitating perfectly His holy virtues, and to draw out of the sea of this world the souls of such as are drowned in it. And the second is founded upon the first, for it would be a great folly to draw others out of the dangers of the sea, and to drown myself in it by not following Jesus Christ, and yet cause others to follow Him.

POINT IV.

Consider the excellent *obedience* which the apostles showed to their vocation, for as the Evangelists say, " Peter and Andrew his brother, were casting a net into the sea," and the sons of Zebedee in like manner were mending theirs in the ship of their father, and Matthew was actually engaged in receiving tolls,(18) but when Christ called them, *continuo, et statim*, " forthwith" they forsook all to follow Him.

In this obedience, they discovered *three excellent perfections* contained in this virtue.

1. The first perfection was that of their *understanding* and judgment, which they captivated to the service of Jesus Christ, submitting themselves to His holy ordinance, without replying or alleging the reasons they had, to omit, or defer the accomplishment of it. For S. Peter might have said that he was obliged to support his daughter, and his family, and to dispose first of his affairs.—S. John and S. James, that they had both father and mother, who, being aged, stood in need of their assistance.—St. Matthew, that he was to account and reckon with many;

(18) Mat. iv. & ix.; Marc. i. & ii.; Luc. v. 27.

that he had disbursed much money in traffick, and that therefore it was necessary for him first to set all things in good order.—None of all this did they allege, but wholly submitted their judgment to the commandment of Christ, and casting themselves confidently upon the divine providence, they obeyed Him with blind obedience, yet not imprudently, but very discreetly, because the inward illustration, the force of divine grace, and the divinity which beamed in the face and words of Christ our Lord, induced them to submit and yield to His commandment.

2. The second perfection was that of their *will*, which they most readily subjected to that of Jesus Christ, divesting themselves of the carnal love which they bore to their wife, children, fathers, friends, and worldly substance, which although it was but little, yet, as St. Gregory says,(19) they left much, in leaving the will and desire to possess anything but Jesus Christ; and if all the world had been theirs, with the same will they would have forsaken the whole to follow Him. And for this cause St. Peter said to Christ our Lord, " Ecce nos reliquimus omnia" (20). " Behold we have left all;" he said not—We have forsaken all the things which we had, but absolutely " all things," to signify that they forsook all things which they had, and might by possibility hereafter have, namely, fathers, mothers, brothers, sisters, friends, and kindred, with whatsoever riches and right appertaining to them; and finally themselves, together with their own will and liberty, and even if it had been needful, their honour and their life, renouncing all to follow Christ.(21)

3. The third perfection was of *execution*, the which was prompt, punctual, joyful, without the delay of so much as an instant, and without repugnance or any sadness. And

<hr>

(19) Hom. v. in Evang.   (20) Mat. xix. 27.
(21) S. Chrysos. hom. xiv. in Mat.

although they now possessed the things they loved or esteemed, as their fathers, and their money; yet they forthwith forsook all, as if they had fled from a serpent. Those
who had spread or set their nets in the sea suddenly unloosed them.—Those who were mending them, did not
afterwards knit so much as a knot.—And he who held the
counting books open, and the gold and silver lying upon
them, forsook all even as it lay, with the same content with
which he feasted Jesus Christ, His disciples, and other
publicans in sign of joy.

Colloquy.—O miracle of the omnipotence of
Almighty God! O marvellous change of the right
hand of the " most High." (22) O sun of justice who
triply settest on fire the mountains with lightnings
and thunder, and " blindest the eyes " (23) with Thy
excellent brightness, grant unto me a blind obedience
fervent and diligent, such as Thou gavest to these
apostolic mountains, that obeying Thee like them, I
may come to reign together with them, world without
end. Amen.

POINT V.

Consider the great *favours* which Christ our Lord did
to His Apostles for this obedience.

1. First, He *exalted* them to the *most eminent dignity*
above all those which He had instituted in His Church,
which was that of the Apostleship, making them His
legates and ambassadors, that in His name and authority,
they might go and preach throughout the world His holy
Gospel.(24)

2. Secondly, He chose them, as S. Mark says, " *ut essent
secum,*" that they might always be *with Him,* keeping with
them very strict familiarity, discovering to them part of

<hr>

(22) Ps. lxxvi. 11.   (23) Ecclus. xliii. 4.
(24) Marc. iii.; Luc. vi.

His secrets, as He said to them, "I will not now call you servants," but "friends," because "all things whatsoever I have heard of my Father, I have made known to you."

3. Thirdly, imparting to them *greater gifts and graces,* than to all the saints either of the Old or New Testament who succeeded them, as well in all kinds of sanctity, as also in wisdom, with power and authority to work miracles, and with other graces gratis and freely given to them; whence S. Paul says, that they had the " first fruits"(25) of the Holy Ghost, and that they were "the glory of Christ."(26)

4. Fourthly—He *promised* them that on the day of judgment they should "sit " with Him upon *twelve seats judging* the twelve tribes of Israel, (27) for having obeyed in forsaking all things for the love of Him.   He gave them even in this life a hundred times more than what they had left.   And if it be true, as we have said, that with an efficacious will they forsook all riches, honours, and pleasures which they could desire, then that which He gave them was worth a hundred times more than all that, for He gave such graces, gifts and spiritual consolations, as incomparably exceeded all whatsoever they had left: and to encourage us to do as much as the apostles did, He promised us the same as to them, as shall be showed in its place. (28)

Colloquy.—O my Redeemer, since Thou rewardest with such liberality the obedience of man to Thy vocation, it is most just that I should follow Thee in this life, that I may pass from this to a better, where Thou art enjoying Thine everlasting glory.   Amen.

(25) Rom. viii. 23.
(26) 2 Cor. viii. 23.   (27) Mat. xix. 28.   (28) vi. part. med. xlviii.

MEDITATION VII.

ON THE GENERAL VOCATION WITH WHICH CHRIST OUR LORD CALLS ALL MEN TO RENOUNCE THEMSELVES, CARRY THEIR CROSS, AND FOLLOW HIM.

Because Christ our Lord, as St. John says, is come into the world to destroy the works of the Devil, let us first ponder in this meditation, the *vocation which the Devil makes*, soliciting people to follow him, in opposition to the cross of Jesus Christ, and then the *vocation* of the same *Christ*; that *comparing* the one with the other, we may see to which of the two we have reason to *hearken*, and which to follow.(1) This meditation, and that which follows, will give a great deal of light, to make *a safe choice of that state* which is most conducive to our salvation.

POINT I.

1. The first shall be to consider *Lucifer*, the prince of this world, *sitting on a throne of fire full of smoke*, having a horrible figure, and dreadful countenance, surrounded by innumerable devils,—the dukes and princes of this darkness, who consult about making war against Jesus Christ our Lord, and erecting their standard against the standard of the cross.(2) To which effect they have set their snares of temptation for men, to entrap them in those three vices which St. John calls " concupiscence of the flesh, concupiscence of the eyes, and pride of life:" (3) first inviting them to the delights of the flesh, whence proceed the vices of gluttony and luxury—afterwards to the cupidity of having honour, whence proceed the vices of covetousness and ambitions,—after that to the pride of life, which is a

(1) Mat. xvi.; Mar. viii.; Luc. ix.; Joan. iii.
(2) Joan. xiv.; S. Ign. in Heb. 2, die i.   (3) 1 Joan. ii. 16.

desire of our own excellency, with presumption of ourselves, and of our private opinion.(4) And it is called pride of life, because it is pride that is lively and swelling, which always lives and increases, budding forth other vices and sins of the world.

2. Then will I ponder the *rage* with which the *devils range about the whole world*, without leaving any, the least corner unsearched, "seeking whom they may devour," (5) as lions, with the force and violence of persecutions ; and as dragons, with the subtlety of their apparent reasons to deceive men, and to draw them to their service;(6) the destruction which they make being exceedingly great, because they seduce innumerable souls, some of whom give them selves to the seeking of pleasures; others to the greedy covetousness of riches and of wordly honours; others to pride and loftiness of life: and, lastly, they enrol under their standard, all the enemies of the cross of Christ, "whose end is destruction," as St. Paul says, "whose God is their belly, and whose glory is in their shame." (7)

3. With this consideration imitating the same apostle, with tears will I excite my *compassion*, that there are so many who follow the standard of the Devil, wondering that they are so foolish as to follow him, believing that the recompense of their service will be to inhabit with him in hell. And reflecting on my past or present life, I will deplore my having remained for any time in this pernicious error, beseeching our Lord to deliver me from it. Amen.

POINT II.

Secondly, I will consider *Christ our Lord seated in an*

---

(4) Ps. lxxiii. 3, 4, 5.

(5) 1 Pet. v. 8; S. Aug. præf. in Ps. lxvi.

(6) Apoc. xii.; Mat. vii.   (7) Philip. iii. 19.

humble place, with a pleasing and loving countenance, surrounded by His disciples, and with many other persons, saying to all—"Si quis vult venire post me, abneget semetipsum et tollat crucem suam, et sequatur me." "If any one will come after me, let him daily take up his cross, deny himself, and follow me."

1. In *these words*, contrary to the prince of this world, He invites men to three things :—

i. First, *to deny themselves*, mortifying the three concupiscences of the world, and the other vices which proceed from them, that is, that they deny and mortify the love of sensual pleasures, and the greedy desire to get them, vain glory, and interior pride, mortifying their own judgment and their own will, and all presumption and desire of superiority.

ii. Secondly, He calls them *to carry their cross*, offering themselves to all that is repugnant to the three eager desires of the world; that is to say, to suffer labours and sorrows, poverty and contempt, with all manner of humiliation and subjection; because the spiritual cross of Jesus Christ is composed of these three things, pain, poverty, and contempt, each of them comprehending sundry different mortifications which accompany it; and this cross He requires that all men carry every day, bearing that part which daily and hourly shall befal them, with perfect perseverance even to death.

iii. Thirdly; He therefore calls them, that they should *imitate His holy virtues*, and the examples He giveth them of abnegation, and patiently supporting their own cross; as He is resolved to admit none into His school, nor to His company, who do not resolve to embrace the same, and to settle themselves under this standard. And so He says, that whosoever "taketh not up his cross and cometh after me, he cannot be my disciple, and is not worthy of me."(8)

2. Then will I ponder how exceedingly *reasonable this vocation is*, for if I be evil, and from my birth inclined to vices and iniquities, it is most just I should deny myself, and mortify all my wicked inclinations, to emancipate myself from all the evils which spring from thence. And if pleasures, riches, honours, and worldly excellencies, are the source of all sorts of evils, it is but reasonable that I leave the inordinate love I feel towards them, to save myself from such great miseries. And if in this mortal life many labours, toils, sorrows, and tribulations will befall me, how can I do better, than to make a virtue of necessity, and embrace my cross with a willing mind, thus to merit everlasting life? And since Jesus Christ our Lord came down from heaven to carry His cross, and to embrace pain, and disgrace, and contempt, what wonder if I do that which my Captain, my King, and my God has done?

Colloquy.—O supreme Captain, since Thou callest me to renounce and deny myself, come Thou to combat with me against myself, for he ought to have more force than myself, who is to overcome me. And since Thou desirest that I daily carry my Cross, give me daily Thy holy grace, that I neither fall nor stumble, nor yet be oppressed under its weight. Amen.

POINT III.

1. The third shall be, to consider *three most effectual reasons* which Jesus Christ our Lord uses, to persuade us to this vocation.

i. The first is, that "*whosoever will save his life shall lose it;* for he that shall lose it for my sake shall save it:"

(8) Luc. xiv. 27; Mat. x. 38.

that is to say, " Your salvation and your everlasting life is in denying yourselves, taking up your cross, and following me, even to the loss of your temporal life for this cause, if need require, as I lost mine. And whosoever shall lose it after this manner, shall not altogether lose it, because I will return him a better for it, and one eternal." And in the same manner I may imagine Christ our Lord to say to me: " He who for me shall lose his goods, his honour, his pleasures, his friends, or other temporal profit, he shall afterwards find it: and contrariwise, he who seeketh to save or preserve the same, contrary to my will, he shall lose it, and together with it his soul for ever."

ii. The second reason is:—" *What shall it profit a man if he gain the whole world, and suffer the loss of his own soul? Or what exchange shall a man give for his soul?*" As if He had said: " If that thou follow the Devil's suggestion, and not my vocation, sure thou art to lose thy soul everlastingly: for what will it avail thee to have enjoyed all the pleasures, riches, honours, and excellencies of the world, if after all this thy soul be damned? Ask thou of those that are burning in hell, and they will tell thee: ' What hath our pride profited us? or what advantage hath the boasting of riches brought us?(9) Pleasures, honours, dignities, and all the goods upon the whole earth; what profit have they brought us? All is passed like a shadow, and now for our malice we are plunged into perpetual torments.' "

iii. The third reason is, because *the Son of man shall come in the glory* of His Father, with His angels, " *and then will He render to every man according to his works;*"(10) which is to say: " I shall come to judge the world with the sign and standard of my Cross, and those who would not carry the same with me, shall be condemned with the devils to

(9) Sap. v. 8.   (10) Mat. xvi. 27.

everlasting fire, whose colours they followed; but those who have hearkened to my vocation, and have embraced my Cross, I will lead with me to the glory of my Father."

2. Pondering these three reasons, I will *compare* those two vocations,—of *that which Lucifer makes*, with *that which* is made *by Christ our Lord;*—the *disastrous end* which is made by those who follow the one, with that so *fortunate an end* which is made by these who follow the other. And since it is not possible, as our Redeemer says, at once to "serve two" different "masters, God and mammon,"(11) Jesus Christ and vain honours, nor possible to put himself under the banners of such contrary captains, I will endeavour to shut my ears to the suggestion of Satan, and open them to the vocation of Jesus Christ, denying myself, embracing my Cross, and following my Sovereign Captain under His banner. For which purpose it will be a help to consider which of them I would wish to have followed at the hour of my death, and when I shall see myself presen'ed to judgment, before the tribunal of Jesus Christ. Which of the two should I then wish to have chosen? riches or poverty, honours or contempt, pleasures or afflictions, the accomplishment of my own will, or the abnegation of it, and of myself? And I will now make choice of that which I would have wished to have chosen then.

3. And not to put off to the hour of death and judgment, the certainty of this good election, I add, that the vocation of the Devil, which, although at first sight it promises delights, honours, riches, liberty, and repose, yet all these are so intermingled with bitterness, that to say the truth, they *are most painful;* even the damned themselves confessed that they "wearied themselves in the way of iniquity, and that they walked through hard

(11) Mat. vi. 24.

ways." (12) On the contrary, the vocation of Christ, although it treat of abnegation and crosses, it is so proportioned by the Divine Providence, so fitted and accommodated to every ones forces, and mingled with such sweetness and celestial graces, that truly it is most sweet, even in this life; so that those who followed the Devil's standard, find a great refreshment in following Christ, even as our Lord Himself said :—" Come to me all you that labour and are burdened, and I will refresh you; take up my yoke upon you, and learn of me, because I am meek and humble of heart, and you shall find rest to your souls, for my yoke is sweet, and my burthen light;" (13) that is to say: "Although my yoke be abnegation, yet is it sweet, and although my burthen be the cross, yet is it light to such as are meek and humble like myself: for I give my grace unto the humble which renders all that sweet and light, which otherwise of itself is sour and heavy."

Colloquy.—O most sweet master, upon whose sacred shoulders my cross is carried, and that of all mortal men, grant me to hearken to Thy vocation, embracing the labours of Thy cross, remitting to Thy providence the means to support and carry it: that choosing in life that which I would have wished to have chosen in death, I may receive at Thy judgment the crown of glory. Amen.

MEDITATION VIII.

ON THE RESIGNATION NECESSARY TO HEAR THE VOCATION OF JESUS CHRIST AND TO RENOUNCE ALL THINGS TO BECOME HIS DISCIPLE.

Forasmuch as Christ our Lord never ceases to call men

(12) Sap. v. 7.   (13) Mat. xi. 28—30.

to follow Him, I will place in this meditation, the proper disposition which we ought to procure; in order that His holy vocation may be found amongst us, and that it may conduct us to everlasting life. This has our Lord Himself declared in a memorable sentence, which He uttered in St. Luke:—"Every one of you that doth not renounce all that he possesseth, cannot be my disciple." (1)   In which words, He commands not all men to renounce and actually abandon all things, but only to renounce them in heart, to leave the inordinate affection they have for them, and be ready to renounce them entirely, when they shall be any impediment to their salvation, or that the same Lord with a special vocation, shall inspire them to renounce them, as a means much more secure and proper for their salvation. And under the name of all, are comprehended, goods, honour, dignity, and eminent offices. Also fathers, brothers, sons, friends and acquaintance, and any person or thing upon earth, or inordinate affection for which may hinder us from following Christ, and becoming His true disciples. This presupposed, we will set down three sorts of men who seek the end of their salvation, and who desire, in order to attain thereunto, to dispose themselves to follow Christ; that so we may see which amongst them walks the most securely, and to which of them we ought rather to conform ourselves.

POINT I.

1. The first sort is, of those who desire to attain the end of their salvation, *without applying the means* to this end, by reason of the great difficulty they feel in it : they desire to *follow Christ*, but yet wish not to renounce or abandon anything: they desire to leave and forsake their disordered affections, but not to use any effectual means

(1) S. Ignat. ubi supr. Luc. xiv. 33.

whereby they may be freed from them, even as the sick man who desires health, but wishes to have no bleeding, purging, or other remedies necessary to make him well, because of the pain and bitterness which he feels in taking them. These persons have a disposition entirely opposite to the divine counsel and the call of Christ to renounce all, for such as these will never purchase true spiritual health, nor life everlasting, because this is not obtained by bare desires, when works are wanting. And although it seems that they seek to be saved and healed, yet in truth they do not seek it : and for this reason the Holy Ghost says :—"Vult, et non vult piger." "The sluggard willeth and willeth not;"(2) he wills the end, but not the means; where Christ is he would gladly come; but will not follow Christ; he wills virtue in that it is good, but wills it not in that it is difficult, which is the cause that he quite forsakes it.

2. Then will I reflect upon myself, and see if I do not the like in seeking after those virtues which I pursue: for I sometimes say that *I desire to obtain true humility*, and to overcome pride, but I neither humble myself, nor will be humbled by another : I say I desire to keep my patience, and to subdue my anger, and yet will not endure or suffer anything, always remaining proud and impatient: whereas the mortification of passions is a necessary means to vanquish vices; and the practice of virtues is requisite to purchase them.

POINT II.

1. The second sort is of other men who desire the end of their salvation, and *exercise the means* to attain the same, but these means are such as are chalked out *according to their own fancy*, and not according to the will of Almighty God. They seek indeed to follow Jesus Christ,

(2) Prov. xiii. 4.

and to renounce their inordinate affection to earthly things, on condition that what they have may still remain peaceably in their own possession. And although these things are to them an occasion of sin, and Almighty God interiorly calls them to forsake and leave them, yet they obey not, but become sorrowful like the rich young man, to whom Christ said:—"If thou wilt be perfect, go sell what thou hast."(3) These resemble those that are sick, who seek to be healed, and to apply remedies, but not such as the physician orders, but only such as they find to their own liking, seeking to make the will of the physician like their own before they taste them: so that they will draw God's will to theirs, and not conform theirs to that of God, and in consequence, have a disposition repugnant to the divine vocation of renouncing all things, and are in danger of being damned; for perhaps our Lord knows that their cure depends on their forsaking the things which they possess, thereby removing inordinate affections, and the many sins which thence proceed.

2. In short, I ought to believe, that the remedy of my spiritual infirmities, consists not in the *means which I choose with my blind judgment*, but in those *prescribed by Almighty God*, the true physician of my soul; like Naaman the leper,(4) who although he greatly desired to be healed of his leprosy, yet would not apply the remedy which the prophet Elias prescribed him, which was to wash himself seven times in the river Jordan, but wanted an easy means, which he invented in his own brain, which was,—that the prophet should only touch him with his hand. But he would never have been thoroughly healed of his infirmity, had he not changed his opinion, and resigned himself into the hands of the holy prophet: as Almighty God had determined to heal him, not by the

<hr>

(3) Matt. xix. 21.   (4) Reg. v. 10.

means which he himself had chosen, but by another which was more convenient.

3. I will likewise turn the reflection upon myself, and, looking into different parts of my life, see if I *am not deceiving myself*, and falling into the same error. For when I confess, it is wrong if I will not receive the remedy prescribed for my cure by a prudent confessor, but prefer one which my own inclinations suggest to me. And if I be a religious, it is a great abuse to pretend to arrive at the perfection of my state, by the means which my own judgment prescribes, seeking to incline my superiors to will that which I will, and not to incline my own to will that which they will, so that Christ our Lord may say to me what He said to S. Peter, in a similar case:—" Vade post me, Satana ;" " Go behind me, Satan, thou art a scandal unto me;"(5) for I will not fulfil Thy will, but it is Thy part to fulfil mine; the master is not to follow the disciple, but the disciple the master; nor is the subject to govern his superior, but the superior the subject.

Colloquy.—O sovereign master, since Thou art the way, the truth, and the life, suffer not that I should choose any other *way* than Thine, nor follow any other *truth* than Thine, nor live any other *life* than Thou didst live ; walking after Thee who descendest from heaven, not to fulfil Thine own will, but the will of Thy Father in the way which He assigned Thee. Amen.

POINT III.

1. Hence it is, that the third and far happier sort of men consists of those who desire to attain the end of their salvation, the victory over their *inordinate appetites*, and the *perfection* of *virtue*, by the *means* which *Almighty God appoints*, resigning themselves entirely to His will, being

(5) Matt. xvi. 23.

ready to hold or let go whatsoever they possess with equa-
nimity, as will be best for the honour and glory of Almighty God, and for the salvation of their souls: like those
sick men who desire to be healed, and commit themselves
wholly into the hands of the physician, fully prepared to
take those remedies which he shall judge best for the
recovery of their health, without inclining on their part
more to one side than the other.

2. These have indeed an admirable disposition for hearing the divine vocation, and receiving the illuminations
and inspirations of God, ever confiding in the providence
of our great Lord, who, as the prophet Isaiah says,(6)
manifests to us the things most profitable and most convenient for us, and guides us in the way to heaven by Himself, and by means of His appointed ministers. So that
those who suffer themselves to be guided by Him, embracing all those means which He inspires and commands, will
possess a flood of peace, and a sea of sanctity, and will, with
great security, arrive at the port of their salvation and
perfection; because the divine providence calls every one
to that state and manner of life which is fittest and most
convenient for him, as will be shown in the sixth part.

3. Accordingly, I will make a comparison between these
three sorts of men, and seeing the abuses and errors of the
first and second, I ought to make *choice of the third condition*, and then in the presence of God our Lord, say to
Him from my heart, like another Saul newly converted:—
" Domine, quid me vis facere?"—" Lord, what wilt Thou
have me to do?"(7)   Behold Thy servant desirous to serve
and follow Thee; but I am very infirm through my inordinate affections: I put myself into Thy hands, dispose of
me as Thou shalt please, I am prepared to fulfil Thy will;
inspire me, and teach me the means most proper for the

<hr>

(6) Is. xlvii.   (7) Act. ix. 6.

health of my soul; I offer myself with the help of Thy grace to execute the same, be it in retaining the things which I possess, or renouncing them entirely for the love of Thee.

4. Others there are who will proceed yet further, and to imitate Jesus Christ more perfectly, incline and desire, as much as they may, to be *poor, despised, and afflicted as He was*; rather than to be rich, honoured, and comforted as some just and holy persons have been, although they always keep themselves *indifferent* to accept or forsake all according as God wills. And notwithstanding that His Majesty imparts not this grace to every one, to call them to follow Him in actual voluntary poverty in a Religious life, or to suffer injuries and persecutions for the love of Him, yet I ought to procure with all my strength this disposition, in imitation of the Apostle, who said:—" God forbid that I should glory, saving in the cross of our Lord Jesus Christ, by whom the world is crucified to me, and I to the world,"(8) because I abhor and despise the world, and the world likewise in effect abhors and despises me, using me as one crucified, who am held by all men as infamous and unhappy."

Colloquy.—O eternal God, grant me, for Thy mercy's sake, such a disposition, that I may be worthy to be called by Thee to do and suffer great things for Thy glory. Amen.

(8) Phil. i.; Gal. vi. 14.

MEDITATION IX.

ON THE FIRST MIRACLE WROUGHT BY CHRIST OUR LORD AT THE MARRIAGE IN
CANA OF GALILEE.

POINT I.

"There was a marriage in Cana of Galilee, and the mother of Jesus was there. And Jesus also was invited with His disciples, and the wine failing, the mother of Jesus saith to Him : They have no wine." (1)

1. The first point will be, to consider the *benignity* and *charity of Christ* our Lord, in courteously accepting this invitation, to take this occasion to do good to others, and to draw thence some spiritual profit for His disciples. And at the same time I will contemplate the purity, the modesty, and the gravity, with which He sat at table, amidst those merriments and rejoicings: to teach us, that the spiritual man, in every place, ought to be the same, without suffering himself to be carried away by profane things, according to what David says :—" Let the just feast and rejoice before God ;" (2) for by this means they will do nothing contrary to their health which they seek to conserve, nor yet of the majesty of Almighty God, in whose presence they are.

2. Secondly I will weigh:—

i. The *compassion and care of the Virgin* our Lady, who seeing the want of wine, was sorry for the distress and disgrace which was there felt; and of her own accord, without being requested by another, she herself sought a remedy for this misfortune by means of her son; shewing

(1) Joan. ii. 1, 2, 3. S. Th. 3. p. q. xliii. art. 3.
(2) Psal. lxvii. 4.

by this the great affection and love, which she bore to them that had invited her. The very same does she to this present in favour of her devout clients, taking compassion on their necessities, although they sometimes forget themselves, or are careless to seek redress or a remedy for them: for, as St. Augustine says, (3) forasmuch as the Virgin far surpasses all the Saints, so much the more is she solicitous for our good than all they together.

Colloquy.—O sovereign Virgin, how shall I not be solicitous to serve thee, since thou art so solicitous to succour me? If thou art so careful to show thyself grateful for so slight a service, it is but reasonable that I hold myself bound to thank thee for the favours which thou hast done me, with confidence that thou wilt do me others far greater. Amen.

ii. I will weigh that *loving hope*, and that *resignation* with which the Blessed Virgin composed that short petition, "They have no wine:" as she was assured of the bowels of compassion of her son, to whom it sufficed only to lay before Him the present necessity, that He might redress it if it were expedient; for neither love nor power, were wanting for this purpose.

Colloquy.—O glorious Virgin, behold in me the want of the "wine" of fervent charity and devotion: and since thou hast such great compassion for the want of corporal wine, thou wilt have much more for the want of spiritual wine; and since thou askedst a remedy for the one, ask it also for this other, saying for me to thy blessed Son: "Son, this my servant wanteth the wine of celestial love, grant it him abundantly, that he may serve Thee with great fervour." Amen.

3. In *imitation* of this sacred Virgin, I should exercise this manner of prayer, which she has taught me by her

(3) Serm. iv. de Nat.

example, representing to our Lord, my wants and necessities, with great *love, confidence,* and *resignation,* trusting in His liberality and His mercy, that He will send me a remedy when the same is most expedient for me· and so instead of this word, "Wine," I may put other like words, saying to our Lord:—

Colloquy.—O my Father, I have no fervour.—O my God, I have not humility,—I have no patience,—behold my misery, and take pity on me.

Of this sort of prayer we will treat more at large in the meditation of the raising up of Lazarus, Med. xli., part 3.

POINT II.

To this demand Christ our Lord made answer. "*Woman, what is to me and to thee? my hour is not yet come.*" (4) Concerning this answer, in appearance so harsh and distasteful, I will ponder the *mysterious causes* of it.

i. The first was, to make it known that He was *more than man,* and that He was also Almighty God, to whom it appertained to do that miraculous work which was required of Him, in which He was to follow His own course both as to the time and the hour, which, as He was God, He had assigned, without either changing or anticipating it for any respects of flesh and blood; teaching us in this, that we must not afflict nor vex ourselves exclusively for our wants, by seeking to anticipate the hour which God has set down, nor assign to Him the time to redress them, as those of Bethulia did, whom holy Judith (5) for the like occasion, and with great reason, reprehended justly; but doing on my part all that is possible for me, I must rely upon His divine providence for the rest, that He send me a remedy in such hour and season as shall be best and most expedient for me.

(4) Joan. ii. 4.   (5) Judith. viii.

Colloquy.—O most sweet Saviour, Thou hast assigned the time for labour and for working miracles, follow Thine own divine course ; for my will is wholly resigned, always to obey and to follow Thine, without withdrawing myself from the same, any hour or moment of time.   Amen.

ii. The second cause was, to *instruct us* how much *mortified* and diverted He was from all *carnal love of His parents.*   Wherefore, conforming His words to the affections of His heart, we find it nowhere written that ever He called the most holy Virgin by this tender title or name of " Mother," but " Woman;" as is seen both in this place, and upon the cross, when He recommended her to His well-beloved disciple; (6) and at another time, others who heard His sermon saying unto Him, that His mother and brethren sought for Him, He made them answer with great seriousness:—" Who is my mother and who are my brethren?   Whosoever shall do the will of my Father that is in heaven, he is my brother, and sister, and mother."(7)   Whence I will learn to divest myself of all carnal affection to creatures, and not to use the name of mother nor of brother, if they carry my heart after them, studying to prefer before all things, the accomplishment of the will of Almighty God; (8) since on this subject Moyses says:—" Who hath said to his father and to his mother, I do not know you, and to his brethren, I know you not, these have kept Thy word and observed Thy covenant." (9)

iii. The third cause was, to *give the most holy Virgin an occasion to manifest her most excellent virtues ;* especially her incomparable patience, humility, and confidence, for at this harsh answer, she did not trouble herself, she did not

(6) Joan. xix. 26.   (7) Mat. xii. 47.
(8) S. Igna. in exam. c. iv. lit. c.   (9) Deut. xxxiii 9.

complain nor answer a word, nor consider herself slighted by it: and what is more to be admired, she lost not the hope of being heard, as we shall see by and by; after whose example I should encourage myself to keep patience, and not lose confidence, if God refuse to grant my prayers, or defer for a time to hear me, or when men return me distasteful answers, remembering what the prophet Isaiah says:—" In silence and in hope shall our strength be," (10) for by such means we obtain of Almighty God what we ask at His holy hands.

POINT III.

Then the Virgin said to those that served at table, " *Whatsoever*" my son " *shall say to you, do ye.*" (11)

In which words we are to consider—i. The *excellency* of this most sovereign *counsel;* the *end* for which it was given; the *words* which she used: and the *heroic virtues* which she discovered in the whole.

i. First, she discovered a most *heroical confidence:* because, if her son had expressly said to her, I will do what you demand of me, she could do no more than what she did.

ii. Secondly, she *received a great light* to know the *mind of Christ* our Lord, and His intention, that He would supply this want, either by creating new wine, or multiplying the little which remained, without being perceived by those who served at the table; by all which and the rest, the Blessed Virgin well understood that her son meant to command the servants something: for it is the property of Almighty God, to will that men co-operate on their part to remedy their own necessities, disposing themselves by this obedience and diligence, to procure redress and remedy for them.

iii. Hence it is, that the Virgin our Lady, by the coun-

(10) Isa. xxx. 15.   (11) Joan. ii. 5.

sel which she gave to the servants, admonishes us, that to obtain of Almighty God what we demand, *we have no means more effectual than confidence joined with obedience* to what is commanded us: because, as holy David says:—" God will do the will of them that fear Him." (12)   And St. John says:—" If our heart does not reprehend us, we have confidence towards God, that whatsoever we shall ask of Him, we shall receive, because we keep His commandments, and do those things which are pleasing in His sight."(13)   And Christ our Lord said to His apostles: " If my words abide in you, you shall ask whatever you will and it shall be done to you."   And, generally, the more obedient we are, the more Almighty God will yield and condescend to our petitions." (14)

Colloquy.—Therefore, O my soul, obey fervently, if thou wilt be heard speedily ; for much sooner is one obedient prayer heard, than ten thousand slothful and rebellious ones.

iv. Finally, I will ponder the *love which the Blessed Virgin* bore to *silence and brevity of words;* both those which she spake to her son, and to the servants, were so brief, so measured, and so weighty ; and I will particularly engrave them in my heart, as spoken by such a mother, and by such a mistress, and will labour to accomplish all that Christ our Lord shall command me without omitting anything, though difficult,—though it appear to be from the purpose,—though contrary to my petitions,— though He insinuates to me by Himself with secret inspirations, or by the mouth and means of my superiors, appear to me of little importance.

Colloquy.—O sovereign Virgin, mistress of all virtues, teach me truly to practise these which thou hast here practised, that by the means of them I may

(12) Psal. cxliv.   (13) 1 Joan. iii. 21 ; Joan. xv.
(14) Euseb. hom. 3. ad monach.   S. Aug. de opera monach. c. 17.

render myself agreeable to thy son, and may be worthy to obtain that which I ask for.   Amen.

POINT IV.

Consider how Christ our Lord *commanded* the *ministers* to fill *with water, six water pots* there standing, which immediately He converted into most *excellent wine*, commanding the same to be carried to the chief steward who sat at the table.

1. Whence I am to reflect, first, on the *obedience of the ministers*, so well instructed by the counsel of the Virgin, for without reply, or delay, or without asking to what purpose He commanded them this—or what sense there was in carrying water instead of wine—they submitted their judgment to that which Christ our Lord commanded them, and by this means, (never thinking of it,) they obtained the thing which they desired.   Whence I will gather how secure it is for me to obey Almighty God, and His substitutes or vicars, without discussing with vain curiosity the cause of that which they command me, as well not to be deceived by the subtle serpent—(who by the selfsame means abused Eve, enquiring of her the cause why God had forbidden them not to eat of the fruit of the tree of knowledge) (15)—as also, because oftentimes our Lord, to accord us what we ask of Him, is wont to command us something which seems contrary, to teach us by that to captivate our judgment to His obedience: and if I obey in those things that humble me, or discomfort me, by the selfsame way will He exalt and comfort me.

2. Secondly, I will dwell on the *almighty power of Christ* our Lord, who by His only will, without once touching the water, altered and converted it into wine; rejoicing that I have a Saviour so omnipotent, and beseeching Him

(15) Gen. iii.

to change my heart, and to turn it from evil to good, from cold to fervent, and from imperfect to perfect, offering up myself in no way to contradict Him; because, as St. Augustine says:—" He that made me without me, will not save me without me," (16) that is to say, will not change me from evil to good, not from lukewarm to fervent, if I resist Him.

3. I will likewise ponder the *great liberality of our Lord*, in recompensing the services which are done to Him, since for one glass of wine given to Him in this banquet—and that but of inferior quality—He turned six flagons or water pots full of most excellent wine, "even to the brim," as full as they could hold, and to this time does still the same, recompensing a cup of cold water with "good measure, and pressed down, shaken together, and running over;" (17) and gives to Religious a hundred-fold more than they have left or forsaken for the love of Him.

4. Finally, to those souls who *give themselves to prayer*, solemnizing with them these spiritual marriages, He causes to *enter into His " cellar* of wine," (18) and gives them to taste, to their unspeakable joy, of the *six vessels* which there are full of celestial affections, that is—of the heroic acts of six most excellent virtues;—zeal of His Divine glory, and of the salvation of souls;—fervent devotion with great promptitude to all things belonging to His divine service;—gratitude and thanksgiving for benefits received; —and obedience with resignation to do and suffer for the love of God, whatsoever shall be agreeable to Him.

Colloquy.—O Almighty and most liberal Saviour, I will have none but Thee for my Lord, my God, and my all; bring me into the cellar of Thy delicious wines, inebriate me with the wine of these six affec-

---

(16) Tract. 71. In Joan. xiv. 14.

(17) Luc. vi. 38. 　　　　　　　　　　(18) Cant. ii. 4.

tions, filling me full of them even to the top of perfection proper to my state, that, burning like a seraph, I may fly with these six wings (19) to unite myself to Thee, and never cease to love Thee and praise Thee, world without end.   Amen.

POINT V.

Consider the *effects of this miracle.*

1. First, the *joy of the Virgin* when she beheld this miracle, and saw that her hope had not deceived her.   Oh how confirmed did she remain in her former confidence, and what infinite thanks did she render to her Son for this singular favour!   I am likewise to consider how important are the prayers and intercessions of this incomparable lady, for Jesus Christ having said that His hour to work miracles was not yet come, yet in consequence of this prayer of His mother hastened the time and wrought this miracle immediately, so that this prayer was the cause that He anticipated the hour, which but for her sake He would not have anticipated at that time.

It is likewise a thing deserving of remark, that Christ our Lord took His mother for an *instrument of the first sanctification,* which was that of John the Baptist, and of *the first miracle,* which was this at the marriage, both which miraculous works He hastened by the means of His blessed mother, to teach us that she was to become our favourable mediatrix, to obtain for us speedily both temporal and spiritual benefits, the works of sanctity, and the miracles which Almighty God works by her intercession.   Wherefore I ought greatly to rejoice to have such a mother, who on the one side is so solicitous for my good, and on the other, is so powerful to procure it for me.

Colloquy.—O my mother, shew thyself a mother

(19) Isa. vi.

in my behalf, in hastening by thy prayers the hour of my help, that being delivered from this luke-warmness, I may begin to serve thy son with most increased fervour. Amen.

2. Secondly, I will reflect how *confirmed in faith the disciples* of Christ were when they saw this miracle, since as St. John says, they believed in Him with a new fervour of faith, and with extraordinary joy, seeing the omnipotency of their Master, comforting themselves that they were in His company, assuring themselves that nothing could be wanting to them while He should remain with them. Nor was it without mystery, that our Lord would that His first miracle should be showed in a *temporal thing*, so domestic and so necessary, to confirm the faith of those who were yet ignorant, and only beginners in divine things, disposing them by little and little to other things of greater consequence.

3. Thirdly, I will ponder the *great admiration of the chief steward*, having tasted the sweetness of that excellent wine, for not having any longer power to suppress his feelings, he presently caused the bridegroom to be called, blaming him for having infringed the common custom among men, who first give their guests the best wine, and afterward the worst, for he had reserved the best wine till afterward, insomuch, that the wine which at first seemed good, when he had tasted that which Jesus Christ had made, seemed inferior. But he noted not in this case the order and proceedings of Almighty God, who gives not the most precious wine made by His hand, until the former finish, and begin to fail, and this for two most high reasons:—

i. First, that we may hold in *greater estimation that which God gives us*, having first learned by experience our own misery, and seeing how opportunely He assists and succours us, verifying by experience that which David said, That

God " is a helper in due time in our tribulations," (20) sending us succour and a remedy for them, in the time and season most expedient for us.

ii. Secondly, to signify that God does not impart the gifts of *the Spirit, until we first have mortified the gratifications of the flesh ;* neither does manna fall from heaven, till first the meal of Egypt be quite consumed; for as St. Bernard says, (21) we cannot well mingle these two wines together, viz., the wine of celestial and terrestrial comforts, so that it is proper that first the earthly should fail in me, that so I may taste of the heavenly, although sometimes our Lord gives us to taste of the heavenly, that we may leave and more easily loathe that which is earthly.

Colloquy.—O sweet lover of souls, give me to taste of the wine of the Spirit, which may render that of the flesh distasteful unto me ; grant me to feel the sweetness of Thy celestial breasts, which may breed in me a loathsomeness of all terrestrial delights.   O my soul, animate thyself to mortify these sensual delights, that so thou mayest be worthy to obtain those which are eternal.   Amen.

MEDITATION X.

ON OUR LORD'S INDIGNANT EJECTION OF THE BUYERS AND SELLERS FROM THE TEMPLE.

POINT I.

Christ our Lord *going up* to the Temple of Jerusalem, and seeing oxen, sheep, and doves sold therein, and others sitting at their changing tables to receive money, " when He had made as it were a scourge of little cords, and therewith *drove them all out of the Temple,* the sheep also and

(20) Psal. ix. 10.   (21) Ep. 3. et Ser. de Ascen.

the oxen, and the money of the changers He poured out, and the tables He overthrew; and to them that sold doves He said, Take these things hence, and make not the house of my Father a house of traffick." (1)

1. First, I will consider the *great zeal* which Christ our Lord had for the *glory of His Father*, and the *purity* of His holy Temple,—zeal being an ardent desire to take away, or hinder all that is contrary to the thing that is loved, or repugnant to its will, honour, or profit, (2) and the greater the love is, so much greater is the zeal, and consequently greater the grief for the damage which is done to his friend, and greater the desire to remedy the same; and because Jesus Christ our Lord infinitely loved His Father and His Church, so likewise had He a most ardent zeal for whatsoever was connected with it. On this account He took a whip, and drove out of the Temple those that profaned it, as St. John observes, citing this passage of David, "Zelus domus tuæ comedit me." "The zeal of Thy house hath eaten me up." (3) In which words He signifies the greatness of this zeal in two ways:—

i. The first, that it was as a *consuming fire*, which did not only torment His heart, but also consumed His honour, His peace, and His life, despoiling Him so far as to leave Him naked, dishonoured, forsaken, and dead on the cross, to repair the honour of Almighty God, and of His house.

ii. The second, that this zeal had *wholly transported and transformed* Him into itself, in the same manner as the meat which one eats is turned into him that eats it. For even so Jesus Christ was eaten up by this zeal, as all His thoughts, words, and works were totally transformed into zeal; zeal it was which led Him and incited Him to all He said and did for our salvation;—even to this time this zeal

(1) Joan. ii. 16.   (2) S. Tho. i. 2. q. xxviii. art. 4.

(3) Ps. lxviii. 10.

eats up Jesus Christ, for, as we shall hereafter see, zeal is the cause why He has made Himself our meat, to become the food of all the faithful.

Colloquy.—O most sweet Redeemer, I give Thee thanks for the burning zeal which Thou hadst of Thy Father's house, which is the Church, and of my soul, which likewise is His temple and Church. Drive, O Lord, from thence whatsoever is displeasing to Thee, and consume with Thy fire whatsoever pollutes it. Give me likewise a zeal resembling Thine, whereby I may repair Thy honour although it should be with the loss of mine, for most happy and blessed should I be if zeal might consume me as it consumed Thee. Amen.

2. Then I will contemplate the *force of Christ, proceeding from this fervent zeal,* and showing such a countenance as affrighted that great assembly, which might have risen and rushed upon Him, but His divine and fervent love put to flight all human fear, zeal being " strong" and hardy " as death;" (4) which also, when it is needful, makes a whip, with which to chastise all delinquents, and drives out of the house of God whatsoever is prejudicial to it, and for this cause God Himself, as the Scripture says, " chastiseth" him "whom He loveth," (5) and " every son whom He receiveth," (6) that he forsake his imperfections.

Colloquy.—O most sweet Saviour, who with the self-same zeal takest in hand Thy whip to purify the house of Thy Father, and sufferest that Thine enemies take the whip to chastise Thine own most blessed body, paying with Thy bitter scourgings the pains of their sins : fortify me, I beseech Thee, with this holy zeal, whereby I may chastise my flesh for its former offences, and strive most manfully to prevent those of

<hr>

(4) Cant. viii. 6.   (5) Prov. iii. 12   (6) Heb. xii. 6.

others. Withdraw not from me Thy pious zeal when I shall offend Thee, for I had rather be chastised as a son, than live at my own liberty like a stranger. Amen.

POINT II.

The Jews demanding of Christ our Lord some *sign or miracle* to believe in Him, thereby to approve and ratify what He did, He answered to them, saying:—"*Destroy this Temple*, and in *three days* I will *raise it up:*" (7) speaking of His most holy body, the Temple in which inhabited the "fulness of the Godhead corporally," (8) by reason of the hypostatical union which it had. In which is to be considered, what *sign* this is: what *miracles* it contains: what *thing* it *signifies:* and the *effects* which it works.

1. First, Christ our Lord gives them here two signs,— one of His *Passion;*—another of His *Resurrection.*—i. The first is, the *permission* to *destroy* so precious a Temple with whips, thorns, and nails, leaving it disjointed and dead upon a cross.—ii. The second is, the *Resurrection* which He should perform by His own power, restoring His body to its former life, with greater glory than before. The self-same sign He gave at another time, saying :—"This evil and adulterous generation seeketh a sign, and a sign shall not be given it, but the sign of Jonas the prophet," (9) for even as Jonas was cast into the sea to save the ship, and swallowed up by a whale, three days after came forth alive:—even so I, for the salvation of the world, shall be cast into the tempestuous sea of tribulations, and shall be swallowed up by death, but the third day I shall come forth alive as a glorious conqueror.

2. Both these signs are very *miraculous*, because it was a great miracle, that Jesus Christ, God and man, with a

(7) Joan. ii. 19.   (8) Colos. ii. 9.   (9) Mat. xii. 39.

glorious soul, had together a mortal body, and suffered Himself to be slain, dissolving the union which His soul had with His blessed body.

i. And this miracle, in which He yielded to death, was a manifest sign of His infinite charity and mercy, by which He gave permission to His enemies to destroy the temple of His body, to repair the temple of their souls, and make them temples of the living God.

ii. It was likewise a sign of His *omnipotency*, which He testified in *suffering such terrible torments* and scorn, with wonderful patience and meekness, even to die upon a cross. Nevertheless even in dying, He likewise manifested His almighty power, triumphing by His death, over the same death, and over hell, not only in Himself, but also in all His elect, delivering them from its tyranny, and drawing forth of the whale's belly, all those which it had devoured, and so rose again most glorious, enriched with the spoils of innumerable souls, which He drew out of Limbo.

3. With these signs He *wrought so much, that men believed in Him, loved, and obeyed Him:* Hence it was, that the same Lord Himself said :—"*I, if I be lifted up from the earth, will draw all things to myself:*" (10) not with scourges made of cord, or by force of chastisements, but with the "cords of Adam," (11) "with the bands of love," and by the force and number of my benefits.

Colloquy.—I render Thee thanks, O my most sweet Redeemer, for having given to me so singular a sign, so painful to Thee, and so cheap and loving to me. I am that miserable wretch, who, with my sins, have destroyed Thy temple, that is, my soul; but Thou canst build it again "in three days;" quickening me with Thy grace in the first, perfecting me with perseverance in the second, and raising me to

<hr>

(10) Joan. xii. 2.   (11) Ose. xi. 4.

the participation of Thy glory in the third. Repair it, O Lord, by the merits of Thy Passion, and draw me to Thy service by the cords of so many benefits, as for this end Thou has done to me, by which, being renewed in spirit, I may come to enjoy Thee in heaven. Amen.

POINT III.

The third point shall be, to consider, how Christ our Lord, at *another time* nearer to *His Passion*, cast *out of the Temple* the *buyers and sellers*, and overthrew the tables of the money changers, and of those who sold doves, saying unto them :—"My house shall be called a house of prayer to all nations, but you have made it a den of thieves." (12) "*And He suffered not that* any man *should* carry a vessel *through the Temple*." (13)

1. Upon this fact, comparing the same with the precedent, I must ponder :—

i. That the *first time* Christ our Lord *expelled the merchants* from the Temple, both with words, and with a *whip* which He made of cords; but at this *last time*, He added to His words, *great miracles* which He wrought, reserving the whips for His own shoulders; to manifest to us the means which God observes to cleanse and purify His spiritual Temple:—one by chastisements—another by benefits. The first He used in the ancient law, which was a law of fear;—the second in the new law, which was a law of love: and if both these means prove unprofitable, this temple will come to be destroyed like that of Jerusalem, God chastising the same with the last punishment, namely, of everlasting damnation.

ii. Again, the first time He said:—"Make not the house of my Father a house of traffic:" giving to understand,

(12) Mat. xxi.
(13) Marc. xi. 16. Luc. xix. Isa. lvi. Jer. vii.

that the Temple is not to be turned into a house of profane, but divine affairs: that we ought not to come thither to negotiate with men, but to negotiate with God our own affairs, principally that of our salvation, soliciting the same with sacrifices and prayers.—The second time, He would not permit that men should pass with their burthens through the Temple; saying that they made it *"a den of thieves:* to signify, that in these negotiations of buying and selling, thefts, deceits, and injustices are committed, and sometimes simony, forasmuch as *"the desire of money* is *the root of all evils;* (14) which buys and sells the Holy Ghost and His graces, figured to us by those doves.

Colloquy.—O Saviour of the world, upon whom descended the Holy Ghost in the likeness of a dove, and sentest down the same on Thy disciples in the form of fire ; purify my covetousness with the fire of Thy love, that I may obtain the sanctity and purity of a dove, most becoming Thy holy habitation, for ever and ever.　Amen.

2. Here I will enter into the consideration, that *my soul ought to be the house and temple of contemplation;* into which I am to *"enter"* to pray to my heavenly *Father*, (15) who is present there, and sees my praying in the secret of my heart.　And because that house is not called a house of prayer where we only pray occasionally, but that which is an oratory dedicated solely to this purpose, such ought my heart to be, consecrated with great fervour to the frequency of this exercise, so, that wheresoever I be as the saints say, (16) I always carry my oratory with me, and so accomplish that which St. Paul says :—"I will that men pray in every place, lifting up pure hands without anger

(14) 1 Tim. vi. 10.　　　(15) Mat. vi. 6.
16) Amb. l. 6. de sacr. c. 3.　Chrl. hom. 79 ad pop.　Hil. c. 5. in Mac.

and contention." (17) Hence it is, that my soul being a house of prayer, ought also to be a house of humility, obedience, patience, and of other virtues, because they are all found, as we have said in the introduction of this book, in the house of prayer, accompanying and exercising therein their excellent acts, and by consequence it ought not to be a house of profane affairs, nor "a den of thieves," that is, of vices and other earthly cares, which disturb and steal away devotion, and drive prayer out of its own dwelling.

3. Hence I will infer, that *my soul*, to become a worthy house of holy prayer, ought principally to have these *three conditions*, that is to say,—to be *clean from sins*, which bring remorse,—*quiet from passions*, which disturb it,— and adorned with acts of virtue, to entertain it: and then, saith S. Augustine, (18) "'The cleanness of thy heart with its tranquillity" will delight thee, and excite thee to pray, for thus wilt thou be satisfied to dwell within thyself, and to make thy habitation in thine own interior; but if it be foul, disquieted, and disordered, in seeking to enter into it, thou goest forth out of it, and forsakest prayer, even as he that should enter into a church to pray where there were great tumults and clamours, presently departs, because he cannot pray there as he desires.

Colloquy.—O my Saviour, arm Thyself with Thy holy zeal, and take Thy whip into Thy hand : enter into this Thy temple, and drive out of it whatsoever displeases Thee ;—permit not that any thing pass through the same, which may disturb it ;—purify this den of thieves, and make it henceforth a house of prayer, a habitation of angels, and a place of peace, in which Thou mayest dwell for ever and ever. Amen.

(17) 1 Tim. ii. 8.   (18) Serm. 2. in Psal. xxxiii.

MEDITATION XI.

ON THE SERMON ON THE MOUNT: AND THE EIGHT BEATITUDES.

Christ our Lord "seeing the multitudes" of people that followed Him, "went up into a mountain, and when He was set down, His disciples came to Him:" and lifting up His eyes upon them, and opening His mouth, He taught them, saying: "Blessed are the poor in spirit," (1) &c.

Upon this remarkable beginning, may first be considered the mystery which the place itself of the sermon contained, which is a most high mountain;—the seat of the master, which is the bare, or humble earth;—those who approach most near to Him are the apostles; the aspect of His eyes which He casts up to behold them;—the manner of speaking, which is to open His own mouth; the theme of the sermon, which are eight beatitudes; and above all, the interior excellency of the master, from whom the whole proceeds.

POINT I.

1. First, consider, how Christ our Lord, upon this mountain, took *public possession of three very eminent offices,* which His Father imposed upon Him for our profit, that is to say;—of a *master,* a *lawgiver,* and a *councellor,* practising them in most high perfection, figured by the "mountain." For entering into Himself, He from the profound treasures of the science and wisdom of Almighty God "brought out new things, and old," (2) very precious, and profitable for us.—i. As master, He taught us, not vain or curious things, not astrology, or other human sciences, which swell or puff up much, but profit little,

(1) Mat. v. 1 ; Luc. vi. 20.   (2) Mat. xiii. 52.

but taught us the science of the saints, which comprehends the most high mysteries of our holy faith, and the things necessary for us to obtain salvation.—ii. As *lawgiver*, (3) He promulgated and published anew that celestial and divine law, with all the purity and sanctity which it comprises, purging it from those errors with which the malice of man had intermingled it, and perfecting the imperfections of the ancient law.—iii. As *councellor*, He taught us the counsels of the new and Evangelical law, which are the most excellent that can be counselled; and by reason of which, He is called, "Wonderful counsellor," (4) and the Angel of the great council.

2. After this I will consider how He performed these three offices, after an *admirable, new,* and *most excellent manner;* For, i. As master, He did not only exteriorly propound the doctrine, but likewise *interiorly* gave a celestial light, to understand and esteem it.—ii. As Lawgiver, He did not only prescribe most excellent laws and precepts, but also engraved them *in their hearts*, conferring grace to fulfil them with exceeding sweetness.—iii. And as Counsellor, He did not only give the counsels, but moreover, *the spirit and forces to embrace*, and put them in practice. In this He far exceeded all the masters, lawgivers, and counsellors of the world; for which cause with very great reason He commands us, to "call no man master" but Himself, because we have but "one master," which is "Christ:"(5) and for the same reason, but one lawgiver, and one counsellor.

Colloquy.—O eternal Father, I render Thee thanks that Thou hast given me the best master, lawgiver, and counsellor that Thou couldst give me. O Son of the living and everlasting God, how shall I repay this unspeakable favour, for having come in person

(3) Isa. xlviii.   (4) Isa. ix. 6.   (5) Mat. xxiii. 10.

and having opened Thine own mouth to teach me
Thy divine doctrine, since it might have sufficed to
have sent Thine angels, from whose mouth I might
have been taught it. O my soul, behold with Thine
eyes, the teacher and master whom God hath given
Thee: and since He commands thee to choose a
" Counsellor " from amongst a " thousand," (6) choose
thou this one who is the best of all others, and selected
amongst thousands; consult with him about thy
doubts, and let thy counsels be with His divine laws.(7)
O heavenly master, give me light to understand what
Thou teachest me.—O supreme lawgiver, give me
Thy benediction to accomplish that which Thou commandest me. O admirable counsellor, give me force
to follow that which Thou dost counsel me : that by
Thine assistance, ascending " from virtue to virtue," I
may come to see Thee in the holy " Sion."(8) Amen.

3. Christ our Lord *never ceases to execute these three
offices in the behalf of men*, especially towards those who
desire to ascend with Him into the mountain of perfection,
and approach Him by sincere love: because, as the Scripture says, those "who come to our Lord shall be enlightened:" and those who place themselves at His feet, (9)
imitating His humility, shall receive His doctrine. On
these He casts His eyes to behold thee with mercy,
these He teaches by the mouth of His preachers when
they hear them, and by devout and holy books when they
read them: or by themselves alone with His inspirations,
when they pray and meditate, opening His own mouth to
speak effectually to their hearts; and there, as a master,
He infuses into thee a new light, to know the mysteries
of their faith; as a lawgiver, He engraves within them
the affections of the law of grace and of charity; and as

(6) Ecclus. vi. 6.　　　(7) Psal. cxviii.
(8) Psal. lxxxiii. 8.　　　(9) Psal. xxxiii. 6.

a counsellor, He summons and solicits them to follow perfection. And with this spirit I am to repair to a sermon, to reading, or prayer, as one who sets himself to hear this divine master, who speaks to me interiorly through these organs. For this cause the eternal Father said, that the Master whom He would give us, should never cease to execute His office to the end of the world. (10) So that at the beginning of these exercises, I may thus say to Christ our Lord:—

Colloquy.—O Master of masters, open Thy most holy mouth and speak unto me, for Thy servant heareth, with a deire to practise what I hear. Amen.

POINT II.

1. Secondly, consider, the *theme and exordium of this sermon ;* for Christ our Lord, beholding that treasure of virtue enclosed within His noble soul, drew from thence eight principal virtues, which are the *summary* of *Evangelical perfection,*—virtues very ancient and very recent, and never heard of before in the whole world—under a new name of Beatitudes, which, though bitter to the flesh, fulfil that which the spouse in the Canticles speaks of Him, that His lips are (11) as the lilies, dropping choice myrrh, for with great gentleness and sweetness opening His mouth, even this first time, He distilled from His lips these eight acts of most exquisite virtue and mortification, bitter to the taste of the flesh, but odoriferous to Almighty God, profitable to the spirit, powerful to preserve it from all corruption of sin, sweetening them with the reward that Himself has promised, and with the manner by which He propounded them.

Colloquy.—O sovereign master, distil into my heart that "choice myrrh" of these excellent virtues, that

(10) Isa. xxxix. 21.   (11) Cant. v. 13.

"my hands, my fingers," and all my powers, may drop them, (12) by speedily putting Thy doctrine in practice. Amen.

2. Then will I ponder, how Christ our Lord *sustained alone the honour of these virtues* which were rejected and abhorred by the world; reputing them, not blessings or favours, but misfortunes; flying from them, and embracing their contraries. But our Saviour honoured each of them with a most glorious name, and most renowned recompense, and most of all, with His rare example. For being not capable, as He was God, of poverty, tears, and persecutions, He would descend from Heaven, and make Himself man, to practise the acts of these excellent virtues, and to discover to us the divine treasures enclosed within them.

Colloquy.—I give Thee thanks, O sovereign master, that Thou hast drawn us from this error by Thy holy doctrine and example, henceforth I will esteem blessed, that which Thou shalt honour by this name, and with all my strength endeavour to avoid the contrary. Discover, Lord, to all that live in the world, their deceit, that so they may receive these truths, and embrace these virtues, enjoy these recompenses, and finally obtain that true beatitude for which they were created. Amen.

3. Thirdly, I will ponder how these eight beatitudes, *are like* to *eight degrees or steps* of this celestial "ladder," (13) whereby we mount up to the top of *sanctity and union with Almighty God:* and with this spirit will I strive to meditate on them, pondering in each of them, three or four particular things, that is to say:—i. The *acts* of every virtue:—ii. The *example which Christ our Lord has given of it:*—iii. The *reward* which He promised:—iv. The *chastise-*

(12) Cant. v. 5.　　　　　　　　　(13) Gen. xxviii. 12.

ment which He threatens against those who walk a contrary way, as will be seen in the ensuing points; proposing to myself not to repeat one thing often, that I will only quote the examples of Christ our Lord, reserving for another time what is spoken more at large, in the mysteries in which He practised the same virtues, principally on the cross, where He exercised them all in an eminent degree, as will be seen in the beginning of the fourth part. In like manner, I will note briefly something of the rewards, which I will discourse amply in the end of the sixth part, to declare the inestimable riches of the glory of heaven.

POINT III.

"BLESSED ARE THE POOR IN SPIRIT, FOR THEIRS IS THE KINGDOM OF HEAVEN."(14)

i. First, consider the *acts of poverty of spirit*, which are five.

The first act is, to *forsake with our soul*, and with our reason all *temporal things*, renouncing all *inordinate affection* towards them, and to be ready entirely to *renounce* them, when it shall appear to be the will of God.

ii. The second more perfect is, to *forsake actually* all whatsoever I possess, moving myself to it by a spiritual and pure will to please Almighty God only, and to obey the impulse of the Holy Spirit, who inclined me to it.

iii. The third is, to empty and *cleanse my soul* from all evil exhalation, *of vain glory*, from all puffing up and vain presumptions, despising from my heart as much as I can the pomps of the world, or actually renouncing them when I can, and when it is expedient for me the better to serve my God.

iv. The fourth is, to *empty my spirit* of all property, despoiling myself of my own *judgment and will*, together with all its natural desires, unless so far as they are conformable to those of Almighty God, because in such case they are not merely natural, but virtuous.

(14) Mat. v. 3.

v. The fifth and last is, to *despoil myself of myself,* acknowledging myself to be so poor, that *there is no good at all in me, if God do not give it me gratuitously and by favour;* for the very being which I have is not mine own, but God's, without whom I should instantly return even to nothing.

Pondering, therefore, these five acts, I will blush for the want and deficiency which I find of them, beseeching the divine Spirit to assist me to obtain them, as may be expedient for my condition in life.

2. Secondly, consider those rare *examples* which *Christ our Lord gave* of this virtue, in all the stages of His life, and in all such things which *appertain to poverty,* (15) for He chose a poor mother, a poor country, a most poor stable to be born in, was reclined or laid in a poor manger, and in His youth, (16) exercised a poor and despised trade, getting His living by the labour of His hands, as we have seen in the second part. When He preached He lived on the alms which devout women bestowed upon Him; His food was barley bread; house, He had none, nor yet whereon to repose His head, that being wanting to the " Son of Man," which was not wanting to the foxes and birds of the air. (17) He also chose poor disciples—conversed with the poor—loved the despised—fled from honours—and disengaged Himself from His own will, and even from Himself also, and that with a most excellent interior poverty, saying, that He " came not to do His own will," and that He could do nothing of Himself, but what He saw His Father do.

In short, when He died, His poverty reduced Him to such extremity, that His very garments were taken from Him, leaving Him naked upon the cross: and in further

(15) S. Th. 3. p. q. xl. a. 3.   (16) Psal. lxxxvii. 16.
(17) Luc. ix. 58.

confirmation of the love and estimation which He made cf poverty, He took it in this sermon for the first foundation of His Gospel, and as a door by which we are to enter into His school of perfection, saying:—" Every one of you that does not renounce, at least in affection, all that he possesses cannot be my disciple."(18)

Colloquy.—O sovereign master, I beseech Thee by the five fountains of blood, which issued from Thy five wounds, grant me these five acts of poverty, by which I may attain the perfection which Thou hast founded, and established upon them. Amen.

3. Thirdly, consider how to these *poor*, Christ our Lord *promises the Kingdom of heaven*, and on this account calls them " blessed," for so they are even in this life, already possessing the Kingdom of God, which St. Paul called, (19) " justice, and peace, and joy, in the Holy Ghost;" which is granted to those who mortify their covetousness, as we have said before in the first part, meditation twenty-one. And, moreover, they are " blessed" with hope, and with the great and evident pledges which they have to obtain the Kingdom of heaven, which is promised them in the other life, whose riches are inestimable, as we shall see hereafter.

Colloquy.—O my soul, why embracest thou not poverty of spirit, since thy celestial Master embraced it, and that such rewards are reaped thereby? Cast thyself therefore by it, into the arms of Him, whose fatherly providence will neither desert thee, nor fail to accomplish His word to thee; and since thou daily demandest of Almighty God His promised Kingdom, embrace poverty, to whom He has promised it. Amen.

4. Fourthly, consider the *terrible threat* which Christ

(18) Luc. xiv. 33.   (19) Rom. xiv. 17.

our Lord *pronounces against the rich*, who abhor this poverty of spirit, and love their deceitful riches inordinately, saying to them:—"Woe that you are rich, because you have your consolation :"(20) which is to say, "Woe be to you unfortunate men, for all your reward shall end in the satisfaction which you take in your riches, receiving your recompense here below. Woe be to you, for you shall not receive the consolations of God, which is both true and pure, but only your own, which is mixed with a thousand encumbrances. Woe be to you, who shall never possess the Kingdom of heaven, which is 'justice, peace, and joy in the Holy Ghost,' but you shall be filled with injustice, trouble, and affliction. Finally, you shall fall into extreme poverty, and into everlasting misery, like to the avaricious rich man, who here received comfort, and afterwards torment, quite contrary to the distressed Lazarus."

Colloquy.—O my soul, if the desire of recompense does not move thee to love poverty, let the fear of punishment at the least affright thee so as to fly from temporal riches, placing thy comfort in contemning of them, to love and enjoy those that are eternal. Amen.

POINT IV.

"BLESSED ARE THE MEEK, FOR THEY SHALL POSSESS THE LAND." (21)

1. Perfect meekness embraces these several acts, that is to say, i. First, to *repress the swellings of anger* together with the vexations and disquietnesses of the heart, preserving both interior and exterior tranquillity, as well in the countenance as in the comportment of the body.—ii. Secondly, to be *affable towards all*, using such speech as is pleasing, without injuring or sneering at any one, without loud crying or contention, which causes trouble.—iii. Thirdly, not only not to revenge injuries, nor to return evil for

(20) Luc. vi. 24.   (21) Mat. iv. 5.

evil, but not to resist with an *injurious violence him that injured me*, supporting any abuse of myself with serenity, and offering, if it be needful, " the right check" to him that has smitten me on the left, requiting good for evil, excusing him that wronged me, and praying God to pardon him.

And this meekness ought to be observed towards all, as well to superiors as to equals and inferiors, on all occasions and occurrences, without losing my temper even when it shall be necessary to do justice.

2. After this I will consider the most *excellent meekness of Christ* our Lord, of which He made so great account, that He exhibited Himself for a pattern thereof, saying:— " Learn of me, because I am meek and humble of heart:" (22) and by it He desired to be known in His very first entrance into the world, the prophets foretelling that He should not be contentious nor stubborn, that His voice should not be heard abroad, nor should He quench the smoking flax,(23) but patiently suffer the smell in His nose. And in His Passion He demonstrated a most rare meekness, even so much as to pray for His persecutors, as we shall see in its proper place.

Colloquy.—O most meek Lamb, who being shorn and fleeced, didst not open Thy mouth : (24) grant me Thy abundant grace, that I may imitate Thy humble meekness. Amen.

3. Thirdly, consider how the *meek shall have for their reward the inheritance of the earth.*—i. First, forasmuch as they are *lords of the earth, of their own hearts and passions*, possessing securely their own souls, together with their Lord and their God, who dwells within them, with whom they hold most close familiarity, as the most meek Moses

(22) Mat. xi. 29.   (23) Isa. xlii. 2.   (24) Isa. liii. 7.

and gentle David did; (25) for God our Lord takes delight in manifesting His ways to the meek, and in conversing with them.—ii. Hence it is, that they enjoy the earth *of their human hearts*, because they gain the hearts of every one, for doing their works with perfect meekness, they are beloved, as the Wise man says, " above the glory of men." (26)—iii. Lastly, they shall *possess the land of the living*, which is that celestial country for which they were created, where they shall possess God our Lord, who is their inheritance and patrimony, and shall be likewise possessed by Him, who reposes and dwells among the meek, and peoples with them His house of heaven. (27)

Colloquy.—O divine Spirit, who, like a most meek "dove," (28) descendest upon them who are meek lambs, by reason of the resemblance which they have with Thee ; make me like to Thee in perfect meekness, that I may possess securely the union of Thy grace, and hereafter the inheritance of Thy glory.   Amen.

POINT V.

" BLESSED ARE THEY THAT MOURN, FOR THEY SHALL BE COMFORTED."

1. The tears that are *blessed* comprehend these acts.—i. First, to *refrain from inordinate laughter, plays, and pastimes*, cutting off not only the unlawful, but even such as may be lawfully done without sin, saying with Ecclesiastes :—" Laughter I counted error; and to mirth I said, Why art thou vainly deceived?" (29)—ii. The second is, to *weep for my sins*, not so much for my own loss, as for the offence against Almighty God, as both St. Peter and David did, who said:—" My eyes have sent forth springs of water, because they have not kept Thy law." (30)—iii. The third is, *to weep for the sins of other men*, as well for

(25) Ps. xxvi.
(26) Eccles. iii. 19.   (27) Ps. xxxvi.   (28) Joan. i.
(29) Eccles. ii. 2.   (30) Psal. cxviii. 136.

their perdition and damnation, as for the injury done to Almighty God, lamenting to see how ill He is served, as Jeremias lamented the perdition of the people, and desired that his eyes might be converted into "a fountain of tears," (31) to deplore their miseries night and day.—iv. The fourth is, to *deplore my exile* and my *absence* from *Almighty God*, sighing to enjoy His presence, and saying with David: —"My tears have been my bread day and night, whilst it is said to me daily, Where is thy God?" (32)   The first sort of tears are tears of *contrition*, the second of *compassion*, and the third of *devotion*, which resemble those which we shed, when meditating the mysteries of the Passion; and the want which I have of all of them, not only of the cor-poral, which oft are wanting without any fault, but of the spiritual, from whence they spring, I will say to our Lord, what the daughter of Caleb said to her father:—"Thou hast given me a dry land, give me also a land that is watered.   And Caleb gave to her the upper and nether watery land." (33)

Colloquy.—O sovereign father, "my soul is as earth without water," (34) give me the inferior fountain, tears of fear, and the superior tears of love, whereby I may deplore my sins and miseries, and those of all the world, that I may obtain remedy for them.   Amen.

2. We do not read that *Christ our Lord ever laughed*, as St. Basil notes, (35) whereas we know that He *often wept*, as in the manger, at the death of Lazarus, over Jerusalem, and most tender tears on the cross, as will be seen in the meditations on these mysteries; in fine, as St. Paul says, "in the days of His flesh," (36) viz., His mortality, He prayed oftentimes with tears, so that in the garden of Gethsemane

<hr>

(31) Jer. ix. 1.   (32) Ps. xli. 4.
(33) Jos. xv. 19.   Jud. i. 15.
(34) Ps. cxlii. 6.   S. Greg. l. 3. Dial. cap. 34.
(35) Reg. ut xvii. ex fusis.   (36) Heb. v. 7.

He prayed sweating, not drops of water, but of blood, as one that wept tears of blood through all the pores of His natural body, for the sins and miracles of His mystical body.

Colloquy.—O most sweet Jesus, convert my eyes into fountains of tears, which may accompany Thine, since I was the cause of them. Amen.

3. Consider that *tears*, which in the eyes of the world are signs of misery, in the eyes of Christ are *signs of happiness* and felicity, promising to those that weep, that " they shall be comforted," (37) even in that for which they weep. If they weep for their own sins, they shall receive comfort in the remission of them; if they weep for the sins of others, or for their exile, God will " turn their mourning into joy," with hope that their sorrows will have an end, and that everlasting consolations will quickly follow, our tender Lord wiping " away tears from their eyes," (38) and causing their mourning to take an end.

Colloquy.—O blessed tears, which are requited with such consolations: here it is, O my Lord, that I will weep, since even the tears themselves are so wonderfully sweet; and, if it be so sweet to weep for Thee, how sweet shall it be to enjoy Thee? (39) Amen.

4. Ponder the threatening of Christ our Lord, who says: —" Woe *to you that now laugh*, for you shall *mourn* and *weep*," (40) so that if I now give myself immoderately to laughter and such like vain pleasures, afterwards bitter tears and inward sighs will ensue, either in this life "mourning taking hold of the end of joy,"(41) as the Wise man says; or in the other, in which, as our Saviour says:— " Shall be wailing and gnashing of teeth," (42) conformable to the sentence given against Babylon:—" As much as she

(37) Ps. xxix. 12.   (38) Apoc. vii. 17.   (39) S. Aug.
(40) Luc. vi. 25.   (41) Prov. xiv. 13.   (42) Mat. viii. 12.

hath glorified herself and lived in delicacies, so more give ye to her torment, &c." (43) because she has said it in her heart, I shall never taste what it is to weep, or ever know what mourning means.

Colloquy.—O my soul, abhor and detest immoderate laughter, and embrace thou virtuous weeping, since with temporal tears, thou hast the means of delivering thyself from those which are eternal.   Amen.

POINT VI.

"BLESSED ARE THEY THAT HUNGER AND THIRST AFTER JUSTICE; FOR THEY SHALL HAVE THEIR FILL."

The *hunger and thirst after justice* comprehend *these* acts.

1. The first is, a *desire to fulfil* all those *things* which belong to *justice* and obligation, towards *God*, and towards our *neighbour*, without omitting any, performing them with great delight, without disgust or slothfulness, although they be disagreeable to our flesh, even as he who drinks and eats with thirst and hunger, swallows down all with an eager appetite: for as the Wise man says, the "soul that is hungry, shall take even bitter for sweet." (44) —ii. The second act is, to desire to *increase* and profit *more and more* in *virtues*, reputing that which one has done for very little, and that for much which he has failed.— iii. The third act is, to *have a hunger and thirst*, that the *whole world* may have this *justice*, and that all may practise and observe it, offering oneself to suffer any temporal hunger, or any other pain, that this end may be obtained. —iv. The fourth is, to have an *inward hunger* to receive *sacramentally*, or spiritually, *Christ our Lord* who is our "*justice*," (45) with a desire to drink the living water of His grace, and the wine and milk of His divine consolations, running to the sacraments, to prayer and meditation with

(43) Apoc. xviii. 7.   (44) Prov. xxvii. 7.   (45) 1 Cor. i. 30.

exceeding thirst; as being the "fountains of water," (46) whence they flow.—v. The fifth is, *ardently* to *desire the crown of justice, sighing to see Almighty God*, to sit with Christ at His celestial table, and to eat and drink of that which shall feed and satiate me everlastingly.

In this hunger and thirst, consists that which we call fervour of spirit, in opposition to the vice of sloth and tepidity, with which fervour I am to accompany all my actions, ashamed to feel myself so hungry after corporal meats, and to have such disgust for those that are spiritual.

2. Christ our Lord, *had always in His soul so great a hunger and thirst after justice*, that He did not feel the hunger of the body, and so being on a time exceeding weary and in want of meat, He said to His disciple:—"My meat is to do the will of Him that sent me:" (47) as if He had said, Until I have filled my spiritual hunger, I have no care of the hunger of my body, nor does my body feel the want of its food, until the spirit has first received and eaten its food. He likewise had so great a thirst to drink the chalice of His passion, although it was so bitter, that He suffered exceeding great torment for the want and delay of this drink: and upon the cross He said, that He was thirsty, not only for the drought which the body endured, but much more for that which the spirit suffered: as will be seen in meditating those mysteries.

Colloquy.—O beloved Redeemer, inflame me with the fire of Thy love, whence this hunger and thirst proceeds, that I may always have it in Thy service, as Thou hadst it of my salvation. Amen.

3. How *happy and blessed* are the *hungry;* "for they *shall be filled*," Almighty God granting to them the things they desire, giving them in this life abundance of grace,

(46) Isa. xlix. 10.   (47) Joan. iv. 34.

abundance of merits, and great interior spiritual relish, imparting Himself to them for meat, and so uniting Himself to them by love, that they say :—"For what have I in heaven, and besides Thee what do I desire upon earth?"(48) And although the satiety of this life be such, that it awakens a new hunger, and a new thirst, as the holy Scripture says, (49) yet this hunger and this thirst are not painful, but exceedingly delighful, because they take away distaste and augment appetite. In fine, in the other life they shall be filled with the sight of Almighty God, as David says:—" I shall be satisfied when Thy glory shall appear." (50)

Colloquy.—O blessed hunger, which art recompensed with such satiety! Ponder, O my soul, this fulness, for it will excite this hunger in thee. Amen.

4. Consider the threat of Christ our Lord, who says :— " *Woe to you that are filled,* for you shall hunger." (51) He calls those full who abound and are full of temporal goods, and eat and drink even till they burst for voluptuousness sake; whence proceeds that they have no " hunger" nor " thirst" after " justice," but a loathing of it, as the Wise man says:—" A soul that is full shall tread upon the honeycomb." (52) Whose chastisement shall be like to that of the avaricious rich man, who then fared deliciously, and now endures incredible thirst, and has no one to give him a drop of water to refresh him. He also calls the proud " full," who, as St. Paul says, hold themselves for " rich" and " full;" (53) they will come to suffer great hunger and want of all good things, because God our Lord, as the Blessed Virgin says:—" Filled the hungry with good things, and the rich He hath sent empty away." (54)

(48) Psal. lxxii. 25.   (49) Ecclus. xxiv. 29.   (50) Psal. xvi. 15
(51) Luc. vi. 25.   (52) Prov. xxvii. 7
(53) 1 Cor. iv. 8.   (54) Luc. i. 53.

Colloquy.—O eternal God, take away from me, I beseech Thee, this abominable fulness, that so I may be freed from such painful and miserable hunger. Amen.

POINT VII.

"BLESSED ARE THE MERCIFUL, FOR THEY SHALL OBTAIN MERCY."

1. Mercy comprehends *these fourteen acts*, which we call the works *of mercy*, seven of which are *corporal*, and seven *spiritual*, to be exercised with three conditions, by which they may become more excellent.—i. The first is, that I extend it to *all my neighbours* who suffer, without excluding any, even my enemy.—ii. The second is, that I apply myself to *redress all manner of corporal or spiritual miseries*, "according to" my "ability," (55) as Tobias said to his son, giving much if I be rich, and little if I be poor; and if I have no means at all to succour the necessity, at least to have the will and desire to relieve them, praying Almighty God to redress their want, and to procure, if I can, that others supply it.—iii. The third is, to excite myself to *interior compassion* for the misery of others, feeling them as my own, showing first a compassionate heart, and afterwards bestowing the gift itself for pure charity, without expecting any other reward than from God. (56)

2. *Christ our Lord* was *most merciful* in the *highest degree of excellency*, in the three things before mentioned, because He was the *universal remedy* of all our miseries, in which works He wholly employed the years of His preaching, healing the sick, feeding the hungry miraculously, raising the dead, pardoning sinners with sweetness and love, teaching the ignorant, praying, and "doing good" (57) to all manner of persons; and He made so great account of this virtue, that He said to those who would not practise it:—" Go, then, and learn

(55) Tob. 4. 8.   (56) Luc. xiv. 14.   (57) Act. x. 30.

what this meaneth: I will have mercy, and not sacrifice:" (58) teaching that He makes most account of this virtue, and that it is most agreeable to Almighty God, to whom mercy is much more agreeable, and of more estimation than sacrifice, and that He will not accept sacrifice without mercy.

Colloquy.—O God Jesus, who art come into the world, moved thereto by Thy mercy only, and who through mere compassion, tookest upon Thee all our miseries to deliver us from them, shew this mercy in my behalf, and make me imitate Thee in it : And since Thou saidst to all:—" Be ye merciful as your heavenly Father also is merciful," (59) assist me with Thy especial grace, that I may imitate His excellent mercy. Amen.

3. Thirdly, consider that the *reward of the merciful* is to *obtain mercy* of Almighty God, delivering them from all their miseries, both corporal and spiritual, partly in this life, and perfectly and completely in the next, and that with such excess, as there is difference between the misery of a feeble man, and the mercy of Almighty God, which in every way is infinite, as we shall see in the sixth part; and it will be greater towards me in proportion as that has been greater which I myself have showed towards my neighbour, measuring me with the selfsame measure that I have measured him, as has been said in the first part, Med. xxi. And since I am loaded with so many miseries, that none but God can deliver me, what can I do more assuredly to obtain the divine favour, than to be merciful to others, that God may likewise be so to me? O blessed ye merciful, whom the Father of mercy will deliver from all your miseries!

4. Lastly, if I *be not merciful* I shall be *most miserable*,

(58) Mat. ix. 13.   (59) Luc. vi. 36.

for God our Lord will have no compassion on me, as He had no compassion on that wicked servant who took no compassion on his companion. (60)   But on the contrary, as the apostle St. James says:—" Judgment without mercy to him that hath not done mercy." (61)   And on this account, at the day of judgment, mention will be made of the works of mercy in the sentence of the good, and of the want of them in the condemnation of the wicked, as has already been said in its place.

POINT VIII.

"BLESSED ARE THE CLEAN OF HEART, FOR THEY SHALL SEE GOD."

1. *Perfect purity* and *cleanness of heart*, is, *perfect charity*, with the three conditions specified by St. Paul, that is, "*a pure heart and a good conscience, and an unfeigned faith.*" (62)—i. The first condition, is, *purity of heart*, purifying it not only from *mortal sins*, but also as much as we can even from *venial*, in such a manner that although they touch the heart, yet that they make no stay nor be detained therein by usual custom or affection.— ii. The second is, the cleanness and *neatness of the conscience*, filling it with clean thoughts and desires, and with clean, pure, and holy works.—iii. The third is, *true simplicity* in treating either with *God*, or *men*, proceeding sincerely with all persons, with simplicity and sincere intention of heart, without duplicity or deceit.   This cleanness is called cleanness of heart, because it principally appertains to the soul and the will, and thence descends to the body in the cleanness of unpolluted chastity, according to each person's state; although that of virgins and of continent persons is more pure, because, as the apostle says, (63) they are sanctified "both in body and in spirit," purifying themselves from the spots of the spirit, and of the flesh.

(60) Matt. xviii. 30.   (61) Jac. ii. 13.   (62) 1 Tim. i. 5.
(63) 1 Cor. vi. 11. & vii. 34.   2 Cor. vii. 1.

2. I will consider, how *excellent Christ our Lord* was in this kind of *cleanness*, because He neither *sinned*, nor yet *could sin;* nor could the "prince of this world" find in Him aught that was his; nor His enemies "convince Him of sin;" (64) He adorning His whole life with most pure, most holy, and most perfect works, seeking in them no other thing than the glory of His Father, neither was *guile* found in His mouth;" (65)—who hated so much all hypocrisy and counterfeit purity, which proceeded not from the very heart, that He reprehended it most sharply, saying:—"Woe to you hypocrites, because you make clean the outside of the cup and of the dish, but within you are full of rapine and uncleanness." (66) Blind Pharisee, first make the inside clean, that thence the cleanness of the outside may follow, because from the interior cleanness of the heart, proceeds the purity of the exterior works; and even as no man will willingly drink out of a vessel or cup which is very foul within, although it were clean and scoured without: even so Jesus Christ contents not Himself with exterior cleanness, without the interior cleanness of the soul.

Colloquy.—O most pure Saviour, brightness of eternal light, and the unspotted mirror of God's majesty, and the image of His goodness, (67) cleanse me, I beseech Thee, from all my uncleanness, and enrich and adorn me with Thy virtues, that both interiorly and exteriorly, I may be pure in Thy presence, for ever and ever.   Amen.

3. Consider that the *recompense* of this *purity* and cleanness is the *essential beatitude of the saints,* as well that of this life, which consists in the sight of God our Lord by an affectionate contemplation, and joy to possess

(64) Joan. viii. ut xiv.

(65) 1 Pet. ii. 22.

(66) Mat. xxiii. 25.   (67) Sap. vii. 26.

Him, as that of the other life, which consists in the clear vision of the same God, of whose greatness we shall treat hereafter. For this reason the prophet David said:—"Who shall ascend into the mount of the Lord, or who shall stand in His holy place? The innocent in hands, and clean of heart, who hath not taken his soul in vain, nor sworn deceitfully to his neighbour." (68)

Colloquy.—O blessed purity, which art elevated to such excellency! O my soul since anything defiled " with sin, shall not enter " (69) into heaven to see the face of Almighty God, procure thou the greatest purity and cleanness that thou possibly canst, that so thou mayest obtain this blessed sight. Amen.

POINT IX.

BLESSED ARE THE PEACEMAKERS, FOR THEY SHALL BE CALLED THE CHILDREN OF GOD."

1. They are truly *peaceable*, who always study and *endeavour* to *make reconciliation*, in which there are four degrees of great excellence.—i. The first is, that a person should *pacify himself*, subjecting his flesh to the spirit, his passions to reason, and all his powers to Almighty God.—ii. The second is, that he should be *peaceable towards others*, procuring, as much as lies in him, to "have peace with all men," (70) without giving occasion to disquietness, but rather of love and of union.—iii. The third is, that he should *make peace* and agreement *betwixt neighbours*, endeavouring to harmonize one with the other.—iv. The fourth, and most principal is, that he should reconcile *souls to Almighty God*, assisting to restore them to His favour, and to reduce creatures, to the obedience and service of their Creator.

Pondering these degrees of peace, which, as the apostle

(68) Psal. xxiii. 3.   (69) Apoc. xxi. 27.
(70) Rom. xii. 18.

says, "surpasseth all understanding," (71) I will lament the want which I have of them, beseeching our Lord to grant them to me.

Colloquy.—O God of peace and of perfect charity, grant me the peace which Thou gavest Thine apostles, that I may serve Thee with peace and quietness, and that others also may serve Thee by means of me, I having pacified them with Thee.   Amen.

2. *Christ our Lord came down from heaven to bring us this peace,* and who by way of excellence, calls Himself King of peace, and so highly esteemed and prized this holy peace, that He first saluted His apostles with it, and would that they should likewise salute others with it, saying :— "Peace be to this house." (72)   And further, that He might reconcile us to His eternal Father, suffered innumerable persecutions, without losing this peace, but was peaceable even "with them that hated peace :" (73) who "through the blood of His cross," as St. Paul says, maketh "peace both as to the things on earth and the things that are in heaven." (74)

Colloquy.—O most peaceable and sovereign prince, since it hath cost Thee so much to procure this peace, permit not that I lose the fruit of it, nor that all the wars and strifes in the world, be any impediment to me to follow Thy peace.   Amen.

3. I will consider the *reward of the peaceable*, is, to be by excellence *the "children of God;"*—i. First, because they are singularly *beloved* by Him, and will find grace in His presence, because of the *conformity* they have with Him.— ii. Secondly, because He takes them under His *fatherly providence*, beholding them as His dear children, cherishing,

<hr>

(71) Phil. iv. 7.   (72) Joan. xx. Luc. x. 5.
     (73) Psal. cxix. 7.   (74) Colos. i. 20.

ruling, and enriching them with His gifts, and giving them the spirit of true sons, by which they are not only "*called,*" but *are* " the sons of God." (75)—iii. Lastly, because they shall be *heirs of His glory,* where they shall obtain completely this dignity, and with the same, immense and eternal tranquillity.

Colloquy.—O how blessed are the peace-makers, who are elevated to such a dignity! but accursed are the disturbers of peace, because they shall be called sons of the Devil, with whom they have their portion in the inheritance of hell.

POINT X.

" BLESSED ARE THEY THAT SUFFER PERSECUTION FOR INJUSTICE, FOR THEIRS IS THE KINGDOM OF HEAVEN."

1. Consider first:—

i. *What persecutions* the just are to suffer—ii. from *whom*—iii. for *what cause*—iv. and *how.*

i. Persecutions are all *sorts of injuries* and *afflictions,* either in goods, honour, content, health, or life itself, from which, or at least from some of them, none can escape: because it is a general rule, as St. Paul says, that all those who desire to "live godly in Christ Jesus, shall suffer persecution" (76) for Him.—ii. These persecutions bring upon us, in consequence of the *devils,* the hatred which they bear against Almighty God, and against virtue, as also men, his agents and ministers, our open enemies, and those who, under the colour of piety, pretend to be our friends, and even our "parents and brethren, and kinsmen and friends," (77) says Christ our Lord, all these will persecute and deliver us up to death, supposing sometimes that they do good service to God.—

(75) 1 Joan. iii. 1.
(76) 2 Tim. iii. 12.   (77) Luc. xxi. 16.

iii. The *cause of these persecutions*, must not be *their own faults or offences*, as the apostle St. Peter says : (78) but "for *justice sake*," that is, for having kept and defended the *Catholic faith;* for performing the works of virtue, to which they are obliged; for reprehending vices and enormities, for fulfilling and complying with their duties; and for following a more perfect and religious state of life, to which they are called.—iv. The *manner* how they are to suffer, is, with great *patience* and with *inward joy*, reputing it for an especial favour of Almighty God, to suffer anything for the love of Him: for, to suffer for injustice, or with impatience, does not belong to this beatitude.

2. Consider the rare *examples* of our *Lord* in this point, who even from His birth was always *persecuted*, but most of all the three last years of His life, all sorts of persons conspiring to persecute Him, and in all sorts of things, with greater cruelty than ever was seen; and on His part for the most just cause that ever was, viz., for publishing His most holy law, reprehending vices and abuses, and for redeeming man: all which He suffered with most incredible and wonderful patience; (as will be seen in the funda-mental meditation of the fourth part, which wholly treats on this point.)   With this example I will encourage myself to endure and suffer, saying to myself:—"If they have persecuted my Lord, what wonder is it, if they persecute me who am His servant? 'If they have called the good man of the house Beelzebub,' what wonder is it if they call in the same manner 'them of His household?'." (79)

Colloquy.—O my Saviour, I am one of Thy family, and am ready to suffer all sorts of persecutions for

<hr>

(78) 1 Pet. ii. 20.   (79) Mat. x. 25.

Thy glory: grant, that, after Thy example, doing great things in Thy holy service, I may endure great evils without offending Thee. Amen.

3. I will consider the *recompense* of those that are "*persecuted*," is, the *self-same* "*Kingdom of heaven*," which is promised to the "poor of spirit," but with more advantage; forasmuch as it is harder to suffer persecutions which come from the hands of others, than the trials and miseries of poverty, which we undertake from our own choice. This Kingdom Almighty God gives them to taste of even in this life, imparting to them by the means of tribulations, great "justice, and peace, and joy" (80) in their sufferings. For which reason Christ our Lord promised that He would give us even in this life, a "hundredfold" more than the persecutions, and, after this life, "life everlasting;" (81) and therefore adds:—"Blessed are ye when they shall revile you and persecute you, and speak all that is evil against you untruly for my sake. Be glad and rejoice, for your reward is very great in heaven." (82) As if He should say: "The reward is so great, that the only hope of it, is sufficient to cause you to rejoice amidst your persecutions, and that in such a way, as surpasses a hundred times what you endure."

Colloquy.—O blessed persecutions, which elevate the persecuted to become a king in heaven, these shall be all my joy, in these will I place all my glory; let there come, O my God, all persecutions which it shall please Thee to permit, for I offer myself with the help of Thy grace gladly to embrace them "for justice sake," with hope that Thou wilt hereafter grant me to obtain Thy glory. Amen.

4. Lastly, consider, the *threatening of Christ* our Lord, against those who take a *contrary way*, saying :—" *Woe to*

(80) Rom. xiv. 17. (81) Mat. xix. 29. (82) Mat. v. 11.

you when men *shall bless you*," (83) that is, worldlings, feeding yourselves with their flatteries and vain applaudings. And in saying no more than "Woe," He gives us to understand, that the threatening is exceeding great, as if He said, "Woe be to you, who suffer yourselves to be deluded with these benedictions, which cause you to fall into most grievous errors, for being blessed by these wicked persons whom you imitate, you shall have your share in those maledictions which shall fall upon them."

Colloquy.—I will not, O my Redeemer, be blessed by worldlings, nor that the flattery of sinners, like "oil, fatten my head," (84) lest malediction like "oil" penetrate my "bones." I desire here to be accursed by the wicked, to be hereafter blessed by Thee together with the good, and to reign with Thee in the Kingdom of heaven, world without end. Amen.

MEDITATION XII.

ON THE OFFICE RECOMMENDED BY CHRIST OUR LORD TO HIS APOSTLES, IN THE SERMON ON THE MOUNT.

After the eight beatitudes, Christ our Lord charged His apostles and their successors, with those three acts and offices of the celestial and ecclesiastical hierarchy, which S. Denis calls,(1) to *purify, illuminate, and perfect;* using for this purpose, three delightful comparisons, of which this ensuing meditation shall be made, which every one ought to apply to himself for his own profit.

POINT I.

"You are the *salt of the earth*, but if the salt lose its savour, wherewith shall it be salted? It is good for

(83) Luc. vi. 26.   (84) Psal. cxl. 5, & cviii. 43.

(1) c. 3. de Cœlest. Hier.

nothing any more but to be cast out and to be trodden on by men."(2)

1. The *office of apostolical men*, who perfectly desire to follow Christ, is, by their word and doctrine, by their life and example, *to season the hearts of men*, purifying them from the vicious humours of their sins *lest they savour ill*, and be wholly putrefied and corrupted: as also, to render penance, mortification, and the exercises of virtue savory to them, by which they may with delight the better digest them: and that they in like manner make themselves savory to Almighty God, that so He may gladly incorporate them in Himself, and remain in peace and union with them. But this office they have not by nature, nor yet by inheritance, but by the salt of the wisdom and grace which God of His goodness has imparted to them: with which being purified in themselves, they may likewise help to purify others.

2. Next, consider *how well Christ our Lord performed this office* of *salt*, and how dear it cost Him: for, like salt, He consumed Himself in seasoning meat for us to eat, He also "emptied"(3) and *annihilated Himself* by humiliations and labours, to make us to be of a most pleasing taste to Almighty God; as also by His own example, to make virtue agreeable, and of good relish to us, and to merit for us the salt of wisdom and grace, which gives to it this excellent taste; for as no ancient sacrifice was agreeable to God, if first it were not seasoned "with salt;"(4) so none of our works are agreeable to Him, if they be not united with Christ, and salted and seasoned with His grace.

Colloquy.—O sweet Jesus, be Thou the salt of the earth of my heart, so greatly unsavoury, that it may be savoury and agreeable to Thy celestial Father.

(2) Mat. v. 13.

(3) Phil. ii. 7.   (4) Levit. ii. 13.   Marc. ix.

And since it is nauseous and disgustful to eat the meat which is not seasoned first with salt, season virtue in such a manner to me with the salt of Thy grace, that I may take the delight often to taste and feed upon it. Amen.

3. Although this office be *graciously* given by Almighty God, nevertheless its *preservation depends upon our own free-will.* Wherefore he that is salt, and who, preserving his integrity, merits to be set upon the table of our Lord with excellent honour, if afterwards through his pride he melt away, and lose his savour, will be cast forth from the protection of Almighty God upon the dunghill of the world, and shall be trod under the feet of men, and with great ignominy be trampled on in hell by the very devils. Pondering all this, I will consider and see if I have in myself this salt, and with what savour and taste I serve God, and whether I perform the office of salt towards such as are under my charge, with a will to make virtue become well savouring to the whole world.

Colloquy—O sweet Jesus, make me truly " salt of the earth," and although I should pass through fire and water, suffer not that, instead of giving taste to it, I ever come to scandalize it : and that like earth sowed with salt, it become not barren or unfertile through my fault, turning to its disadvantage, the office which Thou hast assigned me for its profit. Amen.

POINT II.

" You are the *light of the world,*" "men do not light a candle and put it under a bushel, but upon a candlestick, that it may shine to all that are in the house. So let your light shine before men, that they may see your good works, and glorify your Father who is in heaven."(5)

1. The *office of apostles* and doctors is not earthly, but

(5) Mat. v. 15.

heavenly, because as "stars"(6) of heaven and of the firmament of the Church, *they ought to shine and give light,* endeavouring through their doctrine and exemplary life, to be the light of worldly men, driving from them the darkness of ignorance and of sin, and communicating to them the light and splendour of truth and virtue; by which they may convert them from children of "darkness," into the "children of light,"(7) and live according thereunto. Here I will consider, how laudably Christ Jesus our Lord performed this office of "light," who said of Himself: "As long as I am in the world, I am the light of the world."(8)

Colloquy.—O sun of justice, from whom the stars of the Church receive their light, make me like to one of them, free from all obscurity, that so persevering in the place in which Thou hast set me, I may readily obey Thy call, (9) and give my light with joy to the world, which Thou hast created for Thy glory. Amen.

2. *How great an error it is,* through cowardice and pusillanimity, to *hide the light* and talent of knowledge, which God our Lord has given to me, or to obscure it for worldly ends, putting myself thus in danger of losing it, and of being left in darkness; as the light of a candle is extinguished when "put under a bushel," or otherwise hid so that it has no air. Nor is it a less error, if God our Lord has placed me upon some candlestick of His militant Church, that is to say, in any state or public office, not to give the light of doctrine and of good example to those that are under my charge and conduct; because, as Christ our Lord says to a careless prelate, He "will move" my

<hr>

(6) Dan. xii. 3.   (7) Eph. v. 8.
(8) Joan. ix. 5.   (9) Baruch iii. 33.

"candlestick out of its place,"(10) depriving me of my office, and chastise the negligence which He finds in me.

3. On the other hand, *how great a desire* Christ our Lord has, that our works should be so holy, so *resplendent and shining*, as to induce those that see them to glorify His Father who is in heaven, and daily to do like them, by which He may be glorified in the same manner, purifying our intention from all sinister ends contrary to this: so that I seek not in doing them my own glory, but the glory of God, holding that for my glory which redounds to His: lamenting that by my evil works I have been the cause that the glory of God has been obscured by me, and blasphemed by others.

Colloquy.—O my Saviour, since Thou so much desirest the glory of Thy Father, grant to me hereafter such holiness of life, as may everywhere increase and dilate His glory.   Amen.

POINT III.

"A CITY SEATED ON A MOUNTAIN CANNOT BE HID."

By this third comparison, Christ our Lord declared to His apostles, that their office was not to be religious hermits, or such as should lead a solitary life, attending only to their own salvation, but *to be as "a city,"* into which many others should be gathered and assembled: nor yet a city seated in a valley, that is, in an imperfect and ordinary life, but *" seated upon a mountain,"* that is to say, in great fortitude and height of perfection, according to that which the prophet Isaiah says:—" Get thee up upon a high mountain, thou that bringest good tidings to Sion, lift up thy voice with strength, thou that bringest good tidings to Jerusalem;"(11) and consequently admonishes them that their office is to gather together, not a few,

---

(10) Apoc. ii 5.   (11) Isa. xl. 9.

but many people, like a populous city, receiving all such
as desire to be perfect, and instructing them in the way of
evangelical perfection, and the science of spiritual life.
For God our Lord desires, that His elect do not content
themselves with mediocrity, nor apply themselves to low
and inferior works, but that they climb up to the height
of a perfect life, and help their neighbours likewise to do
the same, to the end that they, with many others, may
assist to people that sovereign city of His glory.

Colloquy.—O Eternal Wisdom, who commandest
Thy servants, who are the souls of Thy preachers, to
"invite" the people "to the tower and the walls of
the city," (12) by exhorting them to the height of
Christian perfection; call me effectually, that I may
first ascend the same, and help me also to call others,
who may mount and ascend by means of me, to the
end that Thou mayest be glorified by all.   Amen.

MEDITATION XIII.

ON THE EVANGELICAL LAW, PUBLISHED BY CHRIST OUR LORD, IN THIS SER-
MON ON THE MOUNT ; ON ITS EXCELLENCIES; AND ON THE PERFECTION TO WHICH
IT ELEVATES US.

POINT I.

Our Lord Jesus Christ, in order to publish *His Evangelical law*, first declared how much the law of nature,
expressed in the Books of Moses and the Prophets, was
to be esteemed, and the *office* He was to perform in the
world concerning it, saying: "I am not come to destroy
the law, but to fulfil it:"(1) which He did most excellently in three ways.

1. First, He *came not* from heaven to *transgress the law*,
living at His own ease in carnal liberty, or as one that was

(12) Prov. ix. 3.   (1) Mat. v. 17.

obliged to no manner of law;—neither came He to dispense with Himself, nor with His followers;(2) but on the contrary, He came to *fulfil* and *keep it most exactly*, and to give example of it to all His disciples, so that I ought to say, in imitation of Him:—" I came not into the world to live after my own will, treading under my feet the will of God, and casting off the yoke of His holy law, but to submit myself to it, and to accomplish it entirely; neither entered I into Religion to fulfil my own will, but the will of Almighty God, declared in the rules of my institute. Because, if my Lord and supreme lawgiver, being superior to the law, submitted Himself to it, and came from heaven to shew the estimation which He made of it in taking and supporting his own yoke, what great matter do I in submitting myself to it, and what a shame would it be to me to cast it off."

2. Secondly, He came from heaven to *fulfil the law*, concerning the promises which it contained, and that with *such rigour*, that Himself said:—" Till heaven and earth pass, one jot or one tittle shall not pass of the law, till all be fulfilled." (3) So that I may remain certain and most secure, that Almighty God will accomplish all whatsoever He has promised in His law, how little soever, as Christ our Lord accomplished and performed by works, whatsoever was revealed and promised of Him. By this He leads me likewise to keep and accomplish all His commandments: not only the greater, but also the lesser, signified by that jot or tittle, which is the least of all others, taking care likewise to accomplish them with all their circumstances and modes of perfection which they contain, signified by the " tittle," or little point, which is put in the top of the said letter.

(2) S. Aug. lib. 1, ser. Dom. in monte. c. xiv. S. Chrys. hom. xvi.
in Mat.
(3) Mat. v. 18.

3. Thirdly, He came from heaven to fulfil the law by *adding to it the perfection it wanted*, explicating its *precepts more clearly*, giving admirable counsels, and communicating interiorly His grace to accomplish the whole.

Colloquy.—O sovereign Lawgiver, I most humbly thank Thee, as far as I am able, for the various means by which Thou hast fulfilled Thine own law, aid me with Thy grace to fulfil it as Thou commandest me, to the end that Thou mayest perform in me that which Thou hast promised me.   Amen.

POINT II.

Consider two memorable sentences or *conclusions* which Christ our Lord *inferred* from what He had said.

1. The first was:—" He, therefore, that shall *break one* of these least commandments, and shall so teach men, shall be called the *least in the Kingdom of heaven;*" (4) that is, in the triumphant and militant Church.

i. In which words He teaches us, first, that he who *departs from one* of the least commandments, although he keep and *observe the other*, (5) shall be little accounted of " in the Kingdom of heaven," and consequently excluded from it, as one unworthy of such a kingdom, even as Adam was excluded from paradise for having broken one only precept, for he that breaks one, injures, as the apostle says, the Lawgiver who has made them all, and destroys the charity in which they are all united in one, and so shall lose the Kingdom of heaven, as if he had broken and transgressed all.

ii. Secondly, that although the *commandment were of little things*, and such as obliged not to mortal sin, whosoever *willingly* or maliciously shall transgress them, shall be little in virtue, for having made so little account of that which Almighty God commands; for he ought to consider,

<hr>

(4) Mat. v. 19.   (5) Jac. ii. 10.

that, although the thing commanded be but little, yet that He who commands it is very great, who holds it not for any disparagement to His greatness, to command things that are little in appearance; on which account it is no little injury to despise them; and since the vanquisher is greater than the vanquished, he that is overcome in a little thing shall be little; and that which the Wise man says, shall be accomplished in him:—"He that contemneth small things shall fall by little and little, and offend in great." (6)

iii. Thirdly, if not content to have transgressed some commandment, he *persuades others to do the like*, either by word or example, scandalizing them, and provoking them to sin, such an one shall be the "least in the Kingdom of heaven," and shall be shut out of the same for two reasons, namely, for having been wicked to himself, and wicked to others.

2. The second sentence is:—"But he *that shall do and teach*, he shall be called *great in the Kingdom of heaven.*"(7)

In which words He teaches us, that the *measure of sanctity*, of greatness in virtue, and of its recompense in the Kingdom of heaven, is the *keeping* and *observance* of the divine law, which consists in two degrees. One is to do, the other to teach. To do, is to fulfil all the commandments of the law, be they great or little, without omitting any, as has been said.—To teach, is to counsel others to keep the same law which he keeps. And this second degree is much more excellent than the first: nevertheless our Lord Jesus Christ has joined them together, to signify to us that they have a true connection, forasmuch as the second makes him not great who teaches it, unless he do and perform it:—whereas the first, inasmuch as it teaches likewise by example, is also ready to teach by word, when God shall so command him, according to his state and office, or by

<hr>

(6) Ecclus. xix. 1.   (7) Mat. v. 19.

the law and rule of charity. And he that teaches after this manner is very great among the great ones in heaven, because there is no greater greatness than after the imitation of Almighty God, to be both good and perfect in one's self, and to help and procure that others also be good and perfect, (as we shall see in the ensuing point.)

POINT III.

Consider the *greatness* of that *perfection* to which Christ our Lord *exhorted His disciples,* which is the greatest that can be attained in this life, as He declared in these royal words, saying, " Be you perfect, therefore, as also your heavenly Father is perfect."(8)

1. To penetrate the sublimity of this sentence, I am to ponder, how the 'perfection of God our Lord consists principally in three things:—i. The first, in being *without any sort of sin* or imperfection whatsoever, so that it is impossible for him to do anything evil or defective, against His bounty and His sanctity.—ii. The second, in *embracing all the virtues and perfections* that can be imagined, without a single exception : because, all those that are in creatures, with innumerable others which we attain not, are all united in the Creator.—iii. The third, in possessing *every one of these perfections, with the greatest excellence that is possible :* so that there cannot be imagined greater wisdom, bounty, and charity, than that which is in Almighty God, for He is infinite, wise, good, and charitable, and is the same in other perfections.

2. Hence it is that Almighty God being so perfect in Himself, has an *exceeding desire* that all His *works be perfect,* and participate in such degree and manner as they may, of His infinite perfection, especially men, whom He hath created after His image and likeness, and this desire

(8) Mat. v. 48.

is the cause that Christ says to us: "Be you, therefore, perfect, as your heavenly Father is perfect;" that is to say, "Content not yourselves with a mean purity and sanctity, nor take only for a pattern of your perfection, Abraham, or Moses,(9) or some one of the prophets, nor only the angels, Cherubim or Seraphim; but take you an infinite pattern of infinite perfection, by which, after His example, you may procure the greatest perfection which is possible for you, and let this pattern be your heavenly Father, to the end that, like true and legitimate sons, you may aspire to be very like Him, in these three things which His infinite perfection comprehends.

Colloquy.—I give Thee thanks, O Son of the living God, for the favour which Thou dost to Thine adopted sons, exhorting them to become perfect, as Thy heavenly Father is. Illuminate me, O sovereign master, to know the perfection which Thou commendest to me, inflame me that I may love it, and fortify me so to seek it, that I may find it. Amen.

3. Hence I am to draw some *fervent purposes* to *imitate* the perfection of Almighty God.—i. To *withdraw* myself from all *sort of sin*, not only from *mortal*, but even from *venial*, as much as I can, conformably to that which God said to His people:—"Be ye perfect and without spot"(10) before me.—ii. To *endeavour* to *obtain all sorts of virtues*, and to exercise their acts with the most ample extension that I can, not only those of precept or commandment, but also those of counsel, seeing my heavenly Father does not only give me things necessary for my life, but many others for my pleasure.—iii. To endeavour to *exercise virtues* in the most *excellent manner* that is possible for me; in such a way, that my love of Almighty God be after the manner that is prescribed in the commandment, loving

<hr>

(9) Deut. xviii.

(10) Deut. xviii. 13.

Him "with all my heart, with all my soul, and with all my strength:" and that my obedience, humility, and patience, be in the highest degrees that these virtues may attain to, endeavouring, as St. Paul says, that my "charity may more and more abound, approving always the better things:"(11) and since the augmentation of charity is not limited,, my desire shall be, to increase it without limit. (12.)

Colloquy.—O my soul, since this pattern is so boundless, and what imitation soever thou makest, that which remains to be imitated is still infinite, imitate as much as thou canst, to approach the nearer to this infinite perfection. O most loving Father, since Thou wilt have me to be "perfect" as Thou art perfect, "give me what Thou commandest," that I may accomplish what Thou desirest. Amen.

POINT IV.

1. Consider the *sovereign perfection* of the *Evangelical law;* which Christ our Lord promulgated, that we might be perfect, as His heavenly Father is, pondering how it comprises *three particular things,* in which it resembles the perfection of God Himself.

i. The first is, to *prohibit all sort and manner of sins, great or little,* even to a vain or "idle word," without consenting to any thought whatsoever that is defective."(13) And, to divert us the more from all sin, it charges us to avoid the *very least things,* together with all sorts of disordered affections which may any way be an occasion of them; even as Almighty God forbid the Nazarites of old to drink "wine," or to "eat grapes,"(14) or so much as any of their little grains, that they might be the further removed from drunkenness.

(11) Phil. i 9.   12) S. Tho. ii. 2. q. xxiv. a. 7.

(13) S. Tho. i. 2. q. cviii. a. 3, & 4.   (14) Num. vi. 3.

And this I may reflect upon when discoursing on some of the commandments which we call *negative*,—in which something is prohibited or forbidden. (a) In the second commandment, to the end we should be very far from swearing falsely, Christ our Lord forbids us to " swear not at all,"—not so much as by one hair of our head, and that our common speech be, " yea, yea, no no,"(15) because whatsoever is more is evil, dangerous, or at the least imperfect, unless in case of urgent necessity. (b) In the fifth commandment, to divert us from *manslaughter*, he forbids us not to *injure* any one, either by words or by *sign*, nor yet to conceal any anger within our hearts: and that, if any one wrong or injure us, we suffer it with great patience, offering the " left cheek" to him that has struck us on the right. (c) In the sixth commandment, for fear of falling into impurity, He commands that if either our eye, or our right hand scandalize us, we " *cut it off*," that is to say, that we withdraw from any manner of person or thing, which may be to us an *occasion of sin*, how dear and *precious soever* we hold them, and how necessary soever they may be to us. (d) In the seventh, the more to induce us not to steal from any one, He wishes us to give away even that *which is ours*, and to him that would " take away" our " coat," that " we let go our cloak also to him."

Colloquy.—O sovereign purity of the Evangelical law, law most worthy of God most pure! truly, O Lord, Thy commandments are chaste and pure, like the silver that comes from the mint, "tried by the fire—refined seven times." (16) O that I might observe them perfectly, to remain pure and immaculate from all deadly sins, and exempt and free from all imperfections!

<hr>

(15) Mat. v. 34. Jac. v. 12.   (16) Ps. xi. 7.

ii. The second excellence of the Evangelical law is, that it goes on to *command or counsel all sorts of virtues*, as well theological as moral, (17) in reference to God, to ourselves, and our neighbour: so that he that shall keep them, shall be owner of all those virtues which will perfect him with his Creator, as also of those which suppress the passions of the flesh to subject them to the spirit, and which accomplish all the works of justice and mercy towards our neighbour.

iii. To this he adds the third excellence, which teaches every one of these virtues, in the *highest degree of perfection possible for this life*, in such a manner that we cannot attain more profound humility, nor more heroic patience, nor more admirable obedience, nor more perfect charity, than that which this our sacred law inculcates. For what intention can there be more pure, than so to hide our works, " that the left hand knoweth" not what the "right hand doth" to please Almighty God? What greater love of God can there possibly be, than "to love" Him with our " whole heart and with our whole soul, and with our whole mind?" And what love of our neighbour can there be more excellent, than that which extends itself to our very enemies, praying for them, saluting them, and doing them good, after the imitation of our heavenly Father, " who maketh His sun to rise upon the good and the bad, and raineth upon the just and the unjust?"(18) Hence Christ our Lord concluded the sentence beforementioned, " Be you perfect, as your Father in heaven is perfect."

Colloquy.—O heavenly Father, who hast manifested Thy most perfect charity in ordaining that the Sun of justice, Thy B. Son, should be incarnate and born for the good of all, and that the dew of His divine doc-

(17) S. Tho. i. 2. q. c. a. 2.   (18) Mat. v. 45.

trine should communicate itself universally, giving by this means even to Thine enemies, the chiefest medicine that Thou couldst give them for their remedy; grant that I may imitate Thy infinite charity, with all Thy other virtues, even as Thou commandest in Thy holy law, by which I may obtain the perfection of them all.   Amen.

2. Hence I may gather that my *principal end* in a Christian life, or in Religion, ought to be to *accomplish the law of the Gospel*, in the three points or circumstances aforesaid, with the greatest perfection that I can, remembering what St. Paul says, that "the end of the commandment is charity," (19) joined with those three conditions, a "pure heart," and clean from all sin; a "good conscience," adorned with the works of all sorts of virtues; and an "unfeigned faith," persevering faithfully in aiming even at the highest of them, and studying, as the same Apostle says, to "prove what is the good and the acceptable, and the perfect will of God," (20) and in this manner I shall become perfect, because, as St. John says:—"He that keepeth His word, in Him in very deed the charity of God is perfected," (21) and consequently all Christian perfection, which consists in the perfection of charity.

MEDITATION XIV.

In this sermon delivered on the mountain, Jesus Christ taught His disciples that divine prayer, which we call the Lord's Prayer, which of right holds the first place above all other prayers, because the supreme Master of prayer

(19) 1 Tim. i. 5.   (20) Rom. xii. 2.
(21) 1 Joan. ii. 5.   Phil. iii.

composed it to teach us how to pray, (1) and therefore
we will meditate upon it word by word, practising in it
the manner of praying by words, of which we have spoken
in the ninth section of the introduction to this book.

1. Having then placed myself in the *presence of Almighty
God*, Three in One, to whom this prayer is to be directed,
although I may indifferently address the same to every one
of the three divine Persons, yet will I beseech Jesus
Christ our Lord to enlighten my soul with His celestial
light, and inflame it with the fire of His divine love, that
it may feel and understand those truths and excellencies of
spirit, which are included in this compendious prayer, and
to ask Him with confidence all that He desires should be
asked of Him, and that with purity and intention, and
with fervent devotion, like that which Himself had when
He pronounced it, speaking to His Father; for it is very
credible that He so taught it to His apostles, that together
with them He prayed to Almighty God, and daily ceases
not to say it with us, because, as St. Augustine says,
Christ our Lord prays for us as our priest, and prays in us
as our head, inspiring into us the spirit and virtue of
prayer, and so " We say this prayer together with Him,
and He likewise says the same together with us;" (2)
for our prayer ought to be united with the merits of His,
to be heard graciously and granted speedily.

2. Nevertheless we are to remark, that Christ our Lord
taught this prayer two *several times*, once on the mountain *publicly to all;* another time after He had *ended His
prayer*, one of His disciples saying to Him:—"Master,
teach us to pray, as John also taught his disciples." (3)
By this we are taught, that this divine prayer ought to be
both *public* and *private;* when it is repeated in public, as

(1) S. Tho, ii. 2. q. lxxxiii. a. 9.　Mat. vi. 9.　Luc. xi. 2.
(2) Prefat. in Ps. lxxxv.　　　(3) Luc. xi. 1.

in the sacrifice of the Mass, it ought to be pronounced with that brevity which the place requires; but when it is repeated in private, and is taken for the ground and foundation of mental prayer, one may spend many hours in it, saying to Christ our Lord:—" Master, teach us to pray;" not only as John taught his disciples, but as Thou Thyself taught Thine, imprinting on my heart the truths, feelings, and affections, which Thou imprintedst in theirs. This done, I will repeat one word of it only, searching with my understanding, and pondering by profound meditation what it means, accompanying it with affections, petitions, and colloquies, conformably to the subject which I mean to meditate upon, or which the Holy Ghost shall inspire me with.

" OUR."

Upon this word I am to investigate the reason why our Lord would not have us say *my* Father, but *our*.

1. That we might know His *infinite charity and liberality*, which shines in this, that whereas He could have no more than *one natural* Son, He would have *many adopted* sons, communicating this excellent dignity to men and to angels, giving the same to every one of them, without any prejudice to the other; for in such manner is He the Father of all, that He is as much mine, as if He were Father of none but me.

Colloquy.—Blessed be so immense a charity, which embraces such an immense number of sons, and yet is so careful of all, as if there were no more than one.

2. To teach us that, as He is the Father of many sons, so we likewise are all *brethren*, and with this we ought to excite in ourselves the *love of our neighbour*, praying for all, and desiring that all may become the adopted sons of this Sovereign Father, without despising any, since the

rich and the poor, the gentleman and the yeoman, the wise and the ignorant, are equally sons of one and the same heavenly Father, calling to mind the words of the prophet Malachi:—" Have we not all one Father?"......
" why then doth every one despise his brother?" (4)

Colloquy.—O " our Father," let it suffice me to know that Thou art the Father of men, that I may love them as my brethren. I will therefore embrace them all by love, since Thou embracest them all by Thine infinite charity

3. To move us to *reverence*, because the word " my" is too familiar and indulgent for us, and more proper for the Only-begotten Son of this divine Father, with whom therefore I ought to treat jointly with love and reverence together, notwithstanding, that alone by myself, and in my private closet, I may make bold to call Him mine, since He is so mine as if He had no more adopted sons but me only.

" FATHER."

Here will I ponder for what respects God our Lord is likewise *our Father.*

1. He is the Father *of all men*, for He has given them their natural being, *creating* them to His own *image* and likeness. Next, He is the Father of *the just*, because He gives thee the being of grace, *adopting them* for *sons* and heirs of the inheritance of heaven, to whom He is a thousand times a Father, for every time they lose this being, which He gave them in baptism, He is most ready to restore it to them by the sacrament of Penance. And in this He exceedingly desires to be the Father of all, not for His own profit, but for ours; not for our merits, but of His pure mercy and grace. And although He offers

(4) Mal. ii. 10.

Himself to be our Father gratis, yet it cost Him not a little so to be, for he has begotten us upon the cross with most excruciating pains, the Only-begotten Son dying to make us His adoptive children, that so all might have but one Father. From all these considerations I will draw very great and profound affections, to praise and glorify Almighty God, for every one of those respects under which He is found to be my Father.

Colloquy.—O most loving Father, I give Thee thanks that Thou bestowest upon Thy sons the most noble being of Thy grace, without refusing to reestablish them, as often as they come to lose it by their sin. O happy angels, who have Almighty God for Father in heaven, praise Him and glorify Him, because He hath likewise vouchsafed to be the Father of us men who live on earth. Amen.

2. How *well does Almighty God perform the office of a Father*, loving us with tenderness, beholding us with carefulness, protecting us with providence, sustaining us with abundance, and setting us in a state most conducive to our salvation, in such manner that all the fathers in the world together deserve not this name in comparison with Him, and for this reason Christ our Lord commands us, saying :—" Call none your father upon earth, for one is your Father who is in heaven." (5)

Colloquy.—O sovereign Father, what thanks shall I give Thee for that Thou vouchsafest in my behalf, to do the office and function of a Father! I will no more call those fathers that are upon earth, which oftentimes "forsake "(6) me, but only Thee, O heavenly Father, who wilt never forsake me, if I forsake not Thee. O Father, be Thou a Father to me, and shew Thyself a Father in my behalf, fulfilling the name

(5) Mat. xxiii. 9.   (6) Ps. xxvi. 10.

which Thou hast taken upon Thee for the love of me. Amen.

3. For the same reason for which Almighty God will be my Father He give to me the *dignity of a son*, and requires that I reciprocally perform towards Him the *duty of a son* towards his Father, loving, reverencing, obeying, and being zealous of His honour and glory.

Colloquy.—O most heavenly Father, whence comes to me so great a good, that being such a despicable creature, I should be named and called Thy son? (7) What charity hath moved Thee to take for Thy son, so wretched a slave? Since, therefore, Thou performest towards me the office of a father, assist me to discharge towards Thee the office and duties of a son. O silly worm, degenerate not from the dignity of the son of God by doing anything unbeseeming the son of such a Father. Endeavour to be like Him in thy life, since it is meet and proper that sons resemble their own fathers. Amen.

4. I will reflect on the causes why our Lord in this prayer would that we should call Him "Father."—i. To awaken in us the affections of *love* and of *confidence*, for by praying with them, He will grant us what we shall ask.— ii. That we might begin with the *praise of that thing* which *we prize* so much, and of which we boast, glorifying Him because He vouchsafes to be "our Father," which serves us for a title and pretext, that He may grant us what we crave at His hands.—iii. To give us to understand that He will be *served* by us with the *spirit of a son*, and that all whatsoever we shall demand of Him, ought to be only that which a good son may ask and demand of so good a Father.

Colloquy.—O sovereign Father, I am sure that

Thou wilt grant me what I shall ask Thee as Thy son, since Thou commandest me to ask of Thee as of my Father. Amen.

"WHO ART IN HEAVEN."

1. Here is to be considered, how Almighty God, who is in *every* place, only said:—" *Who art in heaven.*"—i. To move me to *reverence*, considering the dignity of this sovereign Father, who is Lord of the heavens, and reigns in them.—ii. To *raise up my heart* from earthly to heavenly things, despising all whatsoever is here below, and sighing after that inheritance of heaven where our Father is.(8)—iii. To the end that I may live in this mortal life like a *stranger* and *pilgrim*, but looking forward to heaven, seeking after celestial purity, without which I cannot enter into it.—iv. That especially in *time of prayer*, I may raise my spirit up to heaven, whence the succour, and other good things which I seek, are to descend.

Colloquy.—O Father, who dwellest and inhabitest above in heaven, draw me up thither where Thou art, and whilst Thou dost not yet draw me thither, assist me here with Thy holy grace, so that my conversation may be above "in heaven," (9) quite forgetting that which I have beneath on earth. O my soul, thou art a pilgrim here on earth, since both thy Father and thy inheritance are above in heaven : sigh, therefore, to go to this habitation, where thou mayest enjoy thy part and thy portion. Amen.

2. The *just* are likewise *called* "*heaven*," whom Almighty God *inhabits* by *His grace*, and of those it is that mention is here made; to give us to understand, that God is principally the Father of the just, who are His heaven : in order, also, that he that prays may wholly rid

(8) Ps. cxx.   (9) Phil. iii. 20.

and cleanse himself of all sin and earthliness, and make himself a heaven which Almighty God may inhabit; (10) and that he may recollect and enter within himself, where Almighty God is, there pouring *forth his* prayer before his Father, who is, and resides in the secret of his heart, and sees into the hidden and interior retreat whence he prays.

Colloquy.—O that the same were a very heaven, adorned and shining with all sorts of virtues, in which Almighty God would delight to dwell! I confess, O my Lord, that I am a man of the earth, even wholly earthly, as being a son of that earthly Adam: nevertheless with Thy holy grace, I desire to convert myself into a heaven, and a heavenly man, as a son of the heavenly Adam. Come, Lord, to this Thy servant, who by Thy coming will become a heaven. Amen.

Note.—(The three words just recited, are the *preamble* of this prayer: the words that follow, contain the seven *petitions* of this prayer.)

"HALLOWED BE THY NAME."

First Petition.—In this first petition we beg, that Almighty God may be *acknowledged, praised, and glorified* by all, and that His name may be worshipped, adored, and held for holy. But weighing every word by itself, I will consider:—

1. Why He rather said, "*hallowed* be Thy name," than, *praised* or *glorified* be Thy name. The reason is, because Almighty God esteems no other thing so much as to be holy, and consequently, we cannot give Him any greater glory, than to hold Him for holy: and in imitation of the Seraphim, and of the four holy beasts of the Apocalypse, to cry out with great affection: "Holy! holy! holy!

(10) Aug. ser. Dom. in monte, c. ix. Ambr. lib. v. de Sac. cap. 4.

the Lord God of hosts," "who was, and who is, and who is to come." (11)

Colloquy.—O most holy Father, I rejoice in that sanctity which Thou possessest, desiring that Thy children may resemble Thee therein. I will be regulated, O holy Father, by no other sanctity but by this, to the end I may accomplish what Thou commandest, and so become holy as Thou art holy. (12) Amen.

2. I will consider why He rather said, "Hallowed be Thy *name*," than "hallowed be Thy *majesty*," or "Thy Almighty *power*." The reason is, because it is most just, that all whatsoever we know of God, and bears His name amongst us, should be reverenced, glorified, and held for holy.

Colloquy—O celestial Father, greatly do I desire that Thy name be sanctified, and that all men acknowledge Thy singular sanctity, call Thee—omnipotent,—wise,—Creator,—governor,—Lord,—and "everlasting Father,"—that so Thy omnipotence and wisdom may be hallowed, and held and esteemed by all for holy. O holy Creator, holy governor, and holy Father, all Thy names are holy, and it is but right that all should bow their knees, to adore and worship the name of Thy Deity, hearing it named, because it is most worthy to be named and heard with especial veneration for its sanctity. Amen.

3. I will meditate upon this word "thy," as who should say :—"I desire that *Thy* name be sanctified, and not *mine*, because Thou only art holy by essence, nor is there any other who deserves the divine honour of sanctity except Thyself, of whom, and by whom, the just participate in a beam of it, for, 'Not to us, O Lord, not to us, but to Thy name give glory.' Let not our name be

(11) Is. vi. 3. Apoc. iv. 8.   (12) Levit. xi. 46.

glorified, but Thy most sweet and blessed name, because to Thee, 'King of ages,' immortal, invisible, is due all 'honour and glory,' (13) and to us all shame, dishonour, and confusion."

Colloquy—I am confounded, O my God and my Saviour, at the pride which impels me to desire that my name be spread and published throughout the world, known and esteemed by every one, deserving as I do to be despised, and utterly forgotten. O that I employed myself in searching the glory of Thy name, entirely forgetting myself for the love of Thee. Amen.

4. Christ our Lord added not,—"Hallowed be Thy name," *by us*. The reason is, that our petitions and desires should be universal, without bounds or limits, desiring that the most holy name of Almighty God might be sanctified both by men and angels; and not only by men on earth, but also by the souls that are in heaven, and by those that are in purgatory; again, not only by men present, but also by those that are yet unborn, and that all the creatures in this visible world, in such manner that they may praise and glorify this holy name, since it is most worthy to be glorified by all, and that "every knee of those that are in heaven, on earth, and under the earth," should " bow"(14) and prostrate themselves at the sovereign name of Almighty God, and of His Only-begotten Son, our Saviour Jesus.

5. *I ought to sanctify this name* myself, and how those also ought to sanctify it, for whom I pray that they may sanctify it, for His chief glory consists in this, that all believe what He reveals, hope what He promises, obey what He commands, reverence and serve Him as He ordains, and finally love Him with all their hearts as He deserves, so that their lives and their works be such, that such as see

(13) 1 Tim. i. 17.(14) Phil. ii.

them, may "glorify" in them our "Father who is in heaven." (15)

Colloquy—O most glorious Father, by the merits of Thy Only-begotten Son, I beseech Thee to infuse the light of faith into all infidels, grace and charity into all the faithful, and fervent love into all the just; to the end that all may sanctify Thy holy name upon earth, even as the Blessed sanctify it in heaven. Woe is me, that through my wicked works, Thy name has been blasphemed "amongst the Gentiles;"(16) help me, O my God, that for the time to come, all my actions may be such, that by means of them Thy name may be glorified, world without end. Amen.

"THY KINGDOM COME."

Second Petition.—1. Here we are to consider *what kingdom* this is which we desire and pray to come.

i. We pray for that Kingdom by which Almighty God in this life *reigns in the just by His holy grace.* This Kingdom comprehends the doctrine of faith which we are to believe,—the laws of government we are to keep,—the sacraments we are to receive,—the sacrifices we are to offer,—and all the virtues with which we are to serve our heavenly King, so disposing us that He may enter into our souls and reign in them everlastingly : and lastly, that Kingdom which S. Paul calls "justice, peace, and joy in the Holy Ghost." (17)

Colloquy.—O King of heaven, let this "Thy Kingdom come to us,—yea, let it come daily with more and more perfection, because it is most meet, that as our lawful King Thou reign over and rule us, and that we all remain subject to Thy sovereign government.

ii. We pray for the *Kingdom of glory* in which Almighty God reigns most peaceably with His elect. He says not:

(15) Mat. v. 16.   (16) Rom. ii. 24.   (17) Rom. xiv. 17.

—"Lift us *up to* Thy Kingdom,"—but "let Thy King-dom come" *down to us*, because, if the Kingdom of God come down to us, it is certain that it will lift us up to the Kingdom of glory; and therefore we ought more to desire the first, than the second, because all desire to reign with Christ in heaven, for this is very delightful to all, but all do not desire Christ to reign in them in earth, because this is somewhat painful.

Colloquy.—O my King, I beseech Thee, that Thy Kingdom may come to me, that Thou mayest reign in me, and in all others by Thy grace. I also pray Thee, that this " holy city, the new Jerusalem," (18) come down from heaven, and discover itself to us, and be manifested to us by a lively faith, that the sight of it may inflame us with its love, and may lift us up to be inhabitants of it. O that I saw myself for ever em-barked in this blessed Kingdom! O that it would come and enter within me, since that ought to be within me which is to make me for ever blessed.

iii. We ask that the *last and consummated Kingdom* of Almighty God may come into us, which will be the day of judgment, at which time the kingdom of the Devil will be destroyed wholly, and come to an end, and Almighty God will reign in the just, glorifying both their souls and bodies, and the Kingdom of glory will be accomplished in all.

Colloquy.—O when will this Kingdom come, so that all sin may cease, and the desire of those holy souls be satisfied, who are hoping to enjoy it together with their bodies!

2. I will meditate on this word " *Thy* ;" let, O Lord, " Thy Kingdom come," so that every kingdom which is not Thine may be destroyed. Suffer not the kingdom of

(18) Apoc. xxi.

" sin," (19) nor of the Devil, to reign in me, but on the contrary, I beseech Thee to destroy this kingdom. I pray not, Lord, that the kingdom of this world come into me, which is founded upon riches, honours, and satisfactions, but Thy Kingdom, which is founded on true virtues.

Colloquy.—O most sweet Saviour, who saidst "My Kingdom is not of this world," (20) I will Thy Kingdom, I desire Thy Kingdom, and ask no other kingdom than Thine. Come, O Blessed Trinity, and enter into us, dwell and reign in those who live upon earth, as Thou reignest in the Saints who live in heaven, that we may everlastingly serve Thee, as they serve Thee Amen.

" THY WILL BE DONE ON EARTH AS IT IS IN HEAVEN."

Third Petition.—1. Consider *what " will " it is* which here we pray to be accomplished; it is the will of Almighty God, declared to us by the commandments of the law, by the counsels of the Gospel, by the secret inspirations of the Holy Ghost, by the ordinances of the holy Catholic Church and its ministers, and of all such superiors as sit in the place of Almighty God.

Colloquy.—O that we might truly accomplish this will of God, since it is in the power of our Creator, to cause all His creatures to accomplish it. Let it be life to me, O my Lord, to fulfil Thy will, and death to me to infringe it. Grant that I may fulfil it always, so that I may live, and never violate it though I were to die. Amen.

2. I will meditate on this word " *Thy*," saying to our Lord—" I will not, O my Lord, fulfil my own will, which is perverse; nor the will of my flesh, which is rebellious against the spirit ; nor the will of the Devil, which is most wicked; nor the will of the world, which is most

(19) Rom. v. 17.   (20) Joan. xviii. 36.

vain; but Thy blessed will alone be fulfilled, because it alone is good, just, and the measure and rule of all good wills.

Colloquy.—O most sweet Jesus, who descendest from heaven, to do, "not" Thine "own will," (21) but the will of Thy Father; assist me with Thy grace, that in all things I may renounce and mortify my own will, to subject it to the divine will.　Amen.

3. Ponder the *manner of accomplishing this divine will,* which is declared in these words following: " On earth as it is in heaven;"—that is to say, in the manner that the angels and blessed spirits accomplish it in the Kingdom of heaven.—i. *Entirely,* without failing in any point of how little importance soever it be.—ii. *With purity of intention,* only to please Almighty God, and not any other.—iii. With *promptitude, dexterity, and great punctuality,* without any manner of delay or repugnance.—iv. With *fortitude* and perseverance to the end.—v. By, and with, most *fervent, continual, intense, and delightful love,* rejoicing to accomplish what Almighty God commands.

Colloquy.—O most loving Father, it was most meet first to demand that Thy Kingdom may come, and that Thy heaven may enter within us, since Thy will is, that while we are yet on earth, we should live like those who are in heaven.　O that I could accomplish Thy will with all perfection, as it is to be accomplished! For I will not be sparing in wishing that, which with such goodness Thou wishest me to ask Thee.

4. Here we likewise demand that the will of Almighty God be accomplished by *terrestrial men,* as it is by *celestial,* and above all, as the celestial Adam, our Lord Jesus Christ, accomplished it, who came down from heaven to accomplish and do this divine will, with most excellent perfection.

(21) Joan. vi. 38.

Colloquy.—O heavenly Father, it is but reasonable that the sons begotten by Thy gracious will, should accomplish that which Thou commandest them, as that Son did who was begotten of Thy substance. "Teach me" therefore "to do Thy will, for Thou art my God," (22) to whom be all honour and glory for ever and ever. Amen.

"GIVE US THIS DAY OUR DAILY BREAD."

Fourth Petition.—1. Consider *what* "*bread*" we ask of Almighty God in this petition, for we do not ask Him for any sort of bread, but principally that which is supersubstantial, and more excellent than all others.

i. Therefore we ask Him to give us that bread which sustains and comforts *the soul*, which is the bread of the *most Blessed Sacrament*, beeseching Him to make us worthy to receive it, and that we may become worthy to receive it daily sacramentally, or at least spiritually, by receiving the fruits of that holy Sacrament, and those innumerable graces which are wont to be conferred upon us through it.

Colloquy.—O bread of life, who camest down from heaven to "give life to the world," (23) give Thyself to me, that I may always live, by Thee, and in Thee, and evermore be united with Thee. Amen.

ii. We ask the *bread* and *ordinary sustentation* of our souls, which are the succours of *celestial grace*, with which the life of the soul is preserved, in which are comprised sacraments, inspirations, illustrations, understanding of divine mysteries, and that bread of which Christ our Lord spoke, saying:—"My meat is, to do the will of my Father who sent me." (24)

Colloquy.—O most gentle and most loving Father,

(22) Ps. cxlii. 10.   (23) Joan. vi. 33.
(24) Joan. iv. 34.

since Thou commandest me to lead a heavenly life, doing Thy will on earth as it is done in heaven, give me these two divine and celestial breads to lead a life so wholly celestial, that I may obtain that life which is eternal. Amen.

iii. We likewise crave the bread and nourishment which is necessary to preserve the *life of the body*, because the will of Almighty God is, that we also preserve that, and ask and require it at His hands, not with excessive care and solicitude, but with that perfect confidence which we ought to have in His holy providence. In all which He gives us to understand, that we are His children, who wholly depend upon the sustenance which our heavenly Father is to give us, without whose providence, by our own strength we cannot live.

2. Consider this word, " *our*," for although this sovereign bread be verily God, because it proceeds from Him, He prepares it, He distributes it—yet He will have us call it *ours*, because it was ordained for our wants; again, because our Redeemer bought it for us, and has granted us the right of all His merits, through which we may demand it; because, also, it is ours by right and title of the promise He made to us.

Colloquy.—Forasmuch, therefore, as this divine bread, is prepared in one manner for the Angels of heaven, and in another manner for men upon earth, in one manner for the perfect, and in another for the imperfect; I crave of Thee, O Lord, for all, our bread accommodated according to our nature and capacity, namely, that which is most profitable for our salvation. I ask not the corporal bread of any other kind, nor the superfluous bread of human comforts, but "our" bread, the bread which is required for our necessities, by which we may employ and spend our life in Thy holy service. Amen.

3. Ponder the word, "*daily*," which is to say—"I demand not, O Lord, that extraordinary portion which Thou art wont to bestow upon Thy particular friends, since I consider myself unworthy of it, but the ordinary allowance of every day, without which my soul cannot live, nor subsist in a spiritual life, nor yet my body. As for other extraordinary favours, I wholly remit them to Thy providence, and to the sweet disposition of Thy everlasting ordinance."

4. Consider the words, "*give us*," or give to us; because I ask this bread, not for myself alone, but for *all men* whatsoever, as being my brethren, united with me by charity, and by natural union, although they may be my enemies, fulfiling that which our Lord has said, "Pray for them that persecute you," (25) and that I may understand, that if I saw that my very enemy was hungry I ought to give him to eat, (26) I beseech Almighty God to give him bread.

Lastly, I will ponder the words, "*this day;*" He says not:—"Give us this bread both for to-day and to-morrow," but only "*this day*," for it is the will of Almighty God, that we demand it of Him every day, that every day we employ habitually prayer, and that we may know that every day we depend on Him, and, therefore, ought to lose that disordered solicitude of to-morrow, because, perhaps, there will be no to-morrow at all for us. In the same manner that Almighty God ordained that the Israelites should every day gather manna, but yet no more than should suffice for that day only (27)—so to fasten them always to His fatherly providence. True it is, that I likewise demand for this day, that supersubstantial

(25) Mat. v. 44.   (26) Prov. xxv. 21.   Rom. xii. 20.
(27) Exod. xvi. 4.

bread, which, as St. Paul says, (28) is for the term of our whole life, which is but one day, in respect of eternity.

Colloquy.—O heavenly Father, give me this bread in great abundance, both for this day, and for ever: but yet so give it me, that I may live and pray so devoutly in this day, as if there were for me no other day but this. Amen.

"AND FORGIVE US OUR TRESPASSES AS WE FORGIVE THEM THAT TRESPASS AGAINST US."

Fifth Petition.—1. Consider what "*trespasses* or *debts*" these are, of which I desire and crave forgiveness.

i. These are all mortal, or venial sins, and the pains to which they oblige us: and these debts Almighty God alone can forgive and pardon, which He still does by the means He has ordained: so that I beseech Him to forgive, by applying to me those means, and by assisting me to make use of them.

ii. Although one may be so holy that he may justly call Almighty God, Father, that His Kingdom come to him, and although he may endeavour to accomplish the will of Almighty God here " on earth, as it is in heaven," yet he ought to acknowledge that he is a sinner, and may assure himself that he daily sins in these kinds of venial sins, (29) and to make scores and debts for which he may daily say: " Forgive us, O Lord, our debts."

Colloquy.—O most gentle Father, I confess that every day I fall, alas, not into one debt, but into many, because I trespass many times, notwithstanding Thou, most full of mercy, desirest daily to pardon me: and since Thou commandest me to ask Thee pardon, I ask pardon of Thee because Thou commandest me : grant me what I ask of Thee, because Thou desirest to grant it me. Amen.

(28) Heb. iii. 13.   (29) Jac. iii. 2.

2. Ponder what *debts* they are which I ought to "*forgive*," and remit to others.

These debts are the *wrongs* and injuries which my friend or neighbour may *do to me*, which I am obliged and bound to pardon, without hating or abhorring him who has offended me, nor yet revenging myself on him by my own authority, or letting him see so much as any signs of indignation, but on the contrary, signs and tokens of common amity. But he pardons more perfectly, who entirely forgets the injury, and who, in a special manner, loves his injurer, doing some particular kindness to him, for he will thus obtain a more copious and plenary pardon of his own offences at the hands of Almighty God.

ii. Hence we may gather *how much Christ our Lord desires* us to forgive and pardon one another, since He specifies and puts it down as a condition of our own pardon, as also how greatly He desires us to pardon presently, and that " the sun go not down upon" our " anger," (30) since in this our daily prayer He commands us to pardon our debtors; and if I do not do this I give sentence against myself, because, saying to Almighty God, Forgive me as I forgive others, if I forgive not, it is as much as to pray Him not to forgive me.

Colloquy.—O most liberal Father, from the bottom of my heart I forgive the debts due to me, that Thou mayest pardon me those which I am indebted to Thee: for that which is due to me amounts not to " a hundred pence, and mine amount to ten thousand talents."(31)

" AND LEAD US NOT INTO TEMPTATION."

Sixth Petition.—Christ our Lord does not desire us to demand of our Father, saying:—" Suffer not that we be

---

(30) Ephes. iv. 26. (31) Mat. xviii. 28.

tempted:" or "give not license to the tempter to tempt us," but plainly *presupposes that we are to be tempted*, and that our heavenly Father ought to suffer the same, and to give His leave for it, and if He give it, His gift will be just and for our profit, and without doubt conformable and proportionable to our strength, so that we ought to be prepared to suffer and endure the temptations of the Devil, and of his ministers who live in the world, and of our own flesh, with its passions, as we have said in the fifth meditation. Nevertheless, Christ our Lord commands us to implore His grace that we be not overcome by the temptation, nor fall into it by consenting to sin; and so we jointly crave that He suffer us not to be tempted with any such sort of temptation, nor in any such occasion in which His Majesty sees that we shall be overcome.

Colloquy.—O heavenly Father, look down upon this Thy son, who lives and sojourns in a land of temptation, combatted on every side by sundry enemies : I refuse not the battle, since it is Thy will, but assist me, I beseech Thee, to come off victorious, since the son's victory is the father's honour.

"BUT DELIVER US FROM EVIL."

Seventh Petition.—In this last petition we demand to be *delivered from all evils*, past, present, and to come, as well eternal as temporal, as well of the soul as the body, as far as is expedient for the good of the soul. We likewise demand that God would deliver us from our *sins past*, pardoning them by His especial grace ; and that He may vouchsafe to draw us from out of all ignorances, errors, passions, affections, and miseries which we suffer at present; that He also may preserve and deliver us from those that are *to come*, especially from everlasting damnation, and the power of the Devil, which is the evil from which of all others we desire to be delivered, when we say:—

"But deliver us from evil," so that neither in this life, nor in the other, he may have any power over us, nor that we ever become his slaves or vassals. I may, therefore, in this petition make a litany, like to that which the Church makes, particularizing the evils from which I desire to be delivered, saying:—"From all evil deliver us, O Lord."—"From all sin."—"From Thy anger."—"From the spirit of fornication."—"From the spirit of pride," &c.

" AMEN."

1. For a full conclusion Christ our Lord added this word "*Amen*," as much as to say, "so be it," which ought to be pronounced with fervent *affection and desire*, that Almighty God would vouchsafe to grant me what I have asked of Him, as the desire of the poor is heard by our Lord. It is likewise to be pronounced with great *confidence* that we shall be heard, since we demand the same things which our Lord commands us to ask of Him, according to that which St. John says:—"This is the confidence which we have towards Him; that whatsoever we shall ask according to His will, He heareth us."—And "we know that we have the petitions which we request of Him," (32) Himself teaching and instructing us what things we are to beg of Him, conformable to His holy will.

2. The doctrine which Christ our Lord unfolded in this sermon, of the providence which He has to relieve our necessities, and to hear our prayers, serves for matter of many meditations, and is very profitable to us, which I shall reserve for the sixth part.

(32) 1 Joan. v. 14.

MEDITATION XV.

POINT I.

Christ our Lord, wishing to send His apostles and disciples to preach throughout the land of Israel, said to them:—"The harvest indeed is great, but the labourers are few. Pray ye, therefore, the Lord of the harvest that He send labourers into His harvest!"(1)

1. In these words He discovers the infinite charity and mercy, and the *desire He has of our good* and welfare.

i. First He says, that "the harvest is *great*," because the number of those is great whom He has ordained and chosen for the Kingdom of heaven: and they many, who expect the aid of Evangelical preachers and prelates, to render them wholly devoted to His divine service; which moved Him to compassion, greatly desiring that they should be assisted.

ii. He says, that "the labourers" and reapers "are *few*," forasmuch as the most part of men are lovers of ease, and enemies of labour, and if they labour it is in seeking their own profit, and not the good and convenience of others. Few there are who dispose themselves to be workmen; and many even withstand those who send them, and this it was which greatly moved Him to compassion, desiring that there should be as many workmen as the greatness and necessity of the harvest required.

iii. He says that it *appertains to the Lord of the harvest*, who is Christ Himself, to assign and *send these labourers :* because none may enter into another man's har-

(1) Mat. ix. 28; x. 5. Marc. vi. 6, 7. Luc. ix. 2; x. 2.

vest without the consent and will of the master of it, for whoever enters into this work without the mission of Almighty God, it is a sign that he seeks not the service and advancement of his Lord, not yet the profit of the harvest, but his own honour and advancement, and so he will lose the fruit of his labour: for he can neither reap nor glean in the harvest of souls, but in the name and merits of Jesus Christ.

2. He commands them to *pray the Lord of the harvest* that He send forth labourers into His harvest to gather it together: thus giving us to understand that He has not forgotten it, and that He greatly desires that it should be brought and gathered together. But still He desires to be prayed to do this, because prayer is a means to execute the designs of His divine providence and predestination; and also to make us understand the greatness and importance of this excellent work, in which Almighty God is not interested, but the harvest and the workmen who labour in it, because upon it depends the salvation of men, which ought to be as a harvest reaped or cut down for the Kingdom of heaven:—the workmen also, because God has committed the charge of it to them. And, therefore, the apostle says, " For a necessity lieth upon me: for woe to me if I preach not the Gospel."(2)

3. Lastly, so great is the charity of Jesus Christ, that in declaring this desire before the apostles and disciples besought Him to send labourers, He Himself resolved to send them, to signify, that although we are slothful in seeking this favour at His hands, nevertheless His infinite charity will not be unmindful of this harvest, but of His own bounty and mercy will choose workmen, and send them, as He does, through the universal Church, even among heathens and unbelievers.

(2) 1 Cor. ix. 16.

Colloquy.—O most sweet Saviour, I give Thee all the thanks that I possibly can, for the care which Thou hast of this Thy harvest, and for sending forth workmen to gather it together : and since Thou wilt be prayed, a thousand times I beseech and pray Thee to send forth many most faithful and exemplary workmen, and such as are free from offending Thee. And if I am fit for it, " lo here am I, send me,'' (3) because if Thou dost call me and send me, it is most just that I should obey Thee, labouring to accomplish what Thou commandest me.

These and such like affections and purposes I am to produce from the three considerations abovementioned, as compassionating the necessity of the harvest, and the want that there is of faithful workmen.

POINT II.

After Christ our Lord had said this, He sent Hi apostles and disciples two and two, to preach throughout the land of Israel, saying to them:—"Cure the sick, raise the dead, cleanse the lepers, cast out devils, freely you have received, freely give." (4)

1. And here first I will ponder the *causes* why Christ our Lord commanded His disciples to go *two and two*, and not one alone—which were,—i. That the one might assist, comfort, and guard the other.—ii. That they might practise amongst themselves the law of perfect charity, and by their example exhort others to observe it also.—iii. To be two uniform witnesses of the same truth.—iv. And lastly, in order that those who were to follow after them might imitate this example, taking care to proceed well accompanied in these sacred negociations, for, as the Wise man says:—" A brother that is helped by his brother is like a strong city." (5) " Woe to him that is alone, for when he

(3) Is. vi. 8.   (4) Mat. x. 8.   (5) Prov. xviii. 19.

falleth, he hath none to lift him up." (6)   And as the same Lord says, "For where there are two or three gathered together in my name, there am I in the midst of them." (7)   O happy assembly, of which Jesus Christ makes the third of the company!

2. I will ponder the *liberality* and *omnipotence of Christ* our Lord in communicating to His disciples, without either envy or jealousy, the power of working miracles, (8) even so far as afterwards to say to them, that they should do much greater than He Himself had done, to authorize and give credit to His doctrine; for as they were men of no consequence they would not have been thought anything of or esteemed, had they wanted this sovereign power.

3. I will also ponder these two memorable sentences of our blessed Saviour, "freely you have received, freely give."

i. For by the first He *grounds them in humility*, by which they might understand that this power, and the other special favours bestowed upon them, were not given to them as a debt due to them, nor yet for their merits, but *entirely by grace*, in order that none should glory in himself, but in Almighty God, from whom he received it. And when, after this, it happened that the disciples returning from their mission, were vain-glorious of the devils having obeyed them, Christ our Lord reprehended their pride, saying :—"I saw Satan like lightning fallen from heaven;" (9) that is to say,—take warning by the very devils who obey you, who fell from heaven by their pride and presumption, attributing to themselves, that which appertains to Almighty God.

ii. By the second He exhorts them *to be liberal to their neighbours*, as He Himself had been in their behalf, who

<hr>

(6) Eccles. iv. 10.   (7) Mat. xviii. 20.
(8) Joan. xiv. 12.   (9) Luc. x. 18.

having given them this power freely, would that they should bestow it freely, and not for any temporal gift, profit, or price : and that the less recompense they sought for from men, the greater should they receive from the hands of God; who is grieved and complains of the defects of His ministers, saying by the prophet :—"Who is there among you, that will shut the doors, and will kindle the fire on my altar gratis?" (10) seeking principally My glory, and not his own particular profit?

Colloquy.—O sweet Jesus, since Thou hast given me all that I have, I will serve Thee with this freely as it is all and entirely Thine, For the love of Thee alone I will shut up the gate of my senses, and upon the altar of my heart, I will light the fire of devout affections, and offer upon it the sacrifice of works acceptable to Thee. And if Thou give me anything for the good of my neighbours, I will impart it to them, without seeking any other recompense than Thyself, to whom is due the glory of whatsoever proceeds from Thee.

POINT III.

Consider the *virtues* which Christ our Lord recommended to them on entering upon this office of preaching, saying to them :—"Behold I send you as sheep amongst wolves, be ye therefore wise as serpents, and simple as doves."(11)

1. In these words He commends six virtues to them, viz. :—i. the *meekness* of sheep, hurting no man, even if they are hurt by them :—ii. *patience* to suffer all evils which may be done to them :—iii. *charity* in freely giving and bestowing themselves, and whatever they have for the good of others, even to their enemies; as sheep give their milk, their wool, and their flesh for the good of men : — iv. Notwithstanding they ought also to have great *con-*

(10) Malac. i. 10.   (11) Mat. x. 16.

fidence in the providence of the pastor who sends them, as sheep wholly rely upon the care of the shepherd, because they have no weapons to defend themselves with, or if they had they know not how to use them. And this is what He meant by these words:—"Behold I send you as sheep amongst wolves:" as much as to say:—"be assured that you shall find wolves, and persecutors of your life and doctrine, and ye for your parts, go amongst them, not as wolves against wolves, nor as dogs or lions, to bite and destroy them, but as sheep and lambs, fighting with the weapons of meekness and patience, of charity and confidence, mindful that it is I who send you,—I who am your pastor, your master, and your God, who will be careful of you, and will defend you in your perils."

Colloquy.—O sovereign pastor, since it is Thou who defendest me, send me wherever you please, under Thy favour I shall be secure, wheresoever Thou sendest me : fortify my feebleness by Thy divine virtue, by which. I may conquer such as are wolves, and convert them into sheep of Thy holy fold, fulfilling that which Thou hast promised by Thy prophet : that "the wolf shall dwell with the lamb, and the leopard shall lie down with the kid: the calf, and the lion, and the sheep shall abide together," under the obedience of an humble pastor, " and a little child shall lead them." (12)

2. He recommended to them, to be meek, patient, charitable and confident, in such a manner as not to be ignorant, imprudent and rash, but that they should have— v. the *wisdom* of serpents : whose wisdom consists(a) in so performing and accomplishing their duties, that the wolves may in no ways injure their souls, although they should tear in pieces their bodies: as the serpent saves her head

(12) Is. xi. 6.

although her body endure and suffer, and "stops her ears against the charmer," (13) for fear of hearing anything which may be hurtful to her.—(b) In observing the time, the place, and fit opportunity to preach and to persuade our doctrine: like the serpent did which tempted Eve. For it stands with reason, that we should be as prudent and wise in good things, as the serpents, that is, the devils are, in doing evil. But Christ our Lord will not have this wisdom be a wolfish wisdom, mixed with duplicity or deceit, with false suspicions, or rash judgments, but with sincerity, uprightness, and purity of life, without any gall of malice or bitterness: and so that it be not contrary to the meekness and mildness of very lambs.—

vi. And for this cause, He adds, that they should be as *simple* as doves, having the eyes of their intention pure, to behold that which makes most for the glory of Almighty God, and the good of souls, without the mixture of human respects.

Colloquy.—O lamb without spot, upon whom the Holy Ghost descended in the form of a dove, join in my soul perfect prudence with simplicity, that I may so do good to others, that I receive no damage from them. Amen.

POINT IV.

In the fourth place, I will consider the manner of walking, or going, which our Lord enjoined them, saying: "*Do not possess gold, nor silver*, nor money in your purses; nor scrip for your journey, nor two coats, nor shoes, nor a staff, for the workman is worthy of his hire. (14) And salute no man by the way. Into whatsoever house you enter, first say: peace be unto this house."(15)

(13) Ps. lvii. 5.   (14) Mat. x. 9.   (15) Luc. x. 4.

1. Here we are to consider the intention of Christ our Lord, in these His counsels, which principally respect three things:—

i. The first, is that they *entirely cut off* all *excess and superfluity* of *temporal things*, contenting themselves with what is necessary, so that they carry no precious thing of gold or silver, nor store of money to treat themselves well. And if one garment suffice them with one pair of hose, that they have not a double suit to change them: and if clogs or sandals suffice, such as poor men wear, that they put not on shoes : and if they have no need of a rod or staff, that they use none: or if they carry a staff to support themselves, as being infirm, that they carry not such a one as may serve to defend or revenge themselves.

ii. The second is, that they *neglect* the *excessive care* of their *sustenance*, apparel, and fare, although necessary, putting their trust in Divine Providence, which will provide them all things, if they themselves are such as they ought to be, and discharge their functions as they ought, forasmuch as the labourer is worthy that his master should receive and nourish him, even God Himself will both give to them, and inspire men to give to them: which they may accept, not as the price of their labour, but as the entertainment and support of their life, so as to travel better. Which was punctually accomplished, as the apostles confessed, when on the night of the Passion, our Lord Jesus Christ said to them: " When I sent you without purse, and scrip, and shoes, did you want any thing? (16) And they said: Nothing."

Colloquy.—O most provident Pastor, the "rod," and "staff" (17) of Thy government, alone suffice to comfort and sustain me, because having Thee, I have

(16) Luc. xxii. 35.   (17) Ps. xxii. 4.

all; and not wanting Thee, nothing can be wanting to me.

iii. The third is, that in the way they should by no means *entangle themselves with frivolous discourses*, or impertinent things, which might disturb or divert them from their intent and purpose; as if He had said to them, that they should salute no man by the way, by entertaining themselves with worldly salutations, though they should not omit those which were convenient. And thus He desires that they should be so humble in the houses or places where they dwell, that they first salute their hosts, or those who receive them, and congratulate them with the peace of the Gospel, craving the same of Almighty God in their behalf, from their first entrance into their lodging. For if there is not peace and tranquillity in the house of the soul, it is not well disposed to hear the truth of this holy doctrine.

Colloquy.—O heavenly Master, since Thou so earnestly seekest our instruction, imprint Thy words so effectually in my heart, that I may conform to them indeed, without diverting myself to anything which may turn or distract me from them. Amen.

2. Lastly, Christ our Lord greatly encourages them to execute their office, saying;—"If that house be worthy of peace, your peace shall come upon it, but if it be not worthy, your peace shall return to you;" giving us to understand *two things.*

i. That their preaching should be profitable to some persons, that is to say, *to those who were worthy of peace*, or were children of peace, chosen by Almighty God to receive the doctrine of the holy gospel, without resisting their preaching.—ii. That when they cannot procure the profit of others, because they refuse to receive it, that *their peace shall return to themselves*; that is to say, that they ought not to lose their own peace, nor to be disquieted by any anger, vengeance or vexation, but leave it to Almighty God, for in doing so they will not lose the fruit of their labours.

POINT V.

In the fifth place, I will consider the *matter* and theme which He delivered them to preach upon, saying—"And going, preach, saying, The Kingdom of heaven is at hand," (18) and publish to all, that they do penance.

In which are to be pondered three things, which this text or theme comprehends.

i. First, the *means* of salvation by which we may enter into the Kingdom of heaven; that is, by repentance and penance for our sins, the extirpation of vices, the exercise of virtues, and the contempt of earthly things, which cause and procure the perdition of souls.

ii. The *end* and *motive* of all such works, which ought to be the Kingdom of heaven: so that they should be induced to do them, not principally for fear of punishment, nor for hope of temporal recompense, but only for the promise of the Kingdom of heaven.

iii. That all this could be done with great *facility*. sweetness, and ease, because the kingdom of heaven was near at hand, and even within themselves, that is to say,— the author of grace, to whom it belonged to open the gates of the Kingdom of heaven, and to give sweet and efficacious means to enter therein, as He began even at that time to give them.

Colloquy.—O King of heaven, who hast placed in the power of the world so glorious a Kingdom, help me that I may conquer and attain to it, since Thou hast said that since the days of St. John Baptist, who first began to preach it, that it should suffer

(18) Mat. x. 7.

"violence," and that "the violent" should "bear it away." (19)   Give me, O Lord, this holy violence, by which I may purchase and bear away this so precious a jewel, since Thou who art the master and owner of it art pleased that all men should violently steal and rob it, and so enrich themselves.

MEDITATION XVI.

ON THE GLORIOUS MARTYRDOM OF S. JOHN BAPTIST.

POINT I.

King Herod, having taken his brother's wife, and espoused her for his own, St. John reprehended him, saying to him, that it was not "lawful for" him to do so.(1)

And here is to be weighed, the energy *and zeal of this our new Elias*, who although he was very familiar, and well-beloved by Herod,—for St. Mark says, that he feared him, knowing him to be a just and a holy man, heard him gladly, and did many things by his direction,—yet notwithstanding all this, he sharply reprehended his sin, so public and so scandalous in the sight of the world, although he clearly perceived that he would thereby lose his love and friendship: for such as are zealous of the glory of God fear not to lose the favour of a terrestrial king, but fear to lose that of the King of heaven; and although S. John knew right well that Herod was cruel, and that Herodias was yet more cruel than he, desiring to have him massacred for these reprehensions, nevertheless he was neither afraid nor affrighted, nor yet did he omit to discharge his duty in that, exposing himself to all sorts of perils, disgrace, and detriment that might befal him: shewing in

(19) Mat. xi. 12.   (1) Mat. xiv. 3.   Marc. vi. 17.

this his invincible courage and constancy, and that he was not a light or inconstant "reed," (2) but "a pillar of iron, and a wall of brass:"(3) for as he little respected either his life or his honour, so he feared not to lose them, nothing moved with threatenings or menaces, but like a lion, remained stable and confident without any fear. (4)

Hence I am to form great and invincible resolutions, to imitate the fortitude and constancy of this holy precursor, withdrawing myself from the inordinate love of the mutable things of this life, whence it proceeds that I shake and waver like a reed, with every little wind of temptation.

POINT II.

"Herod" "added this" great evil, "above all" the evils he had committed; he apprehended John, cast him "in prison,"(5) charged and loaded him with many irons.

1. Christ *our Lord permitted this imprisonment* of St. John Baptist, although he was His beloved friend: forasmuch as until then all things had succeeded prosperously with him, being honoured, extolled, and obeyed by all men: and it was meet for this respect that he should pass through persecutions, as other prophets had done, and through which all the elect are to pass, to the end that, like holy Job, having shewed his excellent virtues in prosperity, he might likewise shew them in adversity, and thus purify and refine himself like gold in the furnace, augmenting the crown of his glory by the excellence of his patience. And here I will excite myself to esteem "persecutions" and troubles, endured and suffered "for justice sake:"(6) for although in the eyes of the world they seem to be punishments, yet in the eyes of Almighty God they

(2) Mat. xi. 7.   (3) Jer. i. 18.   (4) Prov. xx. 2.
(5) Luc. iii. 19.   (6) Mat. v. 11.

are the favours and premiums with which He rewards His dearest friends: and for this cause calls them "blessed," saying that "theirs is the Kingdom of heaven." (7)

2. I will ponder the *manner how St. John Baptist suffered this affliction*, for it is to be believed, that when they came to seize and apprehend him, he neither fled, nor tried to hide himself, but on the contrary went out before the soldiers, exposing and offering himself to prison: and when he saw himself bound with shackles and chains, he rejoiced in them no less than St. Paul, comforting himself that they would help him to mortify his flesh, which he abhorred with so holy a hatred. The prison he converted into an oratory, spending the nights in holy prayer and contemplation, as he did in the desert:—and in the day time, he ceased not to instruct his fellow prisoners and his disciples; and from that time sent them to Christ our Lord, asking, not that He would deliver him from prison but that He would deliver those people from the ignorance in which they were detained and imprisoned.

3. Having, in fine, finished his office of a precursor in the world, *he desired to be freed from the prison of his body*, to go and perform this office *in the prison of Limbo*, and to give notice to the just that their redemption drew near, and from day to day with joy he expected death; for being so great a prophet, he doubtless had revelation of the divine will, and knew that his departure was near at hand.

Colloquy.—O my soul, rejoice with this precursor in thy tribulations, since thou knowest, "that tribulation worketh patience; and patience trial: and trial hope, and hope confoundeth not," since those who suffer in this manner, have "the charity" (8) of the

(7) Mat. v. 12.　　　　　　　　　　　(8) Rom. v. 5.

Holy Ghost, dwelling and inhabiting in their hearts, which is the pledge of life everlasting.

POINT III.

" Herod made a" sumptuous " supper on his birthday for the princes" "of Galilee," and "the daughter" "of Herodias" came in to "dance," "and pleased" the whole company so much, that the king " promised with an oath to give her whatsoever she would ask of him," "though" it were " the half of" his " kingdom."   " She being previously instructed by her mother," demanded " the head of John the Baptist. And the king," to fulfil "his oath," granted and awarded it to her.(9)

1. Consider, first, the *craft and cruelty of the Devil*, put in practice by means of this tyrant, stirring up all the squadron of vices, to cut off the head of the holy Baptist, in hatred of his excellent virtues; for he stirred up the gluttony of the banquet against his abstinence,—the impurity of Herodias against his chastity,—the levity of her daughter against his modesty,—the immoderate mirth of the feasters against his gravity,—the prodigality and vainglory of Herod concerning his promise, against his poverty and humility. In short, cruelty, dissimulation, falsity, and infidelity, conspired against the meekness, sincerity, truth, and the most perfect piety of this excellent saint.

Hence it may be seen, how the Devil, by the means of vices, makes war against virtues, although he does not prevail against those who are well grounded in them. And here I will resolve, with great and invincible courage, to " crush the head" (10) of this subtle serpent, although he should cut off mine; for though he should cut off the head of my body, he cannot separate me from Christ my " head," (11) in whom consists all my good.

(9) Marc. vi. 22. Mat. xiv. 6.   (10) Gen. iii. 15.
(11) Colos. i. 22.

Colloquy.—O most sweet Jesus, the head of all powers and principalities, grant me such fervour of spirit, that neither tribulations, anguish, perils, persecutions, nor death itself, may ever separate me from Thy love and charity : and assist me here, so to fight for Thy service in the church militant, that I may come to reign with Thee in Thy Church triumphant. Amen.

2. I may likewise ponder in this place, the *condition of sin,* and *of that sinner* who becomes disordered and abuses God's gifts, which is always to proceed from bad to worse, since it is not without mystery that St. Luke adds:—" for all the evils which Herod had done, he added this above all, and shut up John in prison." (12)　And after this many more which he committed at the same banquet; that being accomplished in Herod, which David says, that " the pride of them that hate" our Lord, "ascendeth continually." (13)　For first, he was deaf to the correction of St. John Baptist; next he apprehended him, and then consented to his death, seeking like a subtle and crafty fox, some apparent pretext for this purpose, under the counterfeit title of religion, and keeping his oath.

And in the same manner, following the example of Herod, I, who was wont to live in amity with the grace of Almighty God, figured by John, and was accustomed to hearken to His divine inspirations, have since resisted Him, and then imprisoned Him, by my perverse affections and passions, and lastly, have slain Him with my sins, by adding one upon another, at one time feasting them, and at other times thinking it an act of religion to commit them.

3. From all which I will learn to cut off evil in the very beginning, and especially to receive correction with a meek

(12) Luc. iii. 20.　　　　　　　　(13) Ps. lxxiii. 23.

and humble spirit: for the difference betwixt the predestinate and the reprobate, is not in this,—that one sins and the other not; but in this—that the one admits correction and amends them with David, (14) but the others with Saul reject it, and like Herod, pour forth their anger on those who reprehend them, so as even to fall into the most deep pit of malice, and the bottomless depth of hell and damnation. (15)

POINT III.

Herod "sent" an executioner to the "prison" where St. John was, to behead him, which he performed, and delivered the head to Herod, who gave it to the daughter of Herodias, and she to "her mother." (16)

1. Here consider the *great consolation* with which the Baptist received the sentence of death, when it was notified to him, right joyful to die for so good a cause, conforming his will to the will of God, who also suffered it. And it is to be believed that as Jesus Christ our Lord and Saviour died upon the solemn day of Easter, to signify the joy and content it was to Him, and that the chief Paschal feast He had was to die for men, so He would have St. John Baptist die upon the day of this solemn banquet, to testify that it was a feast and banquet to him to suffer death for truth and justice.

2. It is to be believed, that falling down upon his knees, *he first prayed for his enemies*, saying thus to Almighty God:—" Lord, forgive them, for passion blinds them, so that they know not what they do."   Then he prayed for his disciples, and lastly for himself, commending his spirit into the hands of Almighty God, which done, he courageously presented his head unto the executioner, and if he was grieved or sorry for anything, it was because his death

(14) 2 Reg. xii.   (15) 2 Reg. xv.   (16) Mat. xiv. 10.

was not more painful, as he would willingly have suffered more for the service and honour of his beloved Lord.

3. I may consider the *honour with which his holy soul was carried* and conducted *into Abraham's bosom*, for if many angels came to conduct the soul of poor Lazarus, how many thousands more came to conduct the soul of this precursor? For as many rejoiced, according to the saying of the angels, at his nativity, so when he entered into Limbo, the just rejoiced with a most singular joy, which Almighty God communicated to them at his arrival, because of the good tidings which he brought them, about the Messiah whom they were expecting.

Hence I will consider *the glory which he now enjoys in heaven*, in recompense for such great and singular services which he did for Christ our Lord, from the time that He sanctified him in his mother's womb, until he was put to death in prison. For although his life was very short, not having fully attained three and thirty years, nevertheless his merits were exceedingly great, because of his fervour, of which we will speak further in his holy life; for Christ our Lord had dignified and raised him up to one of the highest thrones of heaven, amongst the supreme Seraphim, giving to him those *three* most precious crowns, of Virgin, Doctor, and Martyr, as he was *a virgin, a doctor*—and *doubly a martyr*,—the one of perpetual voluntary martyrdom, by poverty, charity, and continual mortification of his flesh; the other, by a violent martyrdom, shedding his blood in testimony of the truth. Wherefore at the day of judgment, forasmuch as he has left and forsaken all for the love of Jesus Christ, he will be placed by Him in a glorious throne with the apostles, to judge the whole tribes of Israel, and the whole world.

Colloquy.—O holy precursor, I rejoice heartily at thy greatness ; thou wast blessed in thy birth, more blessed in thy life, and much more blessed in thy death, but most of all blessed in the glory which thou possessest in recompense of such a life and such a death. Blessed were thy labours and pains, which have obtained so blessed a reward, such an incomparable crown ; and since thy blessedness was so great, beseech our Lord to assist me to imitate thy life, by which I may attain a share of thy glory. Amen.

4. Finally, I will ponder how *Herod, Herodias, and her daughter triumphed in this day*, with the head of St. John, but that this *their joy lasted them but a short time*, for the justice of Almighty God soon fell upon them, and they all three died disastrously, fulfilling that which is written:— "They take the timbrel and the harp, and rejoice at the sound of the organ," (17) spending their days wholly in pleasure, but come at the last to fall into terrible miseries; for " the death of the wicked is very evil," (18) not only in the eyes of Almighty God, but sometimes also in the eyes of men, being chastised with some unexpected death, for the sins which they have committed in their life. Thus I will compare the life and death of St. John Baptist, most precious in the eyes of Almighty God, with the disastrous life and death of his enemies, and I will rather choose to suffer with John than to reign with Herod, since at this present time Herod is suffering most terrible torments without any remedy, and John is reigning without end in ineffable joy.

(17) Job. xxi. 12.   (18) Ps. xxxiii. 22.

(2.)—MEDITATIONS ON OUR LORD'S MIRACLES.

MEDITATION XVII.

ON THE MIRACLE WROUGHT BY CHRIST OUR LORD OF FEEDING FIVE THOUSAND MEN WITH FIVE LOAVES.

POINT I.

Christ our Lord, having conducted "a great multitude" of people, and having preached to them a long time in the "desert," and "the day" beginning "to decline," the apostles prayed Him to "send them away," "that going into the towns," they might "buy themselves victuals" "to eat." (1)   To whom Christ our Lord answered, They have no need to go, "give you them to eat."

I. Here consider:—The great *devotion* with which *these people followed Jesus* Christ our Lord, which they did for two principal reasons,—the one for the *miracles* which He wrought,—the other for the *food* of that *marvellous doctrine* with which He fed their famished souls, accomplishing that which is written:—"I will draw them" to me "with the cords of Adam, with the bands of love," (2) that is to say, with benefits both corporal and spiritual. With these cords Jesus Christ so held them bound, that although it was late, and that they had not anything to eat, nor knew how nor where to get themselves meat, yet they would not depart from or leave Him, but quite forgetting to eat, entertained themselves with His lovely presence.

(1) Mat. xiv. 15. Marc. vi. 35. Luc. ix. 14. Joan. vi. 5.
(2) Osee xi. 4.

Colloquy.—O most sweet Jesus, draw me to Thee with these cords of charity, and knit and unite me so straitly to Thee, that, forgetting all things created, I may only sigh and aspire after Thee, my sweet Saviour and Creator. Amen.

2. Then I will ponder the *compassion which the apostles took* of these devout people, but much more that which Jesus Christ Himself took of them, beholding the difference of the one and of the other. The compassion of the apostles was but little, as proceeding from frail, weak, and feeble men, who seeing these people fatigued and famished, and that they had not wherewith to sustain themselves, took pity on them, beseeching their Lord and master to dismiss them, that they may seek for themselves food, for as they were truly obedient and submissive to Him, so they would do nothing by their private authority, nor allow them to depart without their Lord's permission. But Jesus Christ beholding the scantiness of this compassion, conceived another a great deal more ample, breaking forth from the bowels of Almighty God, and would efficaciously redress their misery, to which He exhorted His disciples, saying:—"Give you them to eat;" as if He had said:—"Extend the entrails of your compassion, and send not away these famished people to seek food, but do you yourselves seek it for them, and give it to them, since I have bestowed upon you the power and might to work miracles, or at least ask me, that I may give them, knowing I am able to do so." In which He teaches us, that the compassion, especially of prelates, ought not to be penurious, but exceedingly ample, as David said (3) of the mercy of God, using all the means in our power to remedy and relieve our neighbour's misery, and if we have not means of ourselves, we ought to have recourse to Him who

(3) 2 Reg. ix.

can help us in that case, and importunately solicit Him to supply our wants.

3. To ponder more profoundly this mercy of Jesus Christ our Lord; consider what He said at another time like this. "I have compassion on the multitude, for behold they have now been with me three days, and have nothing to eat. And if I shall send them away fasting to their homes, they will faint in their way, for some of them came from afar off." (4) In which words He shows us that it is the property of the mercy of Almighty God to feel our necessities by degrees, and also the respects and motives He has to relieve, together with the peril which we incur if He does not redress them. Of all which Almighty God takes the charge upon Himself, so that He may have compassion upon us, and give us a remedy, as if it much imported Him to assist us.

Colloquy.—O most merciful God, what great matter is it for me to persevere three days in Thy company, since Thou implorest them all to do me good? Thou dost a great deal more for me in vouchsafing to dwell and remain with me, than I do in desiring to be and remaining with Thee; and what wonder is it, if I come from far to seek Thee, since Thou descendest from heaven to seek me? My wicked life has placed me far from Thee, but now I will approach to Thee by perfect penance; dismiss me not, I beseech Thee, from Thy presence "fasting," lest I faint in the rugged way of this wretched life: support me, I beseech Thee, with the continual succours of Thy grace, so that I may walk with strength to the end of this my journey. Amen.

4. Consider, fourthly, how Christ Jesus our Lord, to manifest the care which He had of these His people, said to Philip:—" Whence shall we buy bread, that these may

<hr>

(4) Marc. viii. 2. Mat. xv. 32.

eat?" (5)   And this He said to try his faith, and to show the necessity there was of working this miracle, since He will not work miracles to support us, when He can supply our necessities by natural means. "Philip answered Him: Two hundred penny-worth of bread is not sufficient for them, that every one may take a little;" (6) and the other apostles made the same answer, all of them confessing in this case their inability.

Colloquy.—Hence I gather, O most sweet master, the greatness and immensity of Thy Almighty power, for where Thou art, neither pence or pounds are ever wanting, for with Thy only word, Thou canst give to every man, not only a bit or morsel of bread, but even abundance.(7)   Henceforth, therefore, I will confide no more in money, though all things adore and bow before it, but only in Thee, O most liberal giver and dispenser of gifts, whose hand is always open to fill the hungry with Thy abundant benediction.

POINT II.

Jesus Christ our Lord asked His apostles for the bread which they had, and they forthwith gave it to Him, " five barley loaves, and two little fishes,"(8) which was all they had to support themselves.

Here reflect on *three things* full of mystery :—

1. The *great poverty of Jesus* Christ our Lord and of His disciples, and the little care which they had about feeding their bodies with dainty fare, since dwelling in this desert so many days, they had no more for thirteen persons, (besides some others which they led with them,) but only " five loaves," and those of barley, which of all bread is the least pleasant to the taste, commonly used by the poor ; and although they were fishermen by occupation, yet they had only two

(5) Joan. vi. 5.   (6) Joan. vi. 6.   (7) Eccl. x. 5. Ps. cxliv. 16.
(8) Mat. xiv. 7,

little fishes amongst them all. By this example I will confound myself, seeing with what solicitude I seek after dainty and delicate meat, and will endeavour to content myself with a very little, and of a coarse and ordinary kind, although it be somewhat distasteful.

Colloquy.—O sweet Jesus, who didst feed the ungrateful people in the desert with bread from heaven, and sustainedst Thyself and Thy beloved disciples with barley bread, grant that I may choose for myself that which Thou didst choose for Thyself, treating my body with the same severity with which for my example Thou didst treat Thine. Amen.

2. The second is, the great *charity and obedience of the blessed apostles*, for when Christ Jesus demanded those barley loaves of them, they presented them to Him without any reply, never saying that they should need them for themselves, but were willing to spare them out of their own repast, to supply the present necessity of others. Hence I will learn to join obedience with love and charity for the good of the poor, pitying them, and willingly depriving myself of my own provision, to supply their wants and miseries, since I lose them not, but employ them better, as it chanced in this case to the apostles.

3. And hence we are to see, that although Christ our Lord could have redressed this necessity by many other miraculous means, yet *would He use the bread of the apostles*, which He asked of them, to prove whether their charity and pity were perfect, and that they also might have part in this good work, and to teach me, that if I am not able to remedy all the necessity of the poor, that yet it is good at least to remedy some part of it, and then Almighty God with His liberality will remedy the rest, fulfilling that which Tobias said to his son:—" According to thy ability be merciful. If thou have little, take care

even so to bestow willingly a little." (9)   And the same thing happens in spiritual necessities, as well of my own, as of my neighbours, for Jesus Christ our Lord desires me on my part to offer all that I am able, although it be but little, and He by His mercy and almighty power will never fail to supply the rest.

POINT III.

1. Consider *what Christ our Lord did at the beginning of this banquet.*

i. He commanded His apostles to make all the people sit down upon the grass, by hundreds and fiftys, as it wore by squadrons.   One reason was, to know by this means *the number* of the guests, which amounted to the number of five thousand men, besides women and children, which might be as many more; the other was, to observe by this means order and agreement in the manner of eating and distribution of the bread, so that all might behold and see the greatness of this divine and stupendous miracle.

ii. This done, Christ Jesus our Lord *took the bread* into His holy hands, and lifted up His eyes to heaven, to give us to understand that every good and "perfect gift is from above," (10) and that the Almighty power which He had to work miracles, inasmuch as He was man, came likewise to Him from His Father who is in heaven.

iii. Then He *gave thanks* to Almighty God, as well for that present food, as also for that which He intended to give miraculously, teaching us to be grateful to Almighty God for every gift, how small soever, and for that He vouchsafes to give us bread, though it be but of barley, since it suffices that it is God who gives it, on this account alone it is to be esteemed; and so much the more when He divides it to them to whom He is nothing indebted, and who merited nothing at His hands.

(9) Tob. iv. 8.   (10) Jac. i. 1l.

iv. Afterwards He *blessed the bread* with certain words of holy prayer, with which He imprinted in it the virtue to multiply and to become better, for the benediction of Jesus Christ is not like ours, which asks or desires only, but also is essential *to do* what He *says*.

v. And having given this benediction He broke the bread, and gave it to His apostles, to give and distribute it to others.

2. In doing this Christ our Lord instructs us in *the manner how Christians ought to eat*, Christianly, and religiously, with the four conditions before specified.

i. With *order and agreement*, each one sitting in his place, without contention or emulation, but choosing "the lowest" and most humble "place." (11)

ii. With *elevation of soul to heaven*, considering ourselves in the presence of God, who beholds us: because, having this in view, we may the better bridle our taste and our tongue, observing due temperance and modesty. For which reason holy David said, that "the just feast and rejoice before God,(12) even as Moses, "Aaron, and all the ancients of Israel eat bread with" Jethro, " before God."(13)

iii. With a *grateful mind*, as those who eat and live on alms given them by the liberal hand of Almighty God, from whom both poor and rich receive the bread which they eat;(14) and by this affection we shall repress the complaints and murmurings which the flesh makes, when our food is but little, or but poorly seasoned, or that the time of dinner is somewhat deferred, since he that merits nothing ought to receive whatsoever is given him, and that with gratefulness and thanksgiving.

iv. With *previous petition for blessing*, with devout prayer, which we should also take care to intermingle with our meat, feeding the body, that the spirit also may be

(11) Luc. xiv. 10.　　(12) Ps. lxvii. 4.　(13) Exod. xviii. 12.
. (14) Rom. xiv. 6.

refreshed.   Whence it will come to pass, that the meat, although but little and unsavoury, will seem to thee exceeding sweet, because the taste of the spirit will sweeten its sourness to the flesh, which, as St. Paul says, " is sanctified by the word of God and prayer," (15) receiving it with " thanksgiving."

3. In this act also is represented to us the manner how we are to eat that most holy bread of the *Blessed Sacrament*, figured by this meat, of which we will speak in the fourth part, where Christ Jesus our Lord did the self-same things, when He instituted it the night of His last supper.

POINT IV.

Consider the *greatness* of this sovereign miracle, since, as the bread was miraculously multiplied between the hands of Christ our Lord, between the hands of His apostles, and even of those also that ate it ; so that although they received but a little bread, and also consumed it, yet it did not diminish, but greatly multiplied, till all were filled and much contented, because this bread was exceedingly sweet, as being the bread of Almighty God, given to them by so good a hand.

1. Upon this I will ponder—the almighty *power of Jesus Christ* our Lord, who could with such facility convert five loaves into many thousands, and insipid bread into sweet, and the fishes in the same manner, drawing from this consideration an ardent desire to serve a Lord of such power and might.

Colloquy.—O King of heaven, who will not glory that serves thee, who art so powerful as to feed Thy people in a desert? (16)   Where Thy Almighty power is, we need never doubt, nor fear any desert, for by Thy power Thou drawest " honey out of the rock, and oil out of the hardest stone : (17) Thou sentest quails

(15) 1 Tim. iv. 5.   (16) Ps. lxxvii. 29.   (17) Deut. xxxii. 13.

from the skies, Thou rainedst down manna from heaven, and in the hands of the hungry Thou multipliedst bread and fishes, that Thy children might know that not only the fruit of the earth, but Thy omnipotent word nourishes all that believe in Thee.(18)

2. Here I will contemplate the *fatherly providence* of this great and sovereign God, in feeding those who faithfully serve Him, with so bountiful a hand, and by means so miraculous, *when human help utterly fails*, provided that the confidence fail not which we ought to have in Him, founding ourselves upon the promise which He has made us, saying:—" Be not solicitous, therefore, saying, What shall we eat, or What shall we drink, or Wherewith shall we be clothed, for after all these things do the heathen seek. For your Father knoweth that you need all these things. Seek, therefore, first the Kingdom of God, and His justice, and all these things shall be added unto you." (19) All which appeared in this people, who came to seek Him, and to hear His doctrine of the Kingdom of Heaven, to whom, as the Evangelist, St. Luke, says, He discoursed largely, and after gave them corporal meat in great abundance, both for themselves and for their children, to verify the saying of the prophet David, " I have not seen the just forsaken, nor his seed begging bread."(20)

Colloquy.—O most loving Father, I render Thee thanks for this fatherly providence which Thou hast of those who faithfully serve and hope in Thee. Grant, Lord, that I may have a special care to serve Thee as a son, since Thou takest care to find me all things necessary like a father. Amen.

3. I meditate on God's *providence*, which shines manifestly in this miracle, for *they being many and various in*

(18) Sap. xvi. 2.
(19) Mat. vi. 31.   (20) Ps. xxxvi. 25.

their needs, who were at this banquet, and of different ages
and complexions, young and old, strong and feeble, women
and children, and breaking to all indifferently the same
bread, according to the quantity which the apostles pleased,
it was sufficient for all, filled, satisfied, and contented all;
accomplishing that which is written of the manna, that
every one remained satisfied with the quantity he had
gathered; he not wanting who had gathered little, nor he
having anything over who gathered much, by which appear the bountifulness and magnificence of the benefactor. (21)　In which is set forth to us, the singular sweetness of the Divine Providence, which gives to every one of
the just that which he desires, to some more, to others
less, but yet to all sufficiently; giving to the just as much
satisfaction with a little, as to others with a great deal
more.

4. But much more doth the greatness of the Blessed
Sacrament of the Altar appear in this place, which, being
one selfsame celestial bread, although distributed by the
hands of priests, among millions of men, *never diminishes;*
and, although one host be divided and broken into several
parts, every particle contained as much as the whole,
because, in the whole, and every part of it, Christ is wholly
and entirely; so that he who receives but a little part,
receives as much as he who receives a great deal, the one
affording as much satiety as the other, and, finally, fills
and satisfies all, giving to every one that measure of grace
which his necessity and disposition requires.

Colloquy.—O Almighty God, how marvellous are
Thy works, how rich Thy providence, how ample,
sweet, and affectionate!　Let all the angels praise
Thee for this, let all mankind cheerfully rejoice at
this, and let my soul with all her powers, be wholly

(21) Exod. xvi. 18.　2 Cor. viii. 15.

melted in Thy love, employing them in Thy holy service, since Thou dost so employ Thyself in cherishing me.   Amen.

POINT V.

Consider what followed after the miracle. For, first, Jesus Christ our Lord commanded His apostles to gather together the broken bread which remained, and they gathered up twelve baskets full.

1. In this He showed His *liberality*, in rewarding the good will with which His apostles offered to Him five barley loaves, returning them twelve baskets full of excellent bread, and as they were in number, twelve, so He would that there should be twelve baskets, giving each one for that which they had offered to Him, like the widow, who liberally gave a little meal to the prophet Elias, which multiplied miraculously for many days after. (22)   Hence, also, we may gather, how liberally Almighty God recompenses those who give alms, and all those who offer anything for His holy service, returning them a great deal more than what they gave Him, because, to give to God, is not to lose, but to win, and is as the Wise man says, " to put to interest, since the giver receives a hundred for one." (23)

Hence, I will likewise gather, how bountiful Almighty God will be in the next life, since He is so liberal in this: He will doubtless give, as He Himself says, " a good measure, pressed down and running over," (24) and which infinitely exceed all whatsoever we have done for Him here.

Colloquy.—O infinite God, wherewith shall we repay Thee for so much which Thou hast done in our behalfs ? I desire to give Thee a measure, on every

(22) 3 Reg. xvii. 16.　　(23) Prov. xix. 17.　　(24) Luc. vi. 38.

part perfectly heaped up with holy works, pressed together by strict penance, running over with fervent
affections, accomplishing more than Thou commandest
me, performing also what Thou dost counsel me; and
since by Thy grace Thou hast infused into me this desire, grant me also strength to fulfil it.   Amen.

2. Lastly, I will contemplate the *joy and admiration* of
the people, seeing and beholding so great a miracle, which
was so great that they fully resolved to make Jesus Christ
their king, holding themselves highly honoured, to serve so
powerful, and so liberal a Lord.   But our Blessed Redeemer, understanding their thoughts, forthwith fled, and
retired into the most hidden parts of the desert, so to
frustrate their determination, because He sought not
honours, nor temporal dignities, teaching me by His example not to seek after temporal rewards at the hands of
men, for my good works, nor to aspire after dignities, but
as much as may be on my part, to fly from them, and to
shun and avoid the occasions of them.

Colloquy.—O eternal king, who so abhorrest temporal
sovereignty, as Thy kingdom was not of this wretched
world, give me grace, that I may likewise tread under my feet all temporal greatness, contenting myself with those that are eternal.   Amen.

MEDITATION XVIII.

ON OUR LORD'S MIRACLE OF APPEASING THE TEMPEST AT SEA.

After the miracles of the loaves succeeded another
miracle exceedingly famous, in appeasing the tempest at
sea, although He had before wrought another like it, on
which this meditation shall be made, because it will facilitate very much that which follows.

POINT I.

Christ Jesus our Lord having preached to a multitude of people, it growing late He entered into a ship, and commanded His disciples to put from the shore, and began to sleep at the stern of the ship upon a pillow, and at the same time there suddenly arose "a great tempest," and "the waves beat into the ship," (1) and filled it with water, so that it was in danger of foundering.

1. Concerning the sleep of Christ our Lord, I will consider three circumstances which concurred in it.

i. This happened to Him *after great and laborious occupations*, to show that He was *man*, and stood in need of this repose.

ii. That He took it by snatches, and for this reason did not lay Himself down to sleep, like Jonas, in the bottom of the ship, but at the stern, where they might find Him, and easily awake Him.

iii. That although His body slept, *His spirit watched*, knowing all that passed, as if He had been awake. I ought always to sleep with these three conditions, taking care that it be not for ease or idleness, but truly constrained by necessity, with moderation and modesty, and if it were possible to intermingle it with good thoughts, so that I may say with the Psalmist:—The "night shall be my light in my pleasures," (2) and although "I sleep," "my heart watches." (3)

2. Then will I ponder the *mystery of this sleep*, how Christ our Lord, in the ship of His Church, and in every soul seems sometimes to sleep and to neglect it, suffering such a number of tempests, persecutions, and temptations to arise, that the ship is upon the point of being

---

(1) Marc. iv. 37.　Mat. viii. 24.　　(2) Ps. cxxxviii.
(3) Cant. v. 2.

cast away, because the waves do not only beat on the outside, but also, as St. Mark says, they "beat into," and fill the "ship," (4) with interior waves of sadness, fears, scruples, and many other tribulations; but notwithstanding, we must not think that Almighty God is out of the bark, nor that He has ceased to regard what passes in the world, and especially the perils and dangers of His elect. For this cause it was that David said:—"I am with him in tribulation, I will deliver him, and I will glorify him." (5) And again, "He shall neither slumber nor sleep that keepeth Israel." (6)

Colloquy.—O most sweet Saviour, who like a ship was tossed and turmoiled in the sea of this world, with the terrible waves of tempests and labours, the bitter waters of sorrow and fear entering into Thy blessed soul—strengthen me by the example which Thou hast given me, that I may not be drowned with the interior or exterior tribulations which assault me. Amen.

3. Lastly, I will ponder how Jesus Christ our Lord permits *storms*, as has been seen, to prove our faith, to confirm our confidence, to ground us in humility, to purge us from vices, and to provoke us to the exercise of prayer and other virtues. For this reason the proverb says, that those learn to pray who expose themselves to the peril of the sea, and the waves of tribulation entering into the soul, commonly drive away the waves of vices, for humility entering, the wind of pride is driven forth, and anguish entering, sloth is expelled.

Colloquy.—O most wise and skilful pilot, govern as Thou wilt the ship of my soul, only depart not

(4) 2 Cor. vii. 5. Marc. iv. 37.
(5) Ps. xc. 15.   (6) Ps. cxx. 4.

from it, because, if Thou art present, although I may be greatly tossed, I shall not be drowned, but be more confident; waves of tribulation lifting me up to the sovereign exercise of all virtues.   Amen.

POINT II.

The disciples came to Christ our Lord, and awoke Him, saying :—" Lord, save us, we perish."   He said to them : —" Why are you fearful, O ye of little faith?" "have you not faith yet?" (7)

1. Two things are to be considered here,—one on the part of *the disciples*, who in this extremity *had recourse to the only remedy* for all tribulations, which is God Himself, by the means of prayer. Some of them in short, but efficacious words, alleging their peril and necessity, said:—" Lord, save us, we perish."   Others in a more pathetic kind, said to Him:—" Master, doth it not concern Thee that we perish?"(8)   As much as to say, " It concerns Thee to take care of us, because Thou art our Master, in Thee we put our trust, how then dost Thou leave us in such danger?" Imitating these disciples, I will have recourse to Christ our Lord, with these two prayers, saying :—

Colloquy.—" Lord, save me, I perish."   O my Lord and master, to Thee it belongs to deliver my soul, because she is more Thine than mine.   I am Thy disciple, and live under Thy protection.   " I am Thine, save Thou me."(9) "Arise, why sleepest Thou, O Lord? arise, and cast us not off to the end.   Why turnest Thou Thy face away, and forgettest our want and our troubles ?"

2. On the part of *Christ our Lord* we are to consider how suddenly He awoke, showing the singular care He

---

(7) Marc. iii. 39.   Mat. viii. 25.   Marc. iv. 40.   (8) Marc. iv. 38.
(9) Ps. cxviii. 94, et xliii. 23.

had to succour His disciples, reprehending them for the little faith and confidence they had in His omnipotence, and for this reason He said to them:—"Why are you fearful, O ye of little faith?" As if He had said, "Although if you weigh your peril and your own resources, you have reason to fear, yet if you consider that you are in my company, you have no occasion to fear, putting your trust in me."

Colloquy.—O my sweet Saviour, I confess, that beholding Thee I have no reason to fear or doubt, either of Thy knowledge or will to succour me, because Thou art infinitely mighty, wise, and good. Into Thy hands therefore I commend myself with my whole heart, and in proportion as my tribulation increases, so much greater my confidence in Thee, that Thou mayst manifest Thy Almighty power in me. Amen.

POINT III.

Immediately Christ our Lord commanded the winds and sea, saying:—" Peace, be still," and at the selfsame instant "the *wind ceased,*" and the sea on a sudden "became calm." (10)

1. I will contemplate the *omnipotency* of Christ Jesus our Lord, and the power which He has over all creatures, and their punctual obedience to whatsoever He commands, rejoicing because it is an honour to my Redeemer, and humbling myself for my little obedience and manifest rebellion.—These two words are not void of great mystery, —" Peace, be still," as the works of Almighty God are most perfect, so that when He will show His Almighty power, He gives command not only to be silent and still, but what is more, to *be mute,* healing the root of trouble and causing perfect peace.

(10) Marc. iv. 39

2. And so, when I see myself troubled with divers thoughts or passions, I am to beseech our Lord to command them not only to be still for a time, but also to be dumb, so that they may never trouble me more in that in which they troubled me before. And if it be expedient for me, He will *so bring it to pass*, that with great admiration of that which I shall feel within myself, I will say with those who were in the ship:—" Who is this that both winds and seas obey Him?" (11)

Colloquy.—O Almighty Saviour, my heart is in a turbulent sea, tossed with many thousands of waves, and much troubled with the winds of contrary passions,(12) command them to cease, and to be calm, saying, " Peace, be still;" because Thy word is Almighty, they will obey Thee immediately.

MEDITATION XIX.

ON CHRIST'S MIRACLE OF WALKING UPON THE WATER, PERFORMED WHEN HE WAS SUPPOSED TO BE A SPIRIT.

In this meditation, by way of instruction, I will put down certain admonitions, by which one may discern the true spirit of Jesus Christ, and the spirit of true fervour from a phantasm, with the effects which Almighty God works in souls when He visits them in prayer with His sweet presence.

POINT I.

" Jesus obliged His disciples to go up into the boat, and to go before Him over the water," whilst " He went up into a mountain alone to pray," where He remained until the fourth watch of the night, (1) when by and by there

(11) Marc. iv. 40.   (12) Is. lvii. 20.   (1) Mat. xiv. 22, 23.

arose a great tempest, which beat and tossed the little bark.

1. First, I will consider the *love which Christ our Lord* had for prayer, choosing for this purpose solitary places, and the silent time of the night, and leaving the company of His disciples, prolonging His prayer almost until morning with great fervour, as we have said in the introduction to this third part. Whence I will gather with what solicitude I am to pray for my own salvation, since Jesus Christ prayed so much for the salvation of others.

2. I will ponder how *loath the apostles were to leave their Master*, for, as St. Mark says, " He obliged them," for their desire was to go up with Him into the mountain, and al ways to be in His blessed company, and loath to venture without Him upon the perils of the sea. Nevertheless, the virtue of obedience prevailed because God ought to be obeyed in all things, even if He should expose us to imminent peril, and for the same reason we should leave the retirement of prayer, this is, to " leave God for God."

3. I will ponder the *mystery of the tempest*, which the ship of the Blessed apostles suffered. For the other time when the tempest arose, Christ was in the ship, but yet asleep. This time He was absent, the better to try the faith of His disciples, seeing themselves so far from their Master, to signify that Christ our Lord is sometimes wont to absent Himself from those that are His, by withdrawing the sensible succour of His grace, and leaving them in great tribulations to prove their loyalty, giving by this means daily new proofs of them, for the immeasurable good which arises from them.

POINT II.

Christ Jesus our Lord, notwithstanding He was in the mountain, and that it was night, yet saw how His disciples laboured in rowing (for the wind was against them) and taking compassion on them, He came to them, walking on the sea; and the disciples seeing Him, were troubled, saying:—"It is an apparition;" and they cried out for fear." (2)

1. And here is to be considered first, that the disciples did not lose their courage in this tempest, and stood not idle, nor leaning upon their elbows, but *laboured, rowing painfully* against the wind and blustering tempests, to save their bark and to bring her to harbour; from which I am to learn, that in tribulations and temptations I am not to lose courage or to be idle, leaving my remedy wholly to God, but to do on my part all that I can, although it be with pain and travail, like him that rows alone, exercising the works of prayer and penance to the best of my power, that God may come to succour me.

2. I will ponder the *charity of Christ* our Lord, for although He seemed to be absent, yet He did not forget those that are His, but stood beholding their labour and diligence, delighted on the one side to see their endeavours, and on the other side taking compassion at seeing them suffer.

Colloquy.—O my soul, although thou see thyself in the sea and night of this wretched world, full of obscurity, and art tossed with temptations, have great confidence, since thy Saviour is above in the mountain of the heavens, entreating and praying His eternal Father for thee,(3) and beholding from His throne all thy labours, having compassion on them, and assisting thee as He did St. Stephen with His infinite mercy, that thou mayest obtain an eternal crown.

3. Consider the *reasons why* Christ our Lord *came walking* upon the water.

(2) Marc. vi. 48. Mat. xiv. 26.
(3) Rom. viii. 26. 1 Joan. ii. 1.

i. The first was, to show us His *almighty power*, demonstrating the sovereignty which He has over the waters of the sea, and over the tribulations and tempests of the world, who, as superior over them all, holds them underneath His feet; and who, if He would, could have exempted Himself from them, but in fact would not: and consequently, if in the time of His Passion, He was, as it were, overwhelmed by the waves, (4) and borne to the bottom of the vessel, it was not from weakness, but from mere charity, and through a desire to suffer for our good; nevertheless, He suffered in such a manner that He immediately rose again from the depth of tribulations, as superior and conqueror of them all.

ii. Another reason was, to manifest the *virtue of that prayer*, which He had made on the mountain; whence the just arise with such strength, that they fear no tempests, nor are they overwhelmed by them, but with a courageous mind in the virtue of God, pass through them, and surmount them. And when those within the bark fear, those fear nothing who are in the midst of the sea, because prayer and confidence in Almighty God gives them greater assurance than all human helps give those that trust in them. And although they are in the midst of innumerable tempests, and within the belly of the whale, as Jonas was,(5) yet they obtain by prayer that the whale of tribulation cannot hurt them, but, on the contrary, brings them to the port with great security.

Colloquy.—O sweet Jesus, grant that I may ascend with Thee into the mountain of prayer, lifting up myself above myself: that in the virtue of prayer, Thy grace may lift me up above the waters of temptation and tribulation, without being sunk by them. Amen.

4. Ponder the foolish fear of the disciples, when they

(4) Ps. lxviii. 1. (5) Jonas ii. 2.

saw Christ our Lord coming towards them upon the waters, thinking Him to be an apparition, where those who did not cry for the fury of the tempest, cried out for fear of their own imagination; whence we may observe our great feebleness and misery, who oftentimes by the divine virtue surmount and vanquish extreme perils and difficulties, and a little after with great cowardice and pusillanimity, suffer ourselves to be frightened by the foot of a fly; by which we may see that our fortitude in great dangers is not our own, since it abandons us upon the least occasion.

POINT III.

With regard to this saying of the apostles, we have to consider *three sorts of persons*, who treat with Jesus Christ our Lord, and have different feelings towards Him, and what proceeds from Him.

1. Some hold what indeed is a *fancy* and an imaginary shadow, to be truly Christ, their fond fancies or imaginations for true revelations, and their vicious passions for virtues, esteeming their anger, zeal, and their carnal love, spiritual. These for the most part, are proud and presumptuous persons, who trust overmuch to their own judgment. And for this reason Satan sometimes transforms himself into an angel of light,(6) making it appear that his words are very light, though indeed they are very darkness. Sometimes their own judgment performs the office of the Devil, persuading them that all the interior instincts which they feel, assuredly proceed from the Holy Ghost, while they are instincts of their own carnal, worldly, proud, and blinded spirit; and sometimes their own imagination, by means of the weakness of their brain, abuses and deceives them, drawing such lively figures of

(6) 2 Cor. xi. 14.

Jesus Christ, that they seem to be even Christ Himself, losing themselves with this feigned favour, deeming that He speaks to them those very words which a little before they themselves had imagined, or took pleasure in hearing, and in short, even the most spiritual, who are accustomed to feel the inspirations of Almighty God, sometimes think that their own discourses come from God, as it happened to the prophet Nathan, as St. Gregory well observed, (7) for even so they deceive themselves in qualifying these spiritual motions which pass in others, easily believing what is said to them, and guiding themselves by exterior appearances; hence it comes that they approve that which is but a shadow, and walk by that " way" of which the Holy Ghost says that it " seemeth good," but " leadeth to death" (8) and to perdition.

2. Others, by another extremity, hold for a . shadow that which is truly *Jesus Christ*, they think virtue a passion, and good inspiration the imagination of their own spirit; these are ordinarily pusillanimous, scrupulous, and ignorant persons, who fear to cry out where there is no cause, through their own imbecility, or through their timorous and melancholy disposition. And sometimes this happens to tried and approved persons, during the time of violent tempests and temptations, as here it happened to the apostles, our Lord permitting these clouds and doubts, (whether that which they see and feel be God or a ghost,) to exercise, prove, and augment their virtue and humility, for then the temptation is most terrible, when I imagine that to be a new deceit, which God sends to succour me. And in the like manner some deceive themselves in judging the spirits of other men, who being very incredulous, and but little experienced, blaspheme whatever

(7) lib. ii. dial. c. 21. et hom. ii. in Ezech.   (8) Prov. xiv. 12.

they themselves do not understand, censuring all visions, revelations, and wonderful works, as so many fantastical ghosts and imaginations, as if Almighty God did not even at this day sometimes sweetly communicate Himself to us, as He did to the saints in former ages. These two extremities are extremely dangerous and pernicious, because it is no less an evil to take Jesus Christ for a shadow or fancy, than a shadow or fancy for Jesus Christ, (9) to leave that which is God, and to mistake it for a devil, than to admit that which is a devil and to deem it God; and even no less perilous is it to follow the motions of the flesh, imagining them to proceed from the Holy Spirit, than to extinguish the inspirations of the same "spirit," (10) imagining them to be motions of the flesh.

3. A third sort of persons *observe* the medium, following the counsel of St. John, who said:—"Believe not every spirit," but "try *the spirits* if they be of God," (11) and by like examination, seconded by the mercy of our Lord, they judge everything for what it is, discerning assuredly that which is Christ from that which is a fantasy or a shadow, as well as in their own affairs, as in those of others, which they examine; and for this end our Lord is accustomed to communicate to them that gift which St. Paul calls the grace to discern " spirits," (12) which grace He especially imparts to the rulers of His Church, whom for this reason we call " triers" (13) or examiners of the metals of spirits, to whom those of lesser experience ought to have recourse, that they may not be deceived, taking counterfeit gold for good, or fine for false. This celestial light all of us ought to crave of Jesus Christ, to the end that we err not, saying:—

<hr>

(9) S. Greg. hom. v. in Ezech.   (10) 1 Thess. v. 19.
(11) 1 Joan. iv.   (12) 1 Cor. xii. 10.   (13) Jerom. vi. 27.

Colloquy.—O heavenly master, the true " weigher of spirits,"(14) suffer not that I do Thee this injury, to call that a shadow or ghost, which is Almighty God : or again, that God, which is but a shadow ; illuminate me with Thy divine light, that I may discern between the one and the other, and assist me with Thy grace, that I may always follow the instincts and motions of the good spirit, and abhor the motions of the bad.   Amen.

POINT IV.

Christ our Lord hearing the cries of His disciples, immediately " spoke to them, saying, Be of good heart, it is I, fear ye not." (15)

1. Hence I should ponder first the *clemency* of Jesus Christ our Lord, in so soon comforting His afflicted disciples, and manifesting Himself by uttering three only words, by which they were freed from their false apprehension.   For it is the property of Christ's spirit to move and persuade us to true confidence, and to take away false fears, imprinting such effects on the soul, that by them she understands the truth of the words, " Ego sum," " It is I," for it would not be enough to say, " It is I," if He did not speak to them with His own voice, and that the words were understood, or giving them sufficient evidence whose it was.   Where I will enter into consideration of that which passes in our hearts, when Jesus Christ our Lord visits them, and speaks to them, giving them to understand, by certain interior signs, who it is that speaks to them; for, as every man has a certain tone of voice, or manner of speaking, by which those who converse with him, distinguish him from others, so the saints who frequently hold discourse and conversation with Jesus Christ, affirm that He uses such a particular manner of speaking

(14) Prov. xvi. 2.   (15) Mat. xiv. 27.

to the heart, with such sweetness, peace, and plenitude of virtues, which represent His divinity, that He easily gives them to understand that it is the good spirit which speaks, because the evil spirit cannot speak nor discourse with such odour and sweetness; (16) this our Lord made to appear by the omnipotence of His word, for in one moment He appeases the heart of the fearful with confidence, changes his heaviness into joyfulness, his troubles into calmness, his hardness into softness, his dryness into devotion, and for his afflictions from temptations of the flesh, of pride, and of covetousness, giving him in exchange chastity, humility, liberality, with affections contrary to his afflictions, so that in the time of storms and tempests, as the spirit of the Devil imprints pusillanimity, dejection, diffidence, and despair, so the spirit of Christ imprints magnanimity, courage, confidence in God, and stability in His service. On the contrary, in time of prosperity and of good weather, temporal or spiritual, the Devil imprints .pride, vanity, presumption, self-confidence, self-complacence, opinion of our own sufficiency, and of our own judgment, and contempt of others. But the spirit of Christ imprints humility, contempt, diffidence of himself, a holy fear lest we fall any more, subjection to God, and to all others for the love of God.

2. As the same man says the same word in a different manner, when he means to show his anger, to make us afraid, and when he means to show his courtesy, to please us, so Christ our Lord, with one and the same words, " It is I," *works contrary effects* on different persons, for by this word He drove fear away from His disciples, and with the same words He so frightened those who came to take Him in the garden, that He made them fall " back-

(16) S. Greg. lib. iv. dial. c. 48.; S. Aug. l. vi. conf. se. 13. de Sancta Monica. Id dicit S. Diadochus, l. de Perfect. c. 30.

wards" flat on "the ground," (17) as we shall see in the fourth part. And in the same manner He gives interior testimony of His presence, both to sinners and to the just, —to sinners terrifying them with reprehensions, threats, and reproaches, to enforce them to come out of sin,—but comforting the just with tender affections of joy and spiritual peace, and thus to encourage them in His service, and if at the first He enters with something of fear, because of the reverence which is due to Him, presently He causes peace, with great joy and security of conscience. (18)

3. Pondering these things, I will *beseech* Jesus Christ our Lord to visit me, and to speak to my heart, that I may know Him, so that I may reverence, love, serve, and put my confidence in Him.

Colloquy.— O Almighty God, who art He, who Thou art, say to my soul, " It is I," manifesting Thy most sweet presence to me, so that with Thy word all my frivolous fears may be appeased, and my fervent desires may be enkindled, putting them in execution to Thy honour and glory. Amen.

POINT V.

St. Peter hearing the words of Christ our Lord, said:— ". Lord, if it be Thou, bid me to come to Thee upon the waters." (19)

In these words five properties of fervent charity are laid open to us, by which true fervour is distinguished from that which is false.

i. The first is, *to have a great perception and esteem of Christ our Lord,* and of the excellencies which these words contain, " It is I," which St. Peter penetrated with divine

<hr>

(17) Joan. xviii. 6.
(18) S. Tho. 3. p. q. xxx. a. 3. ad 3. S. Ign. in reg. de hoc.
(19) Mat. xiv. 28.

illustration, relying on what He said affirmatively, without hesitation:—"Lord, since Thou art who Thou art, wisdom and power itself, bounty and charity itself, show Thyself to be such in my behalf, giving me proof of what Thou art."

ii. The second property is, to have a great *desire to be often commanded* by Almighty God, that I may discover the love which I bear to Him, saying,—If it be Thou, "command me," I am Thy vassal, ready to obey Thee, and shall hold it for a favour that Thou vouchsafe to command me; command therefore what it shall please Thee, behold me ready to obey Thee.

iii. The third is, that one have a cordial desire *to be united with his beloved*, esteeming each little delay very long, wishing and desiring to redouble his paces to approach to Him. And for this reason St. Peter said:—"If it be Thou, bid me come to Thee upon the waters." He spoke not this for vain-glory, or to demand a miracle, but as transported with a fervent desire to be united to his Master; where I am to reflect, that when St. Peter saw in his ship the miracle of the fishes, he desired to withdraw from Jesus Christ, and therefore said to Him :—"Depart from me, O Lord, because I am a sinful man;" (20) but now, seeing Him to walk upon the waters, he desired to draw near to Him, and yet both these spirits were good. The first proceeded from humility, by casting his eyes upon what he was, and seeing *himself* a great sinner; the second from love, by casting his eyes upon *what Christ was*, and upon His almighty power, both which affections I should practise at proper times, because the second assures the first, and the first perfects the second.

iv. The fourth property is, to *expose ourselves confidently* to those things which surpass our forces, although they

(20) Luc. v. 8.

seem impossible to our feeble nature; for such an one measures not his desires with his own might, but with the power of Almighty God. For this cause it was that St. Peter offered to throw himself into the tempestuous sea, believing that in the power of his Master he should walk upon the waters as He walked, without being drowned in them; for many waters of tribulation cannot drown charity, as it is written in the book of Canticles. (21)

(v.) In fine, although charity be fervent, yet it is neither rash nor headstrong, but staid and prudent, and presumes to do no more than it is able to do, without permission, command, and inspiration from God, in whom it trusts, not otherwise than when St. Peter threw not himself into the sea, until Jesus Christ had first commanded him.

Colloquy.—O most sweet master, lead me into the cellar of Thy most precious " wine," and order in me Thy charity with the self same qualities which Thou conferredst (22) on this holy apostle, to the end that fervour do not precipitate me by presumption, nor held me back by too great fear.   Amen.

POINT VI.

Christ answered, " Come: and Peter, going down out of the boat, walked upon the water to come to Jesus."(23)

1. Christ our Lord, who at other times reprehended the fervour of S. Peter, at this time *took pleasure in it*, and condescended to his request, because it proceeded from pure love, and from a spirit of resignation and great confidence, not in his own strength, but in that of Jesus Christ; so when petitions are made after this manner, and proceed from the Holy Ghost, our Lord admits them, for it is His disposition to " do the will of them that fear Him,"(24) and to grant the petitions of them that love Him, when they

(21) Cant. viii. 7.   (22) Cant. ii. 4.
(23) Mat. xiv. 24.   (24) Ps. cxliv. 19.

serve as a proof and sign of their love.   On the contrary,
when S. Peter said, on the night of the Passion, that he
was ready to go to prison and to die with Him, our Lord
answered not "come," because He knew that his offer
proceeded from pride and presumption, with some contempt of his companions, prefering himself before them,
which he did not do here.   Where I will learn how to
ask anything of our Blessed Lord, if I wish that He
should grant me my petition.

2. He likewise *acceded to this petition*, that His disciples
might see by experience, with what great reason He had
said to them, " Fear not, it is I;" for He was so powerful,
that with one only little word, "come," He could do a
thing so prodigious, as to make a man walk on the waters
as if he had been on the firm land; whence they elevated
their spirits to believe, and trust that He was likewise as
powerful to make them walk upon basilisks and serpents,
and to tread under foot lions and dragons, without receiving any manner of injury; as also that they might not
fear the waves of the sea of this world, but that they
might walk upon them, not only without sinking, but even
without so much as wetting, unless it be the soles of their
feet—with some light offences, or involuntary imperfections.

Colloquy.—O powerful Jesus, my soul desires to
go after Thee, by following Thy life, and to go to
Thee to enjoy Thy glory.   Say to her, O Lord, this
word, " Come," for in virtue of this word all will be
most easy to her, for nothing at all is impossible to
Thee.   Amen.

3. S. Peter, hearing this word of Christ our Lord, without delay or fear, *leaped out of the boat*, and began to walk
towards the place where Jesus was, with a desire to

approach Him: to show to us the promptitude and confidence which we ought to have, to execute the will of Jesus Christ, and to accomplish the purposes and resolutions which once we have made in His holy service, not fearing to expose ourselves to all sorts of perils, in virtue of His word, since we do all this in "our Lord," who can "strengthen us."(25)

POINT VII.

S. Peter, "seeing the wind stormy, was afraid, and cried out, saying, Lord save me; and immediately Jesus stretched forth His hand, took hold of him and said to him: O thou of little faith, why didst thou doubt? And when they were come up into the boat, the wind ceased," (26) and the bark arrived at the haven.

1. Christ our Lord *permitted this fear in S. Peter*, that he might not be proud for the time to come, and that he might acknowledge that he had not as yet a perfect faith, seeing he, who was so hardy as to throw himself into the stormy and roaring sea, was afterwards afraid of a blast of wind: this happened to him because he turned away his eyes from Jesus Christ, to look in the direction of the wind, whereupon his faith and confidence failing him, his footing also failed him, and he began to sink into the water.

Colloquy.—O Almighty God, assist, I beseech Thee, my feeble faith, and suffer not that I turn my eyes from Thee in my tribulations, for fear I should sink and be drowned in them. Amen.

2. I will think that whosoever for obedience to Jesus Christ, and faith in His word, shall expose himself to danger, yet shall not perish, but calling upon Him, *He*

(25) Phil. iv. 13.   (26) Mat. xiv. 30, 31, 32.

will stretch forth to him His holy hand, to draw him out and to deliver him from them: if I cast myself into them of my own self-will, or through boasting and vain-glory, Almighty God will withdraw His hand from me, in punishment of my folly and presumption, and permit me to perish with the Machabean priests, who, for the like vainglorious end, entered into battle unadvisedly. (27)

3. Jesus Christ entering into the ship, "*the wind ceased;*" to signify that temptations, which arise in time of His absence, cease by His presence; and with His aid, the bark forthwith, and with good success, arrives at the land of the living, and at the haven of everlasting salvation.

4. Finally, in all this discourse Christ our Lord discovers *the rule which He observes when He calls us to Religion*, or to some important and weighty enterprise; for at the beginning He facilitates our labours, to make us fearlessly plunge ourselves more boldly into them; but soon after he suffers to arise great storms and dangers, yet not to forsake us, but to perfect us in virtues. And lastly, He gives to us a complete peace, with greater joy, by means of the new experiences of the great things we are able to do by the help of His grace, for so He says by the prophet, " I will deceive her by the milk of her consolations, and will allure her and lead her into the wilderness," and after I will place her in the valley of tribulation, where she shall recover new hopes, and sing joyfully, " according to the days of her youth."(28)

Colloquy.—O my dear and best beloved, deceive me, I beseech Thee, with this holy deceit, to deliver me from the deceits of this deceitful world : that afterwards I may go to enjoy eternal repose in heaven. Amen.

(27) 1 Mac. v. 67.　　　　　(28) Osee ii. 14.

MEDITATION XX.

ON THE WORTHY CONFESSION MADE BY ST. PETER OF THE DIVINITY OF CHRIST OUR LORD.

POINT I.

Jesus Christ demanded of His disciples, saying, " *Whom do men say that the Son of Man is ?*"(1)

1. Christ our Lord, as St. Luke quotes, *had first prayed alone,* to give us to understand that it was not from curiosity, but from necessity; not for His profit, but for ours; and to teach us that, in virtue of His prayer, He gave to St. Peter the light which he declared in his answer.   And if I desire the like light, I must obtain by prayer, according to the saying of the apostle:—" If any of you want wisdom, let him ask of God, who giveth to all men abundantly,' (2) so that they ask it with faith and without hesitation.

2. Christ our Lord made this prayer to take an occasion to *give to His disciples a more clear understanding* whence He was, on which, as the same Lord Himself says, depends the seed of our salvation ;(3) as also to teach us the manner how to make our own profit of the speeches of men; for, to desire to know the opinion which they have of us, to ground on it the security of our life, were a very great and evident error, since, as St. Paul says, " He that judgeth is the Lord" God.(4)   Yet it is not amiss for us to inquire and know, to the end that hearing their opinions, we may correct the evils which are in us, or else shun them in such a manner that they may not attribute them to us with truth; and, if they speak good of us, we may endeavour to attain

(1) Mat. xvi. 13.   Marc. viii. 27.   Luc. ix. 18.
(2) Jac. i. 5.   (3) Joan. xvii. 3.   (4) 1 Cor. iv. 4.

it if we be without it, or to perfect it, if already we have it, and thus we may convert to our own profit the opinions of men.

3. I will meditate on the *humility* which Christ showed on this occasion, for He commonly called Himself "the *Son of Man*," which is a name common to all men, how vile and contemptible they may be, suppressing other names much more glorious with which He might have qualified Himself, teaching us by this example to humble ourselves, and always to take the meanest and least accounted titles that we might assume, according to our state; because, "he that exalteth himself shall be humbled." For thus Christ our Lord, calling Himself "the Son of Man," was immediately, by revelation from His Father, called by St. Peter "the Son of the living God."

Colloquy.—O Son of the living God, give me the same humility which Thou didst shew, calling Thyself "the Son of Man," embracing the baseness of the children of men, that by this humiliation, I may come to the dignity of the sons of God, enjoying that glory which they enjoy. Amen.

POINT II.

The apostles answered, "Some say that thou art John the Bapist, and others Elias, and others Jeremias, or one of the prophets."(5)

1. In this we may observe, the *prudence of the apostles* in this answer; for knowing that the scribes and Pharisees said of Jesus Christ, that He was a Samaritan, a glutton, a drunkard, and a friend of publicans, with other injurious imputations, yet they made no mention of them, but only of that which made for the honour of their master: teaching us by this example, that the just and prudent

(5) Mat. xvi. 14.

ought not to relate to others the sayings of their enemies, which commonly are false, and serve to no other purpose than to irritate them to anger and indignation against them, so that it is prudently done to silence them, and not to relate trifles, which choke and stifle brotherly charity. For this reason also, perhaps it was, that Christ our Lord inquired not what the scribes and Pharisees said of the Son of Man, but what men said and thought of Him,—that is to say, the common sort and multitude of " people."

2. We are to ponder, that it is the *property of men*, left to their own miserable nature, *to err in the knowledge of God*, and of Jesus Christ.   Either by reason of their short understanding, or that their passion blinds the light of their reason, or through the deception of the Devil, who labours to take from them this perfect knowledge, to keep them captives under his tyranny, with innumerable sins; according to that which the prophet says, " Therefore is my people led away captive, because they have not knowledge;"(6) that is to say, because they had not the true faith and knowledge of Almighty God, and of the things appertaining to His holy service.   Hence I will draw an inward compassion for all infidels, and ignorant men who err in this point, of whom St. Paul says, " some have not the knowledge of God,"(7) of whom whosoever is ignorant,(8) He will be ignorant of them, because He will not know them to be His, nor will acknowledge them to everlasting life.

Colloquy.—O God of all knowledge, have compassion on our ignorance, and accomplish the promise which Thou hast made, filling the earth " with the knowledge of the Lord."   Amen.(9)

(6) Is. v. 13.   (7) 1 Cor. xv. 34.
(8) 1 Reg. iii. 7.   (9) Is. xi. 9.

3. The most part of men, when they err in things concerning God our Lord, and Jesus Christ, do so in one of these ways:—

i. Some err in *taking from Him that which belongs to Him*, measuring the greatness of Almighty God with the shortness and shallowness of their own understanding, or by their weak judgment, subject to passion: and thus the lower sort of the people denied the dignity of Jesus Christ, affirming that He was a mere man, as was the Baptist, or Elias; others, more passionate, said, that He wanted wit, and called Him fool; (10) others sanctity, and called Him Samaritan ;—others might err, calumniating his miracles; —and others His wisdom, blaming His works like those who said, " Could not He have contrived that Lazarus had not died?" And to this day Christ our Lord endures these injuries of infidels, heretics, and ignorant men: which ought to comfort me in all my injuries, when to mortify me they would deprive me of the honour due to me.

ii. Some Christians, through their evil and wicked conceits, show *by their works* that they hold a *false opinion* of God our Lord, and of Jesus Christ, and practically err in their own knowledge, saying to themselves—"A God severe, cruel, and implacable, who seeks to reap where He has not sowed," as the slothful servant said. (11) Or otherwise, a God so exceeding merciful as to dissemble all things, although they live as they list: for as their own malice lies to them and seduces them, forming to themselves, as St. Bernard says, (12) an idol so far from the truth which is in God, that this is not an imagination or conception of the true God, but of a false Deity and an idol, which can do nothing, and is not at all in the world: because there is not found in the world, (13) a God so cruel, forgetful,

(10) Joan. x. 20.   (11) Luc. xix. 21.

(12) Serm. xxxiii. in Cant.   (13) 1 Cor. viii. 6.

inexorable, accepter of persons, dissembler of sins, &c., and such a one as they imagine.

iii. Moreover, some others also, even spiritual persons, because they are but men, err actually in the knowledge of God, and of the spirit of Christ our Lord, taking from Him what belongs to Him, imagining *a short or limited Christ*, more after the measure of their short understanding. Some think that the spirit of Jesus Christ, is only the spirit of the Baptist, rigorous, austere, and of strict penance.—Others, that it is only the spirit of Elias, zealous and terrible against sins, and all sinners.—Others, that it is only the spirit of Jeremias compassive, and bewailing the sins and miseries of the world.—Others, that it is only the spirit of the prophets, who retire into solitude, or of those who preached to the people, or of those who wrought wonders and miracles, &c.

All these come a great deal short, and err egregiously, so shortening and limiting the spirit of Christ, which, as the Wise man says,(14) is "one and manifold," and embraces great variety of spirits, and various ways of proceeding in the service of God; yet all grounded in the same spirit of love and charity, and all tending to the same end, which is the glory of Almighty God.

4. Hence I will gather, that *it is a great abuse* for me to limit Jesus Christ and His divine Spirit according to that spirit which is in me, wishing that every one should take the same way: for this is to judge with restriction or limit of the perfection of Almighty God, and of the redemption of Jesus Christ, who to some is as the Baptist, —to others as Elias, and to others as Jeremias,—to some He is solitary and contemplative, to others most familiar and active.

Colloquy.—O everlasting Wisdom, in whom are
(14) Sap. vii. 27.

united all the spirits of the saints that do Thee service: grant me that spirit, which is most agreeable to
Thee, and to every one of Thine elect, which is most
convenient for them. Purge my understanding from
errors, whereby I may know Thee for such as Thou
'art in truth, and may lodge Thee within my heart, in
the form and figure which Thou deservest. Amen.

POINT III.

" Jesus saith to them, But whom do you say that I am?
Simon Peter answered and said, *Thou art Christ, the Son of
the living God.*" (15)

1. Christ our Lord having heard what men reported of
Him, would also know what His *disciples* thought of
Him, saying to them:—" You who are more than men, on
account of the heavenly doctrine which you have heard,
and the sublimity of life of which you make profession,
whom say *ye* that I am?" This He said, not that He was
ignorant what opinion they held of Him, but to take occasion to quicken and confirm them in the faith of His
divinity, in imitation of which, when Jesus Christ enters
within my heart, I will demand of my soul:—" What
sayest thou of Jesus Christ? What thinkest thou of Him?
What judgest thou of His bounty and mercy, of His wisdom and omnipotence? What supposest thou of His
humility and obedience, and of the virtues which He practised in the abjections which He embraced for thy salvation?" This proposition will I make to my soul, to
excite myself to conceive very highly of Jesus Christ, and
of His virtues, with infinite esteem and appreciation of
them, reprehending myself for my defectiveness in this
behalf.

2. Though this demand was addressed to all, *St. Peter*

(15) Mat. xvi. 15.

alone returned an answer, and this for two reasons.—i. The first, because he was *more fervent* than the others in the love and service of Jesus Christ, being always the most diligent and foremost in whatsoever concerned the honour of his Master. In imitation of him I will endeavour to become most remarkable amongst the good, and be the first to run to the things which belong to His service, although by humility I esteem myself the least of all others in my own eyes, so that without detriment to myself I may become the first in fervour.—ii. The second was, because Almighty God our Lord, seeing him so well prepared to receive His gifts, favoured *him with an extraordinary light*, to know the excellencies of Jesus Christ, and so being , transported by the force of this light, he anticipated the other disciples, and in the name of them all made answer, saying:—" Thou art Christ, the Son of the living God." (16)

Colloquy.—O my soul, prepare thyself with great fervour, to serve thy beloved, who says, " He that hath to him shall be given, and he shall abound." (17) Hold what thou hast received, diligently making thy profit of it, that Almighty God may multiply to thee the gifts of His grace.   Amen.

3. I will reflect on the words of this illustrious and worthy confession, word by word, as they were spoken.

i. The first was:—" Thou art," as much as to say, Thou callest Thyself the Son of Man,—Thou whom men hold to be the Baptist, or one of the prophets,—Thou who art our Master, and hast elected us for Thy disciples,—Thou art He that art, and art essentially being itself, on whom depends all that has any being.

ii. The second word was:—" Thou art Christ," that is

<hr>

(16) Mat. xvi. 16.   (17) Mat. xiii. 12.

to say, Thou art the Messiah promised to the Jews, and the desired of the Gentiles, "Thou art the King of Israel," (18) the King of kings, and Lord of lords: "Thou art a high priest, according to the order of Melchisedech;" (19) Thou art that supreme "prophet," (20) whom all ought to obey; Thou art the "Saint of saints," (21) anointed of our Lord "with the oil of gladness above my fellows." (22) All this the name of Christ contains, which signifies "anointed," and by excellence belongs to our Blessed Saviour, in whom are united the dignities of those who have been anointed, whom we have mentioned above.

iii. The third word was:—"The Son of the living God;" as if he had said, Thou art not a common Christ, as others who are but only men, but Thou art the Son of Almighty God, yet not His adoptive but His natural Son, who because He is living has the most noble power of action amongst the living, which is, to engender the like, for so He engendered Thee a living God like Himself, and by consequence infinite, immense, eternal, omnipotent, wise, and good, yea, Wisdom and Goodness itself.

iv. All this, with much more, St. Peter penetrated by the light of heaven, confessed by mouth when he spoke these words. And although it be true that St. John Baptist, Nathaniel, and others, had made this confession, and said in a manner the selfsame words, yet St. Peter made himself eminent above the others, in pronouncing them with unspeakable fervour, and with wonderful reverence and devotion. I, therefore, will endeavour to pronounce them with the same spirit, rejoicing in the greatness of my Redeemer, beseeching Him to give me a part of the same light which He gave to His apostle, that

<hr>

(18) Joan. i. 49.   (19) Ps. cix. 4.   (20) Deut. xviii. 15.
(21) Dan. ix. 24.   (22) Ps. xliv. 8.

I may pronounce them with such a lively and fervent faith, as may be agreeable and pleasing to Him.

POINT IV.

Jesus answered, " Blessed art thou, Simon Bar Jona, because *flesh and blood* hath not revealed it to thee, but *my Father*, who is in heaven." (23)

1. Here will I ponder how greatly agreeable this illustrious confession of St. Peter was to our Lord, and the manner how He *confirmed, approved*, and exalted this holy apostle.

i. He calls him "*blessed*," because, from this acknowledgement and confession, began his good fortune, and ours also, for this confession is the beginning of everlasting life (24) and of all happiness.

ii. He called him " *Simon*," as much as to say, " obedient," son of Jonas, that is, of "grace," or of Jonah, which is to say, "done;" to signify that by this noble confession he had showed himself obedient to Almighty God, who had revealed it to him; son of grace, and of the Holy Ghost, who inspired it into him, and in virtue of which he should be obedient to the law of grace, and should be filled with the Holy Ghost, with abundant plenty of His divine gifts.

iii. He said that "flesh and blood had not revealed this to him," because, neither this faith, nor the supernatural goods which proceed thence can be understood, nor come by inheritance or gift of earthly parents, nor by the industry or instruction of worldly men, nor by the force of our human nature; for of ourselves we are not sufficient to think or conceive any such like thing, as proceeding from ourselves, but all " our sufficiency is from God." (25)

(23) Mat. xvi. 17.

(24) Joan. xvii. 3.   (25) 2 Cor. iii. 5.

iv. He says, that His "Father who is in heaven," had revealed it to him, by which He assures us, that He is the Son of the living God, whose Father is in heaven, and who revealed these truths of His mere grace for the glory of His Son, and even for the good of us men, who, for this reason, is named " Father of lights,"(26) because, from Him proceed all true illustrations, by which both Himself and Son are known.

Colloquy.—O celestial Father, for the love which Thou barest to Thine Only-begotten Son, vouchsafe, I beseech Thee, to illuminate my soul, to understand that which flesh and blood cannot attain : and since that none can come to Thy Son, unless Thou " draw him," (27) draw me, Lord, with the bonds of love, (28) that I may obey Him as I am bound, so that being a true son of obedience, I may be likewise a son of grace, through the Holy Ghost, which Thou givest to those which are in charity.   Amen.

POINT V.

Then Christ our Lord added, saying, *Thou art Peter*, and upon this rock *will I build my Church*, and the gates of hell shall not prevail against it; and I will give to thee the *keys of the kingdom of heaven*, and whatsoever thou shalt bind upon earth, it shall be bound also in heaven, and whatsoever thou shalt loose in earth, it shall be loosed also in heaven." (29)

1. In this will I ponder, the *glorious promises* which Jesus Christ our Lord made to St. Peter, wherein is to be seen, how well He rewards, even in this life, the services which are done to Him, and the happiness of those who serve Him with fervour, and are the first in things apper-

(26) Jac. i. 17.

(27) Joan. vi. 44.　　　(28) Osee xi. 4.　　　(29) Mat. xvi. 18.

taining to His honour, since, for this cause, this blessed apostle received four especial favours above the rest of his fellow apostles.

i. The first was, to impose upon him a *most glorious name*, saying, " Thou art Peter," as if He said, Thou hast said of me, that I am Christ, the Son of the living God, and I will now fulfil my word, which I have said to thee, that "thou shalt be called Cephas," (30) or Peter, and so henceforth I will that thou be called, and be, " Peter." And like as the names, which Jesus Christ imposed, are not empty or vain, but full of the reality which they signify; so with this name, He made this apostle partaker of the virtues, which the name of Peter signifies, derived from Petra, or "rock," which is " Christ," (31) making him like Himself, because he was to be the fundamental Rock of the holy Church, in fortitude and constancy, and in the other virtues of this strong and precious stone.

ii. He also adds the second excellence, saying, " *upon this Rock I will build my Church*," (32) as if he had said, " I, who by excellence, am that wise man, who built his house upon a rock, to the end, that neither 'rain,' nor ' winds,' nor ' floods,' (33) might overthrow it, I will build my universal Church upon myself, who am the fundamental stone, and the foundation of all foundations: and I will likewise build it on thee, as on a firm Rock, giving thee the dignity of universal head over all the faithful, who shall rely upon thee, and upon thy confession and lively faith, and shall build upon it the houses of their conscience, and thou shalt confirm and establish them in faith and religion, and in obedience to my holy law." (34)

iii. The third favour was, that He *assured him of the perseverance*, and invincible fortitude of this rock, and of this

(30) Joan. i. 42.   (31) 1 Cor. x. 4.   (32) Mat. xvi. 18.
   (33) Mat. vii. 24.   (34) 1 Cor. iii. 10.

building, saying, that although the gates of hell should open on every side, and that all the infernal powers should issue forth, yet should they never prevail against it; and although the rains, winds, and floods of all the persecutions of the world and of the flesh, should discharge themselves upon this house, yet never should they overthrow it; because it is built upon the omnipotence, wisdom, and protection of Jesus Christ, who is the living stone, who will defend, and give strength to this rock, which is Peter, and to his successors, as being His Vicars, so that they never fail in this holy faith.

iv. The fourth favour was, the *promise of the keys of the Kingdom of heaven,* to open and shut its gates to mortal men; that is to say, that He would give him the key of science to declare the truths, which are enclosed in the holy Scriptures, to make them known to men: and the key of power, to pardon those sins which hinder the entrance into heaven.

2. All this Christ our Lord *truly accomplished,* as shall be seen in the meditations on the fifth part, where we will examine the greatness of these promises, for which I am to thank Him infinitely, reputing those favours my own, which He bestowed on this holy apostle. For he received not these privileges so much for himself, as for the profit of the universal Church, and for me if I can make my profit of them, as if they had been granted to me alone. I will likewise rejoice in the greatness of this saint, with a desire to imitate him as far as I am able.

Colloquy.—O glorious apostle, I rejoice in the new name, which this day was imposed upon thee, and in the new dignity promised to thee : be thou in good time, the fundamental stone of the Catholic Church, dreadful to the devils, the porter of heaven, beloved of the angels, and favourable to men. Beseech our Lord that He make thee a fundamental stone, to help me to build my life upon the same ; in such a manner that the gates of hell prevail not against me. Open unto me with thy celestial keys, the gates of heaven, which I have shut against myself, and do thou shut the gates of hell, which I have opened by my sins : to the end, that being clean from all guilt of sin, I may enter to enjoy with thee the Kingdom of glory. Amen.

MEDITATION XXI.

ON THE TRANSFIGURATION OF OUR LORD JESUS CHRIST ON THE MOUNT OF THABOR.

"After six days, Jesus taketh unto Him, Peter, James, and John his brother, and bringeth them into a high mountain apart," and being in prayer, "was *transfigured* before them; and His face did shine as the sun, and His garments became white as snow." (1)

Upon these words there are to be considered *six things*, distinguished by the following points.

POINT I.

First I will consider the *motives* which Christ our Lord had, to transfigure and shew Himself glorious to His apostles.

1. To give some *proof* of the *glory* which He concealed and suppressed, under His mortal and passible humanity; and of that which His servants shall enjoy, when they shall hereafter reign with Him.

2. To encourage them the rather to carry their cross, even in this life, He gives them a taste of the joys of His

(1) Mat. xvii. 1.   Marc. ix. 1.   Luc. ix. 28.   S. Th. 3. p. q. xiv.

glory, although as it were in a cursory manner: and as He Himself said a little before:—"Amen I say to you, there are some of them that stand here, that shall not taste death, till they see the Son of Man, coming in His Kingdom." (2) This agrees with what we have already said, namely, that the life of him who follows Christ is a cross, that it is a sugared cross of spiritual pleasures, which makes His yoke sweet, and His burden light.

From all which I will draw great desires to serve this so glorious a Lord, in the hope of enjoying Him in His glory, for perhaps He will give me, even in this life, some little taste of it.

POINT II.

Secondly, I will consider the *time* and the *place*, which Christ our Lord chose to work this mystery.

1. The *time* was *in the midst of His preaching*, and six days after He had preached to all to carry their cross, promising that some of them should see Him in His Kingdom: which, as another Evangelist says, He fulfilled on the eighth day, counting the day in which He said it, and in which He accomplished it: to teach us, that Almighty God does not long delay His promises when the speedy fulfilment of them is necessary to fortify us. Moreover, that our perfect glorification will be after the six days of this mortal life, upon the eighth day of the general resurrection. Notwithstanding, all that time is but little in respect of eternity, since as David says:— "a thousand years" before God, are but even as "yesterday:" (3) or as S. Paul says: (4)—"all this is but a moment, and hardly perceptible."

2. The *place* was a *high mountain* and *apart*, very fit and proper for prayer: to signify that Almighty God

(2) Mat. xvi. 28.   (3) Ps. lxxxix. 4.   (4) 2 Cor. iv. 17.

does not impart those favours to those souls who live in public, and in the tumult and commerce of the world, but in the solitude and secret of recollection, and when they are far removed from earthly cares and affections, and elevated to a life of great perfection: even as Moses and Elias, who had not the sight of Almighty God amidst the people, but on solitary mountains.

With this example I will encourage myself to seek out this solitude, and excellent way of life, saying with David:—"Who will give me wings like a dove" (5) to fly, and carry me into the desert, hoping that there Almighty God will speak to my heart, and that I shall find the rest which I desire!

Colloquy.—O my soul, lift up thyself above thyself, and endeavour to make thy heart like a mountain, high, and apart; a mountain, by the perfection of thy works; high, by the contemplation of things that are eternal; and apart, by the mortification of perishable things, that Jesus Christ may delight to come to thee, and to transform thee by love into Himself. Amen.

POINT III.

Thirdly I will consider the *company* which He led with Him on to the mountain, and the *practice of prayer*, in which He employed Himself: His company was the three apostles.

1. They were *the most fervent* of all others, and most beloved: for although God our Lord loves and cherishes all the just, yet to the most fervent He shows the greatest favours. And if He led not all the twelve, it was to give us to understand, that these extraordinary favours were not to be showed to all; and perhaps, because amongst the twelve there was a Judas, an evil and a wicked man,

(5) Ps. liv. 7.

and that it was not expedient to lead him thither to enjoy
the sight of so great a good, nor to leave him alone, for
fear of defaming Him. Whence I will learn, how much
it imports me to be fervent in the love of Jesus Christ :
and what mischief an evil member causes in a community
of good.

2. I ought also to note, that Christ our Lord *imparts* these extraordinary graces *to whom* He pleases, and
how He pleases : and sometimes bestows them on such as
are but imperfectly holy, and leaves another more devout,
by His secret judgments, reserving all His recompense
for the life to come : for although S. Andrew was not led
to the mountain, it does not follow that he was not as
fervent as the others. And this shall comfort me, when I
shall see others favoured of Almighty God, and myself
forsaken, not to lose courage, nor to fall into pusillanimity
and despair, holding for a sovereign good thing, the eternal
disposition of our Lord, and the following His steps, since
they are always the most beneficial and secure.

3. Thirdly, I will ponder the *mystery* of those *three*
companions, or associates of our Saviour, by which are
represented the *three principal virtues*, which accompany
prayer, even to the elevating of it to the transfiguration
of the soul; that is to say, a lively and fervent *faith*,
figured by Peter: steadfast *hope* fighting with valour
against the enemies of prayer, figured by James : and
ardent and affectionate *charity*, figured by John. But it
is necessary that Christ our Lord walk before, and with His
inspiration conduct and lead them, that they may assuredly
mount up to the height of these most perfect affections,
by which they were transformed and united to God
by love.

Colloquy.—O most sweet master, "send forth"

from heaven "Thy light and Thy truth," which may accompany and conduct " me to Thy holy hill,"(6) leading thither my affections, uniting me with Thee by means of them.   Amen.

4. Hence it is that the *exercise* in which Christ our Lord employed Himself on the mountain, was. as S. Luke says, *prayer:* to teach us how in prayer those celest'al favours and delights are conferred, and that prayer obtains the transfiguration of the soul, altering and changing an earthly life into one that is heavenly, and a human into a divine life.   In prayer the soul lifts herself up above herself : her face shines with the light of truth, and the splendour of virtues, which there are communicated, casting forth beams of loving affections, and whitening her garments, which are her works, with most pure intentions.   Briefly she abides there deified, and wholly transformed into Almighty God, according to that which S. Paul says, contemplating the glory of our Lord, transforming ourselves into His own "image." (7)

Colloquy.—O most sweet Jesus, grant me so to meditate and contemplate the glory of Thy virtues, that I may become transformed into them : instruct me to pray with such a spirit, that I may be transfigured into the image of Thy glory.   Amen.

POINT IV.

1. I will consider the *manner* how Christ our Lord transfigured Himself, which was by permitting the glory of His soul, which was suppressed intrinsically, without extending itself to the body, to burst forth extrinsically, and communicate itself to it, and so it became more bright and shining than the sun, yea and a great deal more by many degrees, nor is there splendour in the world to be

(6) Ps. xlii. 3.   (7) 2 Cor. iii. 18.

compared to it. Thence His garments became as white as snow, and His divine face full of ineffable beauty, even the greatest, as David says, that ever was, or ever will be seen· among "the sons of men :" (8) for which I will rejoice me, and congratulate Him, saying to Him:—

Colloquy.—O Jesus of Nazareth, prince of all the Nazarites, I do rejoice to see Thee much " whiter than the snow, purer than milk, more ruddy than the old ivory, fairer than the sapphire."(9)　O how glorious didst Thou appear in the presence of our Lord, with the beauty wherewith He invested Thee!　O my soul, behold thy beloved, more beautiful than the moon, more resplendent than the sun, "white and ruddy, and chosen out of thousands,"(10) rejoice in His glory, ove His beauty, and repose in it.

2. I will likewise draw forth great *affections* of *praise* and thanksgiving to Christ our Lord, for having for our sakes, deprived His body so many years of such great glory: and for having given us then a little taste of it, although for a short time, and with an intention to conceal it again, to prosecute the business of our redemption.

Colloquy.—O good Jesus, I give Thee all possible thanks for the rest and refreshment which Thou gavest in this day unto Thy afflicted and ill-treated body, suffering it to taste of the sweetness of that glory, which it was to enjoy in that miraculous resurrection, before it tasted the pains and outrages of Thy Passion.　Truly, O my Lord, I perceive by this how much I am indebted to Thee, for having deprived Thy most holy body, so many years, of such great glory, that it might be sacrificed upon the cross with great ignominy.　O that I could renounce all the delights and perishing pleasures of this miserable life, to suffer something for thy infinite love : for I had rather, my

(8) Ps. xliv. 3.　　　(9) Thren. iv. 7.　　　(10) Cant. v. 10.

Saviour, find myself with Thee, on the mount of Calvary, suffering, than mount Thabor, rejoicing : now therefore I will choose to suffer with Thee, and afterwards enjoy Thee, when Thou shalt no longer demand my service.

MEDITATION XXII.

ON THE THINGS THAT HAPPENED DURING CHRIST'S TRANSFIGURATION.

POINT I.

Moses and Elias appeared unto Christ our Lord, "in majesty, and they spoke of His decease, that He should accomplish in Jerusalem." (1)

1. Upon this point I am to consider, first, *why* Christ our Lord *chose these two prophets* amongst so many others of the old testament. The *reasons* were,—i. Because these were the most remarkable and most famous, for the great-ness of their sanctity.—ii. They were both very zealous of the observance of the law, and of the good of the people, and for this cause endured many troubles.—iii Both fasted forty days, (2) like Christ our Lord; and both on another mountain, (3) contemplated the greatness of Al-mighty God, and of the mystery of His Incarnation : and for this reason our Lord would honour Himself with them, and honour them also upon this occasion.   Whence I will excite a great desire of the virtues which shone in these saints, especially of fasting, prayer and zeal, to become familiar with our Lord, with whom these saints were so familiar.

2. Secondly, I will ponder how these saints came with *great splendour and majesty ;* both because it was proper

(1) Luc. ix. 30.   (2) Exod. xxxiv. 28.   (3) 3 Reg. xix. 8.

to be so, for the honour of *Jesus Christ*, whom they came to acknowledge for their Redeemer, and also to give us to understand, that *the saints shall be like Jesus Christ in glory and majesty*, as they are now in the labours and ignominies. of this life.   O what contentment did these saints receive, in seeing Him, whom for so many years they had expected and desired! How did they acknowledge Him, and adore Him for their God, for their Saviour and their Lord!   O what thanks, did they give to Him, that He vouchsafed to come to redeem them! And I, filled with these affections, will practise the like virtues in their blessed company.

3. Thirdly, I will consider *what they discoursed upon* with Christ our Lord, telling Him of the *decease* which He was to accomplish in Jerusalem, that is to say, of His *Passion* and *death*, which was an excess of *dolours* and of ignominies, an excess of *satisfaction* for our sins, all which was most excessive, more than our merits, and more than was necessary for our salvation.

Colloquy.—O sweet Jesus, what words are these, on which Thou discoursest amidst these joys? For words of passion and death, what connexion have they with such a glory? If music be displeasing in time of mourning, tears are not less out of season in time of joy: but now I perceive that Thy music is to discourse of suffering, which love renders sweet to thee.(4)

4. Hence, I will learn how Christ our Lord, during His life, would not take one short moment of *repose*, but always mingled with some *labour:* to teach us, that to labour in this life should be our repose and comfort; as also that we may understand, that he that loves with excess, delights to discourse of what he loves: and as He

(4) Ecclus. xxii. 6.

loved His Passion, both to please His Father and for our profit, so He took delight in hearing it spoken of.

Colloquy.—O excessive lover, grant me to love Thee, as Thou hast loved me, by which I may delight to suffer, and to talk of it as Thou delightest. O that all my consolations might aim at this, to suffer contumelies and sorrows with excess, although there could be no excess, since all would be little in respect of what I have deserved for my sins, and in respect of what Thou, my Lord didst suffer for them.

POINT II.

In the meanwhile that these three apostles lay slumbering and oppressed with sleep, awaking they saw the glory of Christ our Lord, and of Moses and Elias, and S. Peter said :—*Lord, "let us make three tabernacles,* one for Thee, and one for Moses, and one for Elias : not knowing what he said." (5)

1. Here I am to consider, first, our *misery* and *frailty*, for whilst Christ our Lord prays, watches, and in His prayer is transfigured, the three apostles fell asleep : yet it is to be believed, that at the first they fell to prayer with their master, but the prayer lasting somewhat long, they being weary fell asleep. Here is represented the difference betwixt the prayer of the fervent, and that of the lukewarm : that of the one, as the Wise man says, is "better" in the "end" than in the "beginning," (6) because at the end it obtains this transfiguration, which was seen in Christ. But the other quite contrary, are better in the beginning than in the end, because they enter with fervour, and immediately give over all at once, and for this reason obtains not the perfect transfiguration to which it should raise him. Where, if I make reflection upon myself, I shall

(5) Luc. ix. 32.   (6) Eccles. vii. 9.

find that I likewise slumber sundry times, losing the favours which God would do me, if I watched with fervour in prayer; notwithstanding sometimes Christ our Lord shows His infinite mercy, and awakes him that sleeps with His sudden illuminations, discovering unto him His glory, and vouchsafing him the comfort, which he had not deserved, as it here happened to the apostles. (7)

2. I will consider that *immense joy which will be in the state of glory*, one only drop of which, when S. Peter tasted it, seeing the body of Christ glorified, so replenished him, that he desired never more to move from thence, and was sorry to see that Moses and Elias would retire; offering himself to build up three tabernacles, which they might inhabit, forgetting both himself and his companions, as if they had not been in the world, nor stood in need of the like tabernacles to dwell in: for the beauty and sweetness of celestial things causes the forgetfulness of all earthly things, and to say with S. Paul: that we esteem all the things of this world but as "dung" in respect of the gaining of "Jesus Christ," (8) and of dwelling with Him in everlasting glory.

Colloquy.—O my God, "how great is the multitude of that sweetness, which Thou hast hidden for them that fear Thee:" (9) give me to taste one little drop that I may loathe whatsoever is earthly, and only desire to seek that which is heavenly.   Amen.

3. The third shall be to consider, that *S. Peter understood not what he said*, partly from being inebriated with that sweetness which he felt in his soul; and partly from the horror which he conceived of the passion and death of Jesus Christ, on which subject he did not delight to discourse, but desired to hinder it, as he also did six days

(7) S. Aug. in Solit. c. xxi.　　(8) Phil. iii. 8.　　(9) Ps. xxx. 20.

before the transfiguration; for which cause Christ our Lord said unto him, that he savoured "not the things that are of God, but the things that are of men." (10)   And hearing now Moses and Elias confirm that which Christ our Lord before had spoken of His Passion, he sought to interrupt and hinder the conversation, and speaking with great fervour, besought them never to depart from thence : but he knew not what he said, God having ordained that Christ should die, for that this life is not for enjoyment, but suffering: and the consolations of prayer are not given that we should rest in them, but to encourage us by them to labours and sufferings : so also it is gross ignorance to fly from discourses, in which Christ takes contentment, and under the pretext of being in His company, refuse to accomplish His holy will.

Colloquy.—O sweet Jesus, grant, I beseech Thee, that I may love what Thou lovest, and take contentment in those sweet consolations which Thou shalt give me on mount Thabor, by which I may be animated to accompany Thee to mount Calvary.   Amen.

POINT III.

And as Peter spake these words there came a *bright cloud* and " overshaded them, and lo! a voice out of the cloud, saying, *This is my beloved Son*, in whom I am well pleased, hear ye Him.''(11)

1. Where I am to consider first, how the Eternal Father, and the Holy Ghost also, would honour Jesus Christ our Lord, and authorise Him in this case to make known the authority of His person, His dignity and doctrine, as they did at His Baptism.

i. The Holy Ghost appeared in the figure of this cloud: which represented the abundant dew of His divine doc-

(10) Mat. xvi. 28.   (11) Mat. xvii. 5.

trine and science, and the number of graces and celestial gifts which should be given to men by Jesus Christ. This cloud was not obscure, as anciently that cloud was, wherein Almighty God manifested Himself, but bright and resplendent: to signify that the shadows and figures were to cease, and that the truth was come which they represented.

ii. The eternal Father also desired to authorise His Son with this voice which issued from the cloud, which likewise represented the divinity of Christ our Lord, fulfilling here what S. John had said:—"There are three who give testimony in heaven" of Jesus Christ, "the Father, the Word, and the Holy Ghost, and these three are one"(12) same thing in the Deity, and most unanimous in the testimony which they give of Him.

2. I will meditate on *the words of the Father*, saying . "This is my beloved Son, in whom I am well pleased." With which words He ratified that which He had spoken at His baptism : and at the same time teaches us, that the state of the sons of Almighty God begins in this life, by the means of baptism, and is perfected in glory, where they shall receive their everlasting inheritance.

These words have already been pondered in the third Meditation, and this time the Father added: "Hear ye Him;" as if He said, hearken to that which He shall teach you, and command you: believe it, and accomplish it, because He is your Master, not Moses, nor Elias, and it is my will that you hearken to Him.

Colloquy.—O sovereign Father, I give Thee thanks for the testimony which Thou hast given of Thine Only-begotten Son, let it be my delight, O Lord, to hear His doctrine, and to embrace it, since His doctrine is Thine : (13) and He has heard from Thee

(12) 1 Joan. v. 7.   (13) Joan. vii. 16.

what He speaks, and that in hearing Him we hear Thee. O sweet Jesus, blessed be this new approbation of the office which is given Thee of a master: and since Thy Father commands me to hearken to Thee, speak, Lord, to my heart, "for Thy servant heareth," with desire to accomplish what I shall hear. Amen.

POINT IV.

The apostles, astonished with the majesty of this voice, *fell to the ground, and greatly feared.* But Christ our Lord went immediately to them, and touching them with His hand, said to them: "*Arise* and *fear not.*"(14)

1. In this is represented the *property of the good Spirit,* when He speaks, which is to intimidate or affright at the first, and afterwards to calm, and to quiet the heart, as it happened to Daniel.(15)

Colloquy.—Consider, O my soul, that if the voice of Almighty God, so affectionate and peaceable, cause so great a fright in His elect, what will His terrible voice do when it shall resound in the ears of the reprobate? Wherefore hear now the voice of Thy sweet master, for fear of being frightened hereafter by the voice of a terrible and rigorous judge.

2. The apostles arose, and "saw no one but only Jesus:"(16) to give them to understand, that this voice had been pronounced *for Him alone,* and that He alone was sufficient for them without Moses, or Elias.

Colloquy.—O my dearly beloved, although all vanish from me and forsake me, if Thou still abide with me, I never will demand more. Depart, Moses, depart Elias, vanish away all creatures, if Thou my God depart not from me, and do not leave me, I shall be secure, content, and satisfied.

(14) Mat. xvii. 7.   (15) Dan. x. 19.   (16) Mat. xvii. 3.

3. Finally, Christ our Lord said to them: "Tell to no man what you have seen until the Son of Man do rise again from the dead." Desiring in this *to conceal this glory,* lest it should be an occasion of hindering His death and holy Passion.

Colloquy—O profound humility, O burning charity of our Redeemer, who to manifest His glory, chose a mountain, a secret place, few witnesses, on whom He imposed silence during their life : and to die with dishonour, chose a mountain, and a public place, seeking to confound my pride, by such rare examples of humility, and alluring me to suffer by such remarkable demonstrations of His charity. Grant me, O Lord, to imitate Thee in these holy virtues, since Thou gavest them to me for my imitation.

MEDITATION XXIII.

CHRIST'S CONVERSATION WITH THE SONS OF ZEBEDEE WHEN DEMANDING TO SIT IN HIS KINGDOM, ONE ON THE RIGHT HAND, AND THE OTHER ON THE LEFT.

In this meditation we will follow the mystery related by S. Mark, because it serves more to our purpose, adding what S. Matthew saith :(1) observing by the way, that to recite and ponder the imperfections of the apostles at this present, is not to aggravate them, but to exalt thereby the great bounty and power of Christ our Lord, who both supported and instructed them, and afterwards changed them, and gave them most excellent sanctity and perfection: and this notice may serve for some other meditations, which have been delivered already.

POINT I.

Christ our Lord, having made known His Passion and

(1) Mat. xx. 20.   Marc. x. 35.

Resurrection to His apostles, " James and John, the sons of Zebedee, came to Him, saying, Master, we *desire that whatsoever we shall ask, Thou wouldst do it for us.*"(2)

Upon this point I am to consider, in the persons of these two brethren, the *quality of ambitious men*, and the *manner* how they *long for and manage to gain* what they desire.

1. First, I will consider that these two apostles, although they had been told of that "decease" which Christ our Lord was to suffer, as also hearing Him say that He was to rise again and to reign, forgetful of the first, they laid hold on the second, desiring the best and most eminent places in His Kingdom, with a kind of ambition and desire of honour. Whence we may see that ambitious affection, which stops our ears, lest it should understand what ignominy is, inclines us to open them to understand what honour is, whetting the desire to procure it.

2. I will ponder how these two apostles, who as then were imperfect, *discovered their ambition in the manner of praying*, and demanding, saying: " Master, we desire that whatsoever we shall ask, Thou wouldst do it for us."(3) Wherein they committed *three improprieties.*

i. The first was, in showing themselves to be over favourable and *friends to their own will*, taking it for the rule of what they desired, and of what Jesus Christ was to grant them.—ii. Whence proceeded the *second*, which was a *want of resignation* of their will to the will of Christ our Lord, for they said not, " Master, if Thou wilt,"—or, "if it be possible,"—or, " if it be convenient for us,"—but absolutely, "we will,"—intending to draw the will of Christ to follow theirs, and not to conform theirs to His.—iii. Whence proceeded the *third*, which was *presumption* in demanding of Jesus Christ with such general terms, that He should give them whatsoever they asked, as if they had been cer-

(2) Marc. x. 35.   (3) Marc. x.

tain they had asked nothing but what was just, or that Christ must deny them nothing which they should ask Him, abusing the promise which He made unto them, saying, " Ask, and it shall be given you,"(4) for whosoever asketh, receiveth.

In all this they erred, as imperfect men, because the prayer which is agreeable to Jesus Christ, ought not to proceed from self-love, but from the love of Almighty God; nor from our own will, but from a desire to fulfil the divine will; nor yet to be done for our own glory, but for the glory of Jesus Christ.

Colloquy.—O sovereign master, never suffer me to ask Thee what my own will desires, but only that which is conformable to Thine : nor permit that I say to Thee rashly, Give me what I will, but in all humility, Give me what Thou wilt.   Amen.

3. I am to ponder how those two brethren *linked themselves together* to make this demand, because flesh and blood ordinarily do link themselves together, to attain their pretensions of honour; but yet, to conceal their ambition, and to negociate so much the better, they would not themselves propose this demand, but *solicit their mother*, that she should demand for them what they desired.   For so St. Matthew says, that the *" mother of the sons of Zebedee"* went to Christ, accompanied with her sons, adoring Him with exterior reverence, saying, that she had a request of great importance to make to Him, serving in place of an interpreter of the will of her sons.

But St. Mark says, that they *themselves* went to ask what their mother went to petition in their behalf. Whence, we see, that ambition, even to them that have it, appears evil, and that they cover it in searching after

(4) Mat. vii. 7.

honour or dignity; will not have it known that they aim at it; but under hand, they are diligent negociators, employing all the means of flesh and blood, and of the world, that their ambition presents to them, to gain their ends. (5) For this reason David calls the temptation of this vice, " A business that walketh about in the dark:" (6) for ambition is a subtle evil, a secret poison, a hidden pestilence, a train of deceits, mother of hypocrisy, fountain of envy, the origin of vices, the rust of virtues, and the consuming worm of all sanctity: and therefore I am to beseech our Lord, that with the buckler of His truth He keep and defend me from this ambitious spirit, which draws so much detriment upon the heads of its followers.

POINT II.

Jesus Christ said to them: " What would you that I should do for you?"(7)   And they said, Grant to us, that *we may sit*, one *on Thy right hand*, and the other *on Thy left, in Thy glory.*

1. Here I am to consider, First, the *prudence* and *wisdom of our Lord Jesus Christ* ; who knowing the very hearts of these two apostles, did not immediately reprehend them, nor say to them: Ask me not what you require, because it is not expedient; but waited till they themselves should discover the wound of their own ambition, and should vomit out of their mouth their own poison.   Nor yet did He say, that He would give them whatsoever they asked: to teach us, that it is not prudence to accord to every ignorant and bold demander what others ask for them, especially when the petitioners are weak and imperfect, because it may happen, that they may demand some evil or imperfect thing: as it chanced to Herod, when he said to Herodias, that she might ask whatso-

<hr>

(5) S. Ber. serm. 6. in Ps. xc.   (6) Ps. xc. 6.   (7) Marc. x. 36.

ever she would, and she demanded the "head" of the
"Baptist." (8)

2. I will consider, that *these two brethren*, knowing that
Christ preferred them before the other apostles, except St.
Peter, grudged that Peter also was preferred before them,
and for this cause they asked those two immediate places
nearest to Jesus Christ, one on the right side, and the
other on the left, that so even Peter himself should not
be before them. And it is very credible, that if this ambition had passed further, it would likewise have taken
place between themselves, and would have separated and
disunited them: because every one desires for himself the
right hand, to be preferred before another.

Whence I will gather the great restlessness of this vice,
which spares neither friend nor brother, and how much
more secure it is to choose, as our Saviour says, "the
lowest place," (9) under which there is no other, without
seeking to be preferred before any one, for there need but
one to trouble the tranquillity of the heart, and destroy
the fruit of humility. (10)

Colloquy.—O Jesus Christ, master of humility,
who being compared with Barabbas, wouldst not be
preferred, no not before him, choosing for Thyself
the lowest place in the eyes of the world: I beseech
Thee to assist me to choose the same likewise for myself, because it is but reasonable that the disciple
should choose that which the master made choice of
for Himself. Amen.

3. I will consider how *ambition creeps into all states,*
as well temporal as spiritual, inordinately desiring pre-eminence in all things : for even so these apostles either
desired the highest excellence, in the Kingdom and glory

(8) Marc. vi. 24.   (9) Luc. xiv. 10.
(1)) S. Ber. serm. xxxvii. in Cant.'

of Christ, imagining that He would no sooner be risen again, than He should possess a temporal kingdom, following in this the opinion of the Jews, or if they believed that it would be spiritual, they still desired the chief place and primacy in it, not because they were the most holy, but to be the most honoured above all the others: and hence proceeded their endeavours to obtain it by inordinate means; their means both of ambition and pride being greatly displeasing to our Lord, as we shall immediately see.

POINT III.

" Jesus said to them, *You know not what you ask.*"(11)

1. On this word, consider the *errors* which we commit in holy prayer, ignorant even of that which we demand. Whence proceeds that, as the apostle St. James says, we ask and receive not, because we " ask amiss."(12)

i. The first error is, to ask for some excellency, and temporal dignity, or other earthly thing, without resignation to the will of Almighty God, and without putting down this condition, namely, if it be conducive to our salvation.

ii. The second is, to petition for some *spiritual* excellency even in virtues, *without due purity of intention,* proposing to ourselves not so much the glory of Almighty God, as our own.

iii. The third is, to petition for such excellencies as far *surpass our merits,* and such as are singular or extraordinary, and greater than we ourselves imagine: which we demand through ignorance and want of humility; such are those who desire ecstasies, revelations, and the like favours, after the manner that the spouse said:—" Show me ...where thou feedest at noon day;" and the answer was, " If thou know not...go forth, &c.,"(13) that is to say, Thou

(11) Marc. x. 38.　　　(12) Jac. iv. 3.　　　(13) Cant. i. 6.

demandest more than thou meritest, because thou dost not know thyself.

iv. The fourth is, to ask spiritual greatness, expecting to obtain it *only by prayers and intercessions, without regard to merits* or good works. For although prayers are necessary, yet are they not sufficient, if works and labours do not second them, which may dispose us to receive them, and much less are they sufficient, when we only allege the respects and titles of flesh and blood, and of kindred only, which are of little force before Almighty God, to obtain a thing of so great excellency.

v. The fifth error is, to demand these great gifts, which are the crown and reward of those who have conquered, before they have fought, or deserved recompense.

2. For all these reasons, according to the minds of divers doctors, Christ our Lord said to these two apostles, " You know not what you ask."(14) And I, taking warning by other men's harms, will be cautious what I ask, and take heed to the intention, means, and manner with which I ask, lest Christ our Lord say to me: Thou knowest not what thou askest.

Colloquy.—O good Jesus, who saidst to Thy apostles, "if you shall ask me in my name, that I will do:" (15) grant that I may only ask that which is just to obtain in Thy holy name, to the end that asking that which is agreeable to Thee, Thou grant me what I shall demand of Thee. O holy Spirit, since I am so ignorant that I "know not what" I "should pray for as" I "ought," (16) nor yet the manner which becomes me to ask, teach me the one and the other, that asking that which Thou hast taught and inspired me, it may not be said to me, Thou knowest not what thou askest.

(14) Marc. x. 38.   (15) Joan. xiv. 14.   (16) Rom. viii. 26.

POINT IV.

Our Lord Jesus Christ presently added, "*Can you drink of the chalice that I drink of, or be baptized with the baptism wherewith I am baptized?*"(17) That is to say, Have you force and courage for the purpose, and are you prepared for it?

1. Here I am to ponder, first, that it is a singular benefit of our Lord Jesus Christ, when we err either in the thing which we ask, or in the manner of asking, *to refuse our request*, and presently to set us right in the one and the other, setting before our eyes what we ought to ask Him, as He did to these His two beloved apostles, both at this time, and at others, when they said to Him:—"Lord, wilt Thou that we command fire to come down from heaven and consume" the Samaritans? And our Lord "rebuked them, saying, You know not of what spirit you are," for "I am not come to destroy souls, but to save." (18)

Hence it is that I ought to thank Almighty God, not only for that which He has granted me, but also for that which He as a Father has denied me, when I know not what I ask for myself, and that He sets me right in asking Him what I ought to obtain.

2. I will weigh the *charity* and *sweetness* of Christ our Lord in this demand, wherewith He *invites* His apostles to the *sufferings of His Passion*, with *words, examples*, and *effectual reasons*, giving them to understand that the means to obtain the seats on the right hand, and the left, which they desired, was to drink that chalice which He drank, and to be baptized with the Baptism with which He Himself was baptized, exciting them to imitate Him in this by His own example; for if the supreme monarch of heaven and earth went to sit on the throne of His glory, drinking

(17) Marc. x. 38.   (18) Luc. ix. 54.

this chalice, how much more reasonable is it that His vassals should not sit with Him on those thrones which He has promised them, unless they drink of the same chalice. And what great matter was it for the disciples to drink of it, since their master drank the same?

Colloquy.—O my well-beloved, it suffices me that Thou hast drunk this chalice, and desirest that I drink the same, the more willingly to offer myself to it. Although there were no place for me, neither on the right hand, nor on the left in Thy Kingdom, yet hold I myself exceeding happy to drink of it, because my principal reward is to do and suffer much for Thee, in thankfulness for so much which Thou hast done and suffered for me.

3. I will ponder the *spirit which is included in this vocation* of Christ our Lord, *to His Passion and death*, to His chalice and baptism, alluding to the ancient custom of killing malefactors, by giving them a poisoned chalice, or by stifling them in water, to signify that as the chalice of death kills when the poison enters within the man; and baptism stifles, hiding or drowning the whole man under the water; even so to His Passion and death two sorts of sufferings concurred, as shall be said in the fourth part—the one interior, which penetrated His most holy soul, the other exterior, which afflicted His body. And although St. Matthew says that He asked them:—" Can you drink the chalice that I shall drink?" (19) yet St. Mark says, " That I drink of ?" Forasmuch as He drank the same always, by desire and inward representation, and was even now upon the point of drinking the same outwardly by His Passion. All which is full of great mystery, ordained by Him to repress the inward and outward ambition of His disciples, inviting them to mortify them by the means

(19) Ps. lxviii. 16.

of this drink and baptism, of so much suffering and contempt, desiring them from their hearts, and accomplishing them in effect.

4. Lastly is to be considered *another mysterious cause* why He said:—"Can you drink the chalice that I shall drink?" Because in Holy Scripture there is mention made of many chalices, (20) and Christ our Lord did not drink them all. The one is of *passion and labours*, the other is of glory and rewards, which is the lot of the Blessed. Another is of the anger and indignation of Almighty God, which is the portion of the damned. The first Christ our Lord drank, and exhorted us to drink of it, and whosoever shall drink this first which Christ Himself drank, shall also drink the second, and shall not drink the last, as Christ did not drink it. But he who refuses to drink of the chalice of tribulations, and overthrows by this means the law of our Lord, shall not taste of the second, nor establish a claim for his portion, but of the latter.

Colloquy.—Wherefore, O my soul, receive gladly the chalice of thy salvation, although it be somewhat bitter, because by this temporal bitterness thou shalt deliver thyself from the eternal, and shalt drink that excellent chalice which inebriates, seeing and loving Almighty God with unspeakable joy.

5. With this consideration I will imagine that Christ our Lord *demands of me*, as of His Apostles, saying *to me,* Hast thou the courage, and art thou prepared, to drink the chalice which I have drunk? and to be baptized with the Baptism with which I was baptized? And then will I enter within my heart to examine whether I have the courage and promptitude to answer affirmatively, after the manner which we shall presently set down, and if I want

(20) Ps. cxv. 13.   Ps. xv. 5.   Ps. lxxiv. 9.   Is. li. 17.

it, to endeavour to obtain it by the considerations next
ensuing.

POINT V.

The two apostles answered, saying, "We can" drink it,
and Jesus said to them, "You shall indeed drink of the
chalice that I drink of, and with the baptism wherewith I
am baptized, you shall be baptized; but to sit on my right
hand or on my left is not mine to give to you, but to them
for whom it is prepared by my Father." (21)

1. Here I am to consider, first, that one may proceed
from three motives, to offer himself to drink this chalice,
and say with much resolution this word, "We can."

i. The first, with a *spirit of ambition*, which, as it provokes to great enterprises, so also suggests the means to
obtain them, suffering certain humiliations to come to
be exalted.

ii. The second is, with a *spirit of fervour*, but blind,
ignorant, and little experienced, which casts itself blind-
fold into labours and sufferings, which is wont to be easy
to many, because war is sweet to those who never were in
it, he thinking it an easy thing to drink this chalice, who
never tasted of it.

iii. The third is, with the *spirit of Christ*, who inspires
the like desires and purposes into His elect, who offer
themselves very particularly to all the labours which
Christ Himself underwent. And it may be supposed that
after this manner these two apostles offered themselves,
which if they did not then, at the least it is certain they
did it since, and put in practice their desire.

And with this spirit I will likewise endeavour to offer
myself, not trusting in my own strength, but in the
strength of Jesus Christ, saying with St. Paul, "I can do
all things" in Christ our Lord, "who strengtheneth me;"

(21) Marc. x. 39.

(22) and so fortified with His grace, I can and desire to drink the same chalice which He drank.

2. I will ponder how it is a *great grace and favour* of Christ our Lord *to give us to drink the chalice of His passion*, and so He granted it to these two His beloved apostles. Notwithstanding it was not without great mystery that the one died for Jesus Christ, and the other, although he suffered much, yet died a natural death, to signify that the chalice of the Passion of Jesus Christ is not only drunk in dying as martyrs, but also in suffering as confessors.

Colloquy.—O sweet master, grant me such favour as to hear from Thy mouth, and to experience in effect, Thou shalt drink my chalice, and shalt be baptized with my baptism: that suffering with Thee, I may likewise reign with Thee.   Amen.

3. We are to ponder the infinite *wisdom, bounty,* and *charity* of Christ our Lord, which shone forth in the *last words* which He spake to these two apostles, for He so denied them the sitting on His right hand, and on the left, for the motive which prompted them to demand it, that at the same time He granted it to them for another motive, as if He had said:—" It is not my office, nor is it fit nor expedient to give to you the sitting on my right hand, or on my left, as due to you because you are my kinsmen, nor otherwise laboured for it; but it is my part to give it to those to whom my Father has assigned it, who are those who shall drink my chalice, and have laboured in my service, to accomplish that which I have commanded. And consequently you are to drink my chalice, I grant it to you under this title, when I shall see you drink it, for my Father, who inasmuch as He is God, predestinates men to

<hr>

(22) Phil. iv. 13.

the Kingdom of heaven, has ordained, that the predestined aspire not to great rewards, but after great labours."

Colloquy.—O most sweet Jesus, true God, to whom it belongs as well as to the Father to dispose of the seats of Thy Kingdom: I rejoice at the uprightness which Thou hast intermingled with so much sweetness: and it is not Thine to give these seats to the unworthy but to the worthy,(23) make me worthy by Thy grace, by which I may obtain one of them in Thy glory. Amen.

POINT VI.

The ten apostles hearing what had passed, "were moved with indignation against the two brethren. But Jesus called them, and said to them, You know that the princes of the Gentiles lord it over them, and they that are the greater exercise power upon them. It shall not be so among you, but whosoever will be greater among you let him be your minister, and he that will be first among you shall be your servant. Even as the Son of man is not come to be ministered unto, but to minister, and to give His life a redemption for many." (24)

1. We are to ponder the *frailty and misery of men*, before they are perfected by divine grace, for when the ten apostles had heard the answer of Christ, which was so powerful as to be able to repress the aspiring ambition of the sons of Zebedee, it made no impression on them until they fell into the same sin, disdaining the two, because they pretended to be greater than they. Hence we may see the mischief which arises from bad example, and how great prejudice ambition breeds in a community, causing amongst them discords, envies, and indignations.

2. We are to ponder the great *meekness of Christ our Lord* in not being angry, either against the ambitious or

(23) Luc. xxii. 29.   (24) Mat. xx. 24. Marc. x. 41.

against the jealous, but with the spirit of love pacified and united them together, admonished each of them of their error, and repressed their ambition with *two examples*, by one teaching what they ought to *avoid*, by the other what they were to *follow*.

i. What they were to *avoid*, was the custom of worldly princes, who place their greatness in this, to command others after an imperious and tyrannical manner, and to hold their subjects under their feet; but you, says He, ought to place all your greatness in serving all, and in becoming the servants and underlings of all, and by this path must you walk, to aspire to the greatness of my Kingdom, which whosoever shall obtain, he is to obtain it by this means.

ii. The example which we are to *follow* herein, is the life of Him who proposes it, "for I," says He, "being your master, greater than you, and the first in the Kingdom of my Father, came into the world not to be served, but to serve, and to give my life with great torments and ignominy, for the salvation of men. Wherefore, if you be my disciples, know ye that as I am come for this purpose into the world, even so you have come for the same into my school."

Colloquy.—O most sweet master, I have heard that sovereign lesson, which Thou hast read to me, I desire not for the time to come to learn any more examples from the world, which are for my condemnation, but only Thine, which are for my salvation and perfection. And since, by Thy grace Thou hast admitted me into Thy school, help me to put in practice the lesson which I have learned in it, for the glory of Thy holy name. Amen.

MEDITATION XXIV.

This history,(1) which Christ Jesus our Lord recounted unto us for our example and instruction, is a lively picture of the *blessed death of the just*, who drink the chalice of His Passion: and of *the disastrous death and punishment of sinners* who refuse it, to drink the chalice of Babylon, which, as St. John says, is of "gold,"(2) because it consists in honours and riches, and yet is filled with abominations and maledictions.

POINT I.

1. The first is, to consider *the life of the beggar Lazarus*, which was a continual exercise of *patience, in three or four remarkable things*, by means of which he attained to singular sanctity, and to be a lively pattern of what Christ our Lord suffered.

i. First, he made himself very like to Him *in suffering grievous pains and sores*, for he was full of them, even from the sole of the foot to the head, like another Job, without being able to move himself from one side to another, lying at the rich man's gate, suffering all this with great conformity to the will of God, without rancour, murmuring, or complaint.

ii. Secondly, in suffering extreme *poverty, beggary*, and *hunger*, all which he bore with such silence, that it is not said of him that he asked an alms with words, but with the showing of his sores.

iii. Thirdly, in suffering great *rejection and contempt of*

(1) Luc. xvi. 19.　　　　　(2) Apoc. xvii. 4.

men, for being so hungry, that he was constrained to crave the crumbs which fell from the rich man's table, none are given him: neither yet for this did he complain of the cruelty of the rich man, nor of his servants. And to this was added, that he suffered all these things, seeing before his eyes the object of the abundance which others enjoyed, which is wont likewise to augment the pain.

iv. Fourthly, this misery was so great, that the *dogs came to lick his sores*, and to cleanse the filth from them, and he was so weak and broken down, that he could not drive them from him, nor had he any one to drive them for him; and, if we impute this to the natural pity of the dogs, this itself augmented his pain, to see that the dogs had pity on him, and not men.

Whence we may learn that perfect patience embraces all sorts of tribulations, as well those which come of their own nature, such as infirmities and the like, as those which come by the hands of men, such as robberies, injuries, and the like, as also those which come from brute and un-reasonable creatures, such as are wild beasts, gnats, wasps, &c. Moreover, colds, frosts, and other like inclement changes of the air, which sometimes the devils effect. Wherein is accomplished that which St. James says: " patience hath a perfect work," (3) to the end you may be perfect and entire, failing in nothing.

2. By these degrees, Lazarus ascended to *great sanctity*, even such that our Lord Jesus Christ would make a chronicle of his life and labours, and propound it for an example of sanctity; and it seems that in it He would draw forth the lively lineaments of His own Passion, in which He remained all covered with sores in extreme poverty, and with so great a dereliction, that desiring one drop of water upon the cross, He found not any to give it

(3) Jac. i. 5, 4.

to Him, nor to take compassion on Him. So that Jesus Christ, by His own labours, confirmed those of Lazarus: instructing us that the most assured and most short way to attain to sanctity, is to suffer pain, neglect, and contempt from men, conforming ourselves in all things to the Divine will: I say in all things, for, to conform in some one of these sufferings only, is not much, but in all conjuctively is a most heroic and generous act. For it is no heroic thing to suffer sickness, if I have store of riches, and the cherishings of men; nor to suffer poverty, if I have them who relieve me with alms; but to suffer all this with extreme dereliction, is an heroic virtue, and closely resembles that of our blessed Lord and Saviour Jesus.

Colloquy.—O Jesus, ulcerated, poor and abandoned, grant me grace to imitate Thy holy patience, as likewise that of this poor beggar, conforming my will with Thine in all my tribulations, since for this end Thou hast set before me these examples. Amen.

POINT II.

Secondly, consider the *glorious death of Lazarus*, whereof Christ Jesus says, that he " was carried by the Angels into Abraham's bosom." Wherein is to be pondered:

1. First, how the death of Lazarus was the end of all his pains, poverty, and temporal dereliction; and the beginning of his rest, riches, and eternal honours. And although his death, as regarded the body, was vile and abject in the eyes of the world, nevertheless as regarded the soul, it was most precious in the eyes of God, who sent His Angels to carry him into Abraham's bosom, there to rest and repose with the just. And although his guardian angel was alone sufficient for this effect, yet would He that many angels should come, as it were an army of them, to

honour and accompany him. O how contentedly did this soul leave its body! O with what joy did it go in such noble company! O what congratulations did the angels use for his glorious victory, and how ashamed did the devils leave him! Verily, O my God, now I see that "the death of Thy "Saints" is "precious" in Thy "sight,"(4) although they have been poor, covered with sores, and despised in the world. Let my soul "die the death of the just, and my last end be like" to them. (5)

2. Secondly, I will ponder *the glory* which the soul of this beggar now *enjoys in heaven*, into which he was transferred from Limbo patrum, and the glorious qualities which the body shall enjoy at the latter day of the resurrection. For his ulcers he now receives immense joys, for his poverty everlasting riches: for his nakedness, garments of glory: for his hunger, never-ending satiety: for being neglected and despised by men, he shall enjoy the protection and honour of God and His angels. Oh how well employed does he prize the mortifications which he endured in this life! Now it seems unto him, that all which he suffered was but little, and the time no more than a moment, "compared with the glory to come,"(6) which they have procured him. O my soul, animate Thyself to suffer in this life, since such happy repose is pre-pared for thee in the other.

POINT III.

Thirdly, I will consider the *great honour* which Christ our Lord *did in this life*, to this beggar, especially in *two things*.

1. The first was to *reveal his name*, which was forgotten in the world, and would that it should be written in His Gospel, that all men might immortalize its memory: not

(4) **Ps. cxv. 15.**   (5) **Num. xxiii. 10.**   (6) **Rom. viii. 18.**

vouchsafing to nominate the covetous rich man, nor to take his name in His holy mouth. By which the poor and despised may understand, that Almighty God has not forgotten them, and that He knows them by their names, has care of them, and in His time will publish their praises and honour them; and that He will have them honoured in His holy Church, as was St. Paul, the first hermit, St. Francis, and others, whose names would have been forgotten, if they had not been saints.—To make us also neglect the desire of being known and renowned in the world, or having published to the world our fame and works, but rather leave the care hereof to Almighty God.

2. The second was, *Himself to canonize him* for a saint, and to manifest the glory which the angels gave him at his death, to the end that all should hold him for such, and that in his honour, churches might be built, his images erected, and if his relics were found, highly reverenced, accomplishing that which Daniel said:—" But to me, Thy friends, O God, are made exceedingly honourable."(7)

And this Christ did, especially, to give us to understand the excellence of patience in afflictions and miseries, since it alone was sufficient to render testimony of his sanctity, and to canonize the patient for a saint: because he who conforms himself to the will of Almighty God in suffering, with more facility will conform himself in obeying: and to be a famous saint, it suffices to obey what God commands, and to suffer patiently what He ordains or permits, after the manner that we have said.

Colloquy.—O eternal God, I give Thee thanks for the honour which Thou hast done unto Thy servant,

(7) Ps. cxxxviii. 17.

lifting up the poor from the dunghill, to place them with the princes of Thy Kingdom: grant me to imitate this his patience and obedience, that by the means thereof I may enjoy Thy glory.   Amen.

To these *three points* may be reduced that which may be meditated in *every saint*, that is to say,—i. *His life*, and the steps of virtue whereby he ascended to so eminent a degree of sanctity, after the imitation of Jesus Christ.—ii. *His glorious death*, and the recompense which Almighty God bestowed upon him for the same.—iii. The *honour* which Almighty God does him, by rewarding him even in this life before men.

POINT IV.

1. The fourth is, to consider the *miserable life* of *the covetous rich man*, in all circumstances contrary to the life of the just Lazarus: forasmuch as his whole life was nothing else but a continual practice of covetousness and pride, of niceness and dainties, towards himself, and of hardness of heart toward others.

i. His *pride* and *sensuality* appeared in his apparel, clothing himself in purple for vanity, and in silk for delicateness; also in his eating, making sumptuous banquets by way of boasting, and feeding on delicate dishes for gluttony sake, eating and drinking every day till he was ready to burst.

ii. Secondly, his avarice appeared in reserving his riches for *himself alone*, showing great *hardness* and cruelty to the *poor*, without showing any pity or mercy towards them, or giving them alms, no not so much as the crumbs that fell from his table, nor had he any compassion on him who was covered with sores, and lay hungry at his gate; showing himself much more cruel than his very dogs, giving meat to them and not to the poor.   Whence it followed, that those of his house were such as himself, for as was the master, so was the servant, there not being one among so many who took any pity on that poor man. For these reasons he fell into many and most enormous sins; drinking down the whole malignant spirit of the world, which consists in " the concupiscence of the flesh," of worldly wealth, and in " pride of life;" (8) wholly contrary to the spirit of Christ.

2. For this cause, chiefly, Christ so *abhorred him*, that in recounting his life, He would *not nominate him*, nor take his name into His mouth, to shew how greatly He despised and detested him, and that He neither knew him, nor approved him, whose name was blotted out of the book of life, nor would He permit that his memory should remain amongst men. In the same manner does He abhor all those who have this spirit, or any particle of it, seeking after vanity, sensuality, and their own convenience, even to the prejudice of their neighbours.

Hence we may see how contrary the judgments of Christ are to those of the world. Lazarus, in the eyes of the world, was accursed; on the contrary, the rich man in the eyes of the world was blessed, but cursed in the eyes of Jesus Christ, who was always humble and austere to Himself, but sweet and indulgent to others, desiring that His servants should be also such.

Colloquy.—O sweet Jesus, I abhor from my very heart the pride of purple and all soft and delicate clothing, since Thou wast clothed in purple for scorn and mockery, and fastened naked on the cross. I wish for no banquets nor delicate dishes, since Thou didst eat bread made of barley, hadst gall given Thee instead of meat, and sour vinegar instead of drink.

<hr>

(8) 1 Joan. ii. 16.

I will not that my name be vainly published in the world, for fear lest Thou blot it out of the book of life, quite forget me, and cast me out of Thy holy Kingdom.

POINT V.

Consider fifthly, the *lamentable death* of this rich man, and the *tormen's* which he suffered in *the fire of hell.*

"*He also died and was buried,*" as Christ says, "*in hell;*" so that his death was the end of all his riches, delights, and vanities, and the beginning of the miseries, torments, and contempts which he suffers and shall suffer for ever and ever without any end.

After this life he carried nothing with him of all he had —only his vices and his sins, which were to be the fuel of his torments, and so was verified in him that which Job said:—" They spend their days in wealth, and in a moment they go down to hell;"(9) for although he died sweetly in appearance, yet the end of his life was the beginning of his pains. O terrible point, the end of a voluptuous life, which lasts not long, and is the beginning of a miserable life, which will never end. If at that moment I descend into hell, to what purpose will " my pride profit me, or what advantage will the boasting of riches bring me?"(10) Better it is for me to pass my days in tribulations, and in a moment to mount to heaven, to enjoy the reward and recompense of them.

2. Then Christ our Lord said, to declare the pains of this miserable man, that " *lifting up his eyes when he was in torments,*" he saw Abraham afar off and Lazarus in his bosom, and cried to him:—" Father Abraham, have mercy on me, and send Lazarus, that he may dip the tip of his finger in water, to cool my tongue; for I am tormented in this flame."(11) Wherein he teaches us, that the damned

(9) Job. xxi. 13.   (10) Sap. v. 8,   (11) Luc. xvi. 23.

suffer torments proportionable to their offences, as this wicked wretch suffered *four* exceeding terrible ones.—i. The first of *flames* which covered him all over, from the feet to the head, because of the vanity, of the soft and purple garments with which he had been clothed.—ii. The second, of his *tongue*, which, as it was the instrument of his gluttony, and his profane discourse, so was it burned in the fire, and tormented with most terrible hunger and thirst.—iii. The third, of *envy*, seeing by revelation the blessed lot of Lazarus, of whom he dare demand nothing, but only of Abraham.—iv. The fourth, of **contempt** and neglect of every one, in chastisement of his cruelty, for which he found no mercy at the hands of Abraham, who did not afford him the drop of water which he demanded, because he had denied those crumbs of bread to the poor; nor did he deserve any mercy, because he himself had showed no mercy.

Colloquy.—O most just God, how just are Thy judgments and how proportionable Thy punishments to our offences! Why do I not fear the rigour of Thy justice, and tremble at the torments of hell? Deliver me, O Lord, from offending Thee, that Thou discharge not Thine anger and indignation on me. Open the eyes of the rich, that they may take example by this wretch: open also the eyes of the poor, that they conceive no envy against the rich. Amen.

POINT VI.

Consider the *answer of Abraham*, denouncing to him the irrevocable sentence of the divine justice, in these words: " Son, remember that thou didst receive good things in thy lifetime, and likewise Lazarus evil things, but now he is comforted, and thou art tormented: and besides all this, between us and you there is fixed a great chaos, so that they which will pass from hence to you, cannot, nor from thence come hither." (12)

1. This sentence embraces and comprehends *two branches.*

i. The first, that the *rich man receives in this life temporal goods,* viz., embraced them with great avidity, placing in them his felicity, and taking them for the reward of certain good works; but in the chastisement of his evil works, the case was otherwise, for which he now endured pains and torments. On the contrary, *Lazarus received in this life evils* and afflictions, embracing and supporting them with singular patience, and by them atoning for the faults he had committed; but in reward of the good works which he performed, the chance turned, and now he receives great goods, and everlasting content. And thus *comparing together* the lots of these two men, I will choose for myself the lot of Lazarus, since it is impossible to obtain in this life, the lot of the rich, and in the other the lot of the beggar; and if I have for the present that of the beggar, I will comfort myself, that the lot of the rich will not hereafter befall me.

Colloquy.—O my soul, take good heed what lot thou choosest in this life, because thereon depends that which is to befall thee in the other. Tremble at temporal prosperities, which perhaps will afterwards turn into eternal adversities. And on the other hand, rejoice in the adversities of this life, since God sends them to thee as pledges of the prosperities which thou shalt enjoy in the other.

ii. The second is, that there is no *passage from hell to heaven,* nor from heaven to hell, so that never will any one of the blessed go from heaven to be damned in hell, because the decree of Almighty God in this case is absolute, firm and irrevocable, as in its place shall be declared.

(12) Luc. xvi. 25.

2. Ponder *another demand*, which this miserable man made to Abraham, which he likewise flatly refused him, saying:—" Then, father, I beseech thee that thou wouldst send him to my father's house, for I have five brethren that he may testify unto them, lest they also come into this place of torments." (13)   This he said, not for any charity, but that the company of his brethren in hell should not redouble and augment his torments, for the sin of evil example, which he had given them.   O terrible misery of the damned sinner, whose pains are increased with the sight of the good whom he contemned, and with the company of the wicked with whom he associated: so that both the good and the bad are his tormentors, and every thing "worketh evil" to him: as to those who love Almighty God, every thing "worketh" to their eternal "good." (14)

3. Abraham answered, (15) "they have Moses, and the prophets, let them hear them," and this will suffice them. The rich man replied:—" No, father Abraham, but if one went to them from the dead, they will do penance."   And he said to him:—" If they hear not Moses, and the prophets, neither will they believe, if one rise again from the dead:" for they may allege that it is a ghost, or a fantasy, and much more certain is the testimony of the Scripture revealed by Almighty God, than that of " the dead."

4. Hence I will conclude, how much it imports me to *know and believe* with a lively faith, *what God has revealed* in His word and Gospel concerning the life to come, and to conform my life to this belief, taking heed by another's harm; for if I stop my eyes, and my ears, not to hear what holy faith dictates to me, I should be more blind and hard to believe, that which the dead should say to me, if they should come in person to speak to me.   And if I will

(13) Med. li. part. 6.   (14) Rom. li. 9.   (15) Luc. xvi. 29.

believe and hearken to what the dead say, much better is it to hear what the holy Scripture reports of them, as if I heard it from themselves, since they are always saying to us that of Ecclesiasticus : (16) " Remember my judgment, for thine also shall be so: yesterday for me, and to day for thee," as we considered in the eleventh meditation of the first part.

(4.) MEDITATIONS ON MIRACLES OF CONVERSION OF SINNERS, AND OF HEALING THE SICK.

Two sorts of works did Christ our Lord exercise towards men, besides those which we have recounted about the insensible creatures, of wine, bread, and water. The one *spiritual*, converting sinners, hardened in their sins. The other *corporal*, healing the incurable infirmities of the sick, and raising the dead. And as St. Thomas says, (1) He ordinarily joined the first to the second, giving the health of the soul with the health of the body, healing, as the Lord says, " the whole man," as well the exterior, as the interior, first disposing him to receive entire and perfect health: and so meditating the corporal miracle, we ought to ponder the *spiritual effect* which He wrought on the sick, and *what is signified for our utility.* For as the infirmities of the body are signs of those of the soul, even so the cure of the one is represented in the mysterious cure of the other.

All this will be seen in the ensuing meditations, beginning with the *conversion of sinners,* of which the Evangelists make mention.

(16) Ecclus. xxxviii. 23.

(1) 3. p. q. xliv. ar. 3. ad 3.   Joan. vii. 23.   Luc. v. 23.   Joan. v. 14.

MEDITATION XXV.

ON THE CONVERSION OF MARY MAGDALEN.

POINT I.

Jesus being invited by a certain Pharisee, named Simon, a sinful woman who was in the city, as he supped, went to the house of the Pharisee to seek Him. (2)

1. Here consider, first, the *quality of this sinner*, for calling her by this name, we are given to understand that her sins were sins of the flesh, deeply rooted and scandalous in her, since for such sins this name is wont to be given to voluptuous women. Nevertheless, the Evangelist does not specify the quality of her sins, because, as St. Paul says, they ought(3) "not so much as to be named" with our mouths; but forasmuch afterwards, as SS. Luke and Mark say, that Christ drove out of her "seven devils,"(4) we thence gather that she was loaded with innumerable sins, signified by the number of "*seven;*" and that the seven deadly sins, and the devils who tempt and seduce to them, had a long time inhabited in her soul. Hence I will draw *two affections;*—i. Of fear of my own frailty, in beholding Mary Magdalen, who, through little defaults, came to fall into so many and heinous offences, since what happened to her may likewise happen to me.—ii. Of *confidence* in the mercy of Almighty God, in whom this heinous sinner found a remedy; hoping that I shall also find the like, if, as I have imitated her in sin, I imitate her in her repentance.

2. The *occasion* which this woman took to have recourse

<hr>

(2) Mat. xxvi. 7.   (3) Ephes. v. 3.

(4) Luc. viii. 2. Marc. xiv. 3.

to Christ our Lord, which was, to hear from Him a *certain sermon*, and to take notice of the meekness with which He received such as were sinners. But above all the *inspiration* of *heaven*, which touched her heart with a wonderful light, not by way of fear, terrifying her with the severity of chastisements, but by the way of love, discovering the obligations which she had much more to love the Creator, than the creatures, placing in Him all that love which she before had placed in them.

Colloquy.—O celestial Father, without whose favour none "can come to" Jesus Christ, (5) draw me to His service with the "bands of love," (6) lamenting that I have offended Him, who for so many reasons deserves to be beloved by me.

3. Admire the *prompt obedience* of this sinner, to the inspiration and grace of Almighty God, who waited not till Christ our Lord returned from thence to His usual lodging, but understanding where He ate, although it were in the house of a stranger,—at a banquet,—and in the presence of many people, hastened immediately to find Him.

Hereby I will learn not to delay good resolutions, and instantly to answer divine inspirations; especially in matter of my conversion, remembering that which the Wise man says:—"Delay not to be converted to the Lord, and defer it not from day to day, (7) because, on a sudden His anger will come, and in the day of vengeance He will destroy thee."

POINT II.

This sinner, entering into the house where Jesus was, " took a pound of ointment, of right spikenard, of great price, and anointed the feet of Jesus, and wiped His feet

(5) Joan. vi. 44.   (6) Osee xi. 4.   (7) Ecclus. v. 8.

with her hair." (8) In which remarkable and singular act is to be pondered the *perfect repentance* of this woman, and the *excellent virtues* which she showed on that occasion.

1. The first was, a great *faith* and esteem, which she conceived of the divinity and mercy of Christ our Lord, because she verily believed Him to be God, to whom alone it appertains to pardon sins; believing that without speaking a word to Him, as she spoke not one, He understood and penetrated her very heart, and knew sufficiently why she came, and what she sought and asked of Him. Others came to Jesus Christ to beg of Him a remedy for their corporal infirmities; but of this sinful woman alone we read, that she came to Him only for the cure of her spiritual infirmities, and for the forgiveness of her sins.

2. The second virtue was, an heroic *humility*, utterly despising her own honour, and what those at the table might say, beholding her in such a manner. Nicodemus came to consult with Jesus Christ concerning his doubts, but he came "by night," (9) and full of human fear; on the contrary, Mary Magdalen came to Christ, to ask of Him the health of her soul, even at mid-day, full of divine love, treading under her feet all human fear, and what the world might censure in her, as her whole desire was placed in this, to seek to please Almighty God. Nor had she humility only before men, exposing herself to be despised by them, but she had also another greater degree of humility before Almighty God, not daring to appear before the face of Jesus Christ—so abashed was she in respect of her sins—but went behind Him, prostrating herself at His holy feet.

Colloquy.—O my soul, humble thyself before Almighty God, humble thyself also before men: because whosoever humbles himself in all points, and to all

(8) Joan. xii. 3.   (9) Joan. iii. 2.

persons, shall not fail to "find grace before Almighty God,"(10) and shall afterward be honoured both by men and angels.

3. The third was an *affectionate internal sorrow*, joined with great affections of prayer and devotion, which she declared by these exterior signs. She watered and bedewed the feet of Jesus Christ with her tears, right sorrowfully deploring her sins past; beseeching Him to wash her soul with His holy grace.—She *wiped* them with her hair, beseeching Him to wipe away the foulness and deformity of her faults.—She kissed them with her lips, begging that He would reconcile her to Himself, and give to her the kiss of peace, and of perfect pardon.—She *anointed* them with precious ointment, beseeching Him to anoint her soul with His divine virtues, taking from her the unsavoury odour of her sins.—And without speaking a word, she poured forth her heart in the presence of Christ, much more abundantly than that " precious" ointment, manifesting to Him all her miseries, with a deep remorse and feeling for them.

From all this *I may learn* a most excellent manner *how to pray*, not by words,(11) but by *affections*, accompanied by deeds, and by ardent tokens bursting forth from the fire of my heart; such are sighs, groans, sobs, beating of the breast, lifting up the hands, bending the knees, even to the ground, kissing it with humility, and other like acts which the saints used, to excite themselves to devotion; because the fire which secretly burns in the bosom, suddenly catches hold of the garment, and the devotion of the spirit breaks forth from the very body.

4. The fourth virtue was, her *external penance*, converting into instruments of satisfaction, the things which had

(10) Ecclus. iii. 20.	(11) 1 Reg. i. Ps. xxxi. et cxli.

occasioned her perdition, employing in the service of Jesus Christ her eyes, hair, lips, precious perfumes, and herself wholly, forgetful of herself, and of all which was not to the pleasure of her Lord; accomplishing that which the blessed apostle S. Paul said:—"As you have yielded your members to serve uncleanness and iniquity, unto iniquity; so now yield your members to serve justice, unto sanctification."(12)

Colloquy.—O fervent penitent, O efficacy and force of divine inspiration! Touch me, O Lord, with such an efficacy, that all that is within me may be melted, and that all my powers and senses may be employed to appease Thee, converting me to Thee "ten times as much"(13) as I have departed from Thee.   Amen.

POINT III.

The Pharisee, who invited Jesus Christ, beholding this spectacle, spoke within himself, saying:—"This man, if He were a prophet, would know surely who and what manner of woman this is that toucheth Him, that she is a sinner."(14)

Where I may notice *two* exceedingly *rash* and pernicious *judgments* of this Pharisee: the one *against Jesus Christ;*—and the other *against Mary Magdalen*, both which he formed, because he was proud and presumptuous.

1. The first was to judge that *Jesus Christ* was *ignorant* what manner of woman Mary Magdalen was, and consequently that He was no "prophet;" or if He knew her, that He was not holy, since He suffered Himself to be touched by her, and .to pollute Himself by such a touching. In both which points he was deceived, following the opinion of other proud Pharisees, who said that of the prophet Isaiah:—"Depart from me, come not near me,

<hr>

(12) Rom. vi. 19.   (13) Bar. iv. 28.   (14) Luc. vii. 39.

because thou art unclean:" to which the holy prophet presently added punishment, saying:—" There shall be smoke in my anger, a fire burning all the day,"(15) punishing their error with the smoke, and their pride with the fire.

Colloquy.—O good Jesus, holy prophet, wise and humble! Thou knowest, O Lord, who it is that touches Thee, and therefore sufferest them to touch Thee, that so they may be satisfied by such touching, without any ways polluting Thee, for Thou refusest not to be touched by sinners, to render them pure and unspotted from their sins.

2. The second rash judgment was, to *censure that woman* because she had been a sinner, supposing that therefore she was so still, although she gave sufficient signs that she was so no more, weeping so heartily at the feet of Christ.

Hence I will gather, how false and erroneous the judgments of proud persons are, who rashly presume to judge of the very hearts and inward intentions, which are wholly reserved to Almighty God, thus drawing evil from good; because whence they had matter to draw compassion and edification, they took occasion to despise their neighbour.

And in particular I will consider in this Pharisee a most pernicious error of some self-opiniated persons in their first apprehensions, who, having noted or observed some sin in another, will not persuade themselves that ever afterwards he can become good, and always distrust him; and although they see evident signs of his change and conversion, yet they will not give him any credit; so that, with greater difficulty do they alter their own perverse judgment, than the others do their evil life. And, if they are superiors, they are occasion of desperation to their

(15) Is. lxv. 5.

subjects, because they do not believe their repentance as well as their fault. In this they likewise greatly injure the infinite goodness of Almighty God, whose property is both to forgive and to forget sins, as soon as a man does penance for them, and even to honour him who has offended and has amended.

POINT IV.

Jesus seeing the thoughts in the heart of the Pharisee, "said to him, Simon, I have somewhat to say to thee. But he said, Master, say it." (16)

1. In these words I will admire—

i. The *sovereign wisdom* of Jesus Christ our Lord, the universal judge, who beholding this sinner and this Pharisee silent, *penetrated their thoughts*, as well the good thoughts of the penitent, as the evil thoughts of the rash Pharisee, and exercised upon them a judgment most admirable, just, and merciful, approving the one and condemning the other, and all for the good of both the parties. For with His sovereign wisdom He defended the honour of this sinful woman, preferring her before the Pharisee, and reprehending his rashness in order to cure him, giving him to understand that He was a prophet, and knew right well who this woman was, seeing He knew and understood his very thoughts.

ii. And at the same time He showed him in His address great *modesty* and *humility*, considering that Simon had invited Him to dinner, and that He was within his house, for purposing to reprehend him He first courteously begged his leave to propose a question to him, and did not forthwith begin to condemn him, but disposed him by the discourse of a parable, to teach us hereby with what meekness and modesty we are to correct those that are

(16) Luc. vii. 40.

learned and persons of note, that the reprehension may redound to their profit, as in a like case it did to the prophet Nathan, when by the commandment of Almighty God he reprehended king David, (17) setting before him and showing him his sin by a parable, and thus moved and induced him to do penance.

2. The *parable* of our Lord and Redeemer was this:— "A certain creditor had two debtors, the one owed five hundred pence and the other fifty, and whereas they had not wherewith to pay, he forgave them both, which, therefore of the two loveth Him most? Simon answering said, I suppose that he to whom he forgave most. And He said to him, Thou hast judged rightly." (18)

3. Upon this parable I am to consider first in *general* the *mystery* which it unfolds,—i. who is this *creditor ;*—ii. who are the *debtors ;*—who *owes most ;*—who *least ;*—iii. how *they have not wherewith to pay ;*—how He *pardons them* gratuitously;—iv. and which of these debtors *love Him most*, who thus pardons them.

i. First, the *creditor is Almighty God*, who is offended by our sins, and has to show against us the writing and obligation which the apostle Paul calls:—" The hand-writing of decree that was against us," (19) or which was contrary to us. Or a bond and obligation of the decree of Almighty God against us, by which we sinners are bound to pay the temporal and eternal pain which our sins have deserved. For as He is infinitely wise and powerful, the debtor or creditor can neither deceive Him nor escape from Him.

ii. Secondly, the *debtors* are *men*, amongst whom some owe *more*, some *less*, because they have committed more enormous sins. Some owe fifty, because with their five senses they have broken the ten commandments of the law of God. Others owe " five hundred," for having infringed

(17) 2 Reg. 12. (18) Luc. vii. 41. (19) Col. ii. 14.

them more often, transgressing as well the precepts of the Church and of their own vocation, as of the law of the Gospel, which is a law of perfection, signified by the number of a hundred. Amongst these I should count myself for one, presuming that I am indebted a great deal more than I imagine, for that the debtor owes many secret and unknown debts, but not unknown to the creditor, on which account David said:—"Who can understand sins? From my secret ones cleanse me, O Lord." (20)

iii. These debtors are *not able to pay* their debts, for it is impossible by our own efforts to satisfy Almighty God for our offences, or deserve that He should pardon us, and cancel our obligations to Him, which would remain for ever unpaid if the selfsame God, out of His infinite mercy, had not made Himself man, and with His Passion and death cancelled them, "fastening" them with Him "to the cross," in virtue of which He freely pardons us our faults, by the means of penance, to oblige us to love Him with all our heart, for the infinite bounty which He showed in pardoning freely so great a debt to so vile a slave, and to invite him by this means anew to love and serve so good a Lord.

iv. Hence it is that he who has been *the greatest sinner*, after that God has pardoned him, is obliged in this respect to *love Him the more*, because he has received a greater benefit in so long expecting his repentance, pardoning him such grievous offences, and delivering him from greater pains. And if he has the light of heaven to confess these favours, let him make it apparent by showing himself grateful to his creditor; and this is the end and scope of this parable, for to love Almighty God much, or to love Him little, depends not so much on his having been a greater or less sinner, as on his having a greater

(20) Ps. xviii. 13.

or less acknowledgment to make for the pardon of his numerous and grievous sins. And as the proud (such as was the Pharisee) in their own opinion, are indebted but little to Almighty God, and have but little acknowledgment of their offences, which appear to them little, even so do they but little love Almighty God, because they hold but for little the benefit of having been pardoned by Him. But those who acknowledge themselves grievous sinners, and have a profound knowledge of the greatness of their sins, greatly love Almighty God when He does pardon them, because they acknowledge this benefit to be exceeding great.

Colloquy.—O most liberal and most merciful Lord, I desire to love Thee with all my heart, since instead of punishing me for having offended Thee, Thou desirest to pardon me, to the end I should love Thee. I acknowledge my sins to be most grievous, and many in number, and for the pardon of them I desire to return Thee very many and great services, to give proof of my amendment.

POINT V.

Next, consider how Christ our Lord *applied* this parable to this *woman*, who held herself so great a sinner, and to the *Pharisee* who reputed himself for just, and a great deal less sinner than she; wherefore, "turning to the woman He said to Simon: Dost thou see this woman? I entered into thy house, and thou gavest me no water for my feet, but she with tears hath washed my feet, and with her hair hath wiped them; thou gavest me no kiss, but she since she came in, hath not ceased to kiss my feet; my head with oil thou didst not anoint, but with ointment she hath anointed my feet; wherefore I say to thee, *many sins are forgiven her because she hath loved much.* But to whom less is forgiven, he loveth less:"(21) that is to say, "This woman esteems herself a great debtor, and so expects from me a greater benefit to remit and pardon her: and for this reason she loves much, as she has manifested by her works, and I have remitted her many sins, because she hath with this love disposed herself to receive the pardon of them. But thou supposest thyself to owe but little, and so expectest but a little benefit and favour from me in pardoning thee, and consequently lovest also but a little."

1. First, by the *example* of great and notorious converted sinners, Almighty God is accustomed to *confound* those who *presume they are just*, and therefore counsels us, behold and consider them attentively, saying: "Dost thou see this woman?" Seest thou her tears, and her sighs? Seest thou her humiliation and confusion? Seest thou the inventions which she has found, whereby to please and appease Almighty God? Seest thou all this? Then I say, consider it well, and be confounded at the little which thou dost, to purchase pardon at the hands of God. "Amen I say to you," says Christ our Lord, "that the publicans and harlots shall go into the Kingdom of God before you."(22)

2. I will reflect that one great sinner, with *one only fervent act*, is wont to mount up to a more excellent degree of *charity* and sanctity, than one *lukewarm just* soul, with *many* acts, and in many years. Where I am to behold what an excellent means it is, to obtain pardon, greatly to love Almighty God, for love disposes to pardon of sins, walks with it, increases and augments with it, when a man sees himself obliged to love him who has pardoned him.

Colloquy.—O my Redeemer, I am confounded in the presence of this so fervent a penitent, beholding my extreme tepidity. "Wash away the filth"(23)

(21) Luc. vii. 44.   (22) Matt. xxi. 31.   (23) Jr. iv. 4.

of this daughter of Sion, my poor soul, with the spirit of judgment and of fervour, giving me the spirit of justice and the fire of charity, whereby I may love Thee much, because Thou hast remitted me much.   Amen.

POINT VI.

Then said Jesus unto the woman, "Thy sins are forgiven thee. And they that sat at meat with Him began to say within themselves, Who is this that forgiveth sins also? And He said to the woman, Go, thy faith hath made thee safe, go in peace."(24)

1. Consider, first, the *efficacy of these words*, "Thy sins are forgiven thee:" by which He absolved her both from guilt and pain, and communicated a superabundant grace, exceedingly rejoicing the heart of Mary Magdalen to hear them. We likewise ought greatly to rejoice, since now our confessors, when they absolve us, say the same words to us, and work in us the same effect, if that we bring the same disposition.

2. The *modesty* of our Lord Jesus Christ likewise shewed itself in this case; for seeing that they were astonished because He pardoned sins, He would impute this pardon not to His own liberality, but to the faith of the sinner, saying, "Thy faith hath made thee safe;"—that is to say, "The lively faith which thou hast had of my power and divinity, and the loving confidence which thou hast taken in my mercy, have been the cause of thy salvation."

3. How *fixedly Mary Magdalen sat at the feet of* Jesus Christ: for seeing she had obtained the pardon she asked for, she would not stir, nor depart from thence, till Christ had said to her, " Go in peace:" thy peace is made with Almighty God, and within thyself, with plenary indulgence of all thy sins, and with complete victory of thy

(24) Luc. vii. 48.

sensual passions; for it may well be presumed that the liberality of our Lord granted all this to her, whom He loved so much. Perhaps for this reason, He said not to her, as to other sinners, "sin no more," as He knew full well the great firmness of her good resolutions, by the abundant grace and love which He had given her.

Colloquy.—O happy those who approach in humility and charity to the feet of Jesus Christ, whence they carry so happy a sentence. O my soul, go and prostrate thyself before them with great confidence, and embrace them with great love, purpose with great firmness to follow His footsteps, and never to depart from them till He say to thee: "Vade in pace." "Depart in peace." Amen.

MEDITATION XXVI.

ON THE CONVERSION OF THE SAMARITAN WOMAN.

POINT I.

Jesus Christ our Lord, walking from Judea into Galilee, through Samaria, " wearied with His journey, sat down on Jacob's well; it was about the sixth hour, there cometh a woman of Samaria to draw water."(1)

Here ponder:

1. First, the *labours* and *weariness* of our Lord Jesus Christ in His voyages and pilgrimages for the good of souls, walking on foot, and without any rest, long journeys, and in the heat of the day.

Colloquy.—O sovereign pastor, how dear does it cost Thee to seek Thy strayed and wandering sheep, taking as much pains for one alone, as for the whole flock! How many times didst Thou sweat by the

(1) Joan. iv. 6. et seq.

way, the weariness of Thy body enforcing Thee to sit down to ease Thyself and repose! I give Thee thanks, O my Lord, for these Thy wearinesses, and take compassion on Thee for them, because they are fore-runners of others far more painful; for within a little time Thou wilt find no other place of repose in the, heat of the day, but the hard bed of the cross.

2. The *charity* of this our Lord, who reposed not so much by the side of this well to relieve His body, as to surprise a soul which He had elected: for He never omitted any occasion to seek the good of distressed souls.

Colloquy.—O wisdom incarnate, how lovely and how admirable is the providence wherewith Thou "seeking such as"(2) wander astray. Those who seek Thee not, find Thee, and Thou sayest to those "that sought Thee not: Behold me!"(3) If the blessed Magdalen went to seek Thee, Thou inspiredst and first drew her to Thee.—If the Samaritan met with Thee, it was because Thou soughtest her. Inspire me, O Lord, to go after Thee, and also vouchsafe to seek me, that I may find Thee. Amen.

3. How *wonderful are the secrets of Almighty God* in the conversion of souls, taking occasion for this purpose, when they least imagine or think of it. This woman was a sinner, and sensual, who after she had had " five husbands," lived now in concubinage or unlawful company with a " sixth," and although St. Chrysostom (4) and other doctors are of opinion, that to all the five she was but their concubine, and that those five men were not her five lawful husbands, yet this woman being such, and going to the well to fetch water, without any care of her salvation, met with Jesus Christ, who showed to her extraordinary favours, with admirable efficacy and sweetness, accommo-

(2) Sap. vi. 17.   (3) Is. lxv. 1.   (4) S. Chrys. in Ps. xiii.

dating Himself to the quality and condition of the person with whom He treated, as shall be declared hereafter.

POINT II.

The woman of Samaria coming to the well, "Jesus said to her: *Give me to drink.*" She answered: "*How dost thou*, being a Jew, *ask of me to drink?*—for the Jews do not communicate with the Samaritans. Jesus answered —If thou didst know the gift of God, and who He is that saith to thee, Give me to drink, thou perhaps wouldst have asked of Him, and *He would have given thee living water.*" (5)

In this first conference is livelily represented, *what man is towards God*, and *what God is towards man;* which are two points of great profit to the spirit.

1. Christ our Lord, although He had a bodily thirst, because He was wearied in the way, and that it was in the middle of the day, nevertheless had a far greater *spiritual thirst* of the salvation of this soul: as He said upon the cross, "I thirst." And as he who is very thirsty greatly desires to drink water, and pours it into his body to quench his thirst, even so Christ our Lord, with most singular delight, drinks and receives souls, and makes them members of His own body, incorporating them with Him by holy love, and with this desire says to thee: "*Give me to drink.*"

Colloquy.—O most sweet Jesus, O that I could present to Thee innumerable souls to quench Thy thirst! Behold here mine, receive it, and incorporate it with Thee, so that it may never separate itself from Thee. Amen.

2. *The Samaritan refused* to give water to Jesus Christ, and likewise reprehended Him that He asked it at her

(5) Joan. iv. 7.

hands, and talked to her: in which is represented how niggardly, uncivilly, and rudely men deal with Almighty God, denying Him that which He demands of them, whether by secret inspiration, or by the mouth of His holy law, or by superiors, or by the poor, who ask them alms, never wanting excuses and pretexts not to give what He demands, and sometimes also covertly reprehending Him, and complaining that He requires too many and too great things of them, and even hold it painful and troublesome to talk or treat with Almighty God. All which proceeds from this, that, like the Samaritan, they do not know who this great God is, that demands of them, not having that estimation of Him which reason requires, because their faith is almost extinguished.

3. The *answer of Jesus Christ our Lord*, in which He discovered His infinite *charity* and *liberality* towards man; because, instead of revenging Himself on us, as David would on Nabol,(6) because he denied what he asked of him, He invites us anew to crave of Him that which we want, and desires that we should know who God is, and how great His gifts and graces are, to stir us up to desire them.   For this cause He says to the Samaritan, " O that thou knewest the gift of God, which is present before thee, which is His only Son given freely to the world, to communicate to it the gifts of the Holy Ghost, and the other gifts of grace, and knewest *the occasion* which I now offer to thee of thy salvation, or who He is that asks drink of thee, thou perhaps wouldst ask of Him, and He is so liberal that He would not refuse thee as thou refusedst me, but would give thee a water, not dead, but living, on which depends thy very life; yea, His liberality passes yet further, declaring a greater desire to give us His gifts, than men have to ask them after they know them; for in the

. (6) 1 Reg. xxv. 39.

first He makes no doubt, but doubts of the second saying:
—" If thou knewest who it is that asketh thee to drink,
thou perhaps wouldst ask of Him; for as thou art free,
perhaps thou wilt not desire that spiritual good which
thou knowest for fear of losing another; but if thou askest
me as thou oughtest, without doubt I will give it to thee.
He would have given it thee, because He has said to all:
—' Ask, and ye shall receive.' " For this reason St. Augustine says:—" Erubescat humana pigritia, plus paratus
est Deus dare, quam nos accipere." " Let human slothfulness be ashamed, that God is more ready to give than we
to receive."

Colloquy.—O my Saviour, illuminate my soul, to
make it understand "the gift of God," and move
me so effectually to ask for, that I may obtain it,
and then will I say to Thee: "Dilectus meus mihi,
et ego illi," Such as "my beloved to me," such am
"I to Him;" I will give Him all He shall ask of me,
as He gives me all I ask of Him; I will desire that
He demand something of me that I may give it
Him; as He desires that I demand much of Him,
that He may give it me: He is to me "a gift," because He gives Himself wholly to me by grace, and
I will be likewise "a gift" to Him, giving myself
wholly to Him, not for my own good, but only to serve
Him, world without end. Amen.

POINT III.

The woman said unto him, " Sir, thou hast *nothing
wherein to draw water*, and the well is deep, from whence
then hast thou living water?" Jesus answered:—" Whosoever drinketh of this water shall thirst again; but he
that shall drink of the water that I will give him, *shall not
thirst for ever*, but the water that I will give him, shall

become in him a *fountain* of water, *springing up unto life everlasting.*"(7)

1. In this discourse of the Samaritan is represented the *property of a carnal man,* of whom St. Paul says that he "perceiveth not the things which are of the Spirit of God,"(8) nor comprehends more than that which appears to the corporeal senses of the body, nor thinks of any other living waters, more than that which springs out of the fountains before his eyes; but the *condition of Christ our Lord is,* to teach us to raise up our spirit from visible things to things invisible, from temporal to eternal, and from creatures to the Creator; reflecting how in the Creator, and in celestial goods, perfections are far otherwise than in creatures, and in earthly goods; viz., without any faults and imperfections, which are found in created things. And so from the "water" of the well, and of the visible "fountain," He instructs us to discover one that is invisible; and by this example teaches us the manner how to meditate in mental prayer concerning these matters.

2. *Five wonderful properties* does Christ our Lord put down of *the "living water" of His grace,* comparing it to this material water, which we are to weigh, that we may know, desire, and earnestly seek to obtain it.

i. The first property is, that it *quenches the thirst for evermore.* In which it differs from material water, which quenches the thirst but for a little time, because it is corruptible, and by and by consumed. But the living water is of itself incorruptible, and abides in the soul everlastingly, unless she herself cast it up by mortal sin.

ii. The second property is, that it so *refreshes* and satisfies the soul, that it *takes away* generally the *thirst of all other waters* and goods of the world, after the manner that Christ our Lord speaks, saying:—" He that believeth in

<hr>

(7) Joan. v. 11.   (8) 1 Cor. ii. 14.

me, shall never thirst;"(9) that is, shall not desire anything created contrary to me, because he shall be filled
and satisfied with me; in which it differs from earthly
goods, which satisfy but a little, and for a little time, and
forthwith fade away, because they are vile, and easily consumed. But celestial goods nourish for ever, without
distaste or loathing, being so precious and so savoury, that
a man no more regards those that are earthly.

iii. The third property is, that the water of life *resembles*
"*a fountain* which *ever* springs, because the Holy Ghost
is within the same soul, which is the fountain of all graces,
from whom, as Christ our Lord says, spring fountains of
living water," with great abundance of celestial gifts: and
the same grace itself has always this inclination to grow,
increase, and augment itself, for which reason it is said of
it: "They that drink me shall yet thirst:"(10) that is to
say, Although they shall not thirst after earthly things,
yet shall they thirst, to increase in that good which they
possess with so great delight.

iv. The fourth property is, that this "water of life"
"*springeth up*" *within the soul*, boiling and leaping up with
great impetuosity even to heaven; that is to say, it inclines
to celestial things, with great joy, delight, and promptitude, not consenting to be detained by earthly things, nor
to suffer delays, nor to admit repugnances or tediousness,
and will not be inclosed or shut up within the heart of
man, but springs with violence out of itself, because,
lifting up itself above itself, it joins itself with its source,
and flows back to the place whence it proceeded, which is
to God.

v. The fifth property is, that it *springs* "*up unto everlasting life*," for, as St. Paul says, it is a "pledge of our
inheritance,"(11) which we hope for, and remains with it for

(9) Joan. vi. 35.   (10) Ecclus. xxiv. 29.   (11) Ephes. i. 14.

ever; wherein it is not only different from material goods, but also from some spiritual goods, which finish together with the life of the body, and enter not into life eternal; such are the virtues of faith, hope, and other graces, given gratis.

3. From these considerations *I am to draw* a very great *esteem* of the gifts of Almighty God, and great *care* to procure them, running with great joy to the fountains of our Saviour,(12) which are the sacraments, whence this water is drawn, and whence the increase and augmentation of it proceeds, pondering how the Samaritan, *understanding* these excellent properties, said to Christ:—" *Lord, give me this water, that I may not thirst, nor come hither to draw.*" In which words she discovered that she was advancing towards her conversion, with a great *desire* of this " living water" which she humbly asked of her Lord, who offered it to her. But her life was carnal and gross, for she asked this favour *for a base end*, viz., to be ever afterwards preserved from thirst, and to be delivered from the labour of going every day to the well for water.

Here is represented the imperfection even of some of the faithful, who desire spiritual goods, not so much for their excellence, as for some temporal profit which they expect to derive from them, such as some honour or interest, or to be delivered from melancholy and sadness, like those who desire sensible consolations from Almighty God, with an affection of self-love, for fear of feeling overmuch the heaviness of the troubles of this life, but those who desire to be perfect ought to seek and ask for this " living water," on account of its intrinsic excellencies, which are those aforesaid, saying, with most fervent affection:—" *Domine da mihi hanc aquam ut non sitiam in eternum.*"

Colloquy.—O Lord of heaven and of earth, give me

(12) Is. xii. 3.

this "living water," that I may never thirst after any other thing, nor fill myself with anxiety in seeking the water of temporal and corruptible goods, since the spiritual and the eternal suffice me.   O sweet Jesus, the fountain of living water, vouchsafe to place in my soul this divine fountain, which ever boils, increases and springs "up to everlasting life." Amen.

POINT IV.

Consider the wonderful *dexterity* with which Christ Jesus our Lord *disposed the Samaritan* by little and little, to renounce that which hindered her from receiving the living water of His grace.   For seeing her desire, He said to her:—"*Go call thy husband.—The woman answered and said, I have no husband.   Jesus said to her, Thou hast had five husbands, and he whom thou now hast is not thy husband: this thou hast said truly.*"(13)

1. *This woman is a figure* of those souls who *run after creatures* to enjoy pleasure by means of their five senses and appetites, granting to them all the delights which they inordinately desire, which is the reason why they are incapable of receiving the living water of grace, and the gifts of the Holy Ghost, which "cannot dwell in a body subject to sins," especially carnal sins, which, as St. Paul says,(14) profane " the temple of the Holy Ghost," and by the abominable union of the flesh with the voluptuary, destroy the precious union of the soul with the spirit of God.   For which reason the same apostle says:—" Fly fornication," and whatsoever is any occasion of it, to join your souls by love, " Uni viro Christo," to one only husband, who is Christ."

2. This being presupposed, I will ponder how Christ our Lord, to heal this woman, *crushed the imposthume of sin,*

(13) Joan. iv. 16.   (14) 1 Cor. vi. 18.

which she kept hidden in her breast, reprehending her not with bitter words, but with a spirit of sweetness and gentleness, saying:—*Having kept five men, now thou keepest one that is not thine.* As if He should have said:—It is now high time that thou shouldst bridle the appetite of thy insatiable desires, and withdraw thyself entirely from them.

3. Then will I ponder *in what good part* the Samaritan woman *accepted this reprehension* at His hands, neither denying the truth nor growing angry, nor yet returning any injurious words on Jesus Christ who thus affronted her, but contrariwise honoured Him, calling Him Lord, and believing Him to be a prophet, as He declared things so secret, and therefore said to Him:—"Lord, I perceive that Thou art a prophet," (15) for all Thou sayest is true.

i. And by this humble confession of her faults she made a beginning to her conversion, for he who suffers reprehension is very near his cure, for which reason Ecclesiasticus says:—"How good it is when thou art reproved to show repentance, for so thou shalt escape wilful sin." (16)

ii. Then she gave a *second sign* of her repentance, and of the faith and esteem which she had conceived of Jesus Christ, desiring to be resolved by Him of certain doubts which she had in matters of religion. "Our fathers," said she, "adored on this mountain, and you say that at Jerusalem is the place where men must adore;" (17) that is to say,—"Lord, since Thou art a prophet, draw me out of the doubt I am in, and teach me in what place I am bound to adore God, and offer sacrifice to Him to please Him, and to make myself agreeable to Him." From which we may learn, that the first care of a true penitent ought to be to know what appertains to the true faith and service of Almighty God, without which "it is impossible to please God." (18)

(15) Joan. iv. 19.
(16) Ecclus. xx. 4.   (17) Joan. iv. 20.   (18) Heb. xi. 6.

Jesus answered:—"Woman, believe me that the hour cometh when you shall neither on this mountain, nor in Jerusalem, adore the Father;—and now the hour cometh when the true adorers shall adore the Father, in spirit and in truth, for the Father also secketh such to adore Him. God is a spirit, and they that adore Him must adore Him in spirit and in truth;" that is to say, " This thy demand is not necessary, as concerning the place of adoring God with sacrifices and ceremonies, with which until this time He has been adored, because they are all to cease, and Almighty God will be adored 'in spirit and in truth,' which was veiled under these shadows and exterior figures."

4. But pondering yet further the *spirit* of these words, our Lord Jesus Christ instructs us by them, the *manner* how He will be *adored* by the faithful in the law of the Gospel, especially in that adoration which every one pays to Almighty God alone in secret.

i. First, this adoration may be made *in every place*, for although there are churches deputed for the sacrifice of the Mass, nevertheless in every place and corner I may adore Almighty God, because He is in every place; on which account St. Paul says:—" I will, therefore, that men pray in every place, lifting up pure hands to Almighty God." (19)

ii. Moreover, this adoration ought to be made *within my soul*, which is the spiritual temple of Almighty God, and the oratory deputed for devout prayer, whereinto Jesus Christ commands us to enter, to pray to our heavenly " Father in secret," (20) who is there, and beholds us when we adore Him.

iii. Thirdly, this adoration ought to be made " *in spirit and in truth*," because it ought to proceed from the inspiration and motion of the spirit of holiness and truth,

(19) 1 Tim. ii. 8.　　　(20) Mat. vi. 6.

which is Jesus Christ, and to follow His direction and dictate, conforming our understanding to the truth of faith, our life to that of our Lord and Saviour, and our exterior works to the interior, without any fiction and dissimulation. For even as " God is a spirit," and "truth" itself, He seeks adorers like Himself, which are spiritual and true, as He Himself is; and consequently I ought not to content myself with only exterior worship, because it is a body without a soul, and a shadow without truth; but I ought principally to produce those *interior acts of virtue*, which give it life and animation, such as are—*faith* in the greatness of Almighty God, joined with humility, and an acknowledgment of my own littleness,—*hope* in His divine promises, with prayer and petition to obtain them,— the *love* of Almighty God, with obedience and submission to His holy will, with acts of devotion, prayer, and thanksgiving. After this manner is Almighty God adored as He desires, " For the Father also seeketh such to adore Him." (21)

Colloquy.—O Father of mercies, it is in Thy hand to find what Thou seekest, and to do what Thou desirest: grant that I may adore Thee "in spirit and in truth" with which Thou desirest to be adored. And since Thou hast made me so happy as to live in the law of grace, grant that I may adore Thee, not only in one, but in every place: not with the body alone, but with the spirit: not with external show, but in truth following Thee, who art "the way, the truth and the life," to whom be all honour and glory, world without end. Amen.

POINT V.

Consider the wonderful *conversion* and sudden change of the Samaritan woman, who as yet rude in things apper-

(21) **Joan. iv 32.**

taining to Almighty God, did not comprehend the sublime doctrine of Jesus Christ, for she said to Him:—"I know that the Messiah cometh, therefore when He come He will tell us all things. Jesus said to her, I am He who am speaking with thee." (22)   In which words we must consider,—

1. The infinite *charity* of Christ our Lord, who sought to discover so clearly a truth so sublime, and of such importance to such a sinful and ignorant woman, which He had concealed from the scribes and Pharisees, or declared only by ambiguous parables, in punishment of their pride.

2. His Almighty *power* also no less shone in the wonders which He wrought in this woman, by the virtue of His word:—"I am He who am speaking with thee."

i. He first clearly enlightened her understanding with a true faith, to make her to understand who He was that talked with her, and to believe Him to be the Messiah.

ii. And next He spoke to her heart, mollifying and softening it, to abhor and detest her former life. Moreover, He gave her the living water of His grace, which she asked of Him, fulfilling the word which He said to her:— If thou hadst asked it of me, I would have given it thee.

iii. *He replenished her with so great an interior joy*, that she quite forgot the material water for which she was come thither, so that leaving her vessel at the well, she ran speedily into the city, to give notice of Jesus Christ, and to tell her neighbours, that they likewise might come to enjoy the same treasure which she enjoyed. In which we must notice the *fervour of a soul touched* with the *hand of Almighty God*, who leaves all it has to be free and ready for all things belonging to His holy service, as the blessed apostles did. (23)

(22) Joan. iv. 25.　　　　　(23) Mat. iv. 22.

iv. He gave her perfect *humility*, by which she disdained not even to defame her own self, that so she might honour Jesus Christ, declaring publicly that He had discovered to her the very secrets of her sinful life, that they might repute Him for a prophet, giving us an example boldly to publish Jesus Christ, as St. Paul says, "by evil report and good report." (24)

v. He gave to her great *prudence*, and the living water of perfect *wisdom*, in the manner of preaching Jesus Christ, for she began not by saying: "Believe me that I have seen a prophet, doubtless He is the Messiah," &c., but confessing the frailty of her sex, and that she was not worthy to be believed she said: "Come and see;" and although she said, Come and see if it be that Christ which is to come, yet was it not doubting, but with great modesty, desiring that they likewise should come to see Him, and to be assured of what she said, hoping that Christ would also teach them, as He had taught her.

vi. Finally, He imparted to her so great a *spirit*, and such *fervour* was in her words, that many people went out of the city to see our Lord Jesus Christ, and by her means they believed in Him.

Colloquy.—O riches of the grace of Almighty God, O wonderful "change of the right hand of the most High!" (25)   Who but Thyself, O my God, could so suddenly touch the heart of this woman, and work in her and by her, so many wonders? I am ashamed, O my Lord, of my own tepidity, when I behold the fervour of this so great a sinner. Enlighten me, O my Lord, inflame and change me, with this Samaritan, that I may serve Thee and publish Thy greatness, that so I may be a worthy instrument of Thy glory. Amen.

(24) 2 Cor. vi. 8.   (25) Ps. lxxvi. 11.

POINT VI.

Consider *what* in this case *befel the disciples and their master.*

1. For as they had left Him behind whilst they went to buy meat, at their return *they wondered* not a little to see Him talking with such a woman, looking upon it as a great humiliation of their master, to talk and discourse *with a simple woman*, supposing that He discoursed with her, according to His custom, on divine things.

Colloquy.—O my Redeemer, although I am astonished at Thy humility, yet I likewise praise Thy exceeding charity, since with so much care Thou seekest after a lost sheep, although it be the least and most contemptible of all Thy flock, conversing familiarly with her, to draw her out of her bad state. Help me, O Lord, with Thy holy grace, by which I may likewise apply myself to gain to Thee, as well the little as the greatest sinner, for Thou art no less desirous of the salvation of the one than of the other.

2. They also greatly wondered to see Him speak *all alone with a woman*, it being a rare thing in Him; nevertheless they said not a word to Him, because they held in great veneration all whatsoever their master did, without thinking any evil of His actions. Hence superiors are to take advice not to indulge in such conversations, unless very rarely, and in case of urgent necessity: inferiors also may take example, not to judge rashly nor to suspect amiss the sayings and doings of their superiors, whom they ought to reverence even as saints, remembering what the Psalmist says:—" Touch ye not mine anointed, and do not evil to my prophets." (26)

3. Then the apostles said to Christ:—" Rabbi, eat. But He said to them, I have meat to eat which you know not,

(26) Ps. civ. 15.

—My meat is to do the will of Him that sent me, that I may perfect His work." (27)

In which words He discovered in what great *estimation* He held the fulfilling of the will of His heavenly Father, which was the conversion of souls, since, being both weary and hungry, instead of eating, He affirmed that His meat was to "do the will" of His Father, yet not as He Himself would, but with great perfection and integrity. And, although He was to taste of gall and vinegar, yet all this seemed sweet to Him, seeing it was the will of Him whom He so greatly loved.

Colloquy.—O sweet Jesus, grant me that my meat may be to fulfil Thy will and not my own, fulfilling perfectly that which Thou commandest, and swallowing so greedily this meat of the soul, that I may forget the meat of the body. Amen.

Hence, also, I will draw a *holy fear*, lest Jesus Christ should say to me:—" I eat a certain meat which thou dost not know;" that is to say, "a meat which thou dost not approve, nor like, and therefore thou eatest not of it with me." For if I be disobedient to the law of Almighty God, to His divine inspirations, and to the commandments of my superiors, I know not, nor eat the meat which Christ eat, and consequently I do not lead the life of Christ, for no one can be united with Jesus Christ if he eat not the like meat which Christ eat.

4. Finally, I will ponder how at this time *the Samaritans came to seek Jesus Christ*, who received them with most singular love, and preached to them the Kingdom of God; and at their entreaty remained with them two entire days, during which time He greatly refreshed Himself with this spiritual meat, as many believed in Him, and that with such certitude and assurance, that being convinced by His

(27) Joan. iv. 31.

divine reasons without having seen His miraculous miracles, they said to the woman:—Now, "not for thy saying"
do we believe, but for that ourselves do " know, that this
is indeed the Saviour of the world," (28) not only of the
Jews, but also of the Gentiles, of which we have sufficient
testimonies.

Colloquy.—O heavenly master, who by the means
of Thy Catholic Church figured by this fervent
Samaritan, givest us to understand who Thou art:
give us the same likewise, by Thyself within the interior of our hearts. Remain with us two entire days,
instructing us well in the two precepts of Thy holy
love, that by observing them from point to point, we
may come clearly to see that Thou art our God, our
Lord and our Saviour, to whom be honour and glory,
world without end.   Amen.

MEDITATION XXVII.

ON THE WOMAN TAKEN IN ADULTERY ;—CHRIST'S DELIVERING HER FROM HER
ACCUSERS, AND MERCIFUL FORGIVENESS OF ALL HER SINS.

POINT I.

Jesus preaching "early" to many people in the Temple,
" the Scribes and Pharisees bring unto Him a *woman
taken in adultery*, and they set her in the midst, and say to
Him:—Master, this woman was even now taken in adultery.   Now Moses, in the law, commanded that we stone
such a one to death; but what sayest Thou?   And this
they said tempting Him." (1)

Here I am to ponder:—

1. First, the wonderful *meekness* of Christ our Lord, in
conversing with sinners, and His great *mercy* in pardoning
them their sins, since even His enemies, by the instiga-

(28) Joan. iv. 42.   (1) Joan. viii. 3.

tion of the Devil, sought to set a snare to entrap Him, making Him judge of this adulterous woman, presuming, that of His mercy He would forgive her, contrary to the law of Moses, changing or correcting somewhat of the law, that so they might take occasion to accuse Him of being contrary to Moses and the law; or if He condemned her, then to publish abroad every where that He was not so merciful as He appeared. Whence I will draw great joy for having so meek and so merciful a Saviour and master, saying:—

Colloquy.—I rejoice, O my Saviour, at Thy wonderful meekness and Thy mercy, desiring to make thereof a snare, not to tempt Thee like the Pharisees, but to attract Thee into my heart, that Thou mayest take compassion on me, and mayest pardon my manifold and most grievous sins. Amen.

2. The second shall be to consider the subtlety of Satan, and of his ministers, in tempting the just, setting snares for them in the virtue which they prize most, and drawing them all, by extremes, into the contrary vice, treading the law of Almighty God underneath their feet, under the colour of this virtue. Him that is inclined to too much *mercy* they tempt, that under the colour of mercy he may violate the laws of justice.—Him that is very zealous they tempt, that under the pretext of zeal he should use vengeance against the law of meekness; for which reason it is needful to know how to join all virtues together, without prejudicing the other, after the imitation of Almighty God, of whom David said:—" Because of truth, meekness, and justice, Thy right hand shall conduct thee wonderfully." (2) And in another place, says:—" Mercy and truth have met each other, justice and peace have kissed."(3)

Colloquy.—O most wise master, teach me how to

<hr>

(2) Ps. xliv. 5.   (3) Ps. lxxxiv. 11.

link together virtues with such dexterity, that complying perfectly with the one I fail not in the perfection of the other. Bring me into the "cellar" of Thy precious "wines"(4) ordaining Thy charity in me, that I may so drink the affections of one virtue, that my judgment be not troubled to prejudice another. Amen.

POINT II.

"Jesus bowing Himself down, wrote with His finger on the ground."(5)

1. Here I am to ponder the *causes*, together with the mysteries of this writing.

i. Jesus Christ our Lord, bowed down Himself to write on the ground, *like to a man wholly pensive*, to signify that He made but little account of such a demand, because it did not then concern Him to judge of such causes in exterior judgment, nor did He at all desire to intermeddle with them, more than with that young man, who besought Him to will his brother to divide the inheritance with him, saying, "Man, who hath appointed me judge or divider over you?"(6) to give us to understand that which St. Paul afterwards said:—"No man being a soldier to God, entangleth himself with secular business." (7)

ii. Christ our Lord, beholding the fury with which they came, and would presently condemn that poor woman, began leisurely to write on the ground; to teach them that in *important matters*, on which the honour and life of our neighbour depends, *we must not proceed with passion* and precipitation, but with pausing, and maturity, thinking of them,—writing, reading, and understanding all that passes, for men easily deceive themselves, in judging the actions of their neighbours: and for this very reason

(4) Cant. ii. 4.   (5) Joan. viii. 7.   (6) Luc. xii. 14.
(7) 2 Tim. ii. 4.

our Lord said to Abraham, "the cry of Sodom and Gomorrah is multiplied, I will go down and see whether it be not so."(8)

And of this advice I will profit, to judge of nothing rashly, although others say to me that it is certain, until I myself am well instructed in the truth.

iii. "He wrote with His *finger* upon the ground," to bring to their memory, *that He was the self-same Almighty God, who,* with His finger *wrote the law of Moses* on tables of stone; so that He knew and well understood all those who brake the same with perverseness, whom He was to write, as Jeremias says, in the earth, and not in heaven, because they were departed from Almighty God, and forsook "the vein of the living waters" (9) of His grace: and consequently He wrote them on the earth, because accusing this woman, they broke the law, breaking it in the manner of accusing her, and in the perverse intention which they had to surprise the judge.

Colloquy.—O most just judge, who searchest the inward hearts of men, write in mine with Thy finger Thy holy law, that I may fulfil it perfectly, that I come not like the damned to be written in the earth, but like the saved to be written in heaven. Amen.

2. Lastly, I may reflect—not on that which Christ our Lord wrote, since it cannot be known, nor would the Evangelist express it—but *on that which it may be believed* that He wrote, fitting to the present purpose, such as that which He said of the hypocrite:—" Why seest thou the mote that is in thy brother's eye, and seest not the beam that is in thine own eye?"(10) Or else He wrote *the sins of these accusers*, for which they deserved to be written in the earth. But they were so blinded with their passions,

(8) Gen. xviii. 26.　　(9) Jer. xvii. 13.　　(10) Mat. vii. 3.

so drunk with envy in accusing this woman, and in bringing to pass their wicked purpose, that they took no heed
at all of the writing: (11) for if they had, perhaps in
reading it they would have trembled, as king Baltasar
did when he saw the fingers which wrote upon the wall
his doom and the sentence of his damnation. (12)

Colloquy.—O heavenly master, enlighten the eyes
of my soul, that I may see the beams of my sins,
without meddling rashly in the sins of others, and
quicken my spirit to make it understand bitter things
which "Thou writest against me"(13) in this life,
that so I may amend in good time, and finally obtain
life everlasting.　Amen.

POINT III.

The scribes and Pharisees persevering in their demand,
" Jesus lifted up Himself, and said to them : He that is without sin among you, *let him first cast a stone at her*.　And
again, stooping down, He wrote on the ground, but they
hearing this, went out one by one, beginning at the
eldest."(14)

1. First, here is to be considered, the *prudence*, and
integrity of Christ our Lord in this His answer, because
without either infringing the law, or condemning the woman, He confounded her accusers, and this with great
equity: which He signified by lifting "up Himself," when
He pronounced the sentence.　He did the same when they
asked Him if it were lawful to give tribute to Cæsar,
answering them: " Render to Cæsar the things that are
Cæsar's, and to God the things that are God's."(15)

Hence I will draw affections of great joy, for the
heavenly prudence of Christ our Lord, beseeching Him to
grant me that part of this virtue, which is called writing,

<hr>

(11) S. Amb. ep. 67.　S. Jer. lib. ii. cont, Pel.　　　(12) Dan. v.
(13) Job. xiii. 26.　　(14) Joan. viii. 7.　　(15) Mat. xxii. 21.

by which I may defend myself against the crafts and subtleties of the Devil, and against the malice and calumnies
of wicked men.

2. Our Lord Jesus Christ, by means of this sentence,
revived the spirits of these accusers, awakening and renewing the remembrance of their own sins, which they had
forgotten, and cast at their backs, that seeing their own
sins and the accusation of their own conscience, they might
cease to accuse this poor woman: for reason requires
that he that will condemn another, ought not to be cul-
pable of the same crimes which he imputes to them, or
of others greater; also that all may learn to have compassion on sinners, since they are sinners themselves, as
well as they; and that myself may easily fall into the same
sin into which my neighbour is fallen: for this reason it
is most unjust that I should throw at him stones of murmurings, calumnies, or other injuries, which I would not
that others should throw at me.

3. Christ our Lord, "again stooping down, wrote on
the ground," to give them an opportunity of doing that
which they were to do, leaving them in the hands of their
own consciences, that thence they might hear their own
sentence. But those miserable men, although they knew
full well their faults and were confounded at them, yet
they would not confess themselves before Jesus Christ,
and ask pardon for them, but shamefully withdrew themselves from His presence. By which we may see how
terrible is the torment of our own conscience, and how it
dreads to find itself before this supreme judge; where we
may remark, the difference that there is between sinners :
for some, obstinate in their sin. although they both know
it and are ashamed of it, yet will not confess it, but fly
from God, and would willingly hide themselves from Him,
as Adam did, after he had sinned; but others, touched

with divine grace, approach Almighty God to obtain forgiveness, like the Publican.

Colloquy.—O most merciful Father and most just judge, although I know my faults, yet seek I not to fly from Thy presence, as did these sons of the earthly Adam, imitating this their own father: but, O Lord, because I am a sinner I come to Thee, as the sick man to the physician, confessing my sins with shame, that so it may please Thee to grant me full forgiveness and pardon of them. Amen.

4. These miserable Pharisees, although they came united together with one common consent against Christ Jesus, yet *fled not away together*, but "*one by one*," first one, then another, because every one of them was so ashamed of his sins, that without making any account of his companion, he fled and forsook him, " beginning with the eldest,"—because as they were greater sinners, so malice and shame wrought sooner this effect in them, to begone. Whence I will gather how great the shame will be, which I shall have in the hour of death and of judgment, and the little succour and comfort I shall receive from those whom I took for companions of my wickedness: and with this consideration, I will carefully attend to the business of my salvation, retiring from all kind of wicked company, to join myself to Jesus Christ our Lord and Saviour, on whom depends both my temporal and eternal felicity.

POINT IV.

" Jesus lifting up Himself, said to the woman, Where are they that accused thee, hath no man condemned thee? who said, No man, Lord; Jesus said, Neither will I condemn thee; go, and now sin no more." (16)

1. Christ our Lord lifted up Himself *twice* from whence

(16) Joan. viii. 10.

He had stooped to write on the "ground." Once to behold the *Pharisees*, and to confound them with justice.—The other, to behold this *woman*, and to set her free by means of His mercy: for the eyes of Almighty God beholds rebellious sinners to chastise them; and contrite sinners to pardon them; and in the one and in the other, He is right, just, and holy, as David says. (17) But as soon as He had beheld the Pharisees, He forthwith bowed Himself down that He might not see them, as being unworthy of His sight, and as a people who departed from His presence, unworthy of it: but He beheld this woman with the eyes of His mercy, and sent her away with a happy sentence, because she was contrite and humble of heart.

Colloquy.—O most sweet Jesus, vouchsafe, I beseech Thee, to look upon me with these eyes of mercy, and never to withdraw or divert them from me, since it depends on Thy merciful looks, that I never withdraw myself from Thee. Amen.

2. This woman being delivered from her accusers, and standing all "alone" before Jesus Christ, *had great compunction for her sins*, blushing with shame for having committed them, and expecting the sentence of our Lord, before whom her accusers had brought her. But He comforted her saying, "Where are thy accusers, hath no man condemned thee?" As if He had said, "It is from me thou hast received this benefit, that thy accusers are departed, and have left thee free. And since they condemn thee not, I will not be more cruel than thy accusers, and therefore neither do I condemn thee, because I am not come to condemn sinners, but to save them; wherefore depart in peace." By which words He set her free, not only from temporal but from eternal death, pardoning her all her

(17) Ps. xxxiii, et cxliv.

sins: for the works of Jesus Christ our Lord were most perfect, so that saying He would not condemn her, was understood, that He neither condemned her with temporal condemnation, nor with eternal, but that He absolved her from the sin, for which she had deserved both the one and the other.

Colloquy.—O most sweet and most merciful Jesus, the rampart and the refuge of sinners, how shall I, O Lord, repair the love and care which Thou takest of me? Who will be so hardy as to accuse or condemn me, if Thou dost justify me and free me?(18) How shall I not trust in Thy mercy, since in Thy presence all my misery wholly vanishes? Thou deliverest me from the calumnies of men,(19) and from the accusations of my enemies, pardoning me so liberally my offences, that there is no cause to impose the pains of condemnation upon me: and Thy mercy is so ample that I will never cease to praise and serve Thee.

3. The last word which Jesus Christ our Lord spake to this woman was:—" Go now, and sin no more;" as if He had said, " Since I have delivered thee from this danger, know that it is not that thou shalt therefore live at thy liberty as thou hast lived hitherto, but that thou lead a temperate, clean, and chaste life, returning no more to thy accustomed sin;" and it is to be believed, that even as her accusers never after came against her to accuse her, because Christ our Lord would have it so, even so she never returned to her former dissolute life, but persevered in the service of Almighty God, not now for fear of chastisement, but for the love of Him who had done her so great a good, to whom be all honour and glory, world without end. Amen.

(18) Rom. viii. 33.   (19) Ps. cxviii.

MEDITATION XXVIII.

ON THE CONVERSION OF ZACHEUS, CHIEF OF THE PUBLICANS.

POINT I.

Jesus entering into Jericho, behold a "man named Zacheus, who was the chief of the publicans, and he was rich; and he sought to see Jesus who He was, but could not for the crowd, because he was low of stature, and running before, he climbed up into a sycamore tree, that he might see Him, for He was to pass that way." (1)

1. Consider the *beginning of the conversion of this man,* rich and powerful amongst the people, though he was an egregious sinner, and exceedingly covetous, even the first and principal of the covetous usurers, who amongst the Hebrew people were held and reputed for notorious sinners. His first grace was a *desire* with which Almighty God inspired him to see Jesus Christ, and to know Him, imagining that this sight alone would be profitable to him. In which really he was not deceived, for the first beginning of all our remedies is, to see Jesus Christ with a lively faith, and to know Him in the manner wherein He conversed and lived in this world, (figured by Jericho,) beholding Him poor, meek, humble, and crucified for us, the only sight of which invites us to forsake our sins and covetousness.

Colloquy.—O good Jesus, give me an efficacious desire to see Thee in this manner: for if the sight only of the brazen serpent erected upon a pole, (2) was sufficient to heal the bitings of real serpents, far

(1) Luc. xix. 2.   (2) Num. xxi. 7.

better were it for me to behold Thee, God and man, fastened to the cross under the figure of a sinner, that so I may be healed of all my sins.

2. Ponder the *efficacy of this desire of Zacheus*, and the diligence he used to accomplish it, treading under foot the honour of the world, and all that men might say, when they saw so rich and leading a man running like a child, getting upon the top of a tree, where it is to be believed that the passers by laughed at him, especially as he was so little. By this example I will learn, that when God shall inspire me with good desires, I am not to resist them from motives of human respect, when I ought to make them efficacious for my salvation; but like Zacheus, I should ascend upon the sycamore, (which is a wild and savage fig tree,) treading under foot the favours of the world, honours, (3) and riches, to embrace that which the world esteems folly, which is the cross of Jesus Christ. (4)

Colloquy.—O good Jesus, who for the love of me didst mount up on the tree of the cross, where Thou wast despised and mocked by men: grant me grace to mount up on this tree, which is the tree of wisdom to the elect and of foolishness to worldlings: for I am sure that if I mount on it spiritually, Thou wilt behold me with the eyes of mercy, as Thou didst behold this Zacheus. Amen.

POINT II.

Jesus drawing nigh to the place where Zacheus was, beholding him, said to him:—" Zacheus, make haste and come down, for this day I must abide in thy house."

Ponder here the infinite *charity* and *mercy of Christ* our Lord, which shines in this work, accomplishing the desires of this publican, not only by suffering Himself to be seen by him, but by offering Himself to go with him, a thing

(3) Theoph. Greg. xxvii. Mor. c. 27.   (4) 1 Cor. i.

which we read not that He did at any other time, every word of which has its particular mystery to be considered.

1. He *calls him by his name*, "Zacheus," to show him that He knew him well, though He had never seen him, knew his name, and had written him in the book of everlasting life, desiring to supply that which was wanting to his name, for Zacheus signifies "pure" or "justified:" but he unjustly usurped this name, being unjust and wholly sinful, nevertheless, Jesus Christ calling him, he began to purify himself, so to become pure and just.

2. He commanded him to "*make haste and come down*," to signify the desire He had to hasten his justification, and that He would not lose a moment of time, nor the occasion that was offered to justify him, before his good desire should grow cold. Teaching those who are engaged in the conversion of souls, that seeing them touched by Almighty God, they are to hasten to accomplish their desires, before the north wind of temptation freeze them, or the summer of persecution wither them. For the selfsame reason it is the pleasure of our Lord Jesus Christ, that I execute promptly and fervently such desires as He inspires me with; and that if I be in a high place, I must abase and humble myself; if I be hindered or withheld, I must advance and run with alacrity to accomplish that which He commands me.

Colloquy.—O my Saviour, who hast taken upon Thee the name of one who hastens: hasten, I beseech Thee, to justify me and all such sinners as Thou hast touched with Thy inspiration, moving them with such efficacy, that they may forthwith obtain Thine abundant grace. Amen.

3. He says:—"*For this day* I must abide in thy house." He said not *to-morrow*, or another day, but "*this day*," for

He desires not that good resolutions be deferred until to-morrow if they can be accomplished that present day, because the present day is certain, and that of to-morrow most uncertain, and so He wills that to-day with diligence and fervour we treat of lodging Him, because perhaps to-morrow we would and cannot, or perhaps He will pass further, and will leave us there, for having omitted the opportunity which He offered us.

Colloquy.—Wherefore, O my soul, if thou hearest to-day the voice of thy Lord who calls thee, "harden not" (5) thy "heart," for He that calls thee to-day perhaps will not call thee to-morrow: if therefore to-day He offer Himself to dine in thy house, and that thou dost not receive Him, perhaps He will not come when thou shalt afterwards call and invite Him.

4. This word, "*I must*," is the most noble and royal of all the rest:—" I must abide this day in thy house."

Colloquy.—O sweet Jesus, this much more imports Zacheus, than it does Thyself, for Thou art our God, who "hast no need of" any of our "goods;" (6) and if one deny his house to Thee, Thou canst find a thousand who will gladly receive Thee : as to Zacheus, if Thou do fail him, all good will be wanting him. Wherefore then sayest Thou that it imports Thee to be "this day" in his house?   The love, O my Lord, which Thou bearest to us, makes Thee to say that that imports Thee which imports us, undertaking both our weal and our woes, as if they were Thine own. Since then it so imports Thee to enter into my house, come thither, Lord, and enter therein, because Thy entrance much imports me, and my importance Thou hast taken for Thine.

5. Finally, He says that it imports him " *manere*," to " *abide*" there, that is to say, to make His residence there,

<hr>

(5) Ps. xciv. 8.   (6) Ps. xv. 2.

until such time as He has done there all that which He intends to do, for that which so much imports Jesus Christ He does not in passing, but in *abiding;* and although He wants to be invited and pressed to come, yet He is not in a hurry to depart, if He be not driven out of the soul into which He has entered.

Colloquy.—O Son of the eternal Father, together with whom Thou comest into the soul of him that loves Thee, and abidest there:(7) come, Lord, into my soul, and make therein Thy residence in such a manner that Thou never forsake her, and that she likewise be never so sinful as to expel Thee.   Amen.

POINT III.

Zacheus understanding this, "made haste and came down, and received Him with joy." "And when all saw it, murmured saying: That He was gone to be a guest with a man that was a sinner." (8)

1. Ponder the *obedience* of Zacheus, so prompt, joyful, and punctual to perform what Jesus Christ commanded him. Before he esteemed himself unworthy, and was afraid to be so bold as to invite Him, contenting himself only with seeing Him; but seeing His modesty and His affability, and hearing those endearing words which He spake to him, filled with joy, and expelling all fear and human respect, he obeyed Him, and lodged Him. Hence I will learn punctually and cheerfully to obey the voice of Almighty God whensoever it calls, as He says in the Apocalypse, " at the gate" (9) of my soul, willing to enter, lodge, and to sup with Him; for if I be slothful, that perhaps will arrive to me which happened to the spouse, who having lingered over long, when she came to the " door," (10) her well-beloved was passed further.

(7) Joan. xiv. 17.

(8) Luc. xix. 7.   (9) Apoc. iii. 20.   (10) Cant. v. 6.

2. Ponder *the ignorance and malice* of those who "*murmured*" at this action of our Lord Jesus Christ, rashly judging and condemning Him, as one indiscreet and ill-advised, to lodge in the house of a sinner, because these ignorant and proud murmurers understood not the end which induced and moved Him to it, esteeming the publican unworthy of the presence of Jesus Christ, who in this was only exercising a duty of His office, for it is not unbecoming that the physician should go into the house of the sick, to visit and heal him; all notwithstanding murmured at this, for one beginning to murmur, it presently passed to another. But our Lord Jesus Christ, although He heard these murmurings, and knew that at other times they had murmured against Him for the same conduct, made no account of it, and omitted not to converse amongst sinners to gain them to Him, but said, that "they that are in health need not a physician, but only those that are sick" and ill at ease.

Colloquy.—O sovereign Physician, who art come down from heaven to call to repentance, not the just but distressed sinners, who stand in need of it: come and vouchsafe to visit my diseased soul, to heal it with Thy holy grace. Amen.

POINT IV.

" Zacheus standing, said to the Lord, Behold, Lord, the half of my goods I give to the poor; and if I have wronged any man of anything, I restore him fourfold."(11)

1. Consider the most perfect *conversion of this sinner*, pondering first, how our Lord Jesus Christ, before or after meat, conferred with him, persuading him to change his life, which he did by such lively reasons, that they wholly altered and changed his heart. Where we may learn how

(11) Luc. xix. 8.

to treat with sinners on the like occasions, receiving from them the food of our bodies, and returning to them that of the soul for their salvation.

2. These *effectual resolutions* of Zacheus, which he made to accomplish and perform what he had purposed. He said not, I will give, I will pay, but "*I give*," I pay, and execute the same immediately; this was even as certain as a thing already done, after the manner that David said: "In the morning I put to death all the wicked of the land;"(12) because he purposed so effectually to perform it, that he held it as already done. With this efficacy I ought to purpose (God's grace assisting me) to amend my life in such a manner, that I begin immediately to renew it, saying with David: "Now have I begun:" and then to add, "This is the change of the right hand of the Most High;"(13) because, if I say unfeignedly that I will begin at once, the change of the heart will suddenly ensue, the hand and interposition of the Almighty power, favouring and assisting me with His grace.

3. Nevertheless, we may further ponder the *efficacy of this purpose*, as being not an easy but a difficult thing, and not a thing only obligatory, but also *voluntarily and of counsel;* for being very rich, and wedded to his wealth, of which the greatest part was ill-gotten, healed of his avarice, he suddenly divided all his goods into two parts; —giving the one "half" "to the poor," to redeem his sins by alms, and with the other half paying that which is by justice due to any man, restoring not only what he took, but together with it four times as much, so to assure himself the more to have made full restitution; and by consequence left so little to himself, that it was in effect to forsake all he had to follow Jesus Christ in all perfection.

(12) Ps. c. 8.   (13) Ps. lxxvi. 11.

Colloquy.—O Saviour of the world, Thou hast most truly said, that although it were more easy to make a "camel pass through the eye of a needle, than for a rich man to enter into the Kingdom of heaven," nevertheless "with men this is impossible, but with God all things are possible." (14) O how "possible," how easy and sweet a thing was it to this rich man, assisted by Thy grace, to despoil himself so soon of all he possessed, the better to pass through the strait gate of penance! Vouchsafe, Lord, to make that possible to me by Thy grace, which is impossible to my feeble nature. Amen.

4. To conclude, Zacheus made not this recital before our Lord for vainglory or Pharisaical ostentation, but *out of humility,* and a desire to be directed by Him in what he ought to do, and that He would approve of his resolution, if He found it good; teaching us by this example to give an account to our confessors of the like resolutions, to walk with the more security and assurance in that which is good: especially we ought to present the same to God Himself, saying:—"My Lord, I have undertaken these resolutions by the help of Thy grace, if it please Thee that I accomplish them, vouchsafe to assist me: because he that has begun a good work, ought to finish and bring it to perfection."

POINT V.

Jesus Christ answered to Zacheus:—"This day is salvation come to this house, because he also is a son of Abraham; for the Son of Man is come to seek and to save that which was lost." (15)

1. In this answer our Lord approved this desire of Zacheus, and *sanctified not only him, but also his whole family:* because, He who is the true salvation, entering into any

(14) Mat. xix. 24.   (15) Luc. xix. 9.

house, saves and sanctifies all, taking it for His own, which He did, by means of the head, who was Zacheus, to discover to us the force and efficacy of good example; for as Zacheus converted himself to Jesus Christ, so all his servants, and those of his family did the same: and, perhaps this was the reason why our Lord said, that "salvation" was "come to" that "house," because Zacheus was the son of Abraham, and a follower of his faith, obedience, and liberality, and so was followed and imitated by all his family. This teaches me to give good example to all, since our Lord ordinarily makes use of such to convert others. True it is, that the principal cause of all this good, was, that which our Lord Jesus Christ added; because the "Son of Man is come to seek and to save that which was lost," as we shall show in the forty-ninth meditation of the lost sheep.

2. All that hath been said in this history may be applied to holy communion in the following way.

i. First, as Zacheus greatly desired to lodge Jesus Christ within his house, but had not the boldness to entreat Him, esteeming himself unworthy of so great a good, which desire incited our Redeemer to offer Himself, who is better invited by our desires than by our words; even so ought I to have ardent desires to receive Jesus Christ in this holy Sacrament, and to procure, like Zacheus, first to see Him with the eyes of faith, pondering the infinite good which He did in this world, in all places where He entered.

ii. And next I will ascend upon the tree of the cross, embracing some mortifications, which may induce our Lord to be pleased to lodge in my soul.

iii. Then I will imagine that He said to me these loving words:—"Make haste and come down, for this day I must abide in thy house." (16) pondering that before He enter,

(16) Luc. xix. 5.

He desires that I myself, with great alacrity and fervour, should first enter, to make ready, sweep, and clean the same by confession, and deck and adorn it with virtues suitable for harbouring such a guest, wondering that so great a Lord used such a word as, that "He must this day abide in my house," I being one so wretched and so miserable. From thence I will collect, that, although He comes to invite me in this Sacrament, imparting to me the gifts of His grace, yet, notwithstanding, He comes, that I should likewise, with Zacheus, invite Him: and the banquet which He most desires, is, that I should stand in His presence with inflamed affections of love, of thanksgivings, of praise, and of jubilation, with great hope that He will make me safe and sound by His holy entrance.

iv. Finally, I will make great offers to this our Lord, with effectual resolutions to serve Him in the works of mercy and justice; not only in those that are of command, but also in those that are of counsel, offering to Him all that I have, and myself also, since He gives Himself to me, and in presenting Him these resolutions, I will beseech Him to approve them.

Colloquy.—O sweet Jesus, since Thou vouchsafest to enter into my poor house by the gate of this sacrament, say to it with Thy Almighty word:—"This day is salvation come to this house;" sanctify the family of her feeble powers and faculties, that Thou mayest take delight to dwell in it, world without end. Amen.

MEDITATION XXIX.

ON THE WOMAN OF CANAAN, WHOSE DAUGHTER OUR LORD JESUS CHRIST
DISPOSSESSED OF A DEVIL.

POINT I.

As Jesus passed through the quarters of Tyre and Sidon, a pagan "woman of Canaan" knowing it, cried out with a loud voice, saying:—"Have mercy on me, O Lord, Thou Son of David; my daughter is grievously troubled by a devil." (1)

1. Consider the *virtues* which are manifested in the prayer of this pagan woman, to imitate them, because they are most excellent.

i. The first was, a great *faith* and *confidence*, thinking very highly of Jesus Christ, confessing Him to be her Lord and the Messiah, so powerful as to expel devils, and so almighty that there needed no more than His will to command them; and so she says not, "Pray for me," but "have mercy on me," and "help me," briefly proposing her misery to Him, whom she believed able to apply a sure remedy.

ii. The second was, a great *charity*, which made her consider her daughter's miseries for her own; and so she prayed, not in the name of her daughter, but in her own name, saying:—"Have mercy on me," and "help me."

iii. Thirdly, her *humility* appeared likewise in this, perhaps she attributed it more to her own sins, than to the sins of her daughter, that she was tormented by the Devil. In these two virtues the saints become remarkable, making their neighbour's evils their own; the father those of his children; the superior those of his subjects; and the sub-

(1) Mat. xv. 21. Marc. vii. 26.

jects those of their superiors: confessing that their sins
are likewise the cause of the evils that others suffer.
From this humility also sprung the respect with which she
prayed: for, as St. Mark says, she "fell down at His feet,
and reverently adored Him." In short, she prayed with
great affection and constancy, as her cries well witnessed,
which proceeded from the bottom of her heart, and the
pursuit which she made after Jesus Christ, running after
Him and redoubling her petitions.

2. With these virtues I ought to accompany my prayers,
and when I find myself tempted with any kind of pride,
gluttony, or anger, falling down at the feet of Christ, I
will say to Him, once and oftentimes:—" Lord, Thou Son of
David, have mercy on me," for my soul is grievously
troubled by the "devil" of pride. " Help me," have pity
on me, and deliver me. And after the same manner, when
I see any one of my neighbours that belongs to me, turning vicious, feeling his misery as it were my own, I will
say to our Saviour:—

Colloquy.—" Son of David have mercy on me,"
because the soul of my brother is grievously "tormented by the Devil;" help me therefore, for in
having compassion on him, Thou hast compassion on
me, inasmuch as his misery is mine, and my sins are
the cause of what he suffers.

POINT II.

" Jesus answered her not a word," but she, persevering
in her cry, He said to her:—"It is not good to take the
bread of the children, and to cast it to the dogs;" that is
to say, That the benefits done to the Jews, who are the
children of God, were not due to the Gentiles, who were
unknown dogs; to which she replied; " Yea, Lord, for

the whelps also do eat of the crumbs that fall from the table of their masters."(2)

1. Here we may reflect on what *Christ our Lord did* in this case: and *what the Canaanite did.*

First, Christ our Lord *held His peace*, as making no account of the petition of this woman, not from contempt, but that by this delay her desire and affection might the more increase, and passing further, made show to deny her what she demanded, calling her dog, and unworthy of the favour which she asked; which He did to prove and humble her, and the better to dispose her to receive what she asked. For the humiliation sent by Almighty God, as S. Bernard says,(3) is a sign that He will hear us, and is also a mark that He finds a suitable vessel; for He is wont to give immediately to the weak that which they demand, as to little children; but to the strong, whose virtue He has tried, He proves them with delays, and with sharp answers, as He proved His Blessed Mother at the marriage; that by this example we may learn not to trouble ourselves, though we are not heard as soon as we desire.

2. Consider the *virtues in which Jesus Christ our Lord proved the Canaanite*, which are the true touch-stones of the rest; viz., patience, humility, and perseverance, which this Canaanite exercised admirably, and with great prudence.—i. For although she heard words so harsh and bitter, she did not grow angry, nor complain, nor murmur against Christ, nor yet desist in her demand, but *persevered* in it with singular constancy.—ii. She confessed with rare *humility*, what she was, saying:—"Yea, Lord, I am a dog and a pagan, and what is yet more, an unprofitable dog." But then she went on to say, that "the whelps also eat of the crumbs which fall from the table of their

<hr>

(2) Mat. xv. 26.   (3) Serm. 34. in Cant.

masters;" and yet she did not say she was worthy of these, and so did not ask that so much as any "crumbs" should be given to her, but held her peace, referring all to the liberality and mercy of our Lord.—iii. With great *prudence*, from the self-same words of our Lord Jesus Christ, and from her own baseness, drawing reasons to obtain what she sued for, as if she had said: "If I be a dog, masters likewise nourish not only their children, but also their dogs with the crumbs that fall underneath their table." With this spirit will I say to Christ our Lord:

Colloquy.—O King of heaven, who art set in Thy Kingdom at the table of Thy glory, giving abundantly to all Thy "children" to eat: Thy "table," Lord, resembles not that of the avaricious rich glutton, of the "crumbs" of which there was none to give any to the begging and hungry Lazarus, for though Thou art rich, Thou art not avaricious but liberal, not sparing, but bountiful and prodigal. I come therefore before Thee as a little dog, waiting for some little morsel of that bread which falls from this table for those who live beneath on earth. I confess, O my Lord, that what is "holy" ought not to be given "to dogs,"(4) when they require it to profane and tread it under their feet: but I, O my God, desire the same, that I may cease to be a dog: and so I crave that celestial bread which hath the virtue of turning dogs into Thy true children. Give me some "crumb" of this blessed bread, although I do not deserve it, since Thou art so liberal in imparting what Thou hast to those of Thy household. Amen.

POINT III.

Then Jesus answering, said to her:—" O woman, *great is thy faith*, be it *done* to *thee as thou wilt*,"—" for this saying, go thy ways, the devil is gone out of thy daughter:—

(4) Mat. vii. 6.

and she immediately departed, and her daughter was cured from that hour." (5)

1. From which we may gather how great is the pleasure which Christ our Lord takes in a *humble, patient,* and *confident soul,* how greatly He praises it and exalts it, and how He satisfies its desire, granting it all it requires; which affection He well declared by this exclamation, saying:— " O woman, great is thy faith." O how great was it, since a God so great styled it great. The very apostles Christ often called men of "little faith," and this Canaanite He calls a woman of " great faith."

Colloquy.—O my Lord, give me this greatness of a lively faith, and of an assured confidence in Thy bounty, by which I may become agreeable to Thee. Amen.

2. I will likewise reflect how much Almighty God praises and *honours* those who have this greatness of faith, because they honour and glorify by it Almighty God, esteeming highly His bounty, and relying wholly upon His providence, it being the property of Almighty God to honour those who honour Him.

3. Finally, we are to note these words :—" For this saying, Go thy way, the devil is gone out of thy daughter." (6) In which Christ our Lord attributed the driving forth of the devil to the humble answer of the Canaanite, for humility terrifies the very devils, and makes them fly out of bodies and of souls.

Colloquy.—O my Redeemer, put into my heart and my mouth words of true humility, with which in virtue of Thee I may banish from my own soul, and from my neighbour's, all the devils who torment them, that being set free from their servitude, we may serve Thee in justice and holiness. Amen.

(5) Matt. xv. 29.   (6) Marc. vii. 28.

MEDITATION XXX.

ON THE CENTURION, WHOSE SERVANT CHRIST OUR LORD HEALED.

POINT I.

A Centurion who dwelt in Capharnaum, having his servant, whom he loved exceedingly, sick of the palsy, not presuming to appear in person before our Lord Jesus, nor to request Him to come to his house, sent to Him by some of the ancient of the people this request:—" Lord, my servant lies at home sick of the palsy, and is grievously tormented." (1)

1. Consider, first:—

i. The *piety of this Centurion*, so solicitous for the health, not of his son, as the Canaanite, but of his servant and slave, loving with charity even the least, besides other good works which he did, repairing the synagogue, and doing much good to the Jews, though he himself was a Gentile.

ii. *His profound humility*, holding himself unworthy to appear before Christ our Lord, and to go in person to the place where He was, judging himself so bad, and Jesus Christ so good, that He was not worthy to come before Him; and although the messengers said to Christ that he was deserving of having granted to him what he requested, for the many good works he had done to them, yet he, forgetful of these works, considered himself wholly unworthy.

iii. *His great faith and confidence*, contenting himself only to manifest to Christ the misery of his servant, who was sick of the palsy, and sore tormented, believing that He had power to heal him, although absent, and believing Him

(1) Mat. viii. 6.   Luc. vii. 3.

to be so merciful, that it was sufficient to present to Him the bare necessity, without requiring Him to redress it.

2. Whence I will *learn the manner how to act* with Christ our Lord, which is not so much with words as *with affections ;* not in approaching Him presumptuously, but rather in retiring humbly from Him, because this manner of retiring is in reality approaching to Him. And on this account it is that St. Matthew says, (2) that the centurion " *came to*" Christ our Lord, to give us to understand, that we come not nor approach to Christ by the motion of the body, but of the spirit, that is, with actions and affection of faith and confidence, of humility, reverence, and of charity.

Colloquy.—O God of my soul, give me light to know myself, as Thou gavest this centurion, by which, forgetful of any good which I may have done, I may repute myself an unprofitable servant, and wholly unworthy to appear in Thy presence : but yet not so to withdraw myself by pusillanimity, that I cease to approach to Thee by perfect charity. Behold, Lord, that my servant, who is this body which serves me, is sick of the palsy, very slothful in obeying the spirit, and inapt and slow in the works of virtue, unless Thou provide a remedy for my necessity there is no one that can free me from it.

POINT II.

And Jesus said to him :—" *I will come and heal him.*" And walking towards the house of the centurion, as soon as he heard the case, he sent to Him a second message, saying :—*Lord, I am not worthy that Thou shouldest enter under my roof,* for which reason I deemed myself unworthy also to go where Thou wast, but only say the word, and my servant shall be healed." (3)

(2) Mat. viii. 5.   (3) Mat. viii. 7.

1. Here consider, first, the great *benignity of our Lord* Jesus Christ, and how much He favours the humble and the little ones, beholding at a distance the powerful and the proud. To the little king who besought Him to come to his house to heal his son, although he was so powerful a man, and came himself in person to request Him, He answered harshly, taxing him of incredulity; (4) but this centurion, who by humility held himself unworthy to make this request, He offered Himself to him, and *de facto* went to his house, and yet not to heal his son, but his servant and slave.

Colloquy.—O humility, how great is thy power, that so drawest the Son of God and movest Him to come and to visit the house in which thou dwellest! O that my heart were thy habitation, that so the Son of Almighty God might delight to enter, and to dwell in it.

2. With this favour which Christ our Lord offered the centurion, he did not grow haughty and proud, but more and more *increased in humility*, rooting himself more and more in the knowledge of himself, and in the faith of the omnipotence of Jesus Christ, that He could heal his servant with pronouncing no more than one only " word," of whom the holy Church took these words to repeat them before communion. Which I will endeavour to repeat these two affections of humility and confidence, of reverence and of lively faith.

Colloquy.—O Lord of heaven and of earth, who am I that Thou shouldst come to my poor lodging? I am not worthy of so great a good, nor is a house so vile worthy to be the receptacle of so sovereign a guest. It suffices, O Lord, that Thou but say one only word to heal my soul, and to do in it whatsoever

<hr>

(4) Joan. iv. 48.

Thou wilt; for saying, "Be light made, and light was made:" (5) say to my soul, "I am thy salvation,"(6) and she will immediately be healed: say to this servant, my body, that it arise whole, and it will presently arise to serve Thee, and to serve me in all that shall be pleasing to Thee.

3. The centurion, by this knowledge of himself, attained *other most excellent acts of virtue*, extolling Christ our Lord by words which he afterwards added:—"I am also a man subject to authority, having under me soldiers: and I say to one, Go, and he goeth: and to another, Come, and he cometh;" (7) that is to say: "I myself am an earthly man, and in my situation am subject to others; but Thou art a celestial man, infinite God, and superior to all, and therefore I am not worthy that a Lord so high should come to the house of a man so mean.—And if the soldiers and servants who serve me obey my word, much more all creatures and all infirmities will obey Thy word, and in saying to them Come, they will come,—and in saying Go, they will begone." After the example of this centurion, by what passes in me I will collect this admirable science (8) of what God is able to do, rejoicing in His most excellent power, saying:—

Colloquy.—I rejoice, O my Saviour, in that Thou art the most supreme Monarch whom all obey, and that Thy power is such, that saying efficaciously, "Let this be done," all accomplish Thy commandment. Give to me, O Lord, this power over my senses, that commanding them anything in Thy holy service, they immediately obey me: and saying to my imagination, "Think not on this," it does not think it: and saying, "Imagine this," it immediately imagines it: saying to

(5) Gen. i. 3.

(6) Ps. xxxiv. 3. (7) Luc. vii. 8. (8) Ps. cxxxviii. 6.

my appetites, "Love and desire this," they immediately desire it, and saying, "Abhor this," they forthwith abhor it, following in all things Thy most holy will.(9) Amen.

POINT III.

Jesus hearing this, marvelled and said to them that followed Him, " Amen, I say to you, *I have not found so great faith in Israel;* and I say to you, that many shall come from the east and the west, and shall sit down with Abraham, and Isaac, and Jacob in the Kingdom of heaven, but the children of the Kingdom shall be cast out into the exterior darkness, there shall be weeping and gnashing of teeth."   And turning towards the messengers of the centurion, He said:—" Go, and as he has '*believed, so be it done to*' *him ;* and the servant was healed at the same hour." (10)

1. Consider, first, the *admiration of Christ* our Lord as to the exterior signs, to signify to us how humility, faith, and such like heroic virtues, are so admirable, that it seems sufficient to ravish in admiration even Him who above all is most admirable; and a great deal more when such virtues are found in captains, soldiers, and worldly persons, drawing from thence great love and estimation of these virtues.

2. Christ our Lord *extolled the faith of this* pagan centurion, thereby to honour him, saying; That since His preaching He had not found His like among the people of the Jews, and thereby confounded those who, from their position in society, ought to be more humble, pious, and subject to Almighty God. I may draw from thence a great fear of my ingratitude, in corresponding with the graces I have received.

Colloquy.—O my King, permit not that having

(9) Cass. Coll. vii. c. 5.   (10) Mat. viii. 10.

called me to Thy faith, and to be Thy child by grace, I come to lose it through my fault, be disinherited from Thy Kingdom, and be "cast out into exterior darkness," from Thy light and from Thy friendship, into the obscure lake of hell and damnation, where there is nothing else but weeping and raging : O that many from the East and West Indies might come to Thy holy Faith, that Thy Church and Thy celestial Kingdom might be peopled with many just :—but suffer not, O Lord, that the faithful who are already within Thy Church should go forth and be driven from the Kingdom to which Thou hast called them. Amen.

3. Christ our Lord *fulfilled the desire* of the centurion, healing his servant with only one word, which He pronounced, saying :—" *Be it done to thee :*" because, as David says :—" God will do the will of them that fear Him."(11)

Colloquy.—Let me then fear and reverence Thee, O my God, that Thou mayest fulfil my will, but in this only, that I may always fulfil Thine.   Amen.

MEDITATION XXXI.

ON THE WOMAN HEALED BY CHRIST OF AN ISSUE OF BLOOD.

POINT I.

" A certain woman who was troubled with an issue of blood twelve years," " and had suffered many things from many physicians, and had spent all that she had, and was nothing the better, but rather worse,—when she heard of Jesus, came in the crowd behind Him, and touched His garment. For she said, ' If I shall touch but His garment, I shall be whole;" wherefore, going behind Him, she

(11) Ps. cxliv. 19.

touched the hem of His garment, and "was made whole from that hour."(1)

1. Here I am to reflect, first, on the *misery of this woman*, and the little remedy which she found in the physicians of the earth, our Lord suffering this that she might have recourse to the Physician of heaven, who is able to cure the diseases that are incurable, as well of body as of soul, because to Him all things are possible. In the person of this woman I will consider my own soul, which suffers an issue of malignant blood, that is to say, of self-love, of greedy, covetous, and inordinate affections; an issue of pride, anger, and of other innumerable sins and vices, which overtake one another, and issue forth with such impetuosity, that there is no remedy on earth to stop their furious torrent, if God Himself vouchsafe not to stop it.

Colloquy.—O most sovereign and most powerful Physician, behold this issue of bloody sins which I suffer : and since on earth there is no remedy to stop it, send, I beseech Thee, a remedy from heaven, by which I may be healed. Amen.

2. Her *great faith* and *confidence*, who, seeing that her infirmity was incurable, and hearing the fame of the miracles of our Saviour Jesus, conceived such a faith of His sanctity and omnipotence, that she verily believed He could heal her without speaking to her, or without so much as touching her with His hand, nay, even with the sole touch of His garment, as being the garment of so great a saint. With this confidence she likewise coupled great humility, reverence, and devotion, approaching to Christ our Lord " behind Him," and very secretly, because she feared to go before Him; and having touched the hem and border of His garment, she was presently healed.

(1) Mat. ix. 20. Marc. v. 5. Luc. viii. 43.

Colloquy.—O ineffable virtue of humble confidence, which obtainest so much by the spiritual touching of Jesus Christ. O infinite virtue of Jesus Christ, which workest such wonderful effects in those who touch Thee with humble confidence : for as many infirm as touched the "hem of His garment," found themselves cured, because there issued forth such virtue from Him, as to heal as many as "touched Him." (2) O sweet Jesus, that I could touch Thee with such a spirit, that virtue might go forth from Thee, to heal my infirmities, and to fill me with Thy holy virtues !

3. I may apply this miracle to the Holy Communion, considering three points, namely :—

i. The *misery of my soul* in the manner beforesaid.

ii. The *infinite virtue* of Jesus Christ, whom I touch in communicating, and

iii. The *manner how* I ought to touch Him.

i. Christ our Lord would remain amongst us covered with the garment of certain sacramental species, that touching them who eat and receive Him, they should be cured of the "bloody flux" of their covetousness and inordinate passions; and perhaps it is for this cause that He remains in the form of bread, that when He is eaten, He may touch those members which are the fountain of this blood, and may heal them.—He touches the tongue, to heal the flux of talkativeness, and murmurings, with many more sins which spring from thence.—He touches the throat, to repress the flux of gluttony and sensual surfeitings.—He touches the breast, to stop the flux of evil thoughts and unrestrained covetousness, of anger, pride, &c.

ii. In short, if we touch and receive Him with a lively faith, all this evil flux will stop its current, be dried up,

(2) Marc. vi. 56. Luc. vi. 18,

and quite consumed. "*Siccatus est fons sanguinis*," says St. Mark. The fountain of her blood was dried up, and although it seem incurable, as that of this person, yet will it find a cure in the omnipotence and mercy of Jesus Christ, who is inclosed in it.

Colloquy.—I give Thee thanks, O most sweet Jesus, for that Thou hast left Thyself with us for the redress of our evils. O fountain of mercy, dry up in my heart the fountain of my misery, and make Thy almighty power appear in me, favouring me that I may touch and receive Thee in such a manner, that this wretched flux which I suffer may cease entirely. Amen.

iii. Then will I ponder the *manner* how I ought to touch and receive Jesus Christ, for I ought to approach with this woman, on the one side, with great faith and confidence in the bounty and omnipotence of this Lord: and on the other side, with great reverence and fear, on account of my unworthiness, judging myself unworthy to touch Him, or even so much as behold Him, saying:—

Colloquy.—Who am I, O my Lord, either to touch or to receive Thee? I deserve that there should issue from Thy garment of this Sacrament, flashes of fire to consume me: notwithstanding, I confide in Thy mercy, that there will break forth beams of Thy love, to dry up the torrent of my evil inclinations: and with this confidence I come to receive Thee.

POINT II.

This miracle being ended, " Jesus said, Who is it that touched me ? Peter answered, Master, multitudes throng and press Thee, and dost Thou say, Who touched me? And Jesus said, Somebody hath touched me, for I know that virtue is gone out from me unto her. And the woman seeing that she was not hid, came tremblingly, and fell down before His feet. and declared before all the people for what cause she had touched Him, and how she was immediately healed.''(3)

Christ our Lord, who sometimes covered His miracles, commanding that they should be kept secret, to give us an example of His humility; this time would Himself *manifest this miracle* which the woman concealed, because of the great utility which He drew from thence, both for her good, and for the good of others: especially He drew three particular motives of most singular profit.

1. The first, to manifest the *great disparity* that there is betwixt those that touch Jesus Christ, His sacraments, and sacred things, *with humility*, reverence and devotion: and those who touch Him *without* these dispositions.   Be cause the first are most agreeable and acceptable to Him, the virtue of grace going forth from Him, together with sundry gifts and favours which He communicated to them. The second displease, grieve, afflict, and offend Him, and consequently do not participate of His virtue; as the most part of all those persons who communicate without a good spirit.   And making reflection upon myself, I will lament the many times that I have touched Jesus Christ, paining and afflicting Him by my little reverence and devotion; pondering how for this respect I have drawn so little fruit from the communions and masses which I have said, or heard, and from the works I have performed.

Colloquy.—O King of glory, permit not that I touch or handle Thy Sacraments without reverence and due devotion.   It is not reasonable that I should touch Thy divine body, and eat the bread of angels, without making a difference betwixt them, and the ordinary bread of men.   Take heed. O my soul, how thou touchest and receivest Him, if thou desirest that

that be not converted into sickness and death, which was ordained for thy health and thy life.

And here also consider, that although virtue proceeds from Christ, to sanctify all those who worthily touch and receive Him sacramentally, yet so much the more virtue goes from Him, how much the more worthily we touch Him. And this virtue which goes and issues from Him, is charity, humility, obedience, patience, prayer, devotion, with other graces and gifts of the Holy Ghost; as also, the virtue of peace, joy, spiritual consolations, inspirations, and celestial illustrations, all which this our Lord communicates to us, according to the measure of our disposition, imparting the greater gifts of His grace to such as receive Him with better preparation.

Colloquy.—O fountain of all virtues, grant that I may receive Thee with a most excellent disposition, that so I may participate in some of Thy most excellent virtues. Amen.

2. Christ our Lord did this, to *heal the imperfection and ignorance of this woman*, who, though devout, thought that she might touch Jesus Christ, without His feeling or perceiving it; touching Him amidst that throng when many touched Him; to draw her forth out of which ignorance, He said, " Who is it that hath touched me?" by which I am to understand, that Christ our Lord knows and understands all that touch Him and approach to Him, how secretly soever they do it, even though they be many, and a mighty troop, yet He sees who communicates with reverence and devotion, and who without it.

Colloquy.—Wherefore, O my soul, open thy eyes, and behold when thou communicatest, who this Lord is whom thou touchest; who, although concealed under the veil of this Sacrament, yet sees thy heart and knows the manner how thou touchest Him. Thou canst not cover nor conceal what thou dost at that moment from Him, who will manifest it to thy glory if it be good, and to thy confusion if it be bad. Endeavour therefore to receive Him, and to approach Him with great purity and cleanness of heart, as one that is seen by Almighty God, and as if thou wert looked upon by the whole world.

3. Our Lord would likewise heal another imperfection of this woman, which was the *shame and impediment* that withheld her from manifesting her *malady*, which seemed to herself so exceedingly loathsome, that she feared that all would drive her thence as most unclean. But to take away from her this impediment, that she might ground herself in true humility, and in the desire of her own contempt, Christ our Lord was the cause that she accused and discovered herself; by which I may understand how the excessive shame which I have to discover my sins in confession is not grateful to Him, nor the artifices which I use to cover my faults and my infirmities, with other like things which might humble me, doing the same for vain fear of humiliation: but will that I break myself of this vain shame, that I myself confess and manifest them, that my spiritual health may be permanent and perfect. And if sometimes, by contrition for my sins in the secret of my heart, I obtain pardon of them, it is notwithstanding also necessary to declare them to my confessor, and that he ratify by his sentence of absolution, that which God has already done.

Colloquy.—Preserve me, O good Jesus, from that pernicious shame which draws after it sin, and shuts the gate against its remedy: and favour, I beseech Thee, my pusillanimity, giving me courage to manifest my faults, without fear or apprehension of disgrace, since this holy shame will cause glory to Thee and glory to me, I remaining glorified by the grace which I shall receive by the means of Thee. Amen.

POINT III.

This woman being prostrate at the feet of Christ, full of fear and trembling, "He said to her, Daughter, thy faith hath made thee whole, go thy way in peace." (4)

1. In this point, consider the *charity of Christ* our Lord in comforting His elect: for this woman being anxious and fearful, not knowing whether she had offended in touching Him, or whether He would take away from her the health He had given her: to comfort and assure her both in the one and in the other, with a dear love He called her "daughter;" and said to her, that by reason of her "faith," she had obtained health, of which He would in nowise deprive her.

2. Whence I will gather the following:—

i. How it is *the property of godly souls to fear lest they have offended*, even where there is no cause of fear, and to doubt whether they be agreeable or not to Almighty God, in their communions and devotions, and so are anxious whether they may dare to touch Christ and receive Him, or not: and this our Saviour suffers, to inure and ground them in humility and diligence, to profit daily more and more in virtue, and to prepare them the better for the holy communion.

ii. Jesus Christ our Lord *desires rather that we approach Him by love*, than that we retire from Him by fear: and therefore He approved of the spirit of this woman, and called her "daughter:" because the spirit of love and of confidence is proper to the children of Almighty God: who manifests His infinite bounty in beholding our actions

(4) Luc. viii.

with a favourable eye, although they go mingled with some imperfections; as He praised the faith of this woman and attributed to it the health she had received, although it was imperfect, that I should not be troubled when I see my works mingled with some imperfections, since as the prophet David says, " O God, Thy eyes did see my imperfect being, and in Thy book all shall be written."(5) And therefore the imperfect being, purified from their imperfections, be admitted to glory, where they will reign with Him, world without end.   Amen.

MEDITATION XXXII.

ON THE SICK BEDRIDDEN MAN CURED BY CHRIST AT THE POND OF PROBATICA.

POINT I.

"Now there is in Jerusalem a pond, called Probatica, which in Hebrew is named Bethsaida, having five porches," wherein were washed the sheep and lambs of the Sacrifice; "in these lay a great multitude of sick, of blind, of lame, of withered, waiting for the moving of the water. And an angel of the Lord descended at certain times and the water was moved, and he that went down first into the pond, was made whole of whatsoever infirmity he lay under." (1)

1. This lavatory, or wash-pool of water, dyed with the blood of the beasts which there were sacrificed, *was a symbol of those sacraments* which Christ our Lord was to institute with the blood which He would shed in that Sacrifice which He offered of Himself upon the cross.

2. These sacraments are, the Baptism of water, and Penance, which is a baptism of fire and tears, whose excellencies and principal properties were clearly figured in

(5) S. Aug. in Ps. cxxxviii. 16.   (1) Joan. v. 2.

this miracle: in which there were three remarkable things, but yet with restriction and limitation.—i. It healed all the infirmities of the body, yet it is not said that it raised the dead.—ii. To this effect descended "an angel" from heaven: for as the water of its own nature wanted this virtue, and the angel did not descend when the sick besought or desired him, nor did his coming depend upon the will of any mortal man, but only of Almighty God, who sent him thither *from time to time.*—iii. That it healed but one only each time, and not many: and this one was the first that could get to enter, in reward of his diligence.

3. There are *three other excellencies* in these our sacraments much greater, and without limitation: presupposing that baptism is conferred only once.

i. The first, that they contain the virtue to wash away all the spots of sins, and to heal all the *infirmities of the soul*, and what is more, to raise her up from the death of guilt, to the life of grace, which the sacraments of the ancient law were not able to do. With this spirit I will approach the holy sacrament of Penance; and if I be dead through my offences, there I shall receive life;—if sick through my vices and evil customs, there I shall receive health;—if blind with errors and ignorance, there I shall receive sight and light to see clearly;—if lame in the service of God, there I shall find feet to walk uprightly with a true intention;—if withered and weak, there I shall find fervour, devotion, and strength to work.

Colloquy.—O blessed be the Lord and author of such a lavatory, and of such singular virtue, taking so mean a creature for the instrument of His almighty power, thereby to deliver me from my misery.

ii. The second excellency is, that "*the Angel*" *of the*

great counsel, Christ Jesus our Lord, on His part is prepared to come and sanctify us in these sacraments, *always, at all times, days, and hours;* accommodating Himself to the will of His ministers, and even of the sick themselves; when, and as often as they will, this great God and our sovereign Lord, being always ready to confer health, life, and fervour of spirit to whosoever receive these sacraments. Hence I will gather the great reverence and confidence with which I ought to receive them, beholding the priest and confessor, not as a man only, but as a visible angel of Almighty God, sent from heaven to heal me: beholding also the invisible God who is there present with His invisible virtue to restore my health, in whom I therefore ought to put my principal hope.

Colloquy.—I give Thee thanks, my most merciful Saviour, for having put into the hands of Thy ministers the remedy which Thou hast left to heal me of my sins, so continually attending to the affairs of my salvation, as if Thou hadst nothing else to do. O that I attended perpetually to the affairs of Thy service, without employing myself in anything which may offend Thee.   Amen.

iii. The third excellency is, that these sacraments have the virtue of *healing all,* although in effect many are not healed on account of their tepidity and indisposition; nevertheless it principally heals those who are "the first." Him I call "the first" who comes with more diligence and fervour, and with better dispositions of sorrow and examen of conscience than others; and in this we ought all to endeavour to be the first, as greatly solicitous of our own salvation; and that we may receive more copious fruit by these sacraments. Yet, the bounty of Almighty God is such, that He also heals the imperfect and lukewarm, which are not so well disposed, supplying with the grace of the holy sacrament the want and default of a perfect sorrow.

Colloquy.—O my Lord, I desire, with Thy assistance, to be the very first in all that concerns Thy holy service, and the good of my soul, shaking off all sloth, and advancing myself before others, for Thy honour and glory.   Amen.

POINT II.

" There was a certain man there that had been eight-and-thirty years under his infirmity.   Him when Jesus had seen lying, and knew that he had been now a long time, He saith to him: Wilt thou be made whole?   The infirm man answered Him: Sir, I have no man, when the water is troubled, to put me into the pond; for whilst I am coming, another goeth down before me."(2)

1. Here consider, first, the *great mercy of Christ* our Lord, who, entering into these vaults or porches all alone and unknown, seeing that no one asked Him anything, fixed His eyes upon this infirm person, more in necessity and more abandoned than all the others, that He might heal him; for the greater is the misery, so much the more does it excite the divine mercy to provide a remedy.

2. Consider *the reason* why Christ our Lord *asked the diseased*: " Wilt thou be made whole?" since it was certain that he heartily desired to be healed.   This He did to signify that in the affairs of our spiritual health two several wills are necessary, that of God—and our own will.   That of God is most assured, for it invites us to health, which through Him we shall never lose;—our own ought to be a will, true, efficacious, and not indifferent.   And for this reason Christ our Lord did not say to the sick man: " Wouldst thou be healed?"   But, Wilt

(2) Joan. v. 6.

thou be healed? because this will ought to be absolute and efficacious, so as quite to remove the disordered affections to sins, together with the occasions of them; and induce him to do on his part all that is necessary for his spiritual health: as this diseased person did, who endeavoured and dragged himself with all his force to the pool. And this is the first disposition necessary to approach the pool of Penance.

3. Consider the *answer of this diseased person*, in which he expressed his *own good will*, and at the same time his inability, saying, that *he had "no man to help" him*, nor strength enough to trail himself into the water. By this example I am taught, that I ought, with humility, to acknowledge and confess my own imbecility and necessity, which is, that of myself I have not sufficient strength to heal myself, and that there is no man, who, of himself, is able to succour me, but that my succour is to come from Christ alone, and, therefore, to Him I will endeavour to have recourse, saying to Him with firm confidence:

Colloquy—O my Redeemer, I am infirm and weak, wanting force to seek my salvation without the aid of any creatures to procure it for me. I cannot say that "I have no man," since I have Thee who art a man, and more than a man, and who canst succour me. Succour me, therefore, O Lord; I put not my trust in a mere man, but in Thee, true God and true man, in whom is health and benediction, world without end. Amen.

4. By what has been said it plainly appears that two *dispositions* are necessary for this sacrament, joining, with the *will* to be healed, the *humble confession* of my own impotence; to which is to be added a third, after the imitation of this sick person, who in his answer manifested great *patience*, without complaining or murmuring against

those who would not help him, but expecting his turn with longanimity; even so ought I to have great patience and perseverance in my endeavours to obtain perfect health, and victory over my passions, without complaining or murmuring, or feeling the delays of Almighty God, and without impatience, that the fight and the infirmity last so long; but, crying out, and still persevering; for, as Job says:—" When thou shalt think thyself consumed, thou shalt rise like the day-star:" (3) and when I least think, Christ will come and restore me to health, as He did this diseased cripple.

POINT III.

" Jesus saith to him, arise, take up thy bed, and walk; and immediately the man was made whole, and he took up his bed and walked." (4)

1. Consider the *almighty power* and *infinite mercy* of our Saviour in this miracle; for, using His plenitude of bounty and power, He did not require of him, faith, nor that he should believe, as He did of others, nor did He touch him with His hand, nor wash him with the water of the pond, as He might have done, but with His word only, gave him entire and perfect health.

Colloquy.—I rejoice, O Saviour of the world, that Thou art so mighty and so merciful; it clearly appears that Thou art more than man, since Thou art so powerful to do what neither man nor angel is able to do. Manifest, I beseech Thee, on me Thy Almighty power, giving to me perfect health with which I may serve Thee. Amen.

2. The *reason why* He said, " Take up thy bed and walk." Not only according to the letter, that it might appear that the corporal health which Almighty God gives is perfect and vigorous; but also to give us to understand

(3) Job. xi. 17.   (4) Joan. v. 8.

the same of spiritual health; forasmuch as the infirm person, who, before has his soul paralyzed, prostrate, and extended on the bed of his miserable body, and drawn away with her desires, and the inordinate passions of the flesh, does, by the virtue of Christ, arise so sound, that the soul leads the body even whither she lists, and governs and directs it according to his will; so that she is no more carried away with the passions of anger, or fear, sadness, or joy, but she rules these passions, and makes use of them conformably to the dictate and rule of reason, which is an evident sign of his perfect health.

Colloquy.—O good Jesus, say to my soul, "Take up thy bed, and walk;" that, in conformity with my body, it may walk in the ways of Thy holy law. Disburden then it, I beseech Thee, of inordinate desires, that so it may support with ease the burden of Thy precepts.   Amen.

3. The *exact obedience of this man*, for, although it was on the Sabbath day, on which the Jews judged it unlawful to bear any burdens, notwithstanding, as soon as Christ had said, " Take up thy bed and walk," he submitted his judgment, and with great promptitude, speed, and alacrity, laid it on his shoulders, and began to walk.   And those who met him, saying to him:—" It is the Sabbath day, it is not lawful for thee to take up thy bed; he answered, He that made me whole, said to me, Take up thy bed and walk." (5)   As if he had said, " He that was so holy, and so powerful as to heal me, commanded me to do it; and it is most certain that I may lawfully do it, since He commanded it, and this alone suffices for me."   This he answered without understanding who Christ was, whose holy will is, that subjects obey their superiors, and penitents their confessors, with the like obedience, prompt,

(5) Joan. v. 10.

punctual, joyful, and submissive, where there is no evident sin, accomplishing all that Almighty God shall command them, and their confessor who has healed them.

Colloquy.—O my God, the true health of my sickly soul, command me what Thou wilt; although it be hard, humiliating, and heavy, and although it appear to me quite from the purpose, I will submit myself to all most willingly. And, if any seek to hinder my obedience, I will say to him; God, who hath healed me, hath so commanded me, it suffices for me to fulfil it, since He commands it.

POINT IV.

The miracle being ended, "Jesus went aside from the multitude standing in the place. Afterwards Jesus findeth him in the temple, and saith unto him, Behold thou art made whole, sin no more, lest some worse thing happen to thee." (6)

1. Here contemplate, first, on the part of Christ our Lord, a rare example of *humility in hiding Himself*, and avoiding the praises of the people, and the care that He had to hasten to the Temple, not only to thank His heavenly Father for this work, but to perfect it by the wholesome advice which He gave to this man, knowing that He should find him there.

2. The good affection and *gratitude* of this *diseased person*, who, seeing himself healed, the very first thing he did was to repair to the Temple, and to render thanks to Almighty God for the singular favour He had vouchsafed to bestow upon him. From him I will take example to repair speedily after confession to render thanks to Almighty God for the favour He has vouchsafed to bestow on me by means of this sacrament, recollecting myself in the Church,

(6) Joan. v. 14.

or in some other convenient place, to reflect with gratitude on this benefit, as has been said in its proper place.

3. Thirdly, weigh the *words* which Christ our Lord said to him:—"*Sin no more, lest something worse happen to thee.*" Within which words there are enclosed three very important instructions.

i. The first is, that infirmities are wont sometimes to befall in *chastisement of offences*, and the same I am to think of mine.—Others, though just, suffer for *the glory of Almighty God*, and for their better inurement in virtue, but I, miserable sinner, suffer for my offences, as the prophet Micheas says:—"I will bear the wrath of the Lord, because I have sinned against Him." (7)

ii. That he "*sin no more.*" He said not to him, thou must sin no more, because it is incident to men to sin, especially in lighter sins, but that he should not have a will to sin any more; that is to say, that he must have a resolute purpose, and hold a strong and steadfast will, with God's assistance, to sin no more. And this purpose and resolution ought to be renewed in confession with sincere desire of amendment.

iii. That the relapse will be worse than the sin itself, by reason of the ingratitude which he shows in offending Him who has so graciously forgiven him, making so small an account of the health he had received, losing it so soon, and consequently it will be chastised more severely than before, because the fault is greater than before.

Colloquy.—O true master, whose "works" are "perfect," (8) and whose detection of deceits is certain and profitable, I have hearkened to Thy admonitions, help me, O Lord, to fulfil them in heart, and to conform my life accordingly. Deliver me, I beseech Thee, from all relapses, and give me a firm and in-

(7) Mich. vii. 9.   (8) Deut. xxxii 4

vincible will to offend no more, preserving what Thou hast given me, that I may live and die in perfect sanctity. Amen.

POINT V.

Then "the man went his way, and told the Jews that it was Jesus who had made him whole." (9)

1. In this example we see the *zeal and fervour of true penitents*, who have received from Almighty God the singular benefit of their health, desiring that God should be known and worshipped by all, publishing everywhere the good they have received from Him, according to that which Christ our Lord said to the man from whom He drove a legion of devils:—"Go into thy house to thy friends, and tell them how great things the Lord hath done for thee." (10) The same may I say to our Lord with holy David:—"Restore unto me the joy of Thy salvation, and strengthen me with a perfect spirit," for if Thou do this, "I will teach the unjust Thy ways, and the wicked shall be converted to Thee." (11)

2. Consider his *prudence*, who did not say, Jesus was He that commanded me to carry my bed, but "He *that made me whole*," not to give occasion to the Jews to calumniate Christ our Lord, against whom they had already begun to murmur, because He healed upon the Sabbath day. I may draw from hence the circumspection which I ought to have in my speeches, and recounting the good which I know without mingling anything on which the wicked may take occasion to feed their malice.

(9) Joan. v. 15.   (10) Marc. v. 19.   (11) Ps. l. 14.

MEDITATION XXXIII.

ON THE LEPER HEALED BY CHRIST, COMMANDING HIM TO GO SHOW HIMSELF TO THE PRIESTS.

POINT I.

"Behold a leper came," and "falling on his face, adored Him, saying, Lord, if Thou wilt, Thou canst make me clean." (1)

1. These words lead us to meditate on the *virtues* of the prayer of this poor leper.—i. The first was, great *exterior and interior reverence*, bowing his knees, prostrating himself on the ground, adoring Christ, and calling Him Lord.—ii. The second was, *great faith* in the omnipotence of Christ our Lord, confessing that He could heal him with His only will; for he said not, If Thou ask it of God, but, "If Thou wilt Thou canst;" confessing that He was the Messiah, and Son of Almighty God. Nor did he say "if Thou wilt," as if doubting of His mercy, but because he knew not if he were unworthy on account of his sins, or whether such corporeal health were expedient for him.—iii. The third was *great resignation*, inasmuch as he demanded nothing absolutely, not adding, "cleanse me," but only discovering his necessity and desire, and that in a few words, confessing the omnipotence of Christ, and remitting himself to His holy will to heal him.

2. With these virtues, should I present myself before Christ our Lord, like a man full of the leprosy of sin, and of other miseries, reflecting on the leprosy of my powers and senses, and of my whole soul, with anger, pride, gluttony, and other vices: and then with great humility, and very profound reverence, with a lively faith, and great

(1) Mat. viii. 2. Marc. i. 40. Luc. vi. 12.

resignation, I will say to Him, " Lord, if Thou wilt, Thou canst make me clean."　And in lieu of the word " Lord," I may add other titles of Almighty God, to excite Him to mercy, and myself to reverence.　And instead of the word " clean," I may place others suitable to the remedies which my miseries may require, saying:—

Colloquy.—My Father, my physician, my Saviour, and all my good, "if Thou wilt Thou canst" heal me of my pride, of my gluttony, and the like.　"If Thou wilt Thou canst" illuminate and inflame me with Thy love.—"If Thou wilt Thou canst make me" patient, meek, humble and the like.　I doubt not Thy omnipotence, for Thou canst do all things, nor of Thy will, touching the health of my soul, for it is that which Thou desirest; I only fear my unworthiness, on account of which I cast myself into Thy hands, and in Thy will I place all my confidence.

This is one of those prayers which are called ejaculatory, to be often repeated very probably in the day: in imitation of which we may make many others, and make use of those which we shall note in the miracles which hereafter ensue.

POINT II.

Jesus having compassion of him, "stretching forth His hand, touched him, saying, I will; be thou made clean; and forthwith his leprosy was cleansed." (2)

1. Meditate on the great *virtues and excellencies of Christ* our Lord.

i. His *mercy,* "Misertus ejus," having immediately mercy on the misery of the leper, without any delay, because He is notably compassionate: and He who is so compassionate on the miseries of the body, how much more compassion will He shew to those of the soul?　For the

(2) Mat. viii. 3.

leprosy of sin which provokes the wrath and indignation of Almighty God, when willingly one remains in it, excites His mercy when it is detested, and when we seek to be healed of it.

Colloquy.—O most merciful Jesus, have mercy on me, since it is by Thy mercy that I am freed from my misery.

The word " Misertus ejus," that is, having compassion on him, the Evangelist uses, to shew that the cause of this miracle was not vain ostentation, but true compassion.

ii. The second was, a most rare demonstration of His *bounty* and *omnipotence*, answerable to the faith and confidence of the leper, saying, " I will; be thou cleansed." " Thou sayest, if I will, I therefore answer that I will. Thou sayest that I can, I therefore say, be Thou made clean;" and so it was done.

Colloquy.—O, the greatness of the bounty and omnipotence of Jesus. Christ, who so satisfies the desires of those who trust in Him! say, O Lord, to my soul, I am thy health; " I will; be thou clean," for Thy *saying*, is absolute *doing*, and therefore in so saying, it shall be healed.

iii. The third was, great *benignity* and *humanity*, because without having any aversion to the leper, whom the Jews so greatly abhorred as neither to touch nor come near him, he being reputed unclean that should but touch him, His majesty " stretched forth His hand," and lovingly "touched him," to restore him to health. Where the Evangelist takes notice of His "stretching forth His hand," to signify that He was to extend it upon the cross, to set us free from the leprosy of sin, and that His most sacred flesh had the virtue of healing whatsoever it touched; as also that whensoever Almighty God " openeth His hand

He filleth with blessing every living creature."(3) In this we see the force of that prayer which is made with the conditions aforementioned, and the end to which I ought to address and direct my prayer, which is to obtain of Christ our Lord, one "I will;" and one, "be thou made clean," and one opening of the hand which he held fast closed, and one touching, to heal the leprosy of my soul.

POINT III.

"And Jesus said to him: Go, see thou tell no man, but go show thyself to the priest, and offer the gift which Moses commanded for a testimony unto them."(4)

1. Consider, first, the *zeal which Christ* our Lord had, that the *ancient law might be observed* so long as it lasted, requiring that the lepers should accomplish that which was commanded them, which was, that being healed, they should present themselves to the priest, and should offer gifts and sacrifices to Almighty God, both as an acknowledgment of the favour they had received, and as a testimony that they were cleansed; He who was so zealous that the precepts of the ancient law should be obeyed, how much more zealous is He, that those of the new be obeyed!

2. He prescribed this to the leprous, to *signify the sacrament of penance in the new law,* in which it is commanded that whatsoever leper defiled with the leprosy of sins, although by contrition he have obtained pardon of them, should present himself to the priest, and discover to him the leprosy he had, offering before him the *"sacrifice of an afflicted spirit," and of "a contrite and humble heart ;"*(5) and should receive the sentence of absolution, by which the pardon received is confirmed, and the soul is more purified and perfected, by means of the sacramental grace, thereby remaining disposed to receive the sacrament of the

(3) Ps. cxliv. 16.   (4) Mat. viii. 4.   (5) Ps. l. 19.

Holy Communion; even as anciently the lepers presenting themselves before the priest, were to cut off the hair from their bodies, to wash their garments and their flesh, and to offer in sacrifice a lamb without spot;(6) and in this manner remained clean from the legal uncleanness, and were admitted to the common intercourse with other men.

3. Hence I will gather two very important lessons:—i. One, that when I recollect myself and examine my conscience, to prepare for confession, I am to excite in myself so *great a sorrow*, that I remain exempt and cleansed from my leprosy, in virtue of contrition; for this is the best preparative for confession, as has been said in its proper place.—ii. The other, that with humility I forthwith *present myself to the priest*, discovering to him all my sins, with a new sacrifice of a contrite heart, endeavouring to cut off the hairs, which are the abuses of my former life, and to wash my soul with the water of tears, as also its garments, which are its works, and then to offer myself, that the confessor, with the sharp instrument of penance, correction, and mortification, may help to purify me. And in this manner I will approach clean and unspotted, to offer the sacrifice of the Lamb without spot, Christ Jesus, and to receive His most holy body.

4. Lastly, Christ our Lord commanded this leper, saying:—"*See thou tell no man.*" And St. Mark says that He "strictly charged him"(7) with threats, and with vehemence, to give us an example of humility, and to let us see that He sincerely shunned the praises of men. Nevertheless, the leper, without any scruple, preached and published the miracle, and was the cause that many people ran to hear Christ, in which he neither erred nor disobeyed, but acted according to the inspiration of the good spirit, through zeal for the glory of Almighty God, and thank-

(6) Levit. xiv. 8.   (7) Marc. i. 43.

fulness to Him that had healed him, that He might be reverenced by all men, and that many might profit by His holy doctrine; for Christ our Lord desires that we be not found defective in the laws of gratitude, and of the glory of Almighty God. Further teaching us in this fact, that if the just, through humility, seek to hide and conceal their good works, yet, when there is no bad consequence to be feared, I may preach and publish them for example to others, and for the divine honour and glory.

MEDITATION XXXIV.

ON THE TEN LEPERS HEALED BY CHRIST, WHOM HE SENT TO THE PRIESTS.

POINT I.

As Jesus "entered into a certain town, there met Him ten men that were lepers, who stood afar off, and lifted up their voice, saying: Jesus, Master, have mercy on us."(1)

Consider, as in the precedent meditation, the *affections* with which the lepers prayed, manifesting their humility and reverence in crying "afar off," reputing themselves unworthy to approach to Jesus Christ: they likewise prayed with great *confidence* and resignation, for they did not say, "heal us," but "have mercy on us," throwing themselves entirely on His mercy. With these virtues they joined *unity in the act of petition*, which is of great efficacy with Almighty God, when many who have the same need, pray together united in charity, for as every one asking for all, they obtain also the favour for themselves. For this cause the blessed apostle St. James says: —" Pray one for another, that you may be saved;"(2) for the continual prayer of the just avails much. The poor of

(1) Luc. xvii. 12.   (2) Jac. v. 16.

this world act in a different manner: they would be alone when they ask alms, for if there be many together, they weary the rich, and fear to be refused by them. But our God is not wearied, though many at once demand of Him, for He has enough to content all; rather He delights that all His poor keep charity amongst themselves, and therefore imparts to them His alms with the better will.

Colloquy.—O liberal and most merciful master, we are many lepers in this world, figured by these ten, forasmuch as we transgress the ten commandments of Thy holy law; although some are much more defiled than others. Have mercy, I beseech Thee on all: cleanse the heretics from the leprosy of their heresy; the proud from the leprosy of their pride; the carnal from the leprosy of their impurity; and me, together with them, from all the leprosy which is in my interior, and exterior powers, that I may be converted to Thee "ten times as much as"(3) I have departed, and been estranged from Thee. Amen.

POINT II.

"Whom, when He saw, He said to them, Go, show yourselves to the priests;" and they obeying, "as they went, they were made clean."(4)

1. All *our good proceeds* from this, that *Jesus Christ* our Lord *vouchsafes to behold us* with the eyes of mercy, as we have elsewhere said; yet our Lord seeing the faith of these lepers, desires likewise to prove their obedience, which springs from faith, and to exercise them in it; and therefore before they were healed He said to them:—" Go, and show yourselves to the priests;" although He knew that the law ordained that they should not go, unless they were first healed. Nevertheless, they submitted their judgment, and without reply or longer delay, obeyed as they were

(3) Baruch iv. 28.   (4) Luc. xvii. 14.

commanded; and beginning their obedience, they were instantly healed; to teach us how much He prizes prompt, submissive, and punctual obedience, and how by it He works miracles; and that he who has a lively faith and confidence in Jesus Christ hesitates not to obey all that is commanded him, either by Himself, or by His ministers, who have authority to prove the submission and obedience of their subjects, as Christ our Lord proved that of these present lepers. In the same manner, Almighty God, knowing the great faith of Abraham, yet would for our example prove his obedience, commanding him to sacrifice his son, by which He proved him wonderfully;" (5) for faith, confidence, and obedience, like sisters accord and jointly set themselves to put in execution whatsoever is conformable to the will of God.

2. Consider the *mystical meaning* of this present fact, which is the same as in the preceding miracle, yet with some particularities, namely, to signify to us *what the leprous in soul are to do*, when they seek for health from Almighty God, who, although He can give it of Himself, yet requires that first they repair to the priests of the Evangelical law, who are the confessors, and lay open to them the leprosy of their sin, without concealing anything how vile and enormous soever it be. And this word, "show yourselves," is not void of mystery; as also that other which He said to the leper, "show thyself," that is to say, discover yourself entirely to the priest, that so he may see and know, both within and without, who you are, without concealing from him any evil which you have done, said, or consented to. And even so, with a spirit of obedience, because Christ has commanded it, and with a spirit of humility for the health of my soul, I will accuse myself to my

(5) Gen. xxii. 2.

confessor, patiently supporting the shame which I am to suffer since—

Colloquy.—O good Jesus, since Thou seest my leprosy, and knowest the same, what imports it if Thy priest see it? I wish for no honour amongst men, further than I may keep and hold it with Thee. Thou mightest command me to manifest my leprosy to the whole world, and hast reason to command it, but since Thou art satisfied that I manifest it only to the priest, I will sincerely accomplish Thy command, that Thou mayest heal me by it. Amen.

3. "And *it came to pass as they went* they were *made clean;*" because, in the eyes of Almighty God, the good will is accepted for the work, and perfect sorrow for sins, with a will to confess them, suffices to obtain the health of the soul, and to cleanse it from leprosy, although the party should afterwards be debarred the assistance of a priest. For all which I am humbly to thank Jesus Christ our Lord, who by so sundry ways has facilitated the remedy for all our evils.

POINT III.

" One of them, when he saw he was made clean, went back, and with a loud voice, glorifying God, fell on his face before His feet, giving thanks : and this was a Samaritan. And Jesus answering said : Were not ten made clean? and where are the nine? There is no one found to return, and give glory to God, but this stranger. And He said to him: Arise, go thy way : for thy faith hath made thee whole." (6)

1. Reflect, first, *on the part of the nine lepers*, that the greatest part of men, when they see themselves in distress and necessity, although they are devout and do much importune God, and have both faith and confidence in His

(6) Luc. xvii. 15.

mercy, because their necessity drives and enforces them to it;—yet as soon as they have received the benefit, and see themselves in health and prosperity, they *become forgetful of God*, and do not render Him due thanks. This thing greatly offends Christ our Lord, as the words witness which, on this occasion, He pronounced with much feeling:—"Were not ten clean, and where are the nine?" This manner of speech Almighty God used after Adam had offended, saying to him: "Where art thou?"(7) Giving us to understand that God does not approve the steps and ways of the ungrateful, and that He knows them not, because they do not acknowledge Him.

2. On the part of *the Samaritan leper ;*—for, oftentimes the *greatest sinners*, when they receive from Almighty God the health of their souls, or any other benefit, *are wont to be much more thankful to* Him because they know their own unworthiness, esteeming the favour so much the more as given to one that least deserves it; although on the other side, it were but reasonable that the just should show greater gratitude; so that, to the confusion of the nine leprous Jews, Christ Jesus said: "There is no one found to return and give glory to God, but this stranger." Hence I will gather, how important it is after confession and absolution, as has been said in Part I. Meditation xxxii., to repair speedily to return thanks to Christ our Lord for the purity and pardon which He has given me, with devotion like that of this Samaritan, of whom the Gospel says, that he returned magnifying Almighty God with a loud voice, and prostrating himself in all humility at the feet of Christ, as he that craved to kiss them in gratitude for the health He had bestowed upon him, and with words giving Him thanks for that great benefit. I may likewise observe the great prudence of this Samaritan,

(7) Gen. iii. 9.

who held his peace when Christ inquired of him where the other "nine" were: for he neither blamed, nor taxed their ingratitude, but only attended to his thanksgiving, by which I am to learn, not to blame my neighbour, although occasion were offered to do so.

3. On the part *of Christ our Lord;*—the *modesty* with which He complained of the ingratitude of the other "nine," saying: "There is no one found to return and give glory to God:" He says not, to give glory *to me*, or to give thanks to me; to teach us, that whosoever does any favour, ought not to seek any acknowledgment, or any praise for himself, but only for God, from whom all good proceeds.

4. Meditate on the *benignity and love* with which He received the Samaritan, and spoke to him, honouring and attributing the health he had obtained *to his faith;* and it is to be believed that He likewise delivered him from the leprosy of infidelity and of other sins, dismissing him sound both in soul and body, for the gratitude and thankfulness which he there declared.

Colloquy.—O Lord of my soul, how gracious dost Thou shew Thyself to those who are grateful to Thee, that they may always have reason to be grateful! I desire always to be grateful to Thee, for the great favours Thou hast always done me, although I always come short and fail in this duty; forasmuch as my gratitude is a new benefit which I receive from Thee, my benefactor; to whom be all honour and glory, for the good which Thou doest to Thy creatures, world without end. Amen.

MEDITATION XXXV.

ON THE BLIND MAN HEALED BY CHRIST OUR LORD ON THE WAY TO JERICHO.

POINT I.

It came to pass when He drew nigh to Jericho, that a certain blind man sat by the way-side begging, and when he heard the multitude passing by, he asked what this meant, and they told him "that Jesus of Nazareth was passing by, and he cried out, saying: Jesus, Son of David, have mercy upon me." And although the people "rebuked him," and bid him "hold his peace," yet "he cried a great deal the more,"(1) repeating the same thing.

1. Consider the *virtues* which this blind person discovered in this prayer.—i. The first was, great *faith and confidence* in Jesus Christ our Lord, believing Him to be the Messiah, "Son of David," and Almighty God, to whom it belonged to have mercy, and to redress our miseries.—ii. The second was, great *fervour and affection* in his prayer, proceeding from the knowledge of his blindness and misery, and the hope which he had in Jesus Christ, that He would heal him: which affection he declared by his redoubled clamour.—iii. Great *constancy and perseverance*, without respecting those who reprehended him, and commanded him silence; but on the contrary, he took thence occasion to raise his voice the higher, and to repeat his prayer.

2. In the person of this blind man, I will imagine *myself spiritually blind*, with the two blindnesses of ignorance and guilt, error and passion, which thrust out the two eyes of the soul, which S. Bernard terms, "knowledge and love."(2)   Whence it follows, that I am all the days of

(1) Marc. x. 47, Luc. xviii. 35. Mat. xx. 31.
(2) Lib. de Dig: Amoris Divini. c. 8.

my life sitting still and idle, without attending to the works of virtue to which I am obliged, spending my time in begging of the creatures that pass by this world, some little delight, honour, or profit to maintain my life.   All which is little, soon passing and perishing, like the alms of poor passengers and wayfaring men.   Pondering this misery of my blind, idle, and beggared soul, I am to cry out to Jesus Christ, who alone can help me, saying: " Jesus, Son of David, have mercy upon me."

3. And this prayer I must accompany with the virtues aforesaid, persuading myself, as S. Bernard says, that there are *four things that trouble my prayer*, if I resist them not courageously; that is to say;—i. A *troop of thoughts* and imaginations which pass through my heart, and permit it not to attend to what my words import.—ii. Many *remorses of conscience* for the former sins I have committed, which reprehend me, and breed distrust, demanding of me how I am so hardy as to cry to God, being such a sinner as I am.—iii. A multitude of *wants*, of corporal miseries, of secular cares and worldly thoughts.—iv. Sometimes also, even some of *those who accompany Christ*, cause me to leave and give over prayer, leading me along with them to their affairs, under the pretext and colour of piety.   Notwithstanding all this, I am to pray and cry out with my heart, and sometimes also with my mouth, saying: " Jesus, Son of David, have mercy on me."   And if these hindrances still continue, I will take occasion from them to pray with greater fervour, saying with David:—

Colloquy.—Deliver me, O Lord, because I am poor and needy, and my heart is troubled exceedingly, I decline like a shadow when the sun goes down, and walk disquieted like a locust, my thoughts violently drawing me hither and thither :(3) appease them,

(3) Ps. cviii. 21, &c.

O Lord, with such stability, that I may both pray and praise Thee with fervour. Amen.

POINT II.

Jesus approaching nearer to the place where the blind man was, and standing, commanded him to be brought to Him, and when he was come near He asked him, saying:—"What wilt thou that I do to thee? But he said, Lord, that I may see. And Jesus said to him, Receive thy sight." (4)

1. Although Christ our Lord understood at the first the cries of this blind man, yet He *pretended not to hear them,* to try his perseverance, and that the desire of his health might the more increase. And the same He also does with us, that our perseverance in prayer may the better dispose us to receive what we ask; but yet He presently showed His clemency and benignity, "standing" still at the cry of this blind beggar, although He was going along with many people, causing the whole troop to make a stand, and the blind man to be brought to Him, that He might heal him.

Colloquy.—O good Jesus, Son of justice, who vouchsafest to obey the "voice of a man," (5) and stoppest in the midst of Thy course to restore light to him who desired it: hear my cry, I beseech Thee, and enlighten my blindness, because I can have no joy unless I see "the light of heaven." (6)

2. Then I will reflect, how the blind man, understanding that Jesus called him, presently "casting off his garment, leaped up and came to Him," (7) full of hope to recover his sight. In this is represented the joy of the soul, that feels the inward vocation of Almighty God, and His divine inspiration, which causes it instantly to abandon all things

(4) Luc. xviii. 40. Marc. x. 50, 51, &c.
(5) Jos. x. 14.　　　(6) Tob. v.　　　(7) Marc. x. 50.

to render itself obedient to His call, hoping to find infallibly that which she desires for her salvation and perfection; as those experience who are called to Religion.

3. The *instruction contained in this demand*—"What wilt thou that I do to thee?" And the *answer of the blind man*, "Lord, that I may see." And our Lord's reply, "Respice," "Receive thy sight:" with which only word Christ our Lord accomplished His desire, according to the great faith with which he begged that he might see, with a similar word.

Colloquy.—O God of my soul, I know well that Thou didst enquire of the blind man what he desired; to signify that Thou wilt not impart the gifts of Thy grace, but to such as dispose themselves to receive them.   O that Thou wouldst vouchsafe to say to me, "what wilt thou that I do to thee?" Lord I would forthwith answer: "That I may see:" Yet not as I will, nor what I will, but that with the eyes of a very lively faith, I may see *Thee*, O my Saviour, both to know, and to love Thee, since in this affectionate knowledge consists life everlasting.—Moreover, I ask of Thee, O Lord, "that I may *see*" *Thy holy will*, and Thy holy *law*, so highly esteeming it, that I accomplish it.   "That I may likewise" see *myself*, to know myself, so that I may abhor and humble myself.—Also "that I may see" *creatures* not with corporeal eyes for curiosity, but with the eyes of the soul, by contemplation, beholding in them, Thee, *my Creator*, of whom I receive so many benefits.— Finally, that at this time, "I may" clearly "see" *Thy divinity, with the Trinity of Persons*, with which sight my soul will remain for ever blessed in Thy sweet company.   O my King, say to my soul, "See" what thou desirest, because Thy *saying* is *doing;* and saying that it see, it will recover its sight.

4. From that which here has been pointed out, I will collect, that the *object* and *matter* of the spiritual sight in mental prayer, embraces these *five particular things*, that is to say,—Jesus Christ, God and man;—His holy law;—my own self;—creatures;—and in them the Creator, with the eternal goods of the blessed in glory. And in all the five I ought to exercise myself by means of meditation and contemplation, with the hope of obtaining what I desire, as shall be presently said.

POINT III.

"And Jesus added, Thy faith hath made thee whole: and immediately he saw, and followed Him, glorifying God."(8)

1. Christ our Lord *attributed to the faith of the blind man* that which was the work of *His omnipotence* and mercy, to honour it, and to give us an affection for this virtue, which disposes us for such wonderful favours, as He Himself declared, saying to two other blind men:— "Do you believe that I can do this unto you? They say to Him, Yea, Lord. Then He touched their eyes, saying: According to your faith be it done to you: and their eyes were opened."(9) And it is especially to be noted, that in both cases these blind persons recovered their sight *in a moment* by their great faith; another blind man receiving the same by little and little, because of his little faith. For first he saw no more than the faces of men, who moved like trees, and afterwards "saw all things clearly." (10) This also represents to us two means which our Lord uses to communicate to men divine light and perfection of spirit;—The one *extraordinary*, upon a sudden and in a moment, as He did to Saul;—Another *ordinary*, by little, and by degrees, communicating first a certain obscure

(8) Luc. xviii. 42.   (9) Mat. ix. 28.   (10) Marc. viii. 24.

knowledge of His mysteries, and afterwards another more resplendent, the light increasing, according as the disposition increases, until that he see divine things with so great clearness, that he remains as fully assured of them as if he saw them; ascending, as the apostle S. Paul says, "from glory to glory," until he be "transformed into the same image."(11) Which proceeds from that which Christ our Lord did to this blind man, spitting and touching him, as we shall declare in the thirty sixth meditation.

2. Lastly, I will consider how the blind man, finding himself healed, "*followed*" Christ "*glorifying God.*" For as the works of our Lord are most perfect, He likewise gave him that gift of the soul, that, forgetful of all other things, he should follow Him from whom he had received so great a good. In this example we also see that the internal light which Christ our Lord imparts in prayer, leads us to follow Him, imitating His virtues, to praise Him with giving thanks for benefits received.

Colloquy.—What wonder then is it, O my Saviour, that when Thou openest the eyes of my soul to behold Thee, I should desire to follow Thee? How shall I not follow so much bounty? And how not imitate so much sanctity? Thou dost me far more favour in suffering me to follow Thee, than Thou wilt ever receive by the service which I shall do Thee. Let mo therefore ever follow Thee in this life, until I come to possess Thee in the Kingdom of Thy glory. Amen.

(11) 2 Cor. iii. 18.

MEDITATION XXXVI.

ON THE MIRACLE OF CHRIST'S HEALING THE MAN THAT WAS BORN BLIND, WITH
CLAY AND HIS OWN SPITTLE.

POINT I.

"Jesus passing by saw a man who was blind from his birth," and looked upon him after a particular manner; whereupon His disciples "asked Him: Rabbi, who hath sinned, this man or his parents, that he should be born blind? Jesus answered: Neither hath this man sinned nor his parents, but that the works of God should be made manifest in him. I must work the works of Him that sent me while it is day; the night cometh when no man can work. As long as I am in the world, I am the light of the world."(1)

1. God our Lord *beholds all*, as the Wise man says, both "the good and the evil,"(2) elect and reprobate : but *some* He beholds after an especial manner, to wit, *with the eyes of mercy*, being greatly desirous to do them good, as He did to this blind man.

Colloquy.—O sweet Saviour, before I can look on Thee, Thou must look on me : for unless Thou look on me, I remain blind, and with Thy look I shall recover sight to look on Thee.

2. The infirmities of the body and other pains, although they are oftentimes sent in punishment of sins, yet at other times they *befal us only through the divine providence, to manifest in us the wonderful works of Almighty God*, not one but many :—that is to say, the great good which God Almighty draws from them, enriching the just whom He afflicts, with a variety of virtues, and making them dis-

(1) Joan. ix. 1.   (2) Prov. xv. 3.

cover and manifest those which they have, for the glory of God :—communicating such gifts to them, as may set forth the almighty power of Him that works them : such are to rejoice in tribulations, cheerfully to embrace them, and to glorify Almighty God by them : for of these works it is that Christ our Lord says, that He "must work" them "whilst it is day."

Colloquy.—O my Redeemer, if Thou must work the works which Thy Father has appointed, whilst the time of this Thy life lasts, work, I beseech Thee, these works in me, for it is much more important for me to will them, than for Thee to work them ; moreover, O my Lord, by reason of the great love which Thou bearest me, Thou sayest, that that imports Thee which imports me. Behold, O my God, how the "day" of this present world is very short for me, because my life is short, and "the night" of death will presently approach, when time will no longer permit me to work these works. And since Thou art the Sun and light of all the world, inflame me, and quicken me now with Thy holy grace, that I may hereafter see Thee in Thy glory. Amen.

3. These words I will apply to myself, saying :—Me it imports particularly "whilst it is day," and whilst life lasts, to work the works of Almighty God—works holy and conformable to the will of Him who created me, for my whole life is scarcely so much as a short day, and death will suddenly seize upon me, when I shall no more have time to work or merit. (3)

POINT II.

"When He said these things, He spat on the ground, and made clay of the spittle, and spread the clay upon his

(3) Eccles. ix. 10.

eyes, and said to him, Go wash in the pool of Siloe ;—
He went therefore and washed, and he came seeing." (4)

1. We must consider, first, the *causes of this* mysterious
cure, applying them to our spiritual profit.

i. The first was, that Christ our Lord might *show His
omnipotence,* in giving sight with a thing which seemed
contrary to it : for to spread clay upon his eyes, was
rather to put them quite out, than to open them.

Colloquy.—O immense power of Jesus! how shall
I not submit myself to the providence of Him that can
do so much, as to convert one contrary into another,
who anoints the eyes with clay to make them see
clearer, who humbles to exalt, and casts into prison
him whom he will draw from thence, and make the
Saviour of all Egypt ?(5)

ii. To show that the means to recover the light of
grace, is to *set before our eyes our own dirt,* that is to say,
our own *nothing;* the earth of which we were formed, and
into which we are to be returned, with the filth and mud
of the sins which we have committed, beholding them,
deploring them, and humbling ourselves in considering
them. But take notice also that this dirt must be composed of earth and of the spittle of Jesus Christ, for
unless His infinite wisdom, figured by His spittle, touch
our eyes, they will never be thoroughly cleared to know
our own vileness as we ought.

Colloquy.—O sweet master, mingle Thy spittle with
my earth, to make a remedy for my blindness : make
me to know what Thou art, and what I am, that
knowing Thee and knowing myself, I may love Thee
and hate myself, and may be replenished with Thy
grace and charity. Amen.

(4) Joan. ix. 6.   (5) Gen. xxxix. 45.

2. Together with this clay, Christ commanded the blind man to "wash himself" in the "waters of Siloe," which is interpreted, "*Sent*," to signify the sacraments of Baptism and Penance, in which the spiritual health of a man is made perfect, by the virtue of our Saviour which is in them. Who is He that was "*Sent*" by His Father for our good? But I am to repair to these baths and sacraments with the disposition of this blind man, who had a lively faith, great humility, and most punctual obedience, suffering his eyes to be daubed with dirt, and going so besmeared through the streets in the open view and sight of every one, without delay or reply, obeying the commandment of Christ: for he answered not as Naaman did, saying:—"I thought he would have come out to me, and touched with his hand the place of the leprosy, and healed me;"(6) or as if there were not other waters better than those of Siloe in which I might wash, and recover my sight: but on the contrary, he subjected his judgment, and by obedience recovered his sight. And in the same manner shall I recover mine, if when I feel the inspiration of our Lord, who sends me to these waters of Siloe, I obey, and make use of the good occasion which God offers me.

POINT III.

1. The third shall be, to consider the *illustrious and bold confession of this blind man*, with the *persecutions* which he suffered, and the *virtues* which he manifested, that we may imitate them.

i. The first was, great *zeal* for the honour of Jesus Christ our Lord, who had healed him, together with a spirit of gratitude, publishing and manifesting the miracle to all those that knew not of it.

ii. The second was, great *fortitude;* for, as his parents

(6) 4 Reg. v. 11.

feared to discover what they knew, for fear of the Pharisees, who held in horror the name of Christ, he without any fear boldly confessed that he had been blind, that Christ had healed him, and the manner how He had done it.

iii. The third was, *great zeal for truth*, with a celestial prudence, in not suffering himself to be deceived nor made to hold his peace out of respect for the Pharisees, who said to him :—"Give glory to God, we know that this man is a sinner, (7) and that it is impossible He could heal thee." He still persevered confidently, confessing the truth, defending Christ, and accusing them for that they knew Him not, even to the inviting them to become His disciples.

iv. The fourth was, great *patience*, to endure the maledictions and reproaches which they disgorged against him, saying:—" *Thou wast wholly born in sins, and dost thou teach us ?*"(8)　He likewise endured their persecution by being cast out of the synagogue as one excommunicated, and unworthy to live amongst the faithful.

2. All these virtues did he practise, assisted by our Lord and Saviour Jesus, who would make use of a blind beggar, and make him His preacher, to confound the wisdom of the Pharisees, giving a constancy more than human, to him who of himself was timid and illiterate.

Colloquy.—O greatness of the omnipotence of Jesus Christ, who, by so abject an instrument, performs works which are so glorious ! Take me. O my Saviour, for Thy instrument, that Thou mayest be glorified by me.

POINT IV.

Consider *that which Christ our Lord did to this man*, after all this had succeeded to him.

(7) Joan. ix. 24.　　　　　　(8) Joan. iv. 34.

1. For, first, knowing that they had cast him out of the synagogue, He *comforted* him; to show us the fatherly care which He has to comfort those who suffer persecutions in His behalf, and that He never forgets those who confess Him before men.

Colloquy.—O Redeemer of the world, who would not willingly suffer for Thy glory, since Thou hast so great a care to comfort those who endure and suffer for Thee ?

2. Since He would *perfect him in faith*, and augment him in the interior light of his mistaken mind, reputing Him for no more than a prophet. For he asked the blessed man:—"Dost thou believe in the Son of God?" He answered:—"Who is He, Lord, that I may believe in Him?" Demonstrating herein the promptitude of his heart, Christ said to him:—"Thou hast both seen Him, and it is He that talketh with thee."(9) As if He had said, "With the sight that I have given thee, thou hast seen me, and I am He that speaks with thee." He hearing this, answered, "I believe, Lord; and falling down, he adored Him." O what eyes did he then give him! O what light did he communicate to his soul! O what perfect sight did so humble an adoration procure! Give me, O Lord, such a sight, that I may believe Thee with a lively faith, and adore Thee with due reverence.

3. He *appeased his fears* and prevented the bad impressions which he, being newly converted, might receive from those things which the Pharisees had said against Him, saying, "For judgment I am come into this world, that they who see not may see; and they who see, may become blind."(10) That is to say, "I am come to judge betwixt man and man, that the rude and ignorant, by their humi-

<hr>

(9) Joan. ix. 35.   (10) Joan. ix. 36.

lity and littleness, may come, like thyself, to recover sight, and to believe the mysteries of my divinity and humanity; and on the contrary, that those who are expert in the law, like the Pharisees, philosophers, and the learned of the world, because of their pride, may become blind; not through my default, but through their own offence, be- cause they did not believe my doctrine, nor profit by it as they might.

Colloquy.—O good Jesus, suffer not that they who, by their obligation, ought to see most, through their pride do see least; and that those who should have their sight more clear than others, come to be more blind than others. Preserve us, O Lord, from the sin of pride, which is the cause of this pernicious blind- ness. Amen.

MEDITATION XXXVII.

ON THE HEALING OF THE DEAF AND DUMB, WHOM CHRIST OUR LORD HEALED WITH HIS SPITTLE.

POINT I.

"And they bring to Him one deaf and dumb, and they besought Him that He would lay His hand upon him."(1)

In the person of this miserable man, contemplate *our spiritual deafness and dumbness, their causes, and their proper remedies.*

1. *Spiritual deafness* is a want of faith and obedience, when a man will not hear or understand the truths of holy faith, the words of Almighty God, the precepts of the law, nor divine inspirations, becoming deaf to all these things. Again, spiritual *dumbness* is a want of prayer, and of con- fession, when a man neither knows how, nor yet desires, to open his mouth to call on God, to crave His mercy,

(1) Marc. vii. 32.

to praise Him, to thank Him for the benefits He has done him, or to confess His sins to obtain pardon.

2. Deafness is wont to be the *cause* that deaf persons are *likewise dumb;* the Devil is the cause of both these things, which therefore St. Luke names, "a dumb devil,"(2) because, shutting the gate of these two interior senses of the soul, the gate of remedy remains shut, which enters by the hearing of faith, and by obedience, and is obtained by hearing the word, praying to Almighty God, and confessing their sins to the priest His minister.

All this will I apply to myself, considering myself deaf and dumb, not as David,(3) for fear of hearing or of speaking evil, but rather to all that is good. And the reason is, because I have always the ears open, both of soul and body, to hear all the curiosities and vanities of the world, and to give credit to its lies and deceits, and to obey its maxims and perverse laws; whence it comes, that I have them also shut to those things which Almighty God and His ministers teach and command me. I have my tongue likewise very ready, to talk and discourse with men on all that pleases me on my own praises, listening to flattery, murmurings, or repinings, in consequence of which it is the more unfit to talk with God, and to confess my sins, sloth and shame having strongly tied it.

Colloquy.—O my Saviour, cast out of my soul this " deaf and dumb devil," which possesses it; and for Thine infinite mercy sake, vouchsafe to provide for me a suitable remedy, since of myself I have no power to redress so great a misery.

3. Consider, that as this deaf and dumb man would never have gone for a remedy to Christ, if others had not brought him and asked for him, supplying thus with their tongues the default of his, even so there are many

.(2) Luc. xi.   (3) Ps. xxxvii. 14.

sinners so deaf, so dumb, and so forgetful of their own misery, that they *would never convert themselves to Almighty God, unless some just person made intercession for them.* This ought much to move me to pray often for the conversion of sinners, and to labour as much as I can to bring them to Christ, and to His ministers, remembering that He pardoned the sins of the man " sick of the palsy," (4) seeing the faith of them that brought him before Him.

Colloquy.—O infinite God, have mercy, I beseech Thee, on so many deaf and dumb persons who are in this world ; cast forth, O Lord, from their souls the Devil, who makes them deaf and dumb, that they may gladly hear, praise, and glorify Thee, world without end.   Amen.

POINT II.

" And taking him from the multitude apart, He put His fingers into his ears, and spitting, He touched his tongue, and looking up to heaven, He groaned, and said to him, Ephpheta, which is, Be thou opened."(5)

1. In this action, Christ our Lord did all these things, of which any one would have been sufficient, to shew the *difficulty there is to heal such souls as are deaf and dumb :* not on the part of Almighty God, but by reason of the evil indisposition which is in themselves: for which reason they cannot be cured but in length of time.

i. " *Taking him from the multitude apart,*" to signify, that this kind of persons, to the end they may be cured, are to separate themselves from those who may any way delay or hinder their cure, and from the entanglements and traffic of temporal affairs, wholly attending to their remedy.

ii. " *He groaned,*" to denote the great calamity of these

(4) Mat. ix. 2,   (5) Marc. vii. 33.

souls, and what exceeding grief they cause Him. O how great is that evil, which causes Almighty God to groan!

Colloquy.—O my soul, how dost thou not weep and bewail thy misery, for which thy Lord so wept and wailed! Wail also for the miseries of thy neighbours, since they are so much to be bewailed, that Christ Himself deigned to bewail them.

iii. Groaning, "*He looked up to heaven,*" to signify that these evils are to be cured with fervent prayer and weeping, lifting up our eyes to heaven, from whence our remedy is to come, which cannot be found on earth.

iv. "*He put His fingers into his ears,*" the one finger into one ear, and another into the other;—to signify the gifts of the Holy Ghost, figured by the fingers of Jesus Christ: for as the finger proceeds from the hand, so the Holy Ghost proceeds from the divine Word, which is as the hand and arm of the eternal Father, by whom He works all things. These gifts, as will be seen in the fifth part, open our ears, so that they may hear and understand the truths of faith, and make them docile and obedient to the divine inspirations, and the entire accomplishment of the divine will.

Colloquy.—O Only-begotten Son of Almighty God, who, with Thy Father, dost produce the Holy Ghost, and with them both dost likewise communicate Thy gifts to men; vouchsafe to infuse them into our souls, that we may all hear and obey Thy heavenly words, fulfilling that which Thou hast said, " A people which I know not, hath served me : at the hearing of the ear they have obeyed me."(6)

v. "*Spitting, He touched his tongue,*" as He spit and touched the eyes of the other blind man to whom He gave sight,—to signify, that the celestial wisdom, figured by

(6) Ps. xvii. 45.

the spittle which proceeded forth of the mouth of Jesus Christ, the Wisdom Incarnate, and our Head, is that which must untie our tongue, that it may know how to speak with Almighty God, with ourself, and with our neighbour, as it becomes us. It is that which teaches prayer, the praises of God, the confession of our sins, and the brotherly correction of other men, in order to cure them. And as amongst men, but most of all amongst the Jews, to spit upon any one, was held as a sign of great contempt, Christ our Lord spit upon his eyes, to signify, that for our blindness and spiritual dumbness, we deserve to be despised and punished; in which sentiment Almighty God exercises us, to give us light, as the "gall of the fish" restored sight to Tobias.(7)

Colloquy.—O sweet Jesus, I desire to receive Thy spittle after this manner, since it is Thyself that dost make use of this remedy, permitting me to fall into tribulations, that my senses may be opened.

vi. "*He said,*" *imperiously,* "*Ephpheta, Be thou opened;*" to signify the virtue of His Almighty word. For although men do not speak to those that are deaf, because it were vain, yet Almighty God can speak to thee, because His word is "living and effectual, and more piercing than any two-edged sword,"(8) and powerful to open the hearing, "reaching unto the division of the soul," and to work in her whatsoever He pleases, so changing her, that she yields consent to what He commands.

Colloquy.—O Almighty God, vouchsafe, I beseech thee, so to open my hearing, that I do not withstand Thee, because I am ready to believe what Thou shalt teach me, and to obey what Thou shalt command me.

2. From these six circumstances together I will collect,

(7) Tob. xi. 13, et seq.　　　　　(8) Heb. iv. 12.

what I am to do on my part for the helping of souls, viz., to draw them from the occasion of sin, to deplore their sins, to pray for them, to bring them to the priests, the ministers of Christ, that they may apply to them the sacraments and the word of Almighty God, by which they may come to be cured in the virtue of Christ, who is the principal physician for these infirmities. And finally, to take compassion on those who, like " the deaf asp," (9) stop their ears against him who desires to take the poison from them, beseeching this most skilful Physician to use His omnipotency to heal them.

POINT III.

" Immediately his ears were opened, and the string of his tongue was loosed, and he spoke right." And although Christ commanded them not to tell it to anybody, "so much the more a great deal did they publish" the miracle, saying:—"He hath done all things well; He hath made both the deaf to hear, and the dumb to speak." (10)

1. Here contemplate the Almighty power of Jesus Christ to *do what He will, in removing the impediments to our salvation*, so that he who before was " deaf and dumb," heard and understood exceeding well. " And he spoke right." Hence I will resolve within myself to speak well, that is to say, of good things, and in such manner as shall be agreeable to Almighty God.

Colloquy.—O good Jesus, set a guard on my mouth, and take into Thy hand the keys of my tongue and hearing, shutting and opening them when it is convenient, that so both my silence and my talking, my deafness and my hearing, may always be agreeable to Thy majesty. Amen.

2. The *effect of this miracle* in this devout and thankful

(9) Ps. lvii. 5.   (10) Marc. vii. 35.

people, saying of Jesus Christ:—"Bene omnia fecit." "He hath done all things well."

Colloquy.—O infinite wisdom, who, "out of the mouth of infants and sucklings" "hast perfected praise," how great a truth hast Thou uttered by the mouth of these men! Well hast Thou, O my God, done all things which Thou createdst at the beginning of the world; for having made them, and looking on them, Thou saidst that "they were very good." (11) Well hast Thou done all those things which Thou hast by Thy providence disposed in this world, forasmuch as all Thy "works" are "perfect." (12)—Well hast Thou done the works of our redemption, being all full of sovereign bounty.—O how well hast Thou done all Thy miracles, Thy sermons, Thy sacraments, Thy humiliations, and Thy virtuous exercises!—Thou hast "done all things well," for the utility and good of men, who, notwithstanding for the same, have returned Thee so discourteous payment, that they have rendered Thee innumerable evils for innumerable goods: but Thou of Thyself art so exceedingly good, that as Thou didst well all sorts of good things, so Thou sufferedst well all sorts of evils. Grant me, O Lord, that in imitation of Thee I may do all things well, so that there may be nothing in me which may appear evil before Thee. Amen.

3. Lastly, *how greatly these people glorified Christ our Lord*, who though He had healed but one who was deaf and dumb, yet they said that He made the "deaf to hear, and the dumb to speak," thus confessing that He who did this good to one could do the same to many, and was most ready to do it to all those who were deaf and dumb in their souls, if they themselves would make use of His mercy, because it is His office, and for this He came into the world.

(11) Gen. i. 31.   (12) Deut. xxxii. 4.

Colloquy.—O good Jesus, do this office to all infidels, that they may firmly believe in Thee; to all sinners, that they may obey Thee; and to all those that are lukewarm in devotion, that they may serve Thee with fervour; so that all may praise and glorify Thee, world without end. Amen.

MEDITATION XXXVIII.

ON CHRIST'S HEALING THE MAN POSSESSED WITH A DEVIL, LUNATIC, DEAF, AND DUMB, WHOM HIS DISCIPLES COULD NOT HEAL.

POINT I.

" And when He was come to the multitude, there came to Him a man, falling down upon his knees before Him, saying:—Lord, have mercy on my son, for he is a lunatic, and possessed with a dumb spirit, who, wheresoever he taketh him, dasheth him against the ground, and he foameth, and gnasheth with the teeth, and pineth away: he falleth often into the fire, and often into the water, and I brought him to Thy disciples, and they could not cure him." (1)

1. Here consider, in the person of this possessed person, the *force* of the Devil against the man whom he possesses, *the evils which he does* both to his *soul* and *body*, and those which hereafter he will do him, having him in hell.

i. Such fierceness and cruel malice has the Devil against man, that he would injure him in all that belongs to his *body*, if Almighty God did not restrain him; and thus would he treat all as he did this poor youth, whom he made deaf, dumb, and lunatic, like one that has the falling sickness, afflicting him with very terrible and continual torments from his youth, attempting sometimes to

(1) Mat. xvii. 14. Marc. ix. 16.

burn him with fire, and sometimes to drown and stifle him in the water: and this with such pertinacity, that he would not obey the apostles of Jesus Christ, but rather in a manner triumphed over them.

ii. But much more violence does he show against the *soul* of the sinner, who surrenders himself to him, whom he makes deaf and dumb, as has been said, and lunatic: that is to say, subject to the world, irregular, mutable, and inconstant in good. He "dashed him against the ground," fastening his affections to earthly things. He makes him to cast out of his mouth the foam of beastly and filthy words, and to gnash his teeth, through the fury of anger and choler.—He makes him stupid, and as it were insensible to things celestial in it. Sometimes he casts him into the fire of carnal concupiscence, to burn him, at other times into the currents of the waters of worldly affairs, to sink him in them. And thus does he trail him from one sin to another, tearing him, and making him perversely to resist the preachers and confessors, that none may be able to reclaim him.

Colloquy.—O eternal God, open the eyes of all men, that those who come to this point of misery may be delivered from it: and that others may escape from falling into it, resisting that spirit from which so many evils come to them. Amen.

2. From hence is to be gathered what fury the Devil *will use in hell against sinners,* who are wholly his, since he uses such cruelty towards them here on earth, when Almighty God permits him to do it. O what deafness! O what dumbness! what gnashing of teeth! what enraged foamings! what hurling into flames of fire, and into waters of snow! what variety and eternity of torments will he inflict on them, revenging himself on God in them.

Colloquy.—O my soul, how dost thou not abhor him, who both in this life, and in the other, is so cruel and so bloody a butcher of those who obey him? O Almighty God, if Thou give leave to this enemy, to treat me like Job with regard to my body, yet restrain him, that he may not hurt nor injure my soul. Amen.

POINT II.

Next consider what Christ our Lord did before He healed this youth.

1. First, He *cried out against the incredulous people* that were there present, and in them, against all others like to them, saying:—"O incredulous generation, how long shall I be with you? And how long shall I suffer you?" (2) By which He discovered the pain which He endured by reason of the incredulity and pertinacity of that people, which emboldened the Devil to torment the possessed person, seeming thus to signify that He was weary of living so long amongst them, to support and suffer their hardness.

Colloquy.—O most patient Jesus, what great reason hast Thou to be weary of remaining with me, doing me great favours, and suffering my great imperfections. But Thy patience, O patient Jesus, is infinite, although Thou showest Thyself offended against the faults, Thou yet hast compassion on the faulty, to free them from them; deliver me, O Lord, from mine, that so I may enjoy the fruits of Thy mercy. Amen.

2. Then *He said, "Bring him unto me,* and they brought him, and when He had seen him, immediately the spirit troubled him, and being thrown down upon the ground he rolled about foaming:" (3) to show as it seemed, how much he detested our Redeemer. And, if in the presence of Jesus Christ, he so treats those whom he possesses, what will

(2) Marc. ix. 18.   (3) Marc. ix. 19.

he do to them in His absence? The father of the youth, afflicted ·at this sight, said to our Lord:—"If thou canst do anything, help us, having compassion on us." (4) But Christ seeing the little faith of this man, to heal him first before He healed his son, set before him a memorable sentence, saying:—"If thou canst believe all things are possible to him that believeth:" He says all things without excepting any, how great or difficult soever they be.

Colloquy.—O omnipotence of my Saviour, who makest almighty those who trust in Thee, so that they trust as they ought in Thy infinite mercy! How shall I not believe and trust in this word of my Lord, since He is most faithful in performing whatsoever He promises, and almighty in executing whatsoever He says !(5) O good Jesus, since Thou canst do all things, and sayest to me, "If" I can "believe," I may do all things; grant that I may believe in such a manner as Thou desirest, by which I may obtain of Thee all that which Thou dost promise me. Amen.

3. The father of the youth hearing this, and seeing that the health of his son depended on his faith, with fervour and humility returned answer, saying: "*I do believe; Lord, help my unbelief;*"(6) as much as to say; I believe as much as is possible for me, and in what my faith is defective, vouchsafe that Thy bounty supply the rest. In which words he teaches us a most useful manner and method of prayer, to wit, that doing what we are able, we demand of God to supply what is wanting. Believing, I am to ask an increase of faith;—humbling myself, I am to beg an increase of humility;—and loving, I am to crave an increase of charity.

Colloquy.—O sweet Jesus, I believe, and a thou-

<hr>

(4) Marc. ix. 21.   (5) S. Ber. serm. 84. in Cant.
(6) Marc. ix. 23.

sand times credit whatsoever Thou sayest, and hope what Thou promisest: but, alas! my faith is very feeble, and my confidence little; wherefore, supply, I beseech Thee, my default, fortifying my faith, and perfecting my hope, since it belongs to Thy bounty to finish the good which Thou hast begun.

POINT III.

Then Jesus threatened the unclean spirit, saying to him:—"Deaf and dumb spirit, I command thee to go out of him, and enter not any more into him."(7) Upon which the Devil went forth, crying out, and greatly tearing him, leaving him for dead; but Jesus, taking him by the hand, lifted him up whole and sound, and delivered him to his father: all admiring the greatness of God.

1. Here contemplate, first, *the dominion of Jesus Christ our Lord over the .devils*, and the *authority* with which He commanded this devil two several things;—the one, immediately to go forth;—the other, never more to return to enter. Nor was it void of mystery, that He said to him at this time, enter not any more into him: forasmuch as Christ our Lord knew well the condition of a devil which has long time lodged within a soul, and is afterwards cast out, who has no rest until he return, bringing "with him seven other more wicked than himself."(8) But to repress this his fury, He would here make use of His complete mercy, commanding him to return no more, neither alone, nor yet with company, which command he was enforced to obey.

2. Consider the great *pain which the Devil feels* in quitting a soul, especially when he has long possessed it, and the pains which the poor soul endures at the time he is to be freed from his tyranny, and to leave the vice wherein he has lived, which are agonies that resemble death, but

(7) Marc. ix. 24.   (8) Luc. xi. 25.

yet are very necessary to recover life; so that, although the Devil deters me, or the world and the flesh affright me, yet ought I not to procrastinate my conversion, driving from me this cruel tyrant as soon as I can; for the longer I defer the holy work, the more enraged will he be against me, and the more difficult it will be to dislodge him.

3. Consider the *bounty and benignity of Christ* our Lord, in giving His hand to him that was fallen, lifting him up, and reviving him; for He only it is who can restore life and perfect health. And although He might have taken this youth for His own service, yet He would not, but would return him to his father; showing in everything His charity, and that he does all the good He can, without any profit to Himself.

Colloquy.—O God of my soul, all these reasons invite me to love Thee, and with gladness to serve Thee; but since Thou hast delivered me from the Devil, command him that he return no more to me, and take me for Thine, for I neither have, nor ever will have any other father than Thyself, to whom be all honour and glory for the wonders which Thou workest by Thy Son for our benefit. Amen.

POINT IV.

Our Lord entering into a house, "then came the disciples to Jesus secretly, and said: Why could we not cast him out? Jesus said to them, Because of your unbelief; for amen, I say to you, that if you have faith as a grain of mustard seed, you shall say to this mountain, Remove from hence hither, and nothing shall be impossible to you. But this kind of devil is not cast out but by prayer and fasting."(9)

1. Consider first, the *great prudence of Christ* our Lord,

(9) Mat. xvii. 18.

who would not tax in public the little faith of His disciples, which was in part the cause why the devil went not out of this man; but reprehended in public the incredulity of the nation, which was public; and in secret, that of His diciples which was secret; teaching us the manner how to reprehend others with discretion.

2. He admonishes us, that, to obtain great things, it is but required *to have faith like "a grain of mustard seed,"* which is little in quantity, but great in sharpness and efficacy. For even so faith and confidence ought to be strong, vehement, lively, and effectual; but yet in a subject, humble and little in his own eyes, and distrustful of himself, that he may wholly trust in Almighty God. With this faith, we may pluck up the greatest mountain from its place, how strongly rooted soever it be;(10) that is to say, drive the Devil from bodies and souls, in which he has long time dwelt, and root up the spirit of pride, of anger, of gluttony, and other earthly impediments, which hinder us in the service of God.

Colloquy.—O Almighty Lord, sow in my soul this "grain of mustard-seed," for I can never get such a faith as this, unless Thou give it me. Give me, O Lord, a vehement faith by the fervour of charity, a secure faith by the littleness of humility, and in both conditions like "a grain of mustard-seed," from which there may grow up a tree of virtues, on which the angels of heaven may sit and recreate themselves.

3. Christ our Redeemer added, that "this kind" of devil, so deeply rooted, "is not cast out but by prayer and fasting." So that with faith and confidence, prayer and fasting, proceeding from the same faith, ought to be joined; for if the faith be like "a grain of mustard seed," in such case it buds forth fumes of prayers to Almighty God, and

(10) Marc. xi. 23.

humiliation of fastings, to obtain what we ask, hoping to obtain it by these means.(11)   And Christ our Lord uses the same words to him whom He heals, and to them who are already whole; because both the one and the other ought to be armed with the same virtues.

4. With these spiritual weapons, I will take courage to war and vanquish the malignant spirits, subjecting my heavy flesh by fasting, and elevating my spirit to Almighty God by praying, by which it may ascend to heaven like a pillar of smoke, issuing forth from "myrrh and frankincense;"(12) from "the myrrh" of penance, and from the "frankincense" of prayer; for the smoke thereof, as the angel said to Tobias, "driveth away all devils,"(13) so that they dare not approach to me.

Colloquy.—O my Redeemer, who on the mount of Thabor, didst spend the night in fasting and prayer before Thou didst cast forth this devil, which Thine apostles could not vanquish ; give to me the spirit of prayer and of penance, by which I may subject my flesh, tame my passions, and cast from me the spirit of pride and of vain-glory ; that ascending with Thee to the mountain of myrrh, and the hill of " frankincense,"(14) joining fasting with prayer, I may merit to ascend with Thee to the mountain of Thabor of Thy glory.   Amen.

<hr>

(11) S. Ber. serm. 40 in Quadrag.   (12) Cant. v. 6.
(13) Tob. vi. 8.   (14) Cant. iv. 6.

(5) MEDITATIONS ON CHRIST'S MIRACLES OF RAISING THE DEAD: AND ON THE SPIRITUAL RESURRECTION OF SINNERS.

The meditations on the three dead persons whom Christ our Lord raised to life, ought to be made, not only on the miracle itself, but also on what it *signifies*, viz. :—the spiritual resurrection of all such sinners who are converted to Christ our Lord; which may be reduced to three sorts, —i. Some sin by frailty or ignorance; figured by the daughter of twelve years old, whom Christ raised in the house of her parents.—ii. Others sin by passion; figured by the only son of the widow of Naim, whom our Lord raised as he was carried to be buried.—iii. Others sin with malice; figured by Lazarus, whom our Lord raised after he was buried ; representing in the manner of raising them, the manner of raising sinners.

MEDITATION XXXIX.

ON RAISING TO LIFE THE DECEASED DAUGHTER OF A PRINCE OF THE SYNAGOGUE.

POINT I.

"Behold there came a ruler of the synagogue and he fell down at the feet of Jesus, beseeching Him that He would come into his house. For he had an only daughter, almost twelve years old, and she was dying."(1)

1. Here meditate on the *quality of this deceased*, and the *cause of her death*, and the same may be done on the only

---

(1) Luc. viii. 41.

son of the widow of Naim : for although she was their only daughter, and born of rich and noble parents, and consequently greatly cherished and beloved by them, yet she was overtaken by death, from whom neither her parents, nor the physicians, nor her riches, nor her flourishing youth could defend her : by which I may understand, that in every age, and in every state of worldly fortune, there is no assurance of life, but that death can at all times suddenly attack me. And although this maiden, and some few others might repair the damage of the first time they died, after Jesus Christ had raised them to life, preparing themselves to die well and blessedly the second time, yet that I cannot do the same, because as we have already seen in the first part of the seventh meditation, it is a general law "unto men once to die." (2)

Colloquy.—O good Jesus, let me not vainly assure myself on the flower of my age, nor on my pleasures, riches, and other fallacies of this life; grant me always to fear with a holy fear, that which always threatens me ; and since my death will be but one, grant that it may be a good one.   Amen.

2. The death of young children sometimes befalls them *for the sins of their parents,* who dote upon them, and pet them inordinately, and for their sakes trample under foot the law of God. Sometimes for their own sin, when without bridle they follow their inclinations, Almighty God stopping their passage, lest they should be damned everlastingly; or be detained in purgatory. Sometimes for favour, taking them away, as the Wise man says, lest "wickedness should alter their understanding, or deceit beguile their souls." (3) Sometimes for other secret causes of the glory of God, which we comprehend not.   Hence I will fear to sin, lest death enter (4) and seize upon me,

(2) Heb. ix. 27.   (3) Sap. iv. 11. .   (4) Rom. v. 12,

casting myself upon the fatherly providence of Almighty God, beseeching Him to send death to me in such time and disposition, as may be most favourable for my salvation, and for His glory.

3. This *deceased person* could neither *go, seek, nor call upon Christ* to give her life, and would have remained for ever dead, unless *her father had interceded* for her: even so it is with the sinner, dead by sin. For although it be true that he is not so dead, that he cannot call upon Christ, yet it much imports him, that he have some intercessors to pray for him, and solicit Almighty God to resuscitate him. And so I must endeavour myself to demand the same of Him, saying :—

Colloquy.—O most pitiful Father, behold the innumerable souls that are in the world, so dead and buried in their sins, that they neither ask Thee life nor resurrection. I, O Lord, although unworthy, beseech Thee to come to their houses, and to touch their hearts with the hand of Thy inspiration, to give them life. Behold also this my only daughter, which is my soul and my will, which is, as it were, dead through the sin and tepidity in which I live. Come, O my God, to my unworthy house, and touch it with the touch of Thy Almighty hand, by which it may be raised up with fervour to newness of life. Amen.

POINT II.

"But Jesus having heard the word that was spoken, saith to the ruler of the synagogue: Fear not ; only believe. And He admitted not any man to follow Him, but Peter and James and John,"(5) with the father and mother of the damsel.

1. Here consider the *gentleness of Christ* our Lord, in going immediately after the governor, although his faith

(5) Marc. v. 37.

was imperfect and deserved not the favour; because he prayed Him, as did the ruler mentioned by St. John, that He would go to his house to "heal his son :" (6) as if He could not have healed him without moving a foot farther. But yet He blamed him not, because He saw him prostrate at His feet, and humbled; humility greatly supplying our other defects, and moving the mercy of Almighty God to pardon them : as the pride of the ruler, and the audacity which he shewed in seeking health for his son, without humbling or abasing himself, moved him to indignation, and to reprove him for his little faith.

2. Christ our Lord chose to work this miracle *in secret:* for it being the most famous of all those He had yet wrought, and the first dead person that He raised to life, He would leave us in this an example of humility, teaching us to fly the vain ostentation of men; in confirmation of which, the miracle being wrought, He immediately commanded those that were present not to publish it : but yet He would have witnesses who might afterwards publish it for our profit. Nor was it without mystery, that He chose for this purpose the three apostles, who likewise were witnesses of His Transfiguration on mount Thabor, and of the sorrow which He sustained in the garden of Gethsemane; to give us to understand, that to His best beloved and those who are more fervent, He communicates more of His secrets, especially in three things :—in the work of the conversion of souls,—in the greatness of His glory,—and in the ignominies of His passion. O how happy would he be who could privately accompany Jesus, and follow this lamb whithersoever He goes, without ever departing one only minute from His delightful company.

(6) Joan. iv. 47.

POINT III.

Jesus "taking the" deceased "damsel by the hand, said to her, Damsel, I say to thee, arise. And immediately the damsel rose up and walked: and He commanded that something should be given her to eat,"(7) leaving her parents astonished at the miracle.

1. Ponder the *almighty power of our Lord* and Saviour, since with one only word, without any prayer, as Elias and Eliseus, but absolutely commanding with authority, He restored life to this dead person, and at an instant the soul of the deceased, which was in Limbo, or wheresoever it was, heard His voice, and came and entered into her body, without being able to disobey, neither could anything detain her.

Colloquy.—I rejoice, O my Saviour, that Thou art so powerful, as to call the things that are not, as if they were, and that the dead do hear and obey Thy voice.   Call, O Lord, all those who are dead by sin, with the voice of Thy inspiration, that they may arise to the life of grace ; and, if they resist Thee by reason of their perverse will, because Thou wilt enforce none, call them once again more forcibly, for if it please Thee to use Thy power, who is he that shall not obey Thee?

2. The *cause why He took the dead person by the hand,* and that she began to walk, and why He commanded that there should be something given her to eat, which He did not do to the other dead. This He did, to show, that such sinners as die and offend through mere frailty, figured by this young maid, are quickened by Christ, who helps them with His almighty hand to surmount their feebleness : and, therefore, being raised by His virtue, He requires of them two things.—i. That they be not idle,

<hr>

(7) Marc. v. 41.

nor remain on the bed of slothfulness, but that immediately they begin to walk, and to exercise good works, profiting and advancing themselves in the way of virtue. —ii. That they eat that bread which fortifies "man's heart,"(8) which is the bread of the most Blessed Sacrament, by virtue of which they will obtain strength. And in commanding others to give food to the deceased, He gives us to understand, that His will is that His ministers should give this bread of life to converted sinners, to fortify them to prosecute the journey they have begun.

Colloquy.—O Saviour of my soul, take me by the hand; for, Thine joining itself with mine, I shall immediately arise, and begin to labour, chasing from me all sort of slothfulness. Give me likewise to eat that supersubstantial bread of life which comforts the feeble, and which nourishes the hearts of the pusillanimous, that in virtue of it I cease not to walk, until I come to " the mount of God, Horeb,"(9) where I shall for ever and ever behold Thy glory. Amen.

MEDITATION XL.

ON THE DECEASED SON OF THE WIDOW OF NAIM.

POINT I.

"Jesus went into a city that is called Naim; and there went with Him His disciples, and a great multitude. And when He came nigh to the gate of the city, *behold a dead man,* the only son of his mother, was carried out, and she was a widow: and a great multitude of the city was with her."(1)

1. In the person of this deceased youth, beside what we have said in the preceding meditation, consider, *a sinner*

(8) Ps. ciii. 15.　　(9) 3 Reg. xix. 8.　　(1) Luc. vii. 11.

dead through the sins arising from *his vehement passions,* whose soul is shut fast within his body, as within a coffin, forasmuch as all that he thinks, speaks and treats, is in flesh and of his flesh.   Those which carry this coffin are four appetites, or vehement passions, viz. :—*luxury,* which is an appetite of sensual delights;—*ambition,* which is an appetite of vain honours;—*covetousness,* which is an appetite of riches;—and *anger,* which is an appetite of revenge against those who thwart their vicious desires. By these four passions, this miserable sinner is carried into the abyss of innumerable sins, and afterwards into the abyss of hell, if Christ our Lord do not withhold him. Hence I will draw affections of compassion, to see the world so full of such dead sinners, who every day show themselves in public, in the streets and gates of the city, saying with Jeremiah :—"Who will give water to my head, and a fountain of tears to my eyes, and I will weep night and day" (2) for the dead of my city?

2. Ponder the *charity and providence of Christ* our Lord, in coming to Naim just at *such a time,* to meet with this deceased : since it was not by chance, but wittingly, and with intention to raise him to life, offering Himself without any asking.   The deceased daughter He raised at the entreaty of her father;—Lazarus at the entreaty of his sisters, but this young man of his own proper motion, to signify, the greatness of His mercy in seeking dead souls, going to meet with them, and to offer them a cure, though they do not demand it, moved by the sole compassion which He takes of them : and even then also when they *do* demand it, He prevents and inspires them, in order that they may demand it.

Colloquy.—O Father of mercies, behold the number of dead sinners, who walk according to the ways of

<hr>

(2) Jer. ix. 1.

this world; take compassion on them, go before them to meet them, and stay their passage, before death surprise them. Amen.

POINT II.

"Whom when the Lord had seen, being moved with mercy towards her, He said to her: Weep not; and He came near, and touched the bier, and they that carried it stood still."(3)

1. Christ our Lord would perform this miracle, not in secret, as the former, but *in public, for the greater glory of His Father*, and to establish the authority of His divine doctrine: yet to the end it might appear that He did it not for vain ostentation, but through compassion, He showed a tenderness of heart, in beholding the misery of this woman who was "a widow," who lost her only son: in which He teaches us the prudence which we must use in our public actions, and that we perform them without ostentation:—as also the compassion which we must have for afflicted and desolate persons, after the example of our great God, "who is the father of orphans, and judge of widows,"(4) and the refuge and shelter of all distressed.

2. *The tears of this widow*, without either speaking or asking anything, *moved Christ our Lord* to raise *her son:* because the tears which we shed for our own sins, or for the sins of others, are a very powerful prayer with God our Lord, to move Him to redress our miseries.

Colloquy.—O most merciful Father, whose eyes are moved to tender compassion, seeing the tears to stand in ours, let the tears of the Church, our mother, move Thee to compassion; a widow by reason of Thine absence, who so laments our offences, as if every one were her only son, issued forth of her very womb;

(3) Luc. vii. 13.   (4) Ps. lxvii. 6.

and grant me by her tears that which I deserve not for my own. Take away, O Lord, the cause of this weeping, saying to her, to comfort her, " Weep not," for I will restore life to the child for whom thou weepest.

3. Christ our Lord "came near the bier, and *touched it. And they that carried it stood still:*" to signify that before He raises a sinner, He first touches him with the hand of His omnipotence, and with forcible inspirations, sometimes with fears and threats, sometimes with hopes and promises, and causes the impetuosity of the four passions which carry him away, to subside; and how furious and violent soever they may be, they will be still at the touch and command of Jesus Christ.

Colloquy.—O hands of Jesus, which touched the wood of the holy Cross, to give life to him that died for touching with his the fruit of the forbidden tree; touch, I beseech Thee, such sinners as are dead by sin, that they may dispose themselves to receive the life of glory.   Amen.

POINT III.

" And He said: *Young man, I say to thee, arise.* And he that was dead sat up and began to speak;" and He " gave him to his mother." (5)

1. Consider here, first, *the omnipotence of our Saviour* in this miracle, who need not, like Elias and Eliseus, (6) to stretch Himself upon the body of the deceased, and to lay face to face, eyes to eyes, nor yet so much as touched them with His hand, as He did the daughter of the ruler of the synagogue, but only with an imperious word He spoke to the dead, as to one asleep.

2. This young man—(and not without mystery)—did *not immediately begin to walk,* as did the daughter of the

(5) Luc. vii. 14.   (6) 3 Reg. xvii. 21.   4 Reg. iv. 32.

ruler of the synagogue, but sitting up in the coffin, began "*to speak*," to signify that sinners who are carried away by their passions, are healed by little and little.—First, they receive the life of grace, and cut off their inordinate appetites to carnal things, although there remain yet some affection which entangles and ties their hearts to them, but at last they come wholly to divest themselves of their vicious customs, and begin to speak, confessing their errors, craving pardon, purposing amendment, and praising Almighty God for the favours He does them. Hence I will learn not to disdain those who forsake not on a sudden the customs of their past life, for although justification be effected in a moment, yet the perfection thereof is attained little by little.

3. Consider the *charity of Christ our Lord*, in giving the son to the mother, "a widow," for although He might have detained him for Himself, yet He would not, but would that he should attend and serve her in her age and widowhood, that so her comfort might be so complete, to signify, that it is the property of Jesus Christ to restore sinners to their mother the Catholic Church. And even as this young man, who was taken out of his mother's house dead, and carried by others, returned alive to her upon his feet, with joy to his mother;—even so the sinner departs from the congregation of the just, carried away by his passions, returns to her, quickened and revived by Jesus Christ, with liberty of spirit, and joy of the Church.

Colloquy.—I give Thee thanks, O most sweet Saviour, for the good which Thou dost to so many souls ; O that all sinners would return and join themselves to the congregation of the just, that so the Church might rejoice to have many living children ! Since then Thou, O Lord, canst give her this joy, deprive her not of it, that Thy name may be glorified, and we may say, as the people did who saw this miracle,(7) " A great prophet is risen amongst us, and God hath visited His people with mercy."

MEDITATION XLI.

ON THE RAISING OF LAZARUS FROM THE DEAD.

POINT I.

Lazarus, the brother of Mary and Martha, who were greatly beloved of Christ our Lord, "was sick. His sisters therefore sent to Him, saying, Lord, behold he whom Thou lovest is sick." (1)

1. First, in these words is taught us *a manner of prayer, brief, perfect*, very effectual, and proper for spiritual men exercised in the active and contemplative life, figured by Martha and Mary, which Hugo of St. Victor calls, (2) a manner of praying by insinuation, and consists in *representing to Almighty God briefly any necessity* which I suffer either in soul or body, enumerating the various titles of love which He bears me, referring wholly the care of my remedy to His divine providence, with great confidence and resignation to His holy will; for if I know that He loves me, it is enough to persuade me that He will do what is salutary for me, although I on my part ask Him nothing. This manner presupposes a great opinion of the love which Almighty God bears us, a great confidence in His goodness, and great resignation to His will, desiring nothing but what He wills, leaving to Him the remedy for all my necessities, the place, the time, and manner of supplying my wants.

2. With these affections *I will endeavour to repeat* often

(7) Luc. vii. 16.   (1) Joan. xi. 2.
(2) Lib. de Modo Orandi, c. 2.

and leisurely this ejaculatory prayer:—"*Lord, behold he whom Thou lovest is sick;*"(3) and instead of this word "sick," I may use others, saying, "Lord, he whom Thou lovest is *sad,*—dejected,—slow,—dry,—and indevout;—is tempted with anger, impatience, and pride,—is exiled from heaven,—is in danger of death, and of being damned for ever," &c.

Again, instead of saying:—"He whom Thou lovest," I may put *other* words which contain *titles of love*, saying: "*Lord, he whom Thou madest after Thy own image and likeness is disfigured,*—he whom Thou redeemest with Thy precious blood is stained with sins,—he whom Thou adoptedst in baptism is surrounded by enemies who oppress him,—he whom Thou hast chosen to be a religious, is full of imperfections which disfigure him." And making a pause at each of these ejaculatory prayers, I will pour forth my heart before Almighty God, hoping He will give me what is most suitable for me, yet still resigning myself to all whatsoever it shall please Him to ordain.

3. This sort of prayer is like the Blessed Virgin's at the wedding:—"Fili, vinum non habent," "Son, they have no wine," as has been meditated in its proper place.—As also that which the spouse insinuated when she said:—"I adjure you, O daughter of Jerusalem, if you find my beloved, that you tell him that I languish with love;" (4) as if she had said, "It suffices that He understand that I am sick, that He speedily remedy my infirmity.

POINT II.

"Jesus hearing it, said to them: This sickness is not unto death," (that is to say, shall not cause death,) "but for the glory of God, and that the Son of God may be glorified by it;"(5) and He still remained in the same place

(3) Joan. xi. 3.   (4) Cant. v. 8.   (5) Joan. xi. 4.

two days, Lazarus dying in the meanwhile. Christ our Lord gave this answer, on the one side to comfort these devout women, and the other to prove the soundness of their virtue, and to discover what the faith and resignation was which accompanied their prayer.

1. Consider, first, the *manner how our Lord comforted* these afflicted sinners, with a reason which gives the greatest comfort that can be in the world, which was to say to them, that the sickness of Lazarus, and the troubles and penalties of His elect, as well of body as of mind, all are " for the glory of" Almighty " God," and their own welfare, and that He knows the success they shall have before they happen, and the good which He will draw from them. This glory of Almighty God appears either in delivering us from them when we least expect it, after a wonderful manner, or in giving us in them great patience, and the precious gifts of His holy grace.

Colloquy.—O my glory and my Lord, if it be so that my infirmities and my troubles are conducive to Thy glory, let them come, then, in good time, for I will not refuse them for fear of diminishing Thy glory: nay, I will glory in them, since Thou art glorified in them : " Gladly, therefore, will I glory in my infirmities, that the power of Christ may dwell in me."(6)

2. It *was a great trial and affliction to these sisters to see their brother die*, when Christ had sent them word that his " sickness was not unto death." But this Christ our Lord did, to prove their faith and submission of judgment, in subjecting themselves to what they understood not, seeing in effect the contrary of that which they so greatly desired. In these two things Almighty God proved some great saints, as He proved Abraham, (7) when He commanded him to sacrifice his son, of whom He had promised

(6) 2 Cor. xii. 9.

(7) Gen. xxii. 3.

him an innumerable succession, who, as St. Paul says, "against hope believed in hope," (8) thinking that God was able to perform His promise. The same did Christ our Lord intend that the sisters of Lazarus should do; and the same ought I to do, when Christ sends me the contrary of that which I crave and ask at His hands, as if I ask Him for health or humility, and He should suffer that my sickness should increase, and that I should be more tempted to pride than I was before:—then am I to say that of Job:—" Although He should kill me, I will hope in Him, but yet I will reprove my way in His sight, and He shall be my Saviour." (9)

Colloquy.—O most sweet Saviour, I cast myself into Thy hands, to Thee I surrender my judgment and will, offering myself to undergo whatsoever it shall please Thee to ordain. Although Thou shalt "kill me," yet will I never lose the hope that Thou canst revive me ; and if Thou say that I shall die, and that I see myself die, yet will I "against hope believe in hope," for I will believe that this very death will give me a better life.

POINT III.

Two days being passed, Jesus "said to His disciples, Let us go into Judea again;" and they " say to Him, Rabbi, the Jews but now sought to stone Thee: and goest Thou thither again?" (10) Notwithstanding this, He said to them that He would go, because the matter concerned His Father's glory He would run through all worldly difficulties.

1. To encourage them to do the like, He laid before them two powerful reasons.

i. First, "Are there not twelve hours of the day?" that is to say, as the day has twelve hours, and so is it

(8) Rom. iv. 18. (9) Job xiii. 15. (10) Joan. xi. 7.

impossible that it should not fulfil them; *even so the day of my life,—that of yours,—and the life of all, has its hours fixed by the high decree of Almighty God*, which no man can shorten before the time, for which reason we may ˙securely undertake what shall be for His glory, without fear of losing our life before the time which He has decreed and ordained. And the rather so, because in "twelve hours" men and many other things change, and God Himself alters their wills, wherefore we must not be afraid on account of what passed in the first hour, which perhaps will quite alter in the next.

ii. The second reason was:—"*If a man walk in the day he stumbleth not, because he seeth the light.*" That is to say, He that walks in truth before Almighty God needs not to fear, because the truth and light of God will so conduct him, that he will not stumble nor die, so long as it shall please Almighty God that he should live. But those who walk by night and in darkness fear and stumble, because the true light both of faith and of grace is wanting to them, and so in punishment of their offences they come to fall, and to lose their lives before the time, for " the wicked and deceitful," as the Scripture says, " shall not live the half of their days," and the sun shall go down on their behalf when it should be but noon-day.

With these two reasons I am to animate myself *not to omit things belonging to the service of Almighty God, for fear of men*, or of their persecutions, since they cannot add one day, nor one hour of a day, to those which Almighty God has assigned, nor can they take one away contrary to His holy decree. And if I be a child of light, and pleasing to Almighty God, I have no cause to be afraid of men, since the same Lord says:—" Fear ye not the reproach of men, and be not afraid of their blasphemies, for the worm shall eat them up as a garment, and the moth shall consume them as wool."(11)—And "who art thou that thou shouldst be afraid of a mortal man, and of the son of man, who shall wither away like grass?" As if He had said, Although considering what thou art of thine own self, thou hast sufficient cause to fear, yet beholding whom I thy protector and Redeemer am, thou hast no cause at all to fear.

2. This said, Christ our Lord *discovered to His apostles by little and little the death of Lazarus*, and that with words very mysterious, saying first to them : "Lazarus our friend sleepeth, but I go that I may awake him out of sleep:" (12) in which words He calls the death of Lazarus, " sleep;" not only because it was to Him as easy to raise him, as to waken one that was asleep, which is a thing common to the death both of good and bad, but also to signify, the *difference* that there is betwixt the death *of his friends*, and that *of his enemies;* for even as he that sleeps rests himself by sleep, and soon returns to live the life which before he led: even so the friends and favourites of Almighty God, die to " rest from their labours," (13) and rise again to that life, which in an eminent manner deserves the name of life, which is that life everlasting, in which is given to them the inheritance of glory :(14) but His enemies die, to remain dead for ever, whose " resurrection" shall not be " to life," but to everlasting death.

3. To this saying of Jesus Christ, the apostles answered: "Lord, if he sleep, he shall do well;" (15) as if they had said, It is a sign of health when the sick sleep, and that therefore it was not needful to take the pains with so great danger to go to awake him. In this is represented *the repugnance of imperfect persons*, who will not understand what they desire not to do, unless it be told them in very

(11) Is. li. 7, 12.   (12) Joan. xi. 11.   (13) Apoc. xiv. 13.
(14) Ps. cxxvi. 2.   (15) Joan. xi. 12.

plain terms, and never want excuses for not accomplishing that which God and His ministers command them; so the apostles, who being loathe to go to the country of Judea, supposed our Lord to speak of common sleep, where it was easy to understand that it was needless to take such a journey to awake one that was asleep.   Wherefore Christ our Lord seeing this, He said to them plainly:—"Lazarus is dead, and I am glad for your sakes that I was not there, that you may better believe." (16)   In which words He discovered the desire which He has that our faith and virtue should increase, seeing He was "glad" of Lazarus's death, because from thence was to result great good to His disciples.   And although the apostles already believed this, He nevertheless says, "that you may believe;" teaching us an exercise of virtue, proper to the most fervent persons, who, upon every occasion on which God discovers His mysteries to them, believe anew, and say to Him:— " Lord, if I had not believed until now, I would now believe, and now I renew my belief."   In the same manner, the perfect Religious man renews his vows various times, as if he then made them for the first time, saying thus to Almighty God: "If I had not already vowed chastity, now I would vow it, and now I vow it again."

4. Lastly, Thomas seeing the resolution of our Lord, and that He said:—" Let us go to him;" answered with great courage, saying to his companions :—" *Let us also go, that we may die with him ;*" (17) as if he had said, Let us not forsake our master, let us pass through the danger to which He exposes Himself, dying in the place where He will die.   By which he showed great fervour in two things,— the one in offering himself to die with Christ,—the other in exhorting his companions to do the like, exercising therein two excellent acts of charity, which are, the love

<hr>

(16) Joan. xi. 15.   (17) Joan. xi. 16.

of God and of his neighbour, loving Christ more than his own life, and inviting his neighbour to love Him likewise in the same manner.

Colloquy.—O sovereign master, I here offer myself to go and to die with Thee, if it were needful, that I may not forsake Thee, for Thou art my life, and it is a " gain " for me to " die" for Thee.(18)

POINT IV.

Jesus going to Bethany, found that Lazarus was dead and buried four days before. And Martha going to meet Him, said to Him:—" Lord, if Thou hadst been here, my brother had not died." As if she had said, " If Thou hadst been present, Thou wouldest have stopped in due time the course of his sickness."

1. By this history we are taught that as Lazarus fell sick and died in the absence of Christ, so *when Christ our Lord absents Himself* from us, hiding His face, and ceasing to do us those spiritual favours which He was wont to bestow on us, *passions and temptations are accustomed to burst forth,* and the sickness of sloth and of spiritual feebleness commonly increase, which sometimes end in the death of sin, but all cease in the presence of Him who entirely dissipates them.

Colloquy.—O my Redeemer, do not Thou utterly forsake me."(20) I do not ask Thee that Thou do not leave me for a time, to try me, but that Thou leave me not so long, till I be vanquished and quite overcome. Amen.

2. Then Martha added:—" I know that whatsoever Thou wilt ask of God, God will give Thee." (21) Wherein she showed the *little faith which she had in the divinity of*

(18) Phil. i. 21.   (19) Joan. xi. 21.
(20) Ps. cxviii. 8. Cass. col. iv. c. 6.   (21) Joan. xi. 22.

Jesus Christ, believing that it was needful for Him to demand of God, that which He intended to do, and, therefore, before He would work this miracle He would first heal her imperfection, saying amongst other things:—"I am the resurrection and the life, he that believeth in me, although he be dead, shall live: and every one that liveth and believeth in me, shall not die for ever." (22)   That is to say, " I am the author of the resurrection of souls that are dead through sin, giving them the life of grace, and afterwards that of glory.   I am likewise the resurrection of dead bodies, restoring them when and how I will the life they have lost, in a far better state than they had it before, and whoever with a lively faith believes this, he shall not die for ever."—" Believest thou this?"   Then she with great fervour, as one that accused herself for her little faith, and felt herself accused for the little she had shown, answered:—" Yea, Lord, I have believed, that Thou art Christ the Son of the living God, who art come into this world," (23) and consequently I believe that Thou art the resurrection and the life, and that Thou canst raise my brother, not only by praying as a man, but by commanding as God.   Whence we see that the true disciples of Christ are docile, and easy to be corrected in their errors, taking occasion thereby to make new acts of that virtue in which they failed to compensate for their former faults.

3. Then weigh the *charity of our Redeemer*, and the tender care which He has of such as love Him; for being resolved to raise Lazarus, *He would have Mary present at the doing of it*, recompensing thus the fervent love with which she served Him, giving her new motives to augment and perfect her love, by seeing such resplendent miracles and benefits; and so He sent for her by her sister Martha,

(22) Joan. xi. 25.(23) Joan. xi. 26, et 27.

who said to her secretly :—" The master is come, and calleth for thee." Who when she heard this, arose quickly, and when she "was come wheré Jesus was, seeing Him," "fell down at IIis feet, and saith to IIim, Lord, if Thou hadst been here, my brother had not died." (24) In this fact Mary discovered *three notable virtues*.

i. Very prompt, punctual, and loving *obedience*, proceeding from the great opinion which she had of Jesus Christ; for in hearing that He called her, " She rose up speedily, and went out" to Him, without taking any leave of those that were with her, not using any compliments which might have detained her for some time, teaching us the promptitude with which we ought to obey the divine vocation, without making any account of " flesh and blood." (25)

ii. A great *reverence to our Lord*, for as soon as she saw Him, she immediately prostrated herself before IIis feet, without noticing that there were many nobles of Judea present, who abhorred IIim, and could not brook that any the least honour should be showed Him. And in this she surpassed Martha, of whom no such thing is mentioned.

iii. A far *greater faith than that of her sister Martha*, with great resignation, being full of love and sorrow, she said: —" Lord, if Thou hadst been here, my brother had not died;" (26) but she concealed the surplus which Martha added, as being better instructed in the faith of the divinity of Jesus Christ, having sat at IIis feet where she had heard this doctrine. And this resignation so loving and so confident, without asking at all of Christ our Lord the resurrection of her brother, resigning herself wholly to IIis providence and charity, was sufficient to obtain that favour which the Church attributed to her in the prayer of her feast, saying, " Cujus precibus exoratus," &c. From

(24) Joan. xi. 28, 32.   (25) Gal. i. 16.   (26) Joan. xi. 32.

whence it is to be seen how much more tender affections can prevail with Christ than many words. And as Mary Magdalen was punctual in obeying Christ, so likewise was Christ in granting her desire, and in accomplishing her request.

4. Lastly, consider the mysteries represented in these two sisters, *Martha and Mary*, who *represent the two lives, active and contemplative,* which concur to bring about the conversion and resurrection of sinners, for preaching, prayer, and contemplation, do as sisters concur to this work. Neither does Christ our Lord, who is the principal author of them, content Himself in doing this by Martha only, but He wills that Mary also concur; to teach the ministers of the Gospel, that if they will labour fruitfully, they must join prayers with their words, and meditation and contemplation with their sermons.—Lastly, as in this work Mary performed more than Martha; so, oftentimes, the prayer of humble and fervent persons performs more than the words of very learned preachers; that we all of us animate ourselves to pray for sinners, seeing that Christ our Lord delighted that Mary should pray, weep, and importune Him with sighs.

POINT V.

1. Consider fifthly, the *remarkable things which Christ our Lord did before the miracle.* The first was, *to weep, groan, and to mourn in spirit,* with external signs of sorrow, troubling Himself, and sobbing: which He did two several times. The first time " He groaned in the spirit," for compassion, to see *Mary Magdalen* and the standers by weeping: for it is the property of charity, to "weep with them that weep;" (27) and Christ being charity and mercy itself, would in nowise fail in its laws. The second time He "wept" for compassion *of the departed,* and for

(27) Rom. xii. 15.

sin, which had brought death into the world, representing them to Himself, how dear it would cost Him to destroy death and sin, and how for the same reason He was to die, and His body to be entombed in another's sepulchre, and His soul separated from it to descend to Limbo.   Likewise He is described as "groaning," for *compassion of the Pharisees*, who were present, who would calumniate so evident a miracle, and take occasion from it to conspire His death. For all these reasons " Jesus wept."   O that I had been so happy as to have been present, to have gathered up these tears of Jesus, to have anointed mine own eyes with them, that they might be converted into fountains of tears, which, joined with His, might wash away the spots of my sins, and might restore to me the life of grace, which by them I lost.   O sweet Jesus, for Thy tender tears' sake, give me the gift of tears.

2. I will further remark in this place, the *diversity of judgments which were given of these tears* of Christ, for the more simple judged that they proceeded from love and compassion, and, therefore, said:—" Behold how He loved him," since being so grave a person, He weepeth for him. Others more malicious, calumniated them, saying:—" Since He loved him so much, why, as He gave sight unto the blind, did He not preserve this His friend from death?" In which I may see how erroneous the judgments of men are, and how little account is to be made of them, since of one and the self-same work some speak well, and others ill.   With this I will comfort myself, if perchance some shall judge amiss of the tears and works of devotion, which I shall practise to fulfil the will of Almighty God.

3. Christ our Lord commanded them to " take away the stone" which lay upon the sepulchre, which He did, that all might evidently see the body of the dead.   And although He could have removed it with one only word,

yet He would not, because He would not show a miracle in those things, *which men could do by themselves*, but in that which surpassed human power. Where I may notice how Martha, moved with a pious zeal, sought to hinder the removing of the stone, saying:—" Lord, by this time he stinketh, for he is now of four days.'' (28) In which is represented, how, sometimes even our own kindred and friends, under the pretext of love, become an impediment to our spiritual good, hindering us from ridding ourselves of such things as are obstacles to it.

4. The stone being removed, Christ our Lord lifted "*up His eyes to heaven*," whence life was to come to that deceased person: teaching me that the remedy of my miseries consists in seeing them, not only confusedly in a heap, or covered with whitened stones, but clearly discovered, that I may feelingly smell the filthy savour of them, and forthwith, "lifting up" my "eyes" to Almighty God, from whom my help and cure is to come, ask it with true humility.

5. Then our Saviour said:—" Father, *I give Thee thanks*, that Thou hast heard me, and I knew that Thou hearest me always, but, because of the people, who stand about, have I said it, that they may believe that Thou hast sent me." (29) This was very common to Christ our Lord, to give thanks before He wrought any miracle, He being assured that it was the will of His Father that He should work it: and this delight and conformity of wills, Christ calls and denominates *to be heard*. This, likewise, instructs us, that he who desires to receive new favours from Almighty God, ought to begin by giving thanks for those already received, for by this act of gratitude he disposes himself to receive others.

(28) Joan. xi. 39.   (29) Joan. xi. 41.

POINT VI.

1. After this, Christ *our Lord* "*cried out with a loud voice,*" as if He had spoken to some one afar off, as indeed the soul of Lazarus was,—which we believe to have been then in Limbo,—representing by this loud cry the voice of that sounding trumpet, by which the dead shall be called to judgment: saying imperiously, " Lazarus come forth:" whose soul, at the same instant, " came forth" from where it was, and joined itself to the body, and the " body came forth" alive out of the grave, bound feet and hands with winding bands, and his face was bound about with a napkin:" by which we see the *greatness of this miracle* in giving both life and perfect health to him that was dead, and in a state of putrefaction, and even bodily motion, though he was bound: and though He could have unbound him, yet would He not, but commanded that others should unbind him and let him go, that those who unbound him might be witnesses of the miracle.

2. From all this will I draw affections, both of *joy and admiration* for the omnipotence of this Lord, as has been said in the preceding meditation. And in particular I will consider in the person of Lazarus, a sinner, who had sometimes been just, and God our Lord, having withdrawn Himself from him, to try him, proved to be ill: for first he *sickened* through tepidity, then he died by consent to sin,—was *buried* by suffering himself to be carried away by affections to earthly things, and to be overwhelmed by them:—afterwards the " stone" of the hardness of heart fell upon him by a continual custom of offending;—lastly, he became offensive by the evil example and scandal which he gave to others;—from which it followed that he neither called upon Christ to help him, nor made any reckoning of Him.

3. It is proper to the just to pray to Almighty God with

a fraternal affection for all sinners, and proper to *Christ to hear their prayers*, and to come to raise them for the glory of His Father, discovering the force of His interior word, which is His inspiration, in drawing them alive from their sepulchre, manifesting the efficacy of His word, in withdrawing them from their abominable sins; that, considering this, we may never despair of any man's conversion how wicked soever he be. But as Lazarus came alive out of his grave, yet bound and wrapt in his " winding bands,'' which the apostles loosed;—even so, sinners, raised again to the life of grace, still remain bound with many consequences of sin, and evil customs of their past life, from which they are afterwards loosed and delivered by the industry and direction of their confessors, to whom also Christ our Lord has given power, according to that which He promised to S. Peter, (30) that, with the voice of sacramental absolution, they may unloose the bands of sinners, whom He Himself awakens with the voice of His divine inspiration, that they may confess their sins and offences.

Colloquy.—O powerful Saviour, since all Thy works are perfect, and that Thou hast drawn me alive out of the sepulchre of my sins, deliver me from the vicious customs which I contracted by them. I refuse not to have recourse for aid to Thy priests, but humbly beg Thy favour, that I may depart free and unbound, by means of their ministry. Amen.

(30) Mat. xvi. 19.

MEDITATION XLII.

ON THE COUNCIL HELD BY THE PHARISEES AGAINST CHRIST OUR LORD, IN WHICH
CAIPHAS DECREED THAT HE SHOULD DIE.

POINT I.

"Some of the Jews went to the Pharisees and told them
the things that Jesus had done. The chief priests therefore, and the Pharisees, gathered a council, saying: What
do we, for this man doth many miracles? if we let him
alone so, all will believe in Him, and the Romans will
come and take away our place and nation."

1. We are to consider how *abominable are those* who
subject themselves *to the sin of hatred and envy*, grounded
upon the pretension of their own honour and particular
interest, seeing that even from the very miracles and
works of Jesus Christ, they drew a motive to commit more
heinous sins, making of so precious a balm, a poison to
kill themselves; and from whence others took occasion of
virtue for their salvation, these took occasion of greater
malice to their damnation!

Colloquy.—O my Lord, deliver me, I beseech Thee,
for Thy sweet mercy's sake, that I may not convert
to my hurt that which Thou workest in others, for my
example and good. Amen.

2. Reflect, secondly, on the *promptitude* with which
those malicious people *assemble together against Christ* our
Lord,(1) and against all such as are His servants, and how
blind they are in their own counsels; hatred like a beam
blinding the eye of their understanding;—for on the one
side, they confessed that Christ wrought many miracles,
that all would believe in Him, and would receive Him as

(1) Ps. ii. 2.

their Messiah;—and on the other side they abhorred even to call Him by His name, or to take it into their mouths, neither would they believe His manifest miracles, nor yet receive Him for their Saviour, that they might still continue in their vices.—Lastly, through the just judgment of Almighty God, in declaring the evil which they apprehended if they put not Christ our Redeemer to death, they discovered the evil they were to incur in procuring His death, which was the destruction of their Temple and their nation.

Colloquy.—O good Jesus, Angel of the great council, deliver me from the passionate counsel of my flesh, which counsels me to do that in which it takes pleasure, and by which it may avoid pain and dishonour, and so falls into them. I desire, O my Lord, no other counsel than Thine, and all my "counsel" shall be Thy "justifications,"(2) endeavouring always to conform my life to them. Amen.

POINT II.

" One of them named Caiphas, being the high priest for that year, said to them: You know nothing, neither do you consider that it is expedient for you, that one man die for the people, and that the whole nation perish not. And this he spoke, *not of himself, but being the high priest of that year*, he prophesied that Jesus should die for the nation; and not only for the nation, but to gather together in one the children of God, that were dispersed."(3)

Here is to be considered the *decree and sentence of Caiphas*, first, inasmuch as it proceeded from the very bottom of *his wicked heart;* and next, inasmuch as it proceeded *from the Holy Ghost*, who spoke by his mouth; for he spake not of himself, as the Evangelist says.

(2) Ps. cxviii. 24.   (3) Joan. xi. 49.

1. As touching the first, consider *the pride of this high priest*, who began his discourse by taxing all the rest with gross ignorance, he meanwhile himself erring most grossly, judging that it was meet to put Christ to death, for fear lest they all should die a temporal death by the hands of the Romans, this being the true cause of their destruction. Where we see that pride is so much the more dangerous, as the person is more qualified in whom it predominates, as it happens when it blinds sages, priests, prelates, and princes, who, as Jeremiah says, break much more than other men, the yoke of the law of God, and violate the bonds of His holy precepts.

2. Concerning the second, I will ponder *the sovereign ways of the Holy Ghost*, who makes use of the tongue of the *wicked* to declare *His intentions*. For when Caiphas determined to pronounce these words in hatred and contempt of Jesus Christ, then did the Holy Ghost inspire him to speak them, prophecying the necessity which the world had of the death of Christ, to prevent an universal death, and to gather together in one faith, and charity, those who in the eternal predestination were the children of God, and were dispersed through the world.

Colloquy.—It is most true, O my God, that it much imports us, that one man die for all, yet not a mere man, but God and man, a man who by excellence is a Man ; a Man one and singular, and such a one whose like is not to be found amongst men. O Man, more than man, Man, one, and singular amongst men, I thank Thee all that I possibly can, that Thou didst choose to die for men, that Thy temporal death might deliver them from eternal death. O my Redeemer, suffer not that the fruit of this death be utterly lost, gather together such as are scattered, assemble all Thy children, people Thy church with many just, and fill heaven with many elect, that Thou mayst be glorified by all, world without end. Amen.

POINT III.

"From that day, therefore," the sentence of Caiphas being approved by all, "they desired to put Him to death. Wherefore Jesus *walked no more openly* among the Jews, but He went into a country near the desert into a city that is called Ephrem, and there He abode with His disciples "(4)

1. Hence I will consider the *delight this perverse generation took in this wicked design*, and the applause which they gave to the sentence of Caiphas; beseeching our Lord to deliver me from the company of those who are glad when they have done evil, and rejoice in most wicked things.

2. I will reflect on the *patience and meekness of Christ* our Lord, who, although He was absent, beheld all, and yet took not revenge of so unjust a decree, but gave place to the anger of His enemies until His time appointed, feigning as if He had been ignorant of their evil pretences: in which He accomplished that which He had foretold in Jeremiah, saying: "Thou, Lord, hast shown me and I have known: then Thou showedst me their doings, and I was as a meek lamb that is carried to be a victim, and I knew not that they had devised councils against me, saying: Let us put wood on his bread, and cut him off from the land of the living, and let his name be remembered no more." (5)

Colloquy.—O sweet Jesus, "Lamb of God," and "bread of life," I give Thee thanks for the meekness which Thou didst manifest, knowing that Thy enemies sought to sacrifice Thee like a lamb, and to fasten Thee with nails to the wood of the cross. Give me part of this meekness, that I may glorify

(4) Joan. xi. 53.   (5) Jer. xi. 18.

Thee in it, offering myself to all sorts of injuries and death, for Thy honour and glory.   Amen.

3. The *fidelity of the disciples*, in accompanying their master in all His travels and retirements, especially in this: pondering how Christ our Lord, in this little city which was bordering upon the desert, prepared Himself to die, exceedingly glad to see that the hour itself was so near at hand.

Colloquy.—O Redeemer of the world, repairer of mankind, the decree of Thy death is already published by the mouth of the high priest, who, though he is wicked, yet is moved to this by the Spirit of Thy Father. This sentence cannot be revoked, and for the salvation of all mankind it is not desirable that it be revoked, nay, Thou Thyself wilt not revoke it, esteeming more the lives of our souls, than the life of Thy own body. Prepare Thyself, O Lord, for the combat which now awaits Thee, that dying, Thou mayst obtain the victory which we all hope for : and since Thou hast already obtained it, permit not that I lose the fruit of it : help me to fight in the battle of this life, that, so, with the help of Thy grace, I may obtain the life eternal.   Amen.

(The meditations on the supper in Bethany, and on the entry into Jerusalem with palms, shall be made in the fourth part.)

(6) MEDITATIONS ON SOME OF OUR LORD'S PARABLES.

In the sermons which our Saviour made the last six days before His Passion, He preached certain mysterious and profitable parables, of which, as also of others, which He had preached at other times, I will select the principal, especially those which the Church proposes in the Gospels of certain Sundays and festival days, that on these days they may be meditated. And as they contain various senses and declarations, I will only here follow that which regards our particular profit, as if the parable were spoken to me alone. Neither will I always observe the order in which they were spoken, in order to join some others, which may be directed to the same intention, although in general all of them are directed to declare the mysteries of the Kingdom of Heaven, which comprehends six several things, in which or in some of them, the similitude of the parable is comprised, namely.—i. The Church militant with her members and her citizens.—ii. The Church triumphant, towards which they walk.—iii. The doctrine of the Gospel which they believe.—iv. The laws and counsels which they keep.—v. The virtues and works which they practise.—vi. The properties of the King who rules and governs;—who is Christ our Lord; who, as He has divers offices, so He propounds divers parables to declare them.

MEDITATION XLIII.

ON THE PARABLE OF THE WISE MAN, WHO BUILT HIS HOUSE UPON A ROCK, AND
OF THE FOOL, WHO BUILT HIS HOUSE UPON THE SAND.

Our Lord Jesus Christ, seeing the different dispositions of those who heard His sermon on the mountain, concluded with this parable, saying: Every one that "heareth my words and doeth them, shall be likened to a wise man, who built his house upon a rock, and the rain fell, and the floods came, and the winds blew, and they beat upon that house and it fell not, for it was founded on a rock. And every one that heareth these my words, and doeth them not, shall be like a foolish man, that built his house upon the sand; and the rain fell, and the floods came, and the winds blew, and they beat upon that house, and it fell, and great was the fall thereof."(1)

POINT I.

1. Christ our Lord presupposes clearly, that amongst those who both hear and believe His doctrine, some are *wise and prudent* and put it in *practice;*—others *foolish* and senseless, contenting themselves to *believe without practising* it, whom, therefore, He names so with great reason. For there is no greater folly, nor more senseless oversight, than to believe what Christ says, and to act quite contrary to their belief; nor is there greater wisdom and prudence than believing, and putting in practice what we believe. Upon this I will wonder at myself, that believing as I believe, I live as I live;—that believing there is an everlasting hell, for such as break the law of Almighty God, I break the same, as if I believed it not;—and believing

(1) Mat. vii. 24. Luc. vi.

that God is present in every place, I offend Him, as if He were not present. This extreme foolishness is found amongst the greatest part of men, because, as Solomon says: "the number of fools is infinite:"(2) and Christ our Lord compared the Church to ten virgins, of whom five were foolish, as we shall see hereafter.

Colloquy.—O good Jesus, deliver me from such folly, for Thy infinite mercy's sake : and since Thou hast given me grace to believe what Thou hast spoken, give me grace likewise to fulfil what Thou commandest. Amen.

2. All the houses and consciences of men, as well wise as foolish, are assaulted *with three sorts of temptations* and tribulations,—figured by the floods which run upon the earth,—by the winds which move in the air,—and by the rains which fall from heaven;—that is to say, either by the temptations and tribulations which spring from our own flesh, and from earthly men with whom we converse, —or which proceeds from the devils, those princes of this darksome air,—or else those which come from heaven by the secret judgments of the divine providence for our trial, such as internal discomforts, spiritual aridities, and many other crosses and persecutions, which befall us even by the means of good men, and from zeal, though not according to knowledge.

3. *Both wise and foolish are equally tempted* with the temptations of *concupiscence* and of covetousness, figured by the floods,—of vanity and curiosity, figured by the winds,—of pride, of ambition, of dignities, and greatness, figured by the rains, which fall upon the roofs of houses;— according to that which St. John says :—" All that is in the world is the concupiscence of the flesh, the concupiscence

(2) Eccles. i. 15.

of the eyes, and the pride of life." (3) Lastly, as the floods
beat the foundation of the house, the winds the sides, and
the rains the roof,—even so some temptations combat us
in the beginning of our life and of our actions, others in
the middle, and others at the end, some at their beginning
to serve God, others after they have advanced in His service, and others when they have arrived even to the summit of it, that all, in whatsoever age, time, and manner of
life, should be prepared against temptation.

4. Hence I will gather, that *the difference between the
wise and the foolish*, between the perfect and the imperfect,
consists not in this, that the house or conscience of the
one is impugned, and not of the other, since both are en-
dangered; (4) but in this,—that *the wise prepare themselves*,
and build their houses after such a manner that they may
not fall, fortifying themselves against temptations,—whereas the *foolish are careless*, and therefore are overcome. Whereupon it follows that temptations do not make a man wicked,
but only discovers what he is, viz., whether he be wise or
foolish in the building of his soul's sanctity. Hence I will
gather that it argues gross ignorance to fly from virtue, or
a Religious life, to which Almighty God has called me, for
fear of temptations and tribulations, seeing that wicked
and secular persons suffer the same, as well as they, and
even oftentimes much greater, because, as Job says:—
"They that fear the hoary frost, the snow shall fall upon
them;" (5) and flying from weapons of iron, they fall on a
bow of brass, falling into greater temptations to escape
from the lesser, so that it is prudence to embrace virtue,
and that state to which Almighty God has called me,
arming myself for the combats which shall assault me.

(3) 1 Joan. ii. 16.　　(4) Cass. coll. xviii. c. 13.　　(5) Job. vi. 16.

POINT II.

The house and conscience of the foolish *falls*, because "*it is built upon sand*" And this was his most evident folly, to build upon so feeble a foundation, knowing that his house was to be battered. In this we are to examine what it is to build upon sand, and what the dangerous fall of the building is, which is built upon it.

1. First, to build upon sand, is to ground our life upon *faith alone*, contenting ourselves with believing what Almighty God says, *without any purpose of conforming our conduct to our faith*, or with a purpose very feeble and inconstant; or it is to ground ourselves on a faith mixed with the earth of our inconstant affections to earthly things, such as are, getting honour, pleasure, and the like. And even as the sand is not fit to build upon, because all its parts are disunited,—even so neither is the heart divided into sundry affections, which are not united in Almighty God. Briefly, to build upon the sand is to ground upon a man's own nature, relying upon his own forces, and upon his own fickle will, and his own counsel and judgment. (6)

2. Hence it comes, that *fools are overcome by temptations*, and that *their house falls* because it wants strength to sustain the weight of them. And as the statue which Daniel saw, although it had "the head" of "gold," "the breast" of "silver," "the belly" of "brass," and "the thighs" of "iron," nevertheless because the feet were partly of iron, and partly of earth, one little stone which struck this earth overthrew the whole statue; (7) even so, although our life be very elevated, and adorned with the gifts of human wisdom, and with great dignities, and even with the grace of prophecy, and of working miracles, if it ground itself

(6) S. Bas. de Const. mon. c. 21.   (7) Dan. ii. 32.

only upon faith, mixed with the things beforesaid, the very least temptation will overthrow it, "and great" will be "the fall thereof," because it loses the grace and friendship of Almighty God, the gifts of the Holy Ghost, the virtues which accompany charity, and sometimes the Religious person ill grounded comes to lose his vocation, and the Christian his faith on which he was founded, by reason of the evil mixture which he joined with it, the fall of which ordinarily makes a great noise, because of the scandal which it causes.

Colloquy.—O my soul, take good heed how thou buildest the house of thy conscience, for fear lest it fall; build it not upon the love of moveable things, for so thou also wilt be borne away with it; rely not upon thine own prudence, nor upon thine "own counsel," for fear lest it draw thee "down headlong" after it.(8)   Ground not thyself upon faith alone, although thou canst do miracles, for fear lest at the fearful day of judgment, Christ say to thee, " I never knew you;" (9) divide not thy heart,(10) like the sand, for fear thou die an everlasting death.

POINT III.

" The house" and conscience *of the wise* falls not, because it " is built upon" a stone, or living rock, that is to say, upon *a lively faith joined with charity*, in which all their affections are united, and all their desires firmly rooted. (11)   Moreover, they ground themselves on the mortification and abnegation of themselves, of their own flesh, of self-love, of self-will, and of self-judgment, as he that digs deep, to root out of his heart all whatsoever is earthly and moveable, until he come to the knowledge of his own nothingness, whereon their earth is grounded with

.(8) Job. xviii. 7.　(9) Mat. vii. 23.　(10) Osee x. 2.
(11) Ephes. iii. 17.

such stability, that it never shall be moved. Finally, they build themselves upon a firm and stable purpose, to do whatsoever God shall command them, not relying upon their own strength, but upon the grace of Almighty God, and upon the virtue of Christ our Lord, who is the living stone, and assured foundation of all sanctity, for which reason they boldly say with blessed St. Paul:—"Who then shall separate us from the love of Christ? shall tribulation, or distress, or famine?—I am sure that" nothing " shall be able to separate" me " from the love of God, which is in Jesus Christ our Lord." (12)

Colloquy.—O sweet Jesus, who, as both God and man, most wise, hast built Thy Church upon a rock so strong, that the powers of hell cannot prevail against it, lay the building of my soul upon Thyself, and upon the imitation of Thy holy life, that neither furious "floods" nor stormy "winds," nor tempestuous "rains," nor the powers of hell may prevail against her,(13) but that in virtue of Thee she may remain stable, until she arrive to life eternal. Amen.

MEDITATION XLIV.

ON THE PARABLE OF THE SOWER.

POINT I.

1. " Behold the sower went forth to sow." (1)

This parable our Redeemer Himself vouchsafed to explicate; it therefore, ought to be meditated, according to His explication.—i. What *seed* this is which he sows.—ii. In *what ground.*—iii. For what *cause.*—iv. *How* he sows it.

(12) Rom. iii. 35. 1 Cor. iii. 11.
(13) Mat. xvi.   (1) Mat. xiii. 3. Marc. iv. 3. Luc. viii. 5.

i. The seed is *the word of God*, as well the outward word, which enters by the ears of the body, as the inward, which resounds within the soul, which is the divine inspiration, from whence principally spring those fruits which our heart produces, because it gives a feeling of that which is heard, and is as the seminal virtue, which is within the grain that is sown.

ii. The principal sower is *Almighty God*,—Three, and One—who sometimes sows the seed of His inspiration, by the means of His preachers, in such as hear them;—or by means of good books, in such as read them;—or by the means of good examples, or devout pictures, in such as behold them; sometimes by Himself alone, He casts the seed of His inspiration on a sudden into our heart.

iii. The *ground* on which this seed is sown, *is the soul, with her powers and faculties;*—in the *memory* are sown holy thoughts and devout imaginations, such are the remembrance of our sins, the pains of hell, the rewards of heaven, the shortness of our life, our death, judgment, the presence of God, and of His benefits.—In the *understanding* are sown celestial illustrations, which suddenly discover the secrets which are enclosed in the mysteries of our faith, and are the seed of meditation and contemplation. He also sows therein good counsels, inspiring it with that counsel which it is to take for itself, or to give to others, sowing likewise, the dictates of *conscience*, which exhort to virtue, and reprehend vice.—In the *will* are sown holy desires and affections, which flash forth like sparks, and produce the fire of perfect love, with the fruit of virtues: such are the effects of the fear of God, of hell, of death, sorrow for sins, love of God, desires to see Him, and to serve Him sincerely.

iv. The *reason why* He sows this seed in the soul, is not His own commodity, which other sowers seek, but *the profit and utility of the same soul;* forasmuch as this seed has a most especial virtue to alter and amend the ground on which it is sown, though of itself it be bad, barren, dry, and unprofitable. And for this end it is that Almighty God sows it, not for the worthiness of the earth, but for His only bounty and mercy, because He is good and liberal, and greatly delighted to sow His gifts in us, to amend us with them. Hence it is that He oftimes sows His seed in all places, times and occasions, especially when it most imports us for our salvation. For which reason Christ our Lord said, "The sower went forth to sow." Giving us to understand that it is His office to sow, and that He evermore fulfils His office in one way or other.

2. From all these considerations, and from every one of them, I am to draw affections of *praise and gratitude* to this divine sower, as also a great esteem of His seed, and very fervent desires, that He sow it within my soul, begging it of Him from my very heart, by colloquies made to all the three divine Persons.

Colloquy.—O celestial Father, who hast sent into the world the eternal Word, Thy Word engendered within Thyself, that He might be the seed of all seeds, and of all Thy words, which are the seeds of our only good; I beseech Thee by this Word Thy Son to sow in my memory the abundant seed of holy thoughts, that there may spring from thence an abundant harvest of good works.—O eternal Word, who camest forth from the bosom of Thy eternal Father, and descendest from heaven into our earth to sow the seed of holy doctrine, seed which properly is Thine own, and not another's, nor begged elsewhere ; come, O Lord, to sow in my understanding abundant seed of divine illustrations, by which I may know Thee, and know myself, and know what I am to believe and do in such sort that I may put the same in practice.—O most sacred Spirit, who inspirest where Thou wilt,(2) and wilt inspire where there is need of Thy inspiration; touch my will, oversow it with the seed of holy affections, and cast into it the sparks of fervent desires, by which there may be enkindled within my heart a vehement fire of divine love, that with Thy seed may bud forth abundant fruits of the spirit which proceed from this love.(3)   O blessed Trinity, I give Thee thanks for the liberality with which Thou sowest Thy seed in a ground so vile and so contemptible.—O divine seed, who can esteem Thee as Thou deservest! O that I were full of Thy holy virtue!   O my soul, unprofitable ground, how desirest Thou not this celestial seed?   Sigh for it, demand it, solicit it, and thou shalt not be denied it.

POINT II.

Although this seed be so precious, and efficacious, and that the sower should sow it in very good season, and with desire that it fructify, yet *three parts of it perish* through the fault and bad qualities of the ground in which it is sown: I will search and examine into myself, what the defects and causes are, and how to redress them, being sorry to have them, and taking compassion of others that heve them, and for the loss of so much seed, with so much injury to the sower.

1. "*Some fell by the way side*," and was trodden upon by the passers by, and the fowls of the air came and ate it, so that it did not fructify.   The earth by the way-side, and without a ditch, is a heart hardened, like a way much trodden and trampled upon, which heareth the word of Almighty God exteriorly, and receiveth it superficially, without penetrating or embracing it, giving entrance to all sorts of earthly thoughts, without any guard or circumspection at all; there tread and trample upon this seed,

(2) Joan. iii. 8.   (3) Gal. v. 22.

and the devils themselves run speedily thither to steal it away out of their heart and memory.—In this condition and state will I put myself, and say,—" Woe is me, who for the hardness of my heart have not desired to receive the word of Almighty God, which, if it has entered in at one ear, has gone out at the other. I am like the " way-side," or way of passengers, admitting all manner of evil thoughts and desires, which seek to have passage through my heart. I have permitted the infernal " fowls," with the beaks of their perverse suggestions, to rob me of the seed of good inspirations, receiving those and rejecting these.

Colloquy.—It grieves me, O my God, for the small account which I have made of this sacred seed, and I purpose to till the earth of my heart with the tillage of true mortification, and to soften its hardness, that it may receive Thy holy word, and hide and cover it, " that I may not sin against Thee."(4) But as Thou knowest my frailty, cause that Thy inspirations soften me, and help me to produce the fruit which Thou desirest for Thy glory. Amen.

2. "*And other some fell upon stony ground,* where they had not much earth," as being nigh unto a rock; this seed " sprung up," and grew high, but the sun with his heat parched it, because it had not deep roots, nor sufficient humidity to nourish it. Such are those who have a certain natural tenderness and facility, to hear the word of God with great delight, and to read good books, conceiving good desires and resolutions, and beginning to put them in execution; but when temptations from the Devil, the flesh, and the persecutions of men arise, immediately that good which they had withered away, and they quite forsake and leave it off, being inconstant, and not deeply rooted in humility, and confidence in Almighty God, nor

(4) Ps. cxviii. 11.

have they the humidity and sap of substantial devotion; and as St. Mark says:—" They are devout for a little time, which presently passes like the dew that goeth away in the morning," (5) or like the flower that withers, and hangs its head with the least heat. Nor is it without mystery, that Christ our Lord compares persecutions to the sun, whose property is to shine with his light, and to scorch with his heat; by which two sorts of persecutions are represented, one of prosperity, praise, flattery, vain-glory, and worldly ambition;—the other, of adversity, calumny, dishonour, poverty, fear, and other afflictions, against which we ought to be fortified and deeply rooted, to the end that the fruit do not wither, which the divine inspiration has sowed within us, showing ourselves like the apostles, faithful ministers of God, in " honour and dishonour, by evil report and good report." (6)

Colloquy.—O eternal God, since Thou knowest my great mutability, fortify me with Thy holy grace, that I may cast such deep roots in charity, that nothing created may be able to uproot me from it. Amen.

3. " *And others fell among thorns,* and the thorns grew up and choked them. These are they who hear the word" of Almighty God, but do not fructify, because the riches, and " cares" of the world, and pleasures of the flesh, after which they go, choke the spirit. So that there are three things which choke and smother divine inspiration, and hinder our spiritual profit, viz., riches, pricking cares, and sensual pleasures; all which three in the school of Christ are called thorns.

Colloquy.—O sovereign master, how different are Thy judgments from ours; that which the world terms riches and delights, Thou termest thorns and thistles:

<hr>

(5) Osee vi. 4.   (6) 2 Cor. vi. 4, et 8.

because, howsoever they delight the body, they prick, hurt, and damage the soul, draw forth a great deal of blood by sins, and pierce it with pains, anguishes, and remorses. Deliver me, O Lord, from these thorns,(7) and crown me with Thine, which, although they prick and pierce the flesh, yet they nourish and comfort the spirit, because there is no greater consolation than to embrace Thy crown of thorns on earth, with the hope of obtaining the crown of glory in the Kingdom of heaven.

POINT III.

"And others, (the fourth part,) fell upon good ground, and they brought forth fruit." "These are they who are sown upon the good ground, who" "in a good and very good heart" "hear the word and receive it, and yield fruit in patience," "the one thirty, another sixty, and another a hundred."(8)

1. In like manner, therefore, as there are three sorts of wicked who destroy this seed, so are there three sorts of good Christians, who bring forth good from it.—Some in the state of beginners, with a little profit;—others in the state of proficients, with greater profit;—others in the state of the perfect, with great excellency; all labouring with patience and longanimity, expecting the reward : and although they are fewer in number than the wicked, yet they compensate by their gain, the loss of the other three parts of the seed.

Colloquy.—I rejoice, O sweet and sovereign sower, that there are to be found such grounds in which Thy seed discovers its virtue, and brings forth a hundred for one. O that there were much such ground, that many might glorify and serve Thee as reason requires. Encourage thyself, O my soul, to serve thy God with diligence, and content not thyself with the fruit of

(7) Ps. xxxi. 4.　　　　(8) Marc. iv. 20. Luc. viii. 15.

"thirty," nor yet of "sixty," but with that of an "hundred fold,"(9) since, proportionable to the fruit of this life will be the recompense of the other; even in this life, God will give thee a hundred for one, if thou serve Him with fervent affection.

2. Other applications may be made, as the saints say, attributing the fruit of "thirty," to the *married;* that of "sixty," to *widows* and *virgins;* and that of "a hundred," to *martyrs,* or to such Religious as profess a contemplative or mystical life; teaching others the way of perfection, which they themselves tread. Notwithstanding in what state soever I be, I ought to aspire after that which is the most perfect : for it may well be, that the state be but of "thirty," and yet the fruit of an "hundredfold," the greatness of the fervour supplying the imperfection of the state.

MEDITATION XLV.

ON THE PARABLE OF THE COCKLE.

POINT I.

"The Kingdom of heaven is likened to *a man that sowed good seed in his field.* But while men were asleep, his enemy came, and over-sowed cockle among the wheat and went his way. And when the blade was sprung up, and had brought forth fruit, then appeared also the cockle." (1)

1. This parable likewise Christ our Lord expounded, saying :—That *He Himself was the sower,* whose office it is to sow in the field of the world, His good seed, which are the children of the Kingdom, namely, the just, who are to be heirs of His celestial Kingdom. And they are

(9) Mat. xix. 29.　　　　　(1) Mat. xiii. 24.

called the seed of Jesus Christ, because they are His children, engendered of His noble and celestial progeny, begotten in the life of grace, in virtue of the seed of divine inspiration, which is sown in their hearts. They are also seed from which others spring, such as themselves : because the perfect after the imitation of their Lord and master, endeavour to engender other just, who may serve Almighty God as they themselves serve Him.

2. *"And the cockle are the children of the wicked one."* For as the cockle, when it is in the blade, resembles the wheat, but after it grows up, blackens and damages the wheat with which it grows, as also the man who feeds on it, because it hurts the sight, provokes to vomit, and troubles the senses; even so the wicked resemble the good, in the nature of men, even in faith itself, and in external Christian ceremonies, notwithstanding they are in very truth black in soul, by sin; (2) have their interior sight greatly troubled, with ignorance, and errors, as well in matters of faith as of manners, causing scandals and dissensions, and in the end provoke Almighty God to "vomit"(3) them, and to cast them forth from Him. Whereupon making comparison of these two seeds, I will say to myself:—"Behold which of these two thou lovest best, to be the seed of Jesus Christ, who is thy friend, and seeks thy salvation;—or the seed of the Devil, who is thine enemy, and seeks thy damnation?"

Colloquy.—O God of my soul, I desire from the bottom of my heart to be Thy seed, promptly obeying Thy divine inspiration; permit not that I obey the suggestion of both mine and Thy enemy, for fear lest I become the cockle of Thy Church, and provoke Thee to cast me forth from it.

3. *"The enemy that sowed them is the Devil,"* men in the

(2) Salmer. tom. vii. tract. 6.   (3) Apoc. iii. 16.

meanwhile being asleep—to signify, that first there *were
good before the wicked:*—as well amongst the angels in
heaven, as amongst men in paradise : and generally, after
Jesus Christ sowed in His Church the seed of the just,
by means of Baptism, and the other sacraments, Satan
has come to sow cockle, to pervert them, and to transform
them into darkness; and this he does while men sleep, that
is, by night, suddenly, and when they are most careless,
or when they are drowsy, and sleep the sleep of slothfulness.

Colloquy.—O most sweet Jesus, the "sower" of all
good seed, since Thou ever watchest, and never sleepest, and seest the cockle which the enemy designs to
sow in Thy field, do not appear to slumber, suffering
him to sow in me that which may separate me from
Thee.   And if through negligence I fall asleep, let
Thy mercy watch to awaken me, to resist the enemy,
before he has dominion over me.   Amen.

4. The enemy, after sowing the cockle, *"went his way,"*
to signify, that he hides himself *lest he should be known,*
like him who throws a stone, and hides his hand;—and
sometimes transfigures himself into a friend, and into an
angel of light to deceive us. (4)—At other times he departs,
ceasing to tempt us, that so we may remain careless, and
immediately returns with greater rage to overthrow us.
Whence it is that the wheat and the cockle, from their
resemblance to each other, are not discerned until they
yield fruit—to signify, that oftentimes the good and the
wicked, are like one another at the first beginning, because the wicked take upon themselves the habit and
figure of the good, and the wolves, as our Saviour says,
cover themselves in sheep-skins; but when the fruit
appears, each one discovers who he is, and whether the

(4) S. Chrys Hom. 47. in Mat. S. Jer. tom. 9.

virtues which he has, are true or feigned, which is made manifest by their works. (5)

POINT II.

"The servants of the good man of the house, coming said to him: Sir, didst thou not sow good seed in thy field? whence then hath it cockle? And he said unto them: An enemy hath done this." (6)

1. The apostles themselves, and apostolical men their successors, *seeing the multitude of the wicked*, of errors and abuses, which are in the world, amazed and wounded, *run to Almighty God*, saying to Him:—"Lord, Thou having sown such good seed in the world, how comes it to be mixed with so much cockle? How comes it to pass, that having chosen twelve apostles, one of them is changed into a Judas? And in the garden of the Catholic Church, amongst the lilies of the just, are found so many thorns and thistles of sinners? (7) In the houses of Religion, amidst the wheat of the perfect, the cockle of scandals?" And entering into myself, seeing a multitude of vices and passions, which disquiet my soul, I may likewise say to Christ our Lord:—"Didst Thou not sow within my heart, the good seed of holy desires, with holy purposes to forsake all things to serve Thee with perfection, whence then proceeds so much cockle as grows in me? Discover, Lord, the cause to me, that so I may apply a remedy."

2. Christ *our Lord answers to this demand*, saying:—"*An enemy hath done this.*" In this, three particular things are pointed out.—i. The first, that Almighty God our Lord, is no sower of cockle, nor of evil seed, but only of good, because He is the sovereign Good, and from sovereign good nothing evil can proceed, nor inducing or tempting to evil. (8)—ii. The second is, that Satan is the principal

(5) Mat. vii. 4.   (6) Mat. xiii. 27.   (7) Cant. ii. 2.

(8) Jac. i. 13.

sower of cockle, from whom spring temptations, by reason of the enmity which he has sworn against God, and against men : and for this reason he is called in holy Scripture, the "Tempter,"(9) and those who are the cockle, are called the "children of the Devil,"(10) imitators of their father, whose desires they endeavour to accomplish.(11)—iii. The third is, that although Satan be the principal sower of this bad seed, yet, as S. Thomas says,(12) men are also, by means of their own free will, "tempted" thereto "by" their "own concupiscence :"(13) and perhaps for this reason our Saviour said:—"An enemy hath done this," which was to say, The man who is an enemy of himself, and "hateth his own soul,"(14) and is also my enemy, has sown this cockle in the world, and in himself, and is the cause of this mischief. From these three truths I will take counsel, to know the origin of my faults and troubles, endeavouring to stop the passage of these enemies, which do me so much evil.

3. There is another more *secret sense* of this demand: "*Didst thou not sow good seed in thy field? whence then hath it'cockle?*" That is to say, " Why, O Lord—the field of the world being Thine, Thou having created it by Thine omnipotence, and redeemed it with Thy precious blood, and having sowed it with so wonderfully good and precious seeds—why dost Thou suffer Thine enemy to oversow it with cockle? Because, unless Thou didst suffer him and give him license to do it, he durst not be so bold as to mingle in Thine own field his bad with Thy good seed." *To this demand*, and in this sense, *Christ our Lord did not give answer*, who wills not that we curiously sound His secret judgments, but that we reverence them in all humility, saying with David: " Thou art just, O

(9) Mat. iv. 3.　　　(10) 1 Joan. iii. 10.　　　(11) Joan. viii. 44.
(12) 1 p. q. cxiv. art. 3.　　　(13) Jac. i. 14.　　　(14) Ps. x. 6.

Lord, and Thy judgment is right."(15)   Notwithstanding
I am to believe that the goodness of Almighty God is so
great, and the love so immense which He bears the elect,
that He will not suffer Satan to sow amongst them this
bad seed, unless He could and would, draw from thence a
greater, nor yet permit the enemy to sow within us the
evil seeds of his temptations, if He desired not to convert
them to our profit.   And although, in particular, I cannot
obtain all these advantages, yet may I come to understand
them in general, believing that God permits wicked men
to exercise the good in patience and humility, that they
should daily advance in all perfection; next, to discover
the efficacy of His grace, in the vessels of His mercy;
next, that the good may be the more honoured, manifesting their loyalty amongst so many disloyal persons; and
lastly, to preserve the liberty of men, leaving every one to
his own free will, yet giving sufficient force to resist evil
and to follow good.

Colloquy.—O most just " sower," who by a sovereign bounty sufferest in Thy Church the cockle of so
many evils, and in my soul the seed of so many strong
temptations; grant that I turn not to my hurt that
which Thou permittest for my good; manifest in me
the greatness of Thy mercy, drawing out of so many
evils great abundance of many good things, that by
them Thou mayst be glorified, world without end.
Amen.

POINT III.

" The servants said to him: Wilt thou that we go and
gather the cockle?   And he said: No; least perhaps
gathering up the cockle, you root up the wheat also together with it."(16)

1. In this second demand of the servants is seen the

(15) Ps. cxviii. 137.   (16) Mat. xiii. 28.

zeal of the just, when they behold so many evils in the world, which zeal is disordered in some, from four causes.

i. Because with this their fervour, they would *root up at once all the cockle* together, and take out of the world, out of the Church, or out of Religion, all the wicked, and out of themselves, all vices and passions at one push, which, according to common reason, is impossible.

ii. The second cause is, that they will needs pluck up the cockle *before the time,* and out of season. Whence ensues greater evil, because perhaps he who to-day is cockle, may to-morrow be converted into good wheat, and supporting with patience and longanimity, such as are wicked, by the sweetness of such correction they become good.(17)   And he who precipitates himself disorderly to gain perfection, comes to be deprived of his health, and to lose that perfection which before he had gained.

iii. The third cause is that which is pointed at in the parable, because they will root up the cockle, *not without danger of uprooting the wheat;* which happens when they imprudently correct or chastise the wicked to the detriment of the good, by scandals, wars, and troubles, which result from thence.

iv. The fourth cause is, that they will pluck it up, *with a spirit of choler,* anger, and revenge, transported more by indignation than by compassion; as it happened to the two apostles, James and John, when the Samaritans would not receive Him;(18) for which they were reprehended by Christ their master.

2. In the answer is manifested the *infinite charity of Almighty God,* which was returned by the Father of the family.   For although our Lord had showed Himself so rigorous to the angels of heaven, that in the same instant

(17) S. Thom. 2. 2. q. xxxiii. art. 2. maxime ad 3.
(18) Luc. ix. 54.

that Lucifer had sown the cockle, He plucked up the sower together with all his seed, and cast them headlong into the fire of hell, yet towards men He would not use this terrible rigour, but would expect with great longanimity, giving them room for repentance, desiring rather to convert them into good seed, than to root out the cockle. For God our Lord wills not the perdition of souls, but their salvation, and although He desires to destroy sins, yet He would not destroy the sinners who commit them.

Colloquy.—O most sweet Saviour, I give Thee thanks for the compassion which Thou hast on such as are cockle, beholding that they are the work of Thy hands by nature, although they be the work of Satan, Thine enemy, through their sin. Destroy, O Lord, in them that which makes them Thine enemies, and reform in them that which Thou formedst, that so they may become Thy seed, and may be stored and hoarded up in the granary of heaven. Amen.

3. The infinite mercy of Almighty God shines in this, that He suffers the cockle, *for the love which He bears to the wheat*, tolerating the wicked for the love of the good, as is to be seen when He said to Abraham, that if there were "ten"(19) just in Sodom and Gomorrha, for their sakes He would bear with the sinners that lived in them, although they were laden with innumerable sins. And when He afterwards decreed to punish them, He first drew forth His servant Lot, putting the wheat under secure shelter, before He would pluck or root up the cockle: a very great comfort for the good, since they may be assured by this that no evil will come to them from the hand of our Lord, notwithstanding they be amongst the wicked. Lastly, I will observe that God our Lord does not prohibit us from rooting up the cockle, when it may be done with-

(19) Gen. xviii. 32.

out hurting the wheat, but to its profit; as, at this present time the Church chastises certain sinners for the example of others, that the cockle increase not, and to enable the good to live in quiet; nevertheless Almighty God wills that they avoid those four disorders before recited;—and in this sense He forbad His servants to do that which they wished.

POINT IV.

The father of the family proceeding in his answer, said: "Suffer both" the wheat and the cockle "to grow until the harvest, and in the time of the harvest I will say to the reapers: Gather up first the cockle and bind it into bundles to burn; but the wheat gather ye into my barn."(20)

1. In this parable Christ our Lord assures us that *until the end of the world*, which is the time of reaping, *there will always be wheat and cockle*, good and bad mingled together; for the divine providence will never cease to sow His good seed in His Church, and in Religion, although the Devil endeavour to sow cockle, nor ought I to be dismayed to see so many bad men. For whereas I think that there are but a few good, because I know them not, yet there are many known to God, and beloved by Him;—as it chanced to Elias, thinking that himself was left alone, amongst the faithful, when Almighty God said to him that He had reserved "seven thousand men in Israel, whose knees have not been bowed before Baal."(21)

2. All the time before the harvest the wheat and cockle *grow aud multiply*—for as well the truly good, as the truly wicked grow during their life, the one in sanctity, the others in iniquity, conformably to what Christ our Lord said in the Apocalypse;—"He that hurteth, let him

(20) Mat. xiii. 60.   (21) 3 Reg. xix. 18.

hurt still; and he that is filthy, let him be filthy still; and he that is just, let him be justified still; and he that is ' holy, let him be sanctified still: behold, I come quickly, and my reward is with me, to render every man according to his works."(22) Nevertheless, all this passes in different manners, because it is the will of Christ our Lord, that His wheat grow, and daily advance from good to better by His assistance.—But concerning the cockle it is only His sufferance to let it grow from bad to worse until the harvest, of which there are two different ones;— the one is the *general* harvest at the end of the world:— the other the *particular* harvest at the end of the life of every one, when their good or evil is grown to that height it was to grow to, according to the order or permission of the divine providence; and then he that shall be found to be cockle shall be cut down, and rooted out of this life, to be cast into the fire of hell;—and he that shall be found clean and pure wheat, shall be reaped and gathered up for the granary of heaven.

3. But when the time of the general harvest shall come, Christ our Lord will "*send His angels*," who are the reapers and ministers of the divine justice, who will *gather together all the scandals of His Kingdom*, and those who work iniquity; and will cast them into the fiery furnace; that is to say, will gather together out of His Kingdom all those who are cockle, as well those who were any scandal and occasion of sin to others by their evil life and doctrine, as also those who only were wicked in themselves;—all of whom will be bound in different "bundles," binding together in one bundle those that were co-partners in the same sin, that they may also be co-partners in the same pain, and so they shall be cast into eternal flames, so that they shall never escape from them. And even as

(22) Apoc. **xxii. 11.**

faggots help to kindle one another; even so those accursed shall be a torment one to another: "Ibi erit fletus et stridor dentium," "there shall be weeping and gnashing of teeth," while they shall roar with rage against themselves, and against those who were the cause of their damnation.

Colloquy.—O my soul, how tremblest thou not at this dreadful judgment, who can resist the power of those mighty reapers? who can unbind himself from such terrible chains? "who can dwell" in everlasting fires, and live, and converse with such accursed companions? who can endure such bitter complaints, and enraged gnashing of teeth? O accursed cockle! who sowest in earth discord amongst the good, and shall for ever suffer discord in hell in company with the wicked! Preserve me, O my God, from such offences, for fear lest I fall into such dreadful pains. Amen.

4. Finally, the same angels shall *gather the wheat into the granary of heaven*, for the good shall be placed upon celestial seats, separated everlastingly from the cockle and company of the wicked; at which time "the just shall shine" like the sun in the Kingdom of their Father.

Colloquy.—O most loving Father, I give Thee thanks for the favour which Thou extendest to the just, raising them from the dust of the earth to reign in Thy Kingdom, and to be as suns in Thy heaven. Those who have been eminent in serving Thee, shining like the sun by the good works they did, will eminently enjoy Thee, shining like the sun by the reward granted for the same works; here they have shone like the sun of justice, Thy Son Jesus Christ, by imitating His holy life, and there they will shine like the same sun, sharing His glory for ever and ever. Amen.

MEDITATION XLVI.

ON THE PARABLE OF THE GRAIN OF MUSTARD SEED.

" The Kingdom of heaven is *like to a grain of mustard seed*, which a man took and sowed in his field, which is the least indeed of all seeds, but when it is grown up it is greater than all herbs, and becomes a tree, so that the birds of the air come and dwell in the branches thereof." (1)

POINT I.

Consider *what this grain of mustard seed signifies*, reducing the significations of it to *three* principal heads.

1. First, it represents Christ our Lord *supreme King of the Kingdom of heaven*. For as the mustard seed is very little in exterior appearance, " the least" of all seeds, contemptible to behold, without colour or grateful smell, but great in the virtue of heat which it contains, which is shown when it is ground or eaten;—so Christ our Lord, as man, was little and humble exteriorly, nay, " the least" of all men, insomuch that He said of Himself by the mouth of David:—" I am a worm and no man, the reproach of men, and the outcast of the people;" (2) but interiorly as to His soul, and much more as to His divinity, He was of infinite virtue and efficacy, containing within Him all the treasures of the wisdom, bounty, and charity of Almighty God, with the love of which He heated and inflamed all those who approached Him;—He so seasoned virtue that they might take delight to taste of it, purged them from their coldness and lukewarmness, and expelled from them the venom and contagion of their sins, dissolving the works of the infernal serpent, and in all points performed

(1) Mat. xiii. 31.   (2) Ps. xxi. 7.

the office which this little but powerful grain of mustard seed represents. And then most of all did He manifest His virtue, when He was ground with torments upon the cross, and now also manifests the same when He is eaten by the faithful in the Blessed Sacrament of the altar, which may be truly called a "mustard seed," because in exterior appearance it is so little, and yet entirely contains Jesus Christ, in every little particle of the host, much less than a grain of mustard, but interiorly it has immense virtue, to inflame with the fire of love the souls of those that eat it, and is as a most delightful seasoning to give a relish to all the asperities of this life.

Colloquy.—O divine Word, Son of the eternal Father, I give Thee all the thanks that I am able, for having so greatly humbled Thyself that Thou mightest be compared to a contemptible grain of mustard, so greatly delighting in this littleness, that by means of the Blessed Sacrament Thou wilt persist in it to the end of the world; grant me, O Lord, that I may imitate Thee to the last hour of my life, humbling myself for Thy sake, as Thou didst humble Thyself for mine. Amen.

2. Hence it follows, that "this grain of mustard" represents likewise *all the just*, who are fellow-citizens in the Kingdom of heaven, and disciples of Jesus Christ, who after His example outwardly are very little, and are contemned in the eyes of men, but inwardly are of great virtue and efficacy, for the greatness of charity and fervour of spirit which dwells in them, which they then discover most of all, when they are persecuted and ill-treated as their captain was, for which reason the Church says of herself, that she is "black" exteriorly, "as the tents of

Cedar," "but beautiful interiorly," as the "curtains of Solomon." (3)

3. Hence also it follows that this "mustard seed" likewise represents *the virtues by which the Kingdom of heaven is gained*, which in appearance are very little, but in strength most effectual. For the faith and belief of the divine mysteries revealed in the Holy Scripture exteriorly seems little and contemptible, but is, notwithstanding, of exceeding virtue to those who grind and ruminate upon the same in devout meditation, which wonderfully enkindles the fire of celestial love; in such a manner that St. Paul says, that " Christ crucified" is a stumbling-block to the Jews, and "foolishness" to the Gentiles, but "the power of God and the wisdom of God" (4) to the faithful. The like consideration may I make of humility, and obedience, and those eight virtues which are called the beatitudes, which in outward appearance are so contemptible, that the world holds them for maledictions, but in truth, and interiorly are so precious, that in them is contained the true benediction and possession of the same celestial Kingdom.

Colloquy.—O Almighty God, who, to show Thy omnipotence, choosest "the foolish things of the world"—to " confound the wise," " and the weak things of the world,"—to " confound the strong,"(5) and by mean instruments performest great things, to the end that no mortal man should glory in himself, but only in Thee ; grant that I may cordially love and embrace those little things which Thou didst choose, that so I may be worthy to obtain those great things which are enclosed therein. Make me, O my Saviour, a grain of mustard, bruised and ground with Thee by contempts and torments, that thus I may finally obtain eternal repose.   Amen.

(3) Cant. i. 4.   (4) 1 Cor. i. 23.   (5) 1 Cor. i. 27.

POINT II.

Consider how this "mustard seed" grows until *it be-comes a great tree*, and in what consists its greatness, reasoning upon the *three* things which this mustard seed represents.

1. And first, as this "mustard seed" must necessarily be *sown in the ground and there die*, and strike root, and afterwards grow and extend its branches, and make itself a great tree, so that if it was "the least of all seeds," it comes in proportion to be the greatest of the garden, and if what was one alone produces innumerable others, resembling itself in its properties;—even so Christ, having humbled Himself and made Himself man for our sakes, would, like a grain of mustard seed, and as He Himself says elsewhere, like "a grain of wheat *falling into the ground*, (6) "*die*" therein; for as the life which He lived was always accompanied with great mortifications, and afterwards in a garden He sustained a mortal sadness, and died in a field with most terrible torments, and in another garden was buried, and placed below the ground, so He cast His roots as low as Limbo, whence He fetched the souls of the Fathers, arose again gloriously to a new life, and came to grow, and to ascend to so high a degree of honour and greatness, that He who a little before was held for the least amongst men, came to be adored as head and Sovereign Lord, both of men and angels, all bowing the knee at the sound of His name, a name "above all names," (7) fulfilling that which was prophesied, that "the bud of the Lord" should grow up with great "magnificence and glory," (8) and that His fruit should be very high, because He should engender innumerable spiritual sons, like to Himself in virtue and sanctity.

(6) Joan. xii. 24.   (7) Phil. ii. 9.   (8) Is. iv. 2.

Colloquy.—O most sweet Redeemer, I rejoice at the greatness which Thou possessest in reward of the littleness which Thou undertookest for the love of me. Blessed be Thy death, without which, as Thyself sayest, Thou wouldst have remained alone, and by which Thou hast multiplied so much fruit, as fills the earth, and peoples heaven; and since by Thy ignominious death Thou hast drawn all things to Thee, draw me also to Thee, that I may be in all things like Thee. Amen.

2. In imitation of Christ our Lord, *all His disciples*, who were all grains of mustard seed, by the same way *came to grow*, and to make themselves great trees;—so the apostles of whom St. Paul says, that they bore about in their "bodies the mortification of Jesus," (9) were daily mortified for His sake, and treated like "sheep for the slaughter," (10) yet came to be princes of the Church, and to spread the faith throughout the world, gaining innumerable souls to Christ, and in such a manner that they far surpassed the patriarchs, prophets, and all the just of the Old Testament. After the same manner grew the martyrs, and confessors, and I also ought to grow, persuading myself that, although I be a grain of mustard, sowed in the earth of the Catholic Church, and in the enclosed orchard of Religion, yet unless I mortify myself and die to the world, I shall not grow up in merits nor virtue, but shall remain alone, without the fruit of good works, and without gaining souls;—alone also in prayer, without the company of Almighty God, who delights not to converse with unmortified men, but if I first "die," I shall grow then fruitfully up in all these things.

3. By the same way it is that *virtues* grow, and come to spread abroad their branches so high that they touch

(9) 2 Cor. iv. 10.   (10) Rom. viii. 36.

heaven. For faith leads a man to the sight of God by contemplation, having his conversation in heaven.—Hope ascends to taste the sweetness of celestial rewards.—Charity grows up even to perfect union with Almighty God.—Obedience to the accomplishment of the Divine will beneath on earth, as it is fulfilled above in heaven; and although my confidence be but as a grain of mustard, yet it is sufficient, as our Saviour says, to pluck up trees by the root, and to " remove mountains,"(11) as will be hereafter declared.

POINT III.

This " mustard seed" does so spread and extend its " branches," that " the birds of the air," as the Evangelists say, " dwell under its shadows, and make their nests in it, and rest upon it."

1. *Christ our Lord cast forth from Himself sundry branches*, viz., *the doctrine of the Gospel* which He preached,—the law of perfection, with all its counsels, which He published,—the sacrament and sacrifice which He instituted,—the marvellous examples which He gave us, the miracles and notable works which He effected, with the other mysteries of His glorious life, until He ascended to that excellent highness which He holds in heaven. To these branches the birds of heaven have recourse; not eagles, nor other great birds, which figure in their pride there, but the little birds, which are the just and humble souls, especially those who leave the things of the earth, desiring by contemplation to converse in heaven. After whose imitation I will place myself in repose under the shadow of these boughs, considering the sweetness of their fruit, rejoicing in the protection and shelter which I receive by them, saying with the spouse:—" I sat under His shadow whom I desired, and His fruit was sweet to my

(11) Mat. xvii. 19.

palate." (12)   I will likewise build my nest and abode upon these branches, meditating these mysteries;—sometimes I will make my nest in the mystery of the manger,—sometimes I will fly up to the tree of the cross,—and other times to the empyreal heaven, placing my whole confidence and love in Jesus Christ.   There will I sing songs of praise and thanksgiving, and there will I rest in the nights of tribulations, and sustain myself with the grain and food which I there find.

Colloquy.—O, who will give me the wings of a bird to fly up to this divine tree?   O most high and sovereign tree, how high soever Thou growest, yet may I fly and mount upon Thee with the wings of contemplation, which Thou canst give me.   Lift me up, O my Lord, above myself, and above everything created, that I may repose in Thee, my Creator, for ever and ever.   Amen.

2. After the same manner the *apostles and saints have budded forth many branches*, and have extended them throughout the world, that is to say, the doctrine which they preached,—the books which they published,—and the heroic virtues which they exercised,—in the meditation of which spiritual souls are exercised, animating themselves to imitate them, in order to grow up like them.

3. And in particular, such as are Religious may reflect that their founder and their Religion is like to a grain of mustard, little in humility; for so some call themselves Minors, others Minims, and our Religion is called by the founder, "Hanc minimam societatem Jesu," "The least company of Jesus;" notwithstanding every one of these is great in virtue, and has grown up like a mighty tree, extending its branches through the whole world, in divers

(12) Cant. ii. 3.

houses and convents, and with exercises of sanctity very elevated, and greatly profitable to the good of souls, who like birds of heaven, moved and inspired by the Holy Ghost, fly upon these boughs, and there make their nests and perpetual dwellings, living with great security under their shadow, meditating and contemplating the lives of their founders, imitating them, as they imitated Christ, observing their rules, praying Almighty God with canticles and music, both with voice and affection, for the continual favours which He vouchsafed them. They likewise endeavour to fly from branch to branch of all their virtues, building their nest in the highest degrees that each one has, that they may attain to the top of that perfection which they profess.

Colloquy.—O divine wisdom, whose branches are " of honour and grace,"(13) which make us pleasing to Almighty God, amiable to the angels, honourable to men, and venerable to all the world; vouchsafe to admit me under His shadow, comfort me with His flowers, heal me with His leaves, sustain me with His fruits, and give me a perpetual dwelling on the top of them, that growing up always in virtue, I may come at length to the top of glory, where I may repose for ever and ever. Amen.

MEDITATION XLVII.

ON THE PARABLE OF THE MERCHANT SEEKING PEARLS.

POINT I.

"The Kingdom of heaven is like to a *merchant seeking good pearls*, who when he had found one of great price, sold all that he had and bought it." (1)

(13) Ecclus. xxiv. 22.   (1) Mat. xiii. 45.

1. The *practice and employment of all men is to seek good pearls*, for all greedily seek after that which is good and precious, although in a different manner.—Some seek after the pearls of temporal riches, dignities, and other like things, which the world esteems and prizes for precious;—others seek after the pearls of human arts and sciences, sometimes only to know them, and sometimes for honours' sake and their own interest;—others seek after the pearls of moral and political virtues, to live like men of command in their commonwealth;—but the duty and employment of a Christian, who aims at the Kingdom of heaven, is to seek after the pearls of divine and celestial virtues, which are truly good and precious, and make them that find them good and precious in the eyes of Almighty God. And like as in Latin, pearls are called " Uniones," (2) because that every one is alone or particular in its excellences, and singular amongst others,—even so every virtue is single and singular in some excellency, yet notwithstanding this variety, they all unite themselves with perfect union, to enrich him that has them, and to join him with his Creator.

2. Hence I will infer *that my principal employment ought to be* to seek after these true pearls, persuading myself that since I am a merchant, and traffic, I ought not to employ myself in traffic that is base, contemptible, and of little profit, and much less in a traffic that procures *loss*. My principal employment ought not to be in seeking the pearls of *temporal goods*, as these neither make me good nor apt to inherit heaven;—nor ought I to hold or repute them for precious, but to tread them under foot, and from my heart to hate and contemn them, so that they are an occasion of worldly pride, ambition, covetousness, and other like crimes. And still less ought my principal at-

(2) Plin. lib. ix. cap. 35.

tention to be to seek after the pearls of human "*know-ledge*," which "puffeth" (3) up, and is the food of curiosity and vanity, and without which I may be saved. Nor ought I to content myself with seeking the pearls of *political virtues*, which ordinarily are only apparent, for that they only shine and glitter with outward works in the sight of men, or else are false and counterfeit pearls, like those of hypocrites, who desire to be held for good and holy, for if I content myself with these, in the hour of my death I shall find myself deceived, and supposing myself to have been rich, I shall be a bankrupt most poor and miserable. But I am principally to search the precious pearls of *divine truths* which God has revealed, to under-stand them and believe them with a lively faith, without which "it is impossible to please God." (4) I am like-wise to seek the pearls of *supernatural virtues*, as grace, charity, obedience, patience, humility, prayer, religion, and other like virtues, with which I shall become good and holy, and enter into the Kingdom of heaven. And as for other temporal goods and sciences, I may seek after them secondly, and so far as they may further me to find those other pearls which are so precious.

3. But above all, my principal employment shall be to *seek Jesus Christ*, true God and true man, *that most precious orient pearl* who, like a dew, descended from heaven, and in the womb of the Virgin Mary, by the virtue of the Holy Ghost, made Himself man, for the honour and ornament of all men; this is that pearl, by excellence good and precious, and from whom all goodness proceeds, which I must seek to possess and to have always with me, and to enrich myself with the treasures of His graces and virtues, studying to be one of those of whom David speaks, saying,

(3) 1 Cor. viii. 1.   (4) Heb. xi. 6.

" This is the generation of them that seek Him, of them that seek the face of the God of Jacob." (5)

Colloquy.—O Saviour of the world, true merchant of true pearls, in this, that Thou descendest from heaven to seek souls and precious pearls, which all true merchants who will enrich themselves, must seek ; since Thou art come into the world to show us the good and precious pearls of celestial virtues and truth ; show them, I beseech Thee, me, that I may seek them, not only in appearance, but in truth : desiring by means of them, not my own honour, profit, or contentment, but to please Thee, and to possess Thee, world without end.   Amen.

POINT II.

Consider *how these pearls are to be sought*, seeing Christ our Lord wills that we seek them, and employ ourselves diligently for that purpose.

1. They are sought *by prayer*, craving Almighty God that He would discover them to us, never ceasing to importune Him for this purpose, since He Himself has said: " Ask, and it shall be given you, seek, and you shall find, knock, and it shall be opened to you." (6)

2. They are sought by *the meditation of the understanding*, prevented and assisted by divine illustration, digging and diving into the truths and mysteries of the faith, and into the excellencies of virtues, until we have found out the meaning and force of them.

3. They are sought by *desires and affections of the will*, prevented by divine inspiration, sighing for these precious pearls, and applying our free will to seek them by those other means which Almighty God has left us to find them out; such as are works of penance, reading of good books, frequenting the sacraments, especially that of the Blessed

(5) Ps. xxiii. 6.   (6) Luc. xi. 9.

Eucharist, which is as it were the shell within which is contained that most precious pearl of all pearls, our Lord and Saviour Jesus, ready to communicate to us those other pearls of virtues; this is to become merchants, and to do " business,''(7) as St. Paul says. And if the merchants of the world be so covetous and solicitous in seeking out their earthly pearls, and expose themselves to so many perils to find them, how much more reason is there that I should be solicitous for these celestial pearls, asking them by meditations, and knocking for them with affections and desires, fulfilling that which Almighty God commands me, in order to find them?

Colloquy.—O my Saviour, make me a diligent and a covetous merchant, that I may seek the pearl of divine wisdom, with the same solicitude that men seek after earthly treasure, and hoard up money, since Thou promisest that if I seek it in this manner, I shall find it.(8)

POINT III.

The merchant having " found one pearl of great price, *went his way and sold all that he had, and bought it.*" (9)

1. That this pearl is called "*one*," and "*precious*," because, that Jesus Christ our Lord is One, true God, and true man. And notwithstanding, that there are sundry sorts of virtues, yet they are so united, and enclosed one within another, as if they were but one, joined by charity, which is " the bond of perfection," (10) it being that which unites man with Almighty God, with Christ our Lord, and with all his neighbours, making them one amongst themselves, as if they were but one soul, and one heart. And as among the shells of the sea, in which the pearls are, there is one as conductor or captain, that the rest fol-

(7) 1 Thess. iv. 11.   (8) Prov. ii. 5.   (9) Mat. xiii. 46. ,
(10) Col. iii. 14.

low, which, being taken, it is very easy to take the others;
—even so charity is the captain of the other virtues,
which, whosoever attains, she draws the other virtues after
her: for, as the apostle says, "Charity believeth all things,
hopeth all things, endureth all things." (11)

2. To find this precious pearl is to *discover the same by
the light of faith*, to behold the excellency and beauty of it,
and to enjoy the pleasantness and suavity which is so great,
that it ravishes the heart of him that finds it, who, forthwith, and with great facility "selleth," and gives the farewell
to all things that may hinder the entire possession of it;
all loves and earthly affections, which may hinder the
buying or possession of it, esteeming all that which he
leaves to be little, according to that of the Canticles, " If
a man should give all the substance of his house for love,
he shall despise it as nothing." (12)

Colloquy.—O most precious charity, O most excellent unity of love, O most loving God! who callest
Thyself charity, and art a pearl of infinite value, One
in essence, and Three in Person, and such a friend of
unity, that all those who join and unite themselves to
Thee, Thou makest " one spirit" with Thee; discover
to me this one, and so precious pearl, enamour me of
it, and give me possession of it, for Thou seest that
I here offer Thee for it whatsoever I have ; and had I
more, more would I give Thee, because all is little in
respect of the inestimable value of it. Give me, O
Lord, Thy grace, that I may also serve Thee by grace,
not for profit, but for pure and perfect love. Amen.

3. Accordingly, I will endeavour to enter into myself,
and to examine well:—i. If I seek *false and counterfeit
pearls*, deploring the time which I have spent, and daily do
spend in this search.—ii. If I seek *these true pearls* with
such slothfulness, that I do not find them, for fault of

(11) 1 Cor. xiii. 4.   (12) Cant. viii. 7.

using convenient means to this purpose.—iii. If I be re-solved to *pay for them the price they are worth*, which is the renunciation and abnegation of all I possess, at least in af-fection, considering whether there be in my heart any self-love, and earthly affections, proposing manfully to mor-tify them, and to root them out of my soul, for that the diminishing of courteousness is the increasing of charity.

POINT IV.

1. This "one pearl," and so very precious, *is likewise the Evangelical perfection*, of which such as are Religious make profession, in imitation of Christ our Lord, which by excellency is called "one," because it comprehends in an eminent manner, the full accomplishment of the two precepts of charity, which are, the one to love God, with our "whole heart, and with" our "whole soul, and with" our "whole mind:"—and the other, which, as Christ says, is like to this, to "love" our "neighbour as ourselves,"(13) or as Christ has loved us. (14) And as among men, two pearls which resemble each other are of great price, and are fastened like earings in the ears: so these two pearls of the love of God, and of our neighbour for God, which are like one another, and become an admirable union, are most precious, and much esteemed by God and His angels, and are most excellently practised in Religion, with which, as with earings, are hung and adorned the ears of the soul, which are faith and obedience; all Religious performing in conformity all the exercises of Religion, not from neces-sity, nor by constraint, but by "obedience, with a brotherly love;" (15)which is so pleasing to the celestial spouse, that He said:—"Thou hast wounded my heart, my sister, my spouse,—with one of thy eyes," (16) that is

<hr>

(13) Mat. xxii. 37.   4) Joan. iv. 11.
(15) 1 Pet. i.   (16) Cant. iv. 9. S. Greg. ib.

to say, with the union that there is amongst the just. For, as the two eyes of man are in all things like one another, and do their office in unity, even so Religious are alike in their customs, and accomplish their religious works with virtue.

2. Finally, so great is the preciousness of this pearl, that when Almighty God discovers the same to man by illustration, immediately, with great joy *he sells whatsoever he has* and forsakes the world, dispossessing himself in effect of all things, and giving them for this pearl, to undertake the state of Religion. For, as S. Lawrence Justinian says, (17) Our Lord hides this pearl on set purpose, and will not show the value and preciousness of it to all, because, if all saw it, all would desire to buy it, and none would be found that would live in the world.

Colloquy.—O eternal God, who hast said, "they who sought me not, have found me," for that Thou preventest them with Thy inspirations, that they may find Thee; show to me the preciousness of these pearls, that I may seek them, and seek them so that I may find them. Suffer not that I wound Thy heart with the wound of sorrow, by means of disunion with my brethren, but with the wound of love, by union with them. Discover the preciousness of a Religious life, to such as are fit for it, that they may gladly buy it: but much more discover it to those who have already bought it, that they may rejoice in the bargain which they have made, and obtain the end for which they have bought it. Amen.

(17) S. Laur. Just. in ejus vita.

MEDITATION XLVIII.

The Pharisees murmuring against Christ our Lord because He received sinners, He laid before them this present parable: "What man of you that hath a hundred sheep, and if he lose one of them, doth he not leave the ninety-nine in the desert, and go after that which was lost until he find it?"(1)

POINT I.

Upon this first part of the parable is to be considered; —*who* this pastor is;—*what sheep* these are;—*which* is the *lost* one;—and *how* its pastor *seeks and finds it.*

1. This man *is Jesus Christ our Lord*, who descended from heaven to be the *pastor of men*, and who, with admirable providence, and with great vigilance, governs His sheep, knows them very particularly, and marks them with the mark of His grace and charity, goes before them showing them the example of a holy life, heals them of the disease of their sins, keeps them from the infernal wolves, gives them the selected pasture of doctrine and sacraments, the love which He bears them being so great, that He made Himself meat, and feeds them with His proper body and blood, veiled under the forms of bread and wine, and lastly for their good gave His own life.

Colloquy.—O good pastor, good by excellency, blessed are the "sheep" which are under Thy government, governed by Thy providence, and guarded by Thy protection; I give Thee humble thanks that Thou tookest this office upon Thee, and for the care

(1) Luc. xv. 4.

with which Thou dost fulfil it; fulfil it with me most completely, for it is written, " The Lord ruleth me, and I shall want nothing."(2)

2. The hundred "*sheep*" in general, *are all the faithful of the Church*, but more particularly they are the just, signified by the number of " a hundred," which is a number of perfection whom Almighty God keeps counted, and knows full well those who are His. These sheep, whilst they are under the subjection of their pastor, know Him full well, by faith and contemplation, hearing His voice, obeying what He commands, following His steps, imitating His virtues, receiving the food of doctrine, and sacraments, which He gives them, without diverting themselves to any object opposed to His will; rejoicing to be fed with such divine pastures, giving to Him all their wool, by offering to His service all their substance; giving Him the milk of their breasts, by offering to Him all the affection of their hearts, and all the pleasures of their body, forsaking them all to serve Him; giving Him their young ones and lambs, by offering to Him their works for His honour and glory;—and if it be needful, they will give Him their own flesh and blood, and even their life also, which they will gladly lose for the love of Him. So that, as the pastor gives Himself wholly to them, even so do they give themselves wholly to Him, each of them saying: " My beloved to me, and I to Him." (3)

Colloquy.—O sovereign pastor, set upon my heart the mark of Thy sheep, and take whatsoever I have for Thy holy service, since Thou givest all Thou hast for my happiness.

3. The *sheep which loses itself, is the sinner*, who strays from the company of the just, and from the subjection and

(2) Ps. xxii. 1.   (3) Cant. ii. 16.

obedience of his pastor, not for the want of a pastor, but through his own pernicious liberty; for the pastor keeps no sheep in His flock against its will. But wherefore then does it stray, and lose itself? Because it wants the properties of a loyal and faithful sheep; that is to say, because it knows not its pastor, nor the goods which it possesses in Him, nor makes any account of being under His protection, and in the company of the just. Moreover, it makes itself deaf to His voice, and it is painful to her to hear His command; it is unwilling to follow the steps of its pastor, because they are cragged and sharp with crosses and mortifications. It loathes the pasture of doctrine and sacraments, and lusts after the pasture of the world, and of the flesh;—in short, it will retain for itself its wool, its milk, its lambs, ordering its goods, dignities, offices, and all its works for its own honour and utility, loving itself with a disordered and selfish love, refusing to offer aught of all this to Almighty God. For these causes, or for part of them, it strays and wanders from the fold, exposing itself to the peril of eternal damnation, and of falling into the mouths of the infernal wolves, who go raging to tear it in pieces and devour it.

Colloquy.—O accursed sheep, who forsakes its pastor! O wretch that I am, who so long time have lived like a wandering sheep, following my fancies, and fulfilling my own will, contrary to the will of Almighty God! O how many sheep are there in the world which stray in this manner, every one walking his own way, whose sheep-fold hereafter shall be hell! O most merciful pastor, recall them with the voice of Thy divine inspiration, and vouchsafe to open their interior eyes, to the end they may see their error, before the time of remedy be utterly past. Amen.

4. Consider the *infinite charity of the pastor*, who left

"the ninety-nine" sheep, in good security in the desert, and went to seek *the lost* sheep, and rested not till he had found it. For this reason He came from heaven down to earth to call and seek sinners, and in this exercise spent the three last years of His life, suffering excessive labours, and persecutions, even to the enduring of death, with most terrible torments;—and although it is true that He died for the whole hundred sheep, because, in virtue of His death, all men received whatsoever supernatural good is granted to them; yet did He seek with more anxiety after the strayed sheep of His own time, not omitting to use various means to find them.

Colloquy.—O sovereign Pastor, how dear do these sheep cost Thee, Thou having no need at all of them. For although they should all have been lost, what losest Thou? Wouldst Thou clothe Thyself with their wool, support Thyself with their milk, or enrich Thyself with their lambs? and if Thou desirest to have sheep, hast Thou not others a great deal better, in Thy Kingdom of heaven, who employ themselves faithfully in Thy service? But Thy charity, O my God, is the cause of all this, and because it behoves them to be under Thy government, Thou sayest that it behoves Thee to bring them to Thy fold—" Them also I must bring;" (4)—Gather them, therefore, O Lord, together, and bring them to Thy obedience, that as Thou art one, and a most perfect Pastor, so Thy flock may be one, and a most perfect flock. Amen.

5. The *manner* how, even *at this present time also*, Christ our Lord *seeks this lost sheep* until He find it, seeking it by heavenly inspirations and illustrations, with interior touches of the heart, sometimes moving the tongues of the preachers to call it, and persuade it to repent;—

(4) Joan. x. 16.

sometimes speaking also to it by the means of spiritual books, of good examples, or of chastisements imposed upon others;—yea, a thousand means does He invent to seek it, never resting until He finds it. And when I feel any of these inspirations in my soul, I am to imagine that Christ our Lord comes to seek me, and acknowledging His divine presence, I must endeavour to obey Him in whatsoever He shall command me, to return with Him into the fold from which I am fled.

POINT II.

"And when he hath found it, he *layeth it upon his shoulders rejoicing*, and coming home calleth together his friends and neighbours, saying unto them. Rejoice with me, because I have found my sheep which was lost."

1. S. Matthew says, proposing another parable like to this:—"*And if it so be that he find it:*"(5) because some sheep do so lose themselves, that, notwithstanding Christ seeks them, He does not find them; not for want of diligence on His behalf, but because they fly from Him, and resist His inspirations and vocations, as Judas lost himself, although his master did very much to recall him.

Colloquy.—O most sweet pastor, " I have gone astray" like a sheep that is lost; " seek Thy servant"(6) before he perish. Give not over seeking me, though I fly from Thee, and with Adam hide myself from Thy sight. Cease not to call me, although I resist and contradict Thee, as Cain did ; take pity on me in my peril, and multiply Thy helps until Thou find me, and bring me back to the fold of Thy elect, with whom I may enjoy Thee, for ever and ever. Amen.

2. The second shall be, to ponder the *immense charity of this divine pastor*, who, meeting with the sheep, did not strike it with his staff, nor drag it along by the heels, but

(5) Mat. xviii. 13.   (6) Ps. cxviii. 176.

with great joy *laid "it upon his shoulders,"* and brought it to his flock :—which is to show us, that He treats sinners with great love, and with singular clemency, in order to convert them, not bringing them back by force, chastisements and blows like slaves, but of their own accord and free will, altered and renewed by His holy grace; neither leaves He them to go on their own feet; and because they cannot of themselves alone, walk one step in the way of heaven, He serves them Himself instead of *eyes*, conferring upon them the light of faith and of celestial wisdom;—He serves them instead of *feet*, directing their steps and affections, for fear lest they stray and forsake the law of Almighty God;—He serves them for *hands*, assisting them in all their good works;—He lays them "upon His shoulders," for He aids them with sweetness to support the burdens of this life,—and pays for them the debt of their sins, by applying to them His satisfaction and His merits.

Colloquy.—O most loving pastor ! what return shall I make to Thee for so many favours, and kindnesses which Thou hast done me? shall I not serve Thee with a right good will, and take up Thy yoke, and burthen on my shoulders, since Thou takest me upon Thine own? With great reason sayest Thou, that Thy " yoke is sweet, and" Thy "burthen is light,"(7) since Thou so helpest me to bear it. I will therefore bear it with great alacrity, for the pure love of Thee, since bearing me Thou likewise bearest the burthen, which Thou hast imposed upon me. Amen.

3. Ponder, how far the charity of our sovereign pastor extends itself, who not only rejoices to find these sheep, and that sinners are converted, but also invites all the angels of heaven, the just upon earth, and all the in-

(7) Mat. xi. 30.

habitants of His house, both of the triumphant and militant Church, to rejoice and congratulate Him, for having recovered the "sheep" that was "lost."

Colloquy.—O most loving Father, this congratulation ought to be given to the sheep, because it is the greatest gainer in being found; but yet Thou wilt that we give this congratulation to Thee, because the sheep is Thine, and it has cost Thee so dear to seek it and to recover it. I therefore, O my Lord, congratulate Thee in the behalf of those sinners, whom, by Thy grace, Thou hast recovered from sin, and exult in the joy which Thou takest therein : grant to all those who are now in the world, that they may be converted to Thee, that I may give Thee a thousand congratulations, and rejoice in the joy which Thou receivest in their conversions. Amen.

POINT III.

"So I say to you, that even so, *there shall be joy in heaven upon one sinner* that doth penance, more than upon ninety-nine just, who need not penance."(8)

1. The conclusion of this parable is; that even as a father, who has many children in health and prosperity, if one of them fall mortally sick, or into any notable adversity, when he escapes from peril, receives an exceeding new and actual joy, different from that which he conceives of others who are in health and prosperity;— even so, when a sinner is converted from his sins, *the angels conceive a new accidental·joy for his conversion*, different from that which they feel for other just who need not penance, to convert them to God, as being already converted to Him.

2. Hence will I gather, that it is the will of Christ our Lord, *that we should rejoice at the conversion of sinners*, and

(8) Luc. xv. 7.

that not only we should not murmur like the Pharisees, against him who endeavours to convert them and dispose them to this end, but also that we ourselves should do the same, assisting and furthering their conversion, becoming co-adjutors of Christ in seeking the lost sheep, and bringing them back again to their fold, esteeming this as a great blessing.

3. Next, if I myself be a "lost sheep," I will endeavour *to return to the fold of Christ*, if I desire to minister to Him this matter of joy, and to rejoice the angels of heaven. And if Almighty God has favoured me so far as to establish me in His holy grace, I will labour not to lose the same, because, as the conversion of the sinner rejoices the angels, and makes sad the devils;—even so the fall of the just rejoices the devils, and as far as lies in him, disheartens the angels, who would most "bitterly weep"(9) over our perdition, if they were capable of tears and bitterness.

Colloquy.—O angels of peace, beseech the supreme pastor, that prince of pastors, to give me His holy love, and to preserve me in it. And if through my wickedness, I come to lose it, beseech Him to help me to recover it immediately, that my conversion may be an occasion of joy to heaven, and that I may enjoy Almighty God in your blessed society. Amen.

MEDITATION XLIX.

ON THE PARABLE OF THE PRODIGAL SON.

POINT I.

Christ our Lord, desiring that all might understand the great kindness with which He receives repentant sinners, proposed this parable:—"A certain man had two sons, and

(9) Is. xxxiii. 7.

the younger of them said to his father, Father, give me the portion of substance that falleth to me.   And he divided unto them his substance.   And not many days after, the younger son gathering all together, went abroad into a far country: and there wasted his substance living riotously."(1)

1. Almighty God our Lord, represented by this father, has *two sorts of sons.*—The one *good*, understood by the elder brother, because virtue is most ancient and most precious, and in her consists true wisdom, in which is venerable antiquity;—the other *evil*, figured by the "younger" son, because with vice, mad imprudence, and levity, which he discovered, in demanding of his father the portion which appertained to him, to manage it; insinuating with a certain secret pride, that God owed him something, and presuming that he could govern himself by his own wisdom, contrary to the custom of good sons, who believe with humility, that what they have is "of grace," and do not trust in their own prudence.

2. Hence I will ascend to ponder the *infinite liberality of Almighty God, in distributing the gifts* and talents of *nature*, with many supernatural goods, both to the good and bad sons, giving them liberty to use them well or ill, and to abide within His house, or to go forth without a will to force any, because, as the Wise man says, He leaveth all in the hands of their "own counsel," and gives them power, to choose "water," or "fire," "life," or "death," "good," or "evil :"(2) yet in such a manner, that He always inspires and helps them to make a good choice, and to use well that which He has given them.

3. The *blessing* of *good sons*, consists in *remaining in the house of their heavenly Father*, under His protection and

(1) Luc. xv. 11.　　　　(2) Ecclus. xv. 14. Deut. xxx. 15.

government, that He may order and direct them in the use of the talents they have received, obeying Him in all things; for he who suffers himself to be governed by God, as He promises by the prophet Isaiah :—his "peace" shall be as a "river," and his "justice" as the "waves of the sea."(3) And contrariwise, the curse of wicked children begins by their desire to go forth from their Father's house, and from His government, governing themselves by their own judgment and self-will, living after their own liberty. Hence it is, that by-and-bye they go into a far country, departing afar off from Almighty God by sin, and dissimilitude of life, and by forgetfulness of His divine presence, spending and employing all they have, living luxuriously,—linked to creatures, and loving them more than the Creator. From whence we may see, that secret pride ends in open luxury, and that to trust over-much to himself, makes a man depart far from Almighty God, and he that is forgetful of God, comes to be so affected and entangled with creatures, that he loses the supernatural goods of grace and charity, deforms and obscures the gifts of nature many times with the loss of his goods, honour, and happiness. In the person of this youth, I will consider myself, saying to our Lord :—

Colloquy.—O celestial Father, behold here a prodigal son, who, having received great gifts from Thy liberal hand, has departed from Thy house, and Thy government, to follow his own will and judgment. I have departed far from Thy presence, by innumerable sins, and dissipated the goods which Thou gavest me, using them for my own pleasure. Dear Lord, how hast Thou suffered me with so great patience! O that I had never gone from Thy house. O wretch that I am! who, like an over great libertine, and lit-

<hr>

(3) Is. xlviii. 18.

tle experienced, have suffered myself to be deceived by my sensuality! O my God, take pity on me, and do not deny me Thy mercy, since I have sinned through ignorance. Amen.

POINT II.

After he had "wasted his substance, living riotously, there came a mighty famine in that country, and he began to be in want, and he went and cleaved to one of the citizens of that country, and he sent him into his farm to feed swine. And he would fain have filled his belly with the husks the swine did eat, and no man gave unto him."(4)

1. Here consider the *spiritual and corporal miseries into which sinners fall by their rebellion*, after they have consumed the goods of grace, and are arrived at the depth of their malice.

i. The first is, a *great hunger and want of spiritual food*, which hunger always reigns in the region of the wicked, without finding amongst them any remedy, that is to say, the sacraments are not received;—the word of Almighty God is not heard;—good books are not read;—good examples, are not seen;—interior comforts of the soul are not received nor felt.

ii. The second misery is, *to subject themselves to the chief citizen* of that country who is the Devil, serving him and miserably loving with a most close friendship, what they ought to abhor;—obeying him in base things, and in vices unworthy of the noble nature of a man.

iii. The third is, *to feed swine*, which is to employ themselves altogether in giving contentment to their senses and carnal appetites, seeking opportunities to indulge them, and feeding the devils, whose food is our luxuries, and sensuality, with which they are delighted.

(4) Luc. xv. 13.

iv. The fourth is, *to be so greedy and hungry after their delights*, that can never be satisfied, nor obtain that which they desire, because the meat which he eats, is not the meat of men, but of most unclean beasts, and therefore cannot sufficiently satisfy. O what greater misery can come to a man who was the son of Almighty God, and might have lived with honour and fulness in the house of his celestial Father! O the blindness of my heart, which leads me to so great an evil! God forbid that ever I be willing to live in a country so exceeding hungry, or to serve so cruel a master, or to employ myself in so base a service.

2. Christ our Lord is wont to afflict sinners with *temporal miseries*, and to sow, and, as the prophet Osee says, "hedge up" their "way with thorns," that at least affliction and punishment may make them become wise, and return to Almighty God. To this end He chastises them with poverty, hunger, dishonour and servitude, and the greater sinners they become, into so much greater miseries is He wont to suffer them to fall, that so they may open the eyes of their souls, and be converted. (5) And this is a greater mercy of God towards them, than if He left them in their temporal prosperity: for, to dissemble with them, although it may in some sort seem to be mercy, yet is it a greater chastisement to withdraw from them His holy zeal, as from persons reprobate and rejected by Him already.

Colloquy.—O God of my soul, do not withdraw from me Thy most merciful zeal, and if I depart from Thee, lay punishments and calamities upon me, until such time as I return to Thee, doing penance for my sins. Amen.

POINT III.

The prodigal son "returning to himself said, How many

(5) Amos. viii. 10.

hired servants in my father's house abound with bread, and I here perish with hunger? *I will arise and go to my father*, and say to him : Father, I have sinned against heaven, and before thee, I am not now worthy to be called thy son; make me as one of thy hired servants :" (6) and as he purposed, so did he, arising up, and walking to the house of his father.

1. The beginning of a sinner's conversion is, to *enter into himself*, and to reflect upon his miseries, which he had forgotten, because, before he was *out of himself*, wandering and lost amongst creatures. To this purpose Almighty God does prevent him with IIis inward inspiration and illustration, which is never wanting, but even in the midst of his wickedness, is wont to say to him that of the prophet : "Return, ye transgressors, to the heart,"(7) and recover the understanding which ye have lost; "Hear me, O ye hard hearted, who are far from justice; I have brought my justice near, and my salvation shall not tarry," come and embrace it if you will.

Colloquy.—O my soul, who goest out of thyself, enter into thy own heart, and study to know thyself, for so shalt thou know Almighty God, who can redress and succour thee.

2. It imports much a sinner, to *compare his miserable state with the state of the just*, although it be of those that are most imperfect, and who serve God as "hirelings," in the hope of recompense; for by this comparison, his hunger and necessity will appear more evident, as also the abundance with which Almighty God provides those who faithfully serve Him, and the favours which IIe vouchsafes them, in the use of sacraments, of holy sermons, and other meats fit for the soul : and thus he will animate himself to desire and ambition, that state which has so many

(6) Luc. xv. 17.   (7) Is. xlvi. 8, 11, 12.

advantages above his. And if sometimes he has been just, and lived virtuously, it will be good to compare his present state with that which is past, by which, as the prophet Osee says, wholly confounded at his present misery, he may return to the "first husband" and spouse of his soul, "because it was better with" him "then than now." (8)

Colloquy.—O my soul, turn to God thy Lord, whose word cannot fail, and who has said : Be converted, and you "shall see the difference between the just and the wicked, and between him that serves God, and him that serves Him not."(9) Quickly shalt thou see by experience, if quickly thou begin to change thy life.

3. It imports us much, to *conceive great purposes to return to Almiyhty God*, grounded on the one part in humility, and in the knowledge of our own unworthiness; and on the other part, on the bounty and mercy of our Father, because by this we shall greatly facilitate our conversion.

Colloquy.—I acknowledge, O my Father, that I am so miserable, that I " am not worthy to be called Thy son," nor is it reasonable that a name so glorious should be given to a wretch so infamous, who has so far debased himself as to keep hogs. Nevertheless, I perceive that, although I am unworthy of the name of a son, Thou hast not ceased to be a Father. I return therefore to Thy house, entirely trusting in Thy mercy, that Thou wilt admit me into it. " I have sinned," O Lord, " against heaven, and before Thee," and before Thy presence, committing so many iniquities in the sight of the angels, and of Thy most pure eyes.—" I have sinned against heaven," using its light and its influences to injure Thee. I have sinned " before Thee," running from Thy house and Thy

(8) Osee ii. 7.   (9) Mal. iii. 18.

government, preferring my own will before Thine; I am grieved for my fault, and deserve not to be admitted to the delights of Thy beloved sons. Admit me, if it please Thee, to those of Thy hirelings, and I will hold it for a great honour to be in Thy house, although I be the very least in it.

4. It is of great importance presently to *put in execution our good purposes*, before they grow cold, as this prodigal son did, who *instantly* arose, and began to walk: for we must not sit still with one hand upon the other, nor expect that God do all, and come to seek us, and draw us out of sin by the hair: but His will is, that since He prevents us with His grace, we shall seek Him, and do something, by abandoning our sinful life, and obeying His inspirations to begin a better.

POINT IV.

The father, seeing his son yet "afar off," moved with mercy, ran to him, "*fell upon his neck, and kissed him. And the son said to him, Father, I have sinned against heaven, and before thee, I am not now worthy to be called thy son. And the father said to his servants; Bring forth quickly the first robe and put it on him, and put a ring on his hand, and shoes on his feet, and bring hither the fatted calf, and kill it, and let us eat and make merry; because this my son was dead, and is come to life again, was lost, and is found. And they began to be merry.*" (10)

1. Here is seen, the *infinite charity and bounty of our celestial Father*, which is resplendent in many things; first, in that He beholds the sinner with the eyes of mercy, even when he is yet "afar off" from Him, and is not fully converted to Him, but only thinking of it: with this pity, He runs with great speed to aid him with inward touches and inspirations, until he be entirely converted to

(10) Luc. xv. 20.

Him; He joins Himself to him by embracing him, and giving to him the kiss of peace, that is to say, restoring him to His former grace and friendship.

Colloquy.—O most loving and pure Father, do not disdain nor abhor to kiss and embrace a swine-keeper, hideous and disfigured, an unkind and ungrateful son: a man filthy, naked, barefoot, and all in rags: it well appears, Lord, that Thou art a Father, and that the love of a Father makes Thee to forego Thy dignity, to give Thyself to Thy sons,

2. He showed His charity, *restoring* to him with great liberality, *what he had lost;* for He gives him "the robe," and vestment of grace and charity;—the ring of the Holy Ghost, and of strict familiarity with Almighty God;—the exercise of good works into his hands;—upon his feet "the shoes" of divine perfection, and of those virtues which mortify the affections of the soul, and which direct his steps, and adorn them to preach to others the Gospel of peace;—He feasts him with the fatted calf of His blessed body in the Sacrament of the Altar, and with the abundance of consolations and spiritual comforts, which there He communicates to his famished soul.

Colloquy.—O Father of mercy, and God of consolation, how many mercies dost Thou show at once to a sinner, and what a multitude of consolations dost Thou give him without any desert of his!

3. This mercy is yet further manifested in *the delight* with which He does all this for the sinner, as if He gained something by his conversion, desiring that all his servants rejoice, and make a feast of joy for his conversion.

Colloquy.—Much do I owe Thee, O my Father, for the goods which Thou dost give me, but I feel myself much more obliged for the delight and excess of love with which Thou givest them to me. I desire to serve Thee with the same love and delight, repaying Thee some little of the much I owe Thee, since love is not repaid but only with love.

4. The prodigal son admired the mercy and charity which his father showed him, and mollified or rather melted by it, demanded not that he would make him "as one of" his "hired servants," as he had proposed, but *threw himself into the arms of his father*, hoping that he would admit him to the dignity of a son.

Colloquy.—O what occasion have I, O my Father, to hope in Thy mercy, since Thou so favourest those who have recourse to it! Moreover, Thou endeavourest that it may be known to all the world, that grievous sinners may not be dismayed, seeing the good entertainment which Thou dost give them, and the great dignity to which Thou dost so liberally advance them.

POINT V.

"Now his elder son was in the field, and when he came nigh to the house, he heard music and dancing, and he called one of the servants, and asked what these things meant. And he said to him, Thy brother is come, and thy father hath killed the fatted calf, because he hath received him safe. And he was angry, and would not go in. His father therefore coming out, began to entreat him. And he answering, said to his father, Behold for so many years do I serve thee, and I have never transgressed thy commandment, and yet thou hast never given me a kid to make merry with my friends; but as soon as this thy son has come home, who hath devoured his substance with harlots, thou hast killed for him the fatted calf. But he said to him: Son, thou art always with me, and all I have is thine. But it was fit that we should make merry and be glad, for this thy brother was dead, and is come to life again, he was lost, and is found." (11)

1. *Some imperfect souls* who have lived innocently, and been preserved from great sins, *are wont to be envious* for the favours which Almighty God does to those who have been great sinners; and murmur and complain that our Lord does not comfort them as He does others, it seeming to them that they deserve better cherishing at His hands. This springs from the want of humility and charity, and is very offensive to Almighty God, who takes great pleasure, when we rejoice in the good which He does to our brethren, and when we say with Moses : "O that all the people might prophecy." (12)   O my Lord, that Thou wouldest vouchsafe to receive all sinners, and exalt them to a great degree of justice and sanctity.

2. Consider, likewise, the *intention of Christ* our Lord, in this discourse of the "elder son," which was, to *exaggerate the mercy* and liberality which had been shown to the younger; which was such as was sufficient to provoke complaints and envy in the very just; although their virtues would not allow them to indulge such vicious thoughts, reverencing the secret judgments of Almighty God, and the greatness of His bounty, in communicating Himself to His creatures, and giving sometimes signs of greater comforts to those who are unworthy of them.

3. Ponder the *words* which the Father of mercy speaks interiorly to the just, who truly serve Him :—"Son, thou art always with me, and all I have is thine."

Colloquy.—O most loving Father, what greater favour can there be than this? what robe, what ring, what shoes, and what " fatted calf" is more to be esteemed than to be always in Thy house, in Thy obedience, under Thy government, and that all Thy things

(11) Luc. xv. 29.   (12) Num. xi. 29.

are mine, and at my disposal? If all be mine, then Thy grace is mine, Thy gifts are mine, Thy heaven is mine, Thy Son, my Redeemer, is mine, and Thou Thyself art also mine, and in whom all Thy good things are contained. O my Father, O my God, and all my good, Thou art my delight, my honour, and my riches, and if Thy things are mine, mine are also Thine. With this favour alone I am content that I be always with Thee, and Thou with me, and that Thy things be mine :—so that I desire nothing but that which comes to me from Thy holy hand, being content only to serve Thee, my celestial Father, to whom be honour and glory, world without end. Amen.

MEDITATION L.

ON THE PARABLE OF HIM THAT FELL INTO THE HANDS OF THIEVES, AND WAS SUCCOURED BY THE SAMARITAN.

POINT I.

A lawyer demanding of Christ our Lord who was his neighbour, that he might love him as himself, He answered him with this ensuing parable, showing by it the great compassion which He has for sinners, saying :—"A certain man went down from Jerusalem to Jericho, and fell among robbers, who also stripped him, and having wounded him, went away, leaving him half dead."(1)

1. Consider—i. *who* this *man* is—ii. *who* these *thieves* are—iii. of what goods they rob him—iv. what wounds they give him—v. and how they leave him half alive, and half dead.

i. *This man* is one of *the sons of the earthly Adam*, who after the imitation of his father, being in the grace and friendship of Almighty God, designed to be an heir of the

(1) Luc. x. 30.

city of the celestial Jerusalem, falls from this state, inclining to the goods of this miserable and mutable world, figured by "Jericho," which signifies the moon. The origin of this fall or descending is, that he addicted himself to the things of this world, with some disorder, and applied himself inordinately to the affairs of the earth.

ii. *Against this man the devils proceed*, in the way of thieves, robbers and our enemies, who with their temptations and wicked suggestions, sometimes openly, sometimes by treason and treachery, endeavour to destroy us. To this effect they make use of our visible enemies, who are "*the world and the flesh*," that is, the wicked who live in the world; and of the passions of our flesh. And he is said to fall into their hands, and miserably to consent to their persuasions, and admit that sin which we call mortal.

iii. The *goods* of which they rob this miserable man *are the grace of Almighty God*, the seven gifts of the Holy Ghost, charity, with the virtues infused, which continually accompany it;—and in particular, some they rob of chastity, others of humility, others of patience, others of temperance, others of obedience, and the like;—and some they rob even of faith itself, precipitating them into infidelity; they also rob them of hope, causing sinners to fall into despair, for all they seek is to rob us, and to destroy all that we hold of God, saying that of the psalm:—"Raze it, even to the foundation thereof." (2)

iv. The *stabs and wounds* which they do give him, *are the damages which they leave in the powers of our soul*, the ignorance of the understanding darkened with the clouds of errors;—the weakening of our free will, making it feeble to resist vice;—the fury of inordinate appetites and passions, inclined to that which is earthly, every one

(2) Ps. cxxxvi. 7.

receiving as many wounds as he has ignorances, passions and perverse inclinations.

v. After this manner, this miserable man *is left "half dead,"* for there remains in him only the light of faith, or the light of natural reason; he is left also half dead, because he is in danger of dying eternally.

2. Considering all this, I will imagine *myself to be the miserable man,* of whom this parable speaks, lamenting my misfortune. I am he who have been careless in preserving the grace which God has given me in holy Baptism, inclining myself to the delights of this present life. I am he who have fallen into the hands of the devils, my enemies. Mine the fault to fall into them, for had I resisted, they had fled from me, and had I called upon God and the angels for help, they would have hastened to have helped me: for the way is as full of angels who guard us as of devils who tempt us, and as the prophet Eliseus said: "More are with us, than with them."(3)

Colloquy.—O wretch that I am, for having suffered myself to be robbed by these "robbers," when I might have defended myself against them. Woe is me, for having lost the grace of Almighty God, and His celestial gifts. O what stabs and wounds have I received in my soul, for, "from the sole of the foot to the top of the head, there is no soundness"(4) in me. There is no power or sense in me which has not its particular wound and perverse inclination :—and although they have left me a little life, yet am I much more dead than alive, and in danger of dying for ever. O eternal God, behold, I beseech Thee, this miserable man with the eyes of mercy, and vouchsafe to succour him with Thy grace, before he come to die this miserable death.

(3) 4 Reg. vi. 16.　　　　　(4) Is. i. 6.

POINT III.

"It chanced that a *certain priest went down the same way*, and, seeing him, passed by. In like manner also a Levite, when he was near the place, and saw him, passed by. But a certain Samaritan being on his journey, came near him, and seeing him was moved with compassion." (5)

Upon this point is to be considered, *who this priest and Levite are*, who pass farther without assisting this man: and *who the Samaritan is* who takes compassion on him.

1. First, the priest and Levite represent to us *men, constituted in whatsoever dignity* and excellence, who yet are *not sufficient to succour a sinner*, and so all leave him, and pass on farther; for although they have eyes to behold his misery, yet they have not means of themselves to afford him redress. Moreover, some have little compassion for the miseries of others, being over careful in seeking their own commodities.—Others, because it seems to them that they have enough of their own to do, and to defend themselves from the "robbers" who lie in wait for them in the way; and that if they should undertake to cure him that is wounded and fallen, they themselves might come to fall. In fine, no pure creature can succour this miserable man, nor heal his wounds, so that, unless he have help from heaven, it is clear that he will perish.

2. The "*Samaritan*" who took pity and "compassion" on him, is the *Word eternal, the Son of the living God*, the guardian and *protector of such as are forsaken*, for so the word "Samaritan" signifies. This divine Word seeing our peril and dereliction, made Himself man, and descended from the celestial Jerusalem into this world, living like other men, walking by the same ways which they do, but yet without sin, although He conversed and kept

(5) Luc. x. 31.

company with sinners; for which reason He was held for
a sinner, a Samaritan, (6) and one that was abominable to
the Jews; yet, notwithstanding this, He casts His eyes on
any sinner whom He sees despoiled of His grace, subject
to the devils, and in danger of everlasting damnation.

Colloquy.—O merciful "Samaritan," true God and
true man, the guardian and keeper of those who neither can nor know.how to keep themselves ; who could
protect us from so many enemies, and deliver us from
so many perils, if Thou didst not preserve us, since
"unless the Lord keep the city, he watches in vain
that keeps it?"(7)   What would become of us miserable wretches if Thou tookest not compassion on our
misery?   Moses passed with all the order of the
priests and ancient prophets, who could not cure infirmity, because they themselves were infirm, and had
need of a cure for themselves.   The race of Scribes
and Pharisees passed, who, proud and obdurate of
heart, had not compassion of those that were in sin :
but Thou, most pious Samaritan, camest from heaven
to pass through this world, "doing good, healing all
that were" wounded and " oppressed by the Devil."(8)
I give Thee thanks for the mercy which Thou hast
shown to us, and for the good which Thou hast done
us, remedying our miseries, who would have remained
without remedy, had it not been through Thy great
mercy.

POINT III.

And going near to him that was wounded, he " bound
up his wounds, pouring in oil and wine, and setting him
upon his own beast, brought him to an inn, and took care
of him.   And the next day he took out two-pence, and
gave to the host, and said: Take care of him, and what-

(6) Joan. viii. 48.   (7) Ps. cxxvi. 1.   (8) Act. x. 38.

soever thou shalt spend over and above, I, at my return, will repay thee." (9)

Upon this point is to be considered *the manner how this divine Samaritan* had pity on us, and the innumerable benefits which He conferred upon us; for His infinite mercy ends not in compassion only, nor contents itself with words only, but with works of infinite charity.

1. He *approaches* and draws near to the wounded, because, unless He came to visit the sinner, the sinner could not go to seek Him.

Colloquy.—O most loving Jesus, I confess that, like the prodigal child, I have departed from Thy house, and have estranged myself from Thee, and am brought to such misery, that prostrate on the ground I had no feet nor force to raise myself up to seek Thee, that Thou mightest give me a remedy; but Thy charity has taken me by the hand, and come to visit me, preventing me with divine inspirations, and approaching to me with interior touches, touching my heart with a desire to be cured and healed. I render Thee thanks, O my Lord, that Thou hast visited me after I had departed so far from Thee.

2. "He *bound up his wounds*," and all his stabs, not leaving so much as any one unbound and uncured: but with what linen, and with what bands did he bind them?

Colloquy.—O most pious surgeon, who drawest blood from us, and stayest the current of our sins, and bindest the fury of our passions with the most pure band of Thy grace and charity, and with other virtues which Thou dost communicate to us to justify our souls, to purge them of all their past faults, and to prevent those which might follow: O how pious art

<hr>

(9) Luc. x. 34.

Thou in our behalf, we having been so cruel to Thee, suffering Thyself for our innumerable sins, to be wounded with most terrible wounds, and to be bound with cruel cords, and fastened on a cross with sharp nails! By Thy bodily wounds, therefore, I humbly beseech Thee to heal mine; and by Thy cruel bands I beseech Thee so to bind me, that I may never go after the liberty of the flesh, nor abandon myself to sinful vices, but firmly embrace all sorts of virtues. Amen.

3. He *washed his wounds* with "*oil and wine,*" for He applies to us most effectual sacraments, full of mercy and celestial virtue, with which He anoints, cures, and heals us, comforting, sustaining, and rejoicing the heart.

Colloquy.—O most sweet Samaritan, how well provided art Thou come from heaven, since so readily, and as it were at hand, Thou hast found the remedy for our wounds! What are the sacraments which Thou hast instituted, but so many vessels of the "oil" of grace, and of the "wine" of charity, which Thou pourest forth upon our wounds, and by which we become perfectly healed? Anoint me, O Lord, with this "oil" of gladness, comfort me with this spiritual "wine, and heal me, that I may consecrate and offer myself to the service of Him, who, with such mercy, has healed me of my wounds. Amen.

He likewise applies to us another medicine, which is *the word of God*, and the holy Scripture, full of oil, and of wine, that is to say, full of sweet and amiable truths, which rejoice, and invite us to penance, by the way of love; and other sharp and terrible truths, which affright and move to sorrow for sins, by the way of fear, and with the one and the other He moves us to various affections, and holy desires, by which we earnestly solicit our conversion.

4. Not content with this, seeing the weakness of the sick man, and that he could not walk on his feet, "*he set him upon his own beast*," because He laid upon His own most sacred body the load of our sins, and with the succour of His inspirations, He assists and supports us as upon the feet of another, in the way of virtue, making the "yoke" of His law, and the keeping of His precepts "sweet" to us.

5. And continuing still His mercy, He draws the sick man out of the road, in which he lay prostrate, drawing him out of the occasions and perils of sin, and *placing him in a house*, honourable, secure, and very commodious, which is the *holy Catholic Church*, where He finds all that which is necessary for his healing and perfect cure, with great security and contentment, where He himself, in His own person, "takes care of him," and as a father, provides for him and cherishes him.

Colloquy.—O infinite charity of Jesus Christ, what thanks shall I give Thee for so many favours and encouragements which Thou hast vouchsafed me! The angels praise Thee for them, and let my soul be quite dissolved in Thy praises.—Blessed be Thou for the "oil and wine," with which Thou hast cured my wounds.—Blessed be Thou a thousand times, for the succour with which Thou hast alienated my weakness. —Blessed be Thou a hundred thousand times, that Thou hast drawn me out of such perils, and placed me in the glorious habitation of Thy Church.—And more than this, blessed be Thou many millions of times, that Thou hast drawn me forth out of the dangers and dealings of the world, and put me with Thy own hand, in the secure habitation of holy Religion, which Thou hast ordained in Thy holy Church, to gather therein those whom Thou hast chosen for the most high degree and state of perfection.

6. Lastly, when this Lord departed to heaven, and absented Himself, according to His humanity, although even then He did not cease to take care of us Himself; He *commanded the host of the house*, that is His vicar upon earth, and all the prelates of the Church, and superiors of Religious orders, that they should *take care of the sick*, and of their cure and recovery; and to this end, gave them "two-pence," which are the necessary means of government. He gave them virtue, and knowledge, the graces of sanctity, and graces given gratis for the good of others; He gave them the power of order, and jurisdiction, and strictly charged them, that, on their part they should do all they were able for the good of the sick, not contenting themselves to accomplish that which is of precept, but adding also works of supererogation, and of favour, for when He shall return to judge, He will repay to all whatsoever they have employed for the good of their needy neighbour.

Colloquy.—Here, O my God, my senses fail me, nor do I know what I shall say, but only in silence praise Thee for the great mercy and paternal providence which Thou hast for the needy, and beseech Thy divine majesty effectually to inspire the prelates of the Church, that they fulfil with great fidelity all that which Thou commandest them, that when Thou comest to judgment, Thou mayest find the wounded sinners healed, and the careful prelates full of merits. Amen.

POINT IV.

Lastly, in thy opinion consider the conclusion of the parable: for Christ our Lord, demanding of the lawyer "which of these three was neighbour to him that fell among robbers. But he said, He *that showed mercy to him.* Then Jesus said: Go and do thou in like manner." (10)

(10) Luc. x. 36.

1. In this we discover much *more the infinite charity of our Lord;* first, in desiring that we all take compassion one of another, using mercy towards them, and assisting them, both in their corporal and spiritual necessities, as the Samaritan did, who, being a stranger, had more compassion on this wounded Israelite, than the priests and Levites that were of his nation.

2. He secretly *puts Himself for an example, saying :* Show mercy one to another, even as I, who am represented by this Samaritan, have shown to you. Consider well what I have done to the sick sinner, and do you practise the like, with such a one as is in need, relieving the best that you can his affliction, both of soul and body, and to be not sparing, but liberal, doing much more than what you are obliged, as I did incomparably a great deal more than what was necessary for your remedy, repaying me with this, the love which I showed you, and when I shall return to judge, I will render you abundantly all you shall have done, with a measure of glory, "full, pressed down, and shaken together, and running over." (11)

Colloquy.—O most sweet Saviour, I purpose with Thy grace to love my neighbour as Thou hast loved us, and to pity him as Thou hast pitied us, to imitate Him to whom I owe so much ; to whom be honour and glory, world without end, Amen,

---

MEDITATION LI,

This parable is a lively description of the liberal mercy of Almighty God, in pardoning injuries with great facility, although they be great: and of the abominable hardness of

(11) Luc. vi. 38.

man, who will not pardon his neighbour his, although they be few and little, and in both these respects it shall be the matter of this meditation.

POINT I.

The Kingdom of heaven is "likened to *a king, who would take an account of his servants.* And when he had begun to take the account, one was brought to him that owed him ten thousand talents;—and as he had not wherewith to pay it, his lord commanded that he should be sold, and his wife and children and all he had, and payment to be made."(1)

1. *God our Lord is to take account of all men,* of what they have done in this life, which happens to every one at the instant of his death, and is there concluded; nevertheless before death also He begins to take this account, when interiorly He advises us what we are owing to Him, and demands payment in this life by penance; but especially when He brings us to some grievous sickness, or danger of death, then it seems that He begins to take an account. But I am to remark this difference: that if in the instant of death God calls me to an account, and find me laden with grievous sins, then is the account concluded without any remedy or hope of pardon;—but if during life, the account be taken, there is still hope that we may give satisfaction, through the infinite liberality of the eternal King.

Colloquy.—Wherefore, O my soul, enter into account with Almighty God during this life, and look what thou owest Him, since now is the time of mercy, but hereafter will be the time of rigorous justice.

2. The servant who owes these ten thousand talents, is, *the sinner loaded with sins,* the properties of which are

(1) Mat. xviii. 23.

represented by these ten thousand talents.—The first is, that they are *contrary to the Ten Commandments* of the law of God, violating them to the injury of the lawgiver: and although the sin be against one only commandment, yet is it, as St. James the apostle says, (2) of such a nature that it does a certain injury to all, as has before been said.—ii. That they are *very many* or innumerable, and for this cause are compared to the number of ten thousand; and if venial sins are accounted in this number, we may say that they are more than the hairs of the head, and the sands of the sea.—iii. That they are *most grievous*, and every one as weighty as a talent, enclosing in it a heavy burden, and a grievous injury, as being against a God infinitely good, and against His innumerable and most excellent benefits, and with the contempt of the blood of Jesus Christ which is of infinite value, and to the prejudice of those souls, which are bought with this infinite price, and with destruction of the talents which God has given us with infinite charity.—iv. The fourth, which follows the former, is that *no man of himself can pay this debt*, nor has he sufficient merit to satisfy Almighty God for one only mortal sin, how much less for so many: for being the enemy of Almighty God, he can do nothing to satisfy Him, and whatsoever he shall give, all is nothing in respect of the infinite debt which he owes.—v. To be *liable to so terrible a pain* as to be sold—he, his wife, his children and all he has;—that is to say, to be condemned to lose his liberty, and to be a perpetual slave of the Devil in hell, with loss of all the goods which Almighty God has given him, as well corporeal as spiritual, being despoiled of them as a traitor, and unworthy of them: in such a manner, that the man as well as his wife, viz. :— his sensuality, and his children, which are his works, and

(2) Jac. ii. 10.

his substance, which are the gifts of grace which he received, all shall be sold and taken out of the power and possession of him that enjoyed them; the goods of nature being left him for his greater torment.

3. Pondering these five things, I will excite in my soul a great sorrow for the injuries which I have committed against our Lord, seeing myself charged with so grievous debts, and a great fear of His justice, and of the chastisement which I have deserved for them, having recourse with this servant to my remedy, which is to ask and obtain pardon of this our Lord.

POINT II.

"But that servant hearing what his lord commanded, falling down besought him, saying, *Have patience with me, and I will pay thee* all. And the lord of that servant being moved with pity, let him go, and *forgave him the debt*." (3)

1. Ponder here, in the person of this servant, *the means that are to procure the pardon of our sins;* resolving to make good use of them.—i. Not to deny the debt, but to *acknowledge* and to confess it entirely, and with great repentance for having incurred it.—ii. To *humble oneself* before Almighty God with profound reverence, even to prostrating oneself on the earth, acknowledging his nothing and his misery.—iii. Humbly to crave and *ask mercy* and time for penance, to satisfy for the offences we have committed against Him.—iv. Lastly, a *firm resolution to pay* the whole debt, that is to say, to do on our part, with His assistance, all that possibly we can to pay it. With these affections I will place myself before Almighty God, and say to Him :—"Patientiam habe in me, et omnia reddam tibi," "Have patience with me, and I will repay Thee all."

(3) Mat. xviii. 26.

Colloquy. —O most patient Lord, who with infinite patience sufferest all those who so many times and so heinously offend Thee, add this patience to that which it has pleased Thee to have hitherto, giving me also this one time for penance, that I may pay Thee what I owe Thee ; and because I have not of myself wherewith to pay, I will offer to Thee the payment which my Redeemer made with the price of His precious blood, by which means, and by the assistance of Thy grace, I will pay Thee all I can in discharge of my debt.

2. In the person of this lord, is seen, the *infinite mercy and liberality* of our great God, in granting to humbled sinners much more than they dared presume, either to ask or desire of Him, since of His free will, He both revoked the sentence of punishment which He had threatened, and pardoned the debt without regard of its being very great, and all this of pure mercy, because the debt of sin and of eternal pain, is never pardoned on account of our merits.

Colloquy.—O most merciful, liberal, and bountiful Lord, let the angels applaud Thy infinite mercy, let men praise Thy immense bounty, and let my soul magnify Thee for Thy unspeakable magnificence. There was need of a God so merciful as Thou art, for a man so miserable as I, such a liberality and magnificence as Thine was necessary to pardon so great a debt as mine. And since Thou hast been so liberal in pardoning the fault and the everlasting pain ; I will not cease to punish myself with temporal pains, paying what I am able in compensation for the eternal punishment which I deserved, with a will never more to offend Him who has used such mercy towards me in pardoning me. Amen.

POINT III.

"But when that servant was gone out, he found one of his fellow-servants that owed him a hundred pence, and laying hold of him, he throttled him, saying: *Pay what thou owest.* And his fellow-servant falling down, besought him, saying: Have patience with me, and I will pay thee all. And he would not; but went and cast him into prison till he paid the debt."(4)

1. How is it an ordinary thing amongst men, *that one owes something to another* for some injury done by words, or works, or for other causes; and this proceeds from our frailty, and is permitted by the divine providence, that the good may take occasion of merit, suffering and pardoning injuries, and so may say to God, " Forgive us our trespasses, as we forgive them that trespass against us." But if we consider well the debts which we owe to Almighty God, they far surpass those which men owe to us, as much as ten thousand talents of silver exceed a hundred farthings;—that is to say, exceed it with great excess; because one only injury done to Almighty God is infinitely greater than all the injuries done to men, because the injury is so much the greater, the more excellent is the person that receives the injury; as God is infinitely greater than all men together, so is the injury which is done to Him, as has been pondered in another place.(5)

2. Ponder the *cruelty of this wicked servant against his companion.*—i. First, in the *rage and rancour* which he showed against him, not contented to demand the debt with words only, but also assaulted him by the throat, to choke and strangle him.—ii. In that, his companion, casting himself at his feet, and asking him with humility to have patience with him, promising to pay the whole debt, and using the same words which he himself had used to his lord;—yet *he had no pity* on him,—would not hear him,—would not pardon him, nor expect with patience for

(4) Mat. xviii. 28.   (5) Med. v. p. 1.

a little time.—iii. In the passionate *fury* with which he cast him into prison, until such time as he had paid the whole, using towards him unreasonably great rigour.—iv. In *the ingratitude* which he showed against the same lord, whose servant also that debtor was; because the injury which he did to the servant, redounded to the dishonour of his master, showing himself very contrary to the condition of so noble a lord, being nothing moved to compassion by the same words, by which he himself had received compassion. All this is found in sinners, who will not pardon their neighbours the injuries they have done them, and the debts which they owe them, but revenge themselves upon them with rancour.

3. The *roots of these evils*, which the parable indicates, saying, that this servant went forth from the presence of his lord;—it being evident that he durst not so oppress his companion in his presence;—that is to say, that the cause of our sins against God and our neighbours is in going from the presence of Almighty God, forgetting that He is present, that He is our judge,(6) and forgetting the favours which He has done us, and the gratitude and service which we owe Him for them, because, if we firmly kept them in mind with a lively faith, we should never be so hardy as to offend Him.

Colloquy.—Wherefore, O my soul, think that God beholds thee, walk always in His presence, remember the benefits He has done thee, and that thou must be accountable for them ; for, if thou remember this, thou wilt also remember not to offend Him, whom for so many reasons thou art bound to serve.

POINT IV.

His fellow-servants seeing what was done, were very

(6) S. Jer. in Ezech. viii.

sorry, and they came to their Lord, and told to him all that had passed. "Then his lord called him, and said unto him; Thou wicked servant, I forgave thee all the debt because thou besoughtest me; shouldst not thou, then, have had compassion on thy fellow servant, even as I had compassion on thee? And his lord being angry, *delivered him to the torturers* until he paid all the debt."(7)

1. *All our malice*, and all the grievances which we do to our neighbours, *are disliked by men and angels*, and all the servants of Almighty God that behold them, are greatly afflicted and grieved at them, partly for the compassion they have for the party injured, partly for the damage which the injurer himself received, and partly for the offence committed against God; for, as it is the effect of the good spirit to be grieved for one's neighbour's offences, so is it much better to forbear committing them, and not grieve the just and the angels. Hence it is that, although our malice and ingratitude cannot be hidden from Almighty God, though He seems to be absent, and not to see us; yet the grief and sadness which the just have for the malice of men, and the desire which they have to comfort the afflicted and oppressed, is like a cry and a declaration, which they make thereof to Almighty God, which sometimes awakes Him to take vengeance upon rebellious and ungrateful persons, and to pluck His little ones out of their cruel paws, conformably to that which the same lord says, " Will not God revenge His elect, that cry unto Him day and night?"(8)

2. *Our Lord presently commands that the servant be called with the last call to judgment :* because, in chastisement of our inveterate malice, God is wont to shorten the days of our life, and immediately to call the sinner to render up his last account, and finding him guilty, He delivers him

(7) Mat. xviii. 32.   (8) Luc. xviii. 7.

to the hangmen and tormentors in hell, until he pay the whole debt; and as he can never be able to pay it, so will his torment never end. Oh, if thou hadst always present before thee this final calling, with what sweetness wouldst thou treat thy neighbour, that Almighty God might treat thee with that sweetness which thou desirest. Oh, if thou didst remember the tormentors and torments which attend thee for the debts which thou hast not paid during this life, doubtless thou wouldst pay them immediately, treating with Almighty God to obtain pardon for them.

3. This evil servant was punished not only for the present sin, but also, in a certain manner, for *those sins which were past*, and had been pardoned him, inasmuch as he redoubled his former sin, for having been ungrateful for the benefit which he had received from his lord, and the manner which he used in pardoning him, of which he made no account, when it behoved him to pardon his neighbour: (9) upon this I will tremble at the vice of ingratitude against God, which so much augments the grievousness of the sin, because as many sins as God has forgiven me, so many acts of ingratitude may I conceive in the sin which I afterwards commit; and although it be only one, yet virtually it includes many.

Colloquy.—O abominable ingratitude, after which enter into the soul " seven other spirits, more wicked"(10) than the first that issued forth ; deliver me, O my God, from so great a mischief, since it is so disagreeable to Thee. Amen.

POINT V.

Then consider the conclusion of the parable, which was this:—" So also shall *my heavenly Father do to you, if you forgive not every one his brother from your hearts.*"(11)

(9) S. Tho. p. q. lxxxviii. art. 3.   (10) Luc. xi. 26.

(11) Mat. xviii. 34.

1. In this we are to admire the *infinite charity of our Lord*, which appears in this, that He will have us to pardon one another, not through compliment, but from the heart, wholly influenced by the laws of charity, which are drawn from the words here set down.

i. First, because our celestial Father, whose sons we are, will have it so; and this suffices to give Him content in what He commands.—ii. Because we are all brethren, sons of the same Father: and it is very reasonable that one brother should forgive another.—iii. Because as every one commits something which his brother is to suffer, and to pardon, so it is very reasonable that he should pardon him as he would be pardoned.—iv. Fourthly, because our celestial Father liberally pardons us our debts, which are incomparably greater.—v. Because if love do not induce us to accomplish the law, the fear of punishment will take place, which will be terrible, because he will not be pardoned the second time, who with obstinacy would not pardon his neighbour, and consequently will be delivered to the devils, executioners of the justice of Almighty God, to chastise him as he deserves.

2. Considering all these reasons, I will make very effectual resolutions to *show mercy towards my neighbours*, and to forgive them whatsoever injury they shall commit against me, desiring (if it may be done without offending God,) to be injured, only to have an occasion to pardon, that so Almighty God may pardon me.

Colloquy.—O celestial Father, I forgive from the bottom of my heart the debts which such owe me as have injured me, that I may resemble Thee, who art so frank in pardoning those who offend Thee, it being just that the son should resemble his Father. Receive this good will, and give me grace, that occasion being offered, I may presently put the same in practice.

MEDITATION LII.

ON THE PARABLE OF THE BAILIFF WHO WASTED THE REVENUES OF HIS LORD.

POINT I.

" There was a certain rich man who had a steward: and the same was accused unto him that he had wasted his goods."(1)

Ponder here *who this rich man was :—who this bailiff* is: —in *what manner he wasted his goods :*—and *how he was accused* before his Lord.

1. This rich man represents *God our Lord,* whose are all the riches of heaven and earth, which either angels or men enjoy; and are of three sorts.—Some are corporal riches, which serve the body for its food, clothing, and ornament. —Others are spiritual, which adorn and enrich the spirit with grace and virtues.—Others are eternal riches, with which the just are rewarded in heaven. These riches Almighty God imparts to men, giving the first both to *good and bad,* to the faithful and unfaithful.—The second, only to the *faithful,* and some to the just only.—But the last only to the *blessed.*

Colloquy.—O sovereign God, " rich in mercy,"(2) and rich to all those who call upon Thy holy name; grant that I may so use corporal riches, that I lose not the spiritual; and in such manner trade with the temporal, that I may obtain the eternal.   Amen.

2. *The "steward"* of this sovereign Lord *is man,* to whom He has committed the government of the riches he possesses, as well in body as in soul: and although He gives him the true dominion over some of them, yet is he al-

(1) Luc. xvi. 1.   (2) Ephes. ii. 4.

ways called steward, because his dominion is not absolute, but subject to the dominion of Almighty God, and to His laws, nor is it lawful for him to distribute or use these goods, but conformably to the will of his supreme Lord, who gave them to him, and to whom he is to give an account and reckoning of the whole, the day and hour when it shall be demanded; for which purpose there is a book of account and expenses, in which is put down that which He commits to us, and the manner how we have laid it out.

3. Hence it ensues, namely, that this steward is said to have wasted the goods of his Lord, and to have spent and used them *contrary to His divine will*, and contrary to the commandments, which He has given us in His holy law. I waste food, if I eat it for gluttony;—I waste apparel if I wear the same for vain-glory;—I waste money, if I spend the same in prohibited things, or detain it, and do not give it to the poor when God commands. And in the same manner I waste life, health, and the senses and faculties of my soul, when I employ them in things which offend Him who gave them to me.

4. *For these causes the " steward" comes to be accused* before his Lord; for our good or evil name before Almighty God depends not upon the words of men, but upon our works. These turn to our credit or discredit, they honour or defame us before Him, nor can they be hidden from Him. And although the whole world should have a good opinion of me, if indeed I be wicked, my own works will cry out against me, as against those of Sodom, and will accuse me before God.(3)

Colloquy.—O eternal God, who of Thy infinite mercy hast made man Thy steward in this great house of the whole world, and " hast subjected all things under his feet;"(4) suffer not that I follow the steps

<hr>

(3) Gen. xviii. 20.   (4) Ps. viii. 8.

of the old Adam, who rendered a bad account of his stewardship in the earthly paradise, but assist me with Thy special grace, that I may perform such works, that I may come to have credit with Thee, and may be admitted by them into the celestial paradise. Amen.

POINT II.

His lord "called him, and said to him: How is it that I hear this of thee? *Give an account of thy stewardship*, for now thou canst be steward no longer."(5)

1. As this rich man, by the knowledge which he had that his steward spent and wasted his goods, discharged him from his office, commanding him to give an account; even so the cry of *our sins*, which enters in before the tribunal of Almighty God, is *a cause that He shortens the days of our life*, and calls us to render Him an account of it. For which reason the Wise man says, "Be not overmuch wicked, and be not foolish, lest thou die before thy time."(6) And this our Lord and Saviour does, partly by justice, and partly by mercy, cutting off the evil steps of him, who, living long time in wickedness, would render up a worse account, and have more terrible pain to suffer.

2. This calling is wont to happen in *two manners.*—The first is more terrible, when, as Almighty God calls sinners *so suddenly*, that they think not of their death, and have not time to make themselves ready for the account they are to render.—The other manner is, calling them *by little and little* by the means of some infirmity, which is a warning of death, and gives us space to prepare ourselves for this account, and then it is that He says, "How is it that I hear this of thee?" In virtue of which He puts us in mind of all the sins of which we are accused before Him, that hearing the accusation we may provide our answer in

(5) Luc. xvi, 2.   (6) Eccles. vii. 18.

time, for otherwise, at the instant of death, He will reproach us, convince us of the fault, and will likewise sentence us for the same.

Colloquy.—Wherefore, O my soul, hearken now to the voice of Almighty God, who, with His inspirations and inward remorses, says to thee :—" What sins are those which thou committest ?—What lukewarmness is this in which thou livest ?—What forgetfulness is this of thy salvation ?—What complaints are these which the poor and afflicted make against thee, and which ascend and come up before me ? What carelessness is this which thou committest in thy office, and in the things I have commended to thee ?—Hearken, then, to this warning, and amend thee betimes in that of which God admonishes thee ; for, unless Thou be amended before the hour of thy death, the warning which now He gives thee for thy salvation, He will then give thee for thy condemnation.

3. Then ponder the *terror of that word*:—" *Give an account of thy stewardship;* for now thou canst be steward no longer."(7)   Which is to say, Give me an account of the house and farm of this world, which I have created for thy dwelling;—of the plants and living creatures, which I have made to support thee;—of the treasures, riches, offices, and dignities, which thou hast possessed;—of the years of thy life, health, strength, and talents which I have given thee. Give me, moreover, an account of all the thoughts which roved in thy memory;—of all the words which have issued forth of thy mouth;—of all the works thou hast done with thy hands, of all the steps thou hast walked with thy feet;—and of all the affections and desires which thou hast framed in thy heart. Lastly, give me an account of all that which belongs to the office of a bailiff,

<hr>

(7) Luc. xvi. 2.

because now thou canst administer the same no more, the day is gone for thee to negotiate, and "the night" is come, "when no man can work."(8) Now the hour is come, in which, though against thy will, thou must appear before my tribunal, to render an account of what thou hast done, and " receive the proper things of the body,"(9) according as thou hast done, and receive recompense or punishment for the same. These words ought I to have always before my eyes, since it is certain that the hour will come in which they will be spoken to me: and it is great wisdom to live so well prepared, that I may render a good account when I am summoned to give it up.

POINT III.

"The steward said within himself: What shall I do, because my lord taketh away from me the stewardship? To dig I am not able, to beg I am ashamed. I know what I will do, that when I shall be removed from the steward-ship, they may receive me into their houses. Therefore, calling together every one of his lord's debtors, he said to the first, who owed him an hundred barrels of oil, *Take thy bill, and sit down quickly, and write fifty*. And to another who owed a hundred quarters of wheat, he said, Take thy bill, and *write eighty*. And the lord *commended the unjust steward*, forasmuch as *he had done wisely*: for the children of this world are wiser in their generation, than the children of light."(10)

1. Ponder here, the *fact of the steward*, according to the drift of the parable, in which is represented a kind of men, worldly, crafty, and wise in all that is evil, who will not labour, nor work to get their living, because they are nice, and friends of idleness; they will not beg, because they are considered gentlemen, and above laborious em-

(8) Joan. ix. 4.   (9) 2 Cor. v. 16.   (10) Luc. xvi. 3.

ployments, so that they seek their living of free cost, with deceit, and at the expenses of other men, providing in this manner for their own wants. But in this sense, Christ our Lord does not produce this act of the steward to the end that we should practise it, but that by the foresight which he used, in providing in time for the necessities of his body, we may learn to be prudent in providing for those of the soul: "for the children of this world," are more prudent, in the art which they use about temporal things, than "the children of light" are, for things eternal: and therefore they may learn of them.

Colloquy.—O my soul, behold the prudence of worldlings in their manner of worldly life, and be confounded to see the defect in thy religious and Christian life. They are diligent in vice, thou negligent in virtue;—they watch and invent means to bring to pass their bad intentions, and thou addictest thyself to sleep, careless to accomplish thy good intentions;—they without delay do all they are able instantly, although it be exceeding painful, thou with delays from day to day, dost not what thou mayest, although it is easy. Blush, then, that thou art less prudent in good than they in evil; and leaving that which is evil in them, imitate with spirit that which is good, providing with like fervour that which is necessary for thy soul, as they provide that which is necessary for their body.

2. The *spirit which is enclosed in the act of this steward,* in which are described sundry exercises, by which we may obtain eternal life. Some there are, that gain their living by *digging,* that is to say, taking for their principal occupation, penance and the mortification of their flesh with great rigours and austerities. But this sort of life, although it be very excellent, yet it is not for all, as S. Paul said to

his disciple Timothy,(11) because many are feeble and infirm, and cannot endure such rigour.—Others there are who gain eternal life by *begging*, that is to say, taking for their principal practice, the exercise of prayer and contemplation, in which nought else is done, but to beg and crave of God and His saints, that which is necessary for our salvation and perfection. But this sort of life, although it be also very excellent, yet it is not for all, because some cannot always occupy themselves in prolonged and retired prayer, like such as are hermits, because the sins of their past life, their vices, and wicked inclinations, make them bashful and confounded to treat with God; and, that their estate, office, or natural complexion, are not proper for this end. Those who are not apt for either of these two sorts of life, and say with the steward, "To dig I am not able, and to beg I am ashamed," they must take some other third sort, by which they may gain eternal life, which is by alms, and other works of mercy, both corporal and spiritual, conformably to their talent or capacity, following the counsel which S. Paul gave to Timothy, saying :—"Exercise thyself in godliness, which is profitable to all things, having the promise of this life that now is, and of that which is to come;"(12) next, because with these works of charity and mercy, is obtained of our Lord pardon of sins, with great gifts of His grace in this life, and afterwards the reward of life eternal.

3. This was that which Christ our Lord inferred from this parable, saying :—"*Make unto you friends of the mammon of iniquity*, that when you shall fail, they may receive you into the everlasting tabernacles."(13) In which words He calls temporal riches, "the mammon of iniquity," although they be lawfully acquired, or that the wicked only esteem them for riches, and place their rest

(11) 1 Tim. v.   (12) 1 Tim. iv. 8.   (13) Luc. xvi. 9.

in them, and call those blessed who possess them :(14) but the perfectly just, as the apostle says, "count them but as dung,"(15) and fly from them, because they are the occasion of innumerable evils of sin and pain, to those that love them inordinately, as has been said before. Notwithstanding all this, they may serve as instruments, to become "rich in good works,"(16) following the counsel which Christ our Lord gave here to certain rich persons, saying, that they should make "friends of" them, that when they should "fail, they may receive" them "into everlasting dwellings," exercising towards the poor all the works of mercy; who are faithful and powerful friends, to intercede with our Lord, as Tobias says : (17) that if they died the death of sin, He would deliver them, giving them the riches of His grace, and when they died a temporal death, He would deliver them from eternal death, giving them the riches of His glory in the "dwellings," which He calls "everlasting;" which so far exceed those of this life in greatness, as they exceed them in being eternal. And this ought to move us to give infinite thanks to Him, that has ordained such an exchange, giving us power to change with so great facility, earthly for heavenly, and with riches so vile, as are those of the earth, to be able to gain two sorts of friends, who may exchange for us those of heaven, viz. :—works of mercy, which being "shut up in the heart of the poor,"(18) pray for us : and the same poor also, whose prayers are heard by Almighty God, when they pray for those that do them good.

Colloquy.—O most merciful God, lighten and inflame the hearts of the rich of this world with the

(14) S. Aug. lib. 2. q Evan. xxxiv. tom. 2.
(15) Phil. iii. 8.   S. Amb. lib. 7. in Luc. c. ult.
(16) 1 Tim. vi. 18.   (17) Tob. iv. 12.   (18) Ecclus. xxix. 15.

light and fire of Thy grace and charity, that with the riches that Thou hast given them, they may become "rich in good works," and may gain for friends the poor and just who are in earth, and the angels and saints who are in heaven, by whose intercession they may be received "into eternal dwellings." Amen.

MEDITATION LIII.

ON THE PUBLICAN AND PHARISEE, WHO WENT UP INTO THE TEMPLE TO PRAY

POINT I.

"And He spoke also to some that trusted in themselves, as just, and despised others, this parable. Two men went up into the Temple to pray; the one a Pharisee, and the other a publican. The Pharisee standing, prayed thus with himself:—O God, I give Thee thanks that I am not as the rest of men, extortioners, unjust, adulterers, as also is this publican; I fast twice in a week : I give tithes of all that I possess." (1)

1. In this part of the parable, is to be considered, *the abominable acts of pride*, which *this Pharisee* discovered in his prayer, making reflection upon myself, to see if the like be not in me, and to leave them.

i. The first was, *to hold himself for holy* and full of virtues : whence in his prayer, he craved nothing of Almighty God, neither pardon of his sins, nor that He would preserve or augment His gifts in him, as if he had no need of them.

ii. The second act was, under pretext of giving thanks, *to praise himself*, and boast of his good works, pleasing himself in them, in such a way, that he gave thanks to Almighty God with his mouth only, for with his heart he

(1) Luc. xviii. 9.

gave the thanks to himself, for so it is said, that he prayed, with himself, and about himself, and not with God, nor about God.

iii. The third was, to *prefer himself before all other men*, holding himself better than all others, and singular in virtue, as if he alone had been good, and none but he.

iv. The fourth was, *to make great account of his own good works*, although very little of themselves, as he compared them with the evil doings of other men, instead of doing the contrary; and only made account of exterior things, such as to fast and to pay tithes, which also he did for vanity and boasting, not observing that himself was a "whited sepulchre," and that within he was "full of dead men's bones," and rotten with most grievous sins.

v. The fifth was, *to contemn all men, and his own companion the publican*, making little account of them : and more than this, to judge rashly of the publican that he was yet a sinner; whereas he might have conjectured by the signs which he saw, that he was amended.

2. In all this may be seen, how blind this Pharisee was, and how blind pride is, in the knowledge of its own and others affairs, which Christ our Lord declares in the Apocalypse, in the person of a prelate, like to this Pharisee, who said of himself:—"I am rich and have need of nothing : and thou knowest not that thou art wretched, and miserable, and poor, and blind, and naked." (2)

Colloquy.—O abominable pride, O monstrous beast, blind to the evils thou hast, and presumptuous of good things which thou hast not! Thou seest "the mote" in the eye of thy brother, and seest not "the beam" in thine own eye, because thou canst not see thyself, who art a beam, that blindest the eyes of thine own soul. I confess, O my God, that I have followed the

<hr>

(2) Apoc. iii. 17.

steps of this Pharisee, for being religious by profession, I have been profane in life, but Thy grace can change me, that my life may be conformed to my profession.

POINT II.

Consider *the prayer of the publican*, who "standing afar off, would not so much as lift up his eyes towards heaven, but struck his breast, and said: O, God be merciful to me a sinner!"(3)

1. Here are to be pondered the *acts of humility of this publican*, contrary to those of the Pharisee, that we may imitate them.

i. The first was, *to hold himself unworthy to approach near to God*, or even to approach near to the Pharisee himself, and so he set himself afar off, in the lower part of the Temple, choosing the lowest place of all others.

ii. The second was, *not to dare to lift up his eyes to heaven*, thinking that he merited nothing of Almighty God, and not wishing that his works might appear before Him, and so, covered with shame and confusion, he held them fixed on the ground.

iii. The third was, *to knock his breast*, showing thus the interior sorrow which he had for his sins, and the desire which he had to chastise his flesh for them, joining together the three parts of humble penance, viz. : a contrite and humbled heart, humble confession of his sins, and satisfaction, in the best manner he could.

iv. The fourth was, *to ask forgiveness of Almighty God* for himself alone, as if he alone were the only sinner in the world, not judging so of any others, no, not of the Pharisee himself: and although perhaps he heard the words with which he despised him, yet he was not offended against him, holding himself worthy to be contemned.

(3) Luc. xviii. 13.

v. The fifth was, *greatly to trust in the mercy of God,* because he prayed not with many words, believing that few words suffice with God, and that one is not the sooner heard for the multitude of words.

Colloquy.—O sovereign virtue of humility, mistress of all virtues, thou teachest me both how to love and to trust in God, both to bear Him reverence and respect, and not to despise any, subjecting myself to all, and holding myself for the most vile of all others.(4) O that we could imitate this happy publican! now no more publican, but a saint, since his humility has published his sanctity.

2. With this spirit of the publican, I am to repeat oftentimes, this his brief and fervent prayer, saying: "God be merciful to me, a sinner,"—yea, a great sinner; God be merciful to this proud, to this impatient, and vindicative man, etc.

POINT III.

Consider *the sentence which Christ our Lord gave,* as a most upright judge, betwixt these two men. "I say this man went down into his house justified, rather than the other: because every one that exalteth himself, shall be humbled; and he that humbleth himself, shall be exalted." (5)

1. In this sentence, Christ our sovereign judge, contents not Himself with exterior things, but *penetrates the mind, the intentions, and the affections of the heart,* whence the works spring, and accordingly pronounces sentence of justification or damnation; contrary to other men, who behold only the exterior, and so oftentimes deceive themselves.

2. How *potent is humility,* and how agreeable to Almighty God, since of public sinners He makes men very

(4) Cass. col. 15. cap. 7.   (5) Luc. xviii. 14.

just;—and contrariwise, how *abominable is pride*, which perverts the just, and changes them into grievous sinners. And the cause is, that the proud man attributing his virtues to himself, with vain complacency destroys them; Almighty God humbling him, because he became proud : but the humble attributing his sins to himself, with shame and displeasure, blots them out; God exalting him, because he humbles himself.

3. Hence I will ascend to consider this *general sentence.—Every man* of what estate or condition soever he be, Ecclesiastical, secular or Religious, noble or plebeian, learned or ignorant, great or little, *if he truly humble himself, "shall be exalted;"* (6) even in that in which he humbles himself, will God exalt him, honouring him even in this world, if it be for his good, making him to be well esteemed amongst men, and ennobling him with His gifts;— and afterwards in the other life more copiously with a resplendent crown of glory, placing him with the princes of His celestial Kingdom. And contrariwise, whosoever shall proudly exalt himself, "shall be humbled," either in this life, or in the other, as has been pondered in the first part, and in the seventeenth meditation.

From all this I will draw a love of humility, and detestation of pride, having firm hope in this promise of Christ, that for humbling myself, I shall not lose that exaltation which is conducive to my salvation; and will fear and tremble to grow proud, since it will certainly cause my fall and confusion.

(6) Prov. xvi. 18. Luc. xiv. 11. Mat. xxiii. 12.

MEDITATION LIV.

ON THE HOUSEHOLDER WHO HIRED WORKMEN FOR HIS VINEYARD.

POINT I.

"The Kingdom of heaven is like to a householder, who went out early in the morning to hire labourers into his vineyard. And having agreed with them" for their wages, he afterward went forth "about the third hour," which is the ninth of the day, and hired others, saying, he would give them what should "be just." He did the same at the "sixth," "ninth," and "eleventh hour," which is at the twelfth and third hour of the evening, and one hour before night, reprehending these last because they stood "all the day idle."(1)

1. Here we may ponder,—i. *Who this householder* is:—ii. *What this vineyard* is:—iii. *Who the workmen* are:—iv. *How he calls* them:—v. At *what hours:*—vi. And in *what manner.*

i. The "*householder*" *is God* our Lord, true Father of two families, which He has in heaven and on earth: viz., the blessed spirits and men who are pilgrims; exceeding careful of the good of His, and so particularly of every one, as if He had no more but him to keep: and for this reason, although He is King and supreme monarch, yet He calls Himself "Father" of a family, whose cares are wont to be very especial, and in particular of those who are in His house. O happy he who is in His house, under His safeguard and protection!

ii. His *vineyard is the congregation of the faithful*, but more particularly of the just, who are the principal gates or plants of it, who bring forth fruits of benediction, and

(1) Mat. xx. 1.

the wine of divine love, and from thence He cuts them, and transplants them into the vineyard of heaven, which is the company of the Blessed.

iii. The *labourers of this vineyard are men*, to *whom it belongs to cultivate their souls*, digging and pruning them with the pick-axe and vine knife of mortification and penance, procuring that they bring forth good and copious fruit, not of sour, but of ripe grapes, that is, works pleasing to Almighty God. And the most perfect labourers are those who, both by word and example, labour to instruct and to teach others to labour, that they may truly serve Almighty God, such as prelates and sincere Religious.

iv. For this effect Almighty God Himself calls them,(2) because without His calling none can enter into the "vineyard," nor work nor labour in it. And He calls them interiorly *with His inspirations and illustrations*, taking for instruments *preachers* and other exterior things, and sometimes by Himself immediately, sending them on a sudden an inward light and forcible inspirations.

v. He goes forth "*in the morning*," because His desire is that all men, from the time they have the use of reason, should be good labourers, and not be idle, and so He calls and invites all, with a vocation most sufficient to cause them to come, though all obey not and will not come, but yet His mercy is so great that He ceases not to call them *in all the ages of their life*, once, even oftentimes.—Some receive effectual vocation, and convert themselves to Him from their very infancy; others in their youth, others in the midst of their life, others when they are old, and others a little before their death.

vi. Some He calls with conditions and promises, who are converted like labourers for interest and hope of gain. —Others He calls with *inward reprehension*, by showing

(2) Joan. vi. 44.

them their wicked life, and offering to give them what is just. Others he calls with *absolute authority*, commanding them to go and labour for the love of virtue and virtuous labour.

2. From all these considerations I will draw affections of gratitude and praise to this Father of the family, for the care which He has to call us; and affections of pain and sorrow, to see so many resist His vocation, and for the sundry times that I have resisted it, greatly desiring to obey Him now.

Colloquy.—O sovereign Father of Thy family, careful of Thy vineyard, and to call labourers into it. Thou, in the law of nature, and in the written law, hast oftentimes gone forth to call us, and hast chosen a great number of patriarchs, of prophets, and of other just, Thy beloved servants, and hast since gone forth by Thy Incarnation, making Thyself man, and with Thy preaching hast called and chosen many apostles, and disciples, and by their means innumerable others, and never'ceasest to go forth every day to call workmen;—go forth, Lord, at this present, effectually to call Pagans, and Infidels, that so they may receive Thy faith. Go forth by the means of Thy holy Church, and call sinners effectually, that they may be converted to Thee. Go forth through the world, and call many just, that they may follow Thee with perfection;—and forget not, I beseech Thee, to go forth to call me seriously to the exercise of all virtues, by which my soul, being well cultivated and pruned, may bring forth that abundant fruit which Thou desirest. Amen.

POINT II.

"And when the evening was come, the lord of the vineyard saith to his steward, Call the labourers, *and pay them their hire*, beginning from the last even to the first.

When therefore they were come that came about the eleventh hour, they received every man a penny."(3)

1. The eternal Father has *made over to Jesus Christ our Lord, as He is man, the judgment of the workmen*, and the calling of them to receive their hire, and this is done at the end of the life of every one, which is counted but for a "day" in respect of eternity, as also because every day we ought to labour as if it were the last of our life.

Colloquy.—Remember, O my soul, this latter calling to receive a crown ; for with this remembrance thou wilt encourage thyself to consent to every vocation, with which thou shalt be called to labour ; for if thou resistest this first, thou mayest not be favoured with the second.

2. *All the labourers are to receive their hire*, the first and the last; those who began betimes, and those who began but late, and no hour of labour will pass without a reward, and consequently, by how much the works were more numerous and better, by so much will the reward be more abundant, conformably to that which Christ our Lord says, that He will come to judgment, and "render to every one according to his works,"(4)

3. Above all, to reward this labour, *we must not so much regard* the time that it lasts, *as the fervour, diligence, and love* with which it has been performed, whence it follows that the latter labourers in one only hour merited as much hire as the first who laboured all the day; for some labour with much fervour, with great humility and charity, holding themselves unworthy of any reward; and others work with slothfulness, and for base and avaricious ends, and with some presumption of themselves, and of their labour, for having endured long: but Almighty God much more esteems one hour of fervent labour, than twelve of slothful

(3) Mat. xx. 8.   (4) Mat. xvi. 27.

and lazy; and so, beside the essential reward, He gives to the latter another accidental honour, which the Gospel calls, " beginning" the payment "from the last."

4. Hence I will draw for my profit some considerations; for if the latter labourers in one hour merit so great a recompense, *how great shall the reward be* if they had laboured after the same sort the whole day! And if the saints in heaven could suffer pain, how great pain would they endure for not having answered very timely the divine vocation, and begun from their infancy to serve God. And those who began to serve Him from that time, and have served Him long, but yet with slothfulness and lukewarmness, what pain will they receive therefore, seeing that if they had served Him all that time with fervour, they had obtained much greater glory.

Colloquy.—O my soul, since thou hast time to labour, labour now as thou wouldst wish to have laboured on the day in which thy hire will be paid thee; hasten thee, because the time is short, and the reward great, and every degree of glory which thou deservest is eternal, nor is it just to lose by slothfulness the greatness which will last for all eternity.

POINT III.

The first labourers, seeing that no more reward was given to them than to the latter, " *murmured against the master of the house,* saying, These last have worked but one hour, and thou hast made them equal to us, that have borne the burden of the day and the heats. But he, answering, said to one of them: Friend, I do thee no wrong: didst not thou agree with me for a penny? Take what is thine, and go thy way; I will also give to this last even as to thee. Or is it not lawful for me to do what I will? Is thy eye evil because I am good?"(5)

(5) Mat. xx. 10.

1. Consider *the intent of our Lord in these words*, which is to signify that the rewards and favours, which are done *to the servant*, who in a little time labours much, and with great perfection, are so great that if those of the Blessed, who were not so fervent, had not the divine light to know the justice and bounty of Almighty God, and only considered the same as *earthly men* consider the like things, they would complain, and murmur, and would envy those favours which God does to the fervent.

Colloquy.—O blessed be the liberality of this master of the house, who, giving to every one what he deserves, rewards liberally whatsoever is done for the love of Him.

2. Christ our Lord here paints the *properties* of those *who serve Him in this life many years, but with lukewarmness*, contrasted with those of the others who serve Him less time, but with greater fervour; showing that:—

i. They *presume upon their own works* and services, because of their continuance, and so suppose they ought to receive great recompense; whereas the other neither presume on themselves, nor repute themselves worthy of any reward.

ii. They *bear the burden of the day* and the heats: for lukewarmness is the cause that they feel the labours of virtue painful, although they be little; and on the contrary, that fervour is the cause that they feel them not, although they be great: and so the lukewarm take much pains, and profit little;—the fervent take little pains, and profit much.

iii. The lukewarm are *hirelings and mercenaries*, seeking their own particular profit, and so walk full of complaints, and secret murmurings against Almighty God that He does not cherish and favour them; and against men, that they do not honour and help them: but the other serve Almighty God without interest, only for love, and so find no cause of complaint, receiving with humility the least favour which God may vouchsafe them, esteeming it much and reputing themselves unworthy of it.

iv. The lukewarm *are envious*, and grudge the favours which Almighty God does to the fervent, seeking to depress them: for which reason they despise them, noting them for novices in virtue, and for coming late to travail in His holy Church. But the fervent travail and talk not, desiring that God do well to all.

Colloquy.—O celestial Father, who so greatly favourest the diligent and careful labourers in Thy service, drive from my heart all tepidity and luke-warmness.—Assist me, that I may serve Thee with true fervour, and that I may rejoice that many others serve Thee after this manner: suffer not that I become so wicked as to let my eye be envious, because Thou art so good. I rejoice that Thou art so good as to do good to all, and I am delighted in the good which Thou dost to others more than to me, for well I know that Thou art good, just, and holy in all things.

POINT IV.

Christ our Lord concluded the parable, saying: "So shall *the last be first, and the first last*. For many are called, but few are chosen."(6)

1. Consider in the first part of this sentence, that there are *many in this life* who are reputed to be the "first" in sanctity, either for the continuance of years that they have served God, or for the appearance of exterior works, which move much;—or by reason of the excellency of their state, and office, which is a state and office of perfection;—or for the reputation which they have obtained of

(6) Mat. v. 16.

having been just for some time; who yet *at the day of judgment and of the last account, will be held for the " last,"* because in the eyes of Almighty God they were lukewarm, mercenary, and much imperfect. On the contrary, some who, in this life, seemed " the last," because at some time they had been grievous sinners, or had served God but a little time, or hid themselves with humility and patience, employing themselves in base and humble works, *will afterwards be " the first,"* because, in the eyes of Almighty God, they were very fervent and pure. As also it will come to pass, that some of those who here appeared just will be damned for sinners, and others who seemed sinners will be exalted amongst the just. Hence I will take warning and consider how I live, and desire to be the " first," not in the eyes of men, but in the eyes of Almighty God, who sees all, and who will judge me, not respecting the high nor the low place which I hold in the opinion of men. And I will likewise draw forth affections of fear, trembling at the judgments of Almighty God, and the lot which will befall me; for it may happen that I may be to-day " the first," and by my fault to-morrow, " the last."

2. Ponder, secondly, the other part of the sentence: " *Many are called, but few are chosen.*" For even as amongst the men of this world, who are called by Almighty God to receive His faith and grace, the most part are sinners who resist this calling, and but few just who consent to it, and remain elect for the Kingdom of heaven; —even so amongst the just who are called to a perfect life, there are very many who resist this calling, and live in lukewarmness, contenting themselves with mediocrity, and few are the "chosen" and perfect, because always what is precious is also rare.

Colloquy.—O infinite God, who callest and invitest

all to follow perfection, I beseech Thy divine majesty to augment the number of the chosen, to the end there may be many perfect, as Thou art perfect; grant, Lord, that I may be one of those, answering promptly to my vocation, so that in me and by me Thou mayst be glorified, world without end. Amen.

MEDITATION LV.

ON THE PARABLE OF THE VINEYARD.

POINT I.

"There was a man, an householder, who planted a vineyard, and made a hedge round about it, and dug in it a press, and built a tower, *and let it out to husbandmen*, and went into a strange country."(1)

1. Consider first, the *sovereign providence of Almighty God in the vineyard of His Church*, which shines eminently in three things, figured by the *hedge*, the *press*, and *tower*.

i. The "*hedge*" is the *protection of the angels*, who encompass and defend it from the Devil, and hinder the wild beasts of persecution from entering and laying it waste,"(2) keeping every one with such particular care, as if he alone were the whole vineyard. But a much more strong hedge is the protection of God Himself, who is the " keeper of little ones,"(3) guarding them with the succour of His inspirations, and encompassing them with precepts, fortified with promises of great rewards to those that keep them, and with threatenings of terrible punishments to those that break them.

ii. The "*press*" *is the multitude of sacraments and sacrifices*, in which are *gathered the blood of Jesus Christ*, pressed and strained with the tree of the cross, in virtue of which

(1) Mat. xxi. 33.   Is. v. 2.   (2) Ps. lxxix. 14.   (3) Ps. cxiv. 6.

He imparts the pardon of sins, and the wine of charity. And of them all the principal is the most holy Sacrament, and sacrifice of the altar, in which this divine press-man laid down His own body and blood, to inebriate us with the wine of His love. The "press" is also the divine law, with its commandments and counsels of perfection, the end of which is the pure wine of charity, separated from the sour verjuice of earthly things, and from the lees of our faults, presssed with the press and stone of mortification and penance, and with the weight of humiliation and obedience.

iii. The "*tower*" *is the special providence of our great God*, who foresees the things which are to come for the good of His Church, and for the good of every soul in it. It is also the temple and house of prayer, in which we invoke the name of our Lord, which " is a strong tower" (4) for our defence;—as also the multitude of prelates, and masters, and doctors, who like watchmen keep this vine, lest wild beasts spoil it, or foxes destroy it.(5)—Lastly, this "tower" is the high and sovereign doctrine of the Sacred Scripture, and of the Gospels, by means of which our heart is raised from earthly to heavenly things, and like the tower of David, is furnished with offensive and defensive weapons, of great counsels, and remedies against the temptations and molestations, both public and secret, of our enemies.

Colloquy.—O sovereign Father of the family, I give Thee thanks for the good which Thou hast done to this vineyard, which Thou hast planted with Thine own hand,(6) and since Thou hast placed me therein, take me under Thy protection and safeguard : inebriate me with the wine of Thy love, gladden my soul in the house of prayer, govern me by means of Thy

(4) Prov. xiii. 10.   (5) Cant. ii. 15.   (6) Psal. lxxix. 6.

ministers, and give me light to make my profit of Thy doctrine in such a manner that I may attain the perfection to which it disposes us.

2. God our Lord *let out this vineyard* to labourers and farmers, who are men: He does not sell it them, but only lets it out for rent, because He will retain the dominion Himself, and He requires us to cultivate it, that it may produce fruit of benediction; of which every one is to cultivate and prune the part which is allotted to him, which is his own soul, and the souls of those who are in his charge.

And the agreement being made, it is said, that "He went into a strange country:" to give us to understand that He treats with us as one absent, leaving us to our own liberty, without forcing us, and as if He did not see us, although He actually sees all things, and is in every place. With these considerations, speaking to myself, I will say:

Colloquy.—Endeavour to be liberal to Almighty God, as God is to thee, and seeing God has made thee farmer of so precious a " vineyard," render Him abundant fruit, making thy profit of the " hedge," " press," and " tower," which are in it. And since He makes Himself as absent to prove thy fidelity, serve Him as faithfully as if thou sawest Him, that thou mayest come to see Him as thou desirest. O most liberal God, who requirest rent of me for this vineyard, not for Thine own profit, but for mine, grant that I may bring forth abundant fruit, not for my glory, but for Thine, world without end. Amen.

POINT II.

" And when the time of the fruits drew nigh," the householder " sent his servants to the husbandmen, that they might receive the fruits thereof." But they *treated them evilly and killed the servants.* He seeing this, "sent to them his son, saying: They will reverence my son: but they seeing him, said: This is the heir, come let us kill him, and we shall have his inheritance. And taking him, they cast him forth out of the *vineyard and killed him.*" (7)

1. Meditate on the *providence of Almighty God towards these husbandmen,* soliciting them to good by sundry means; and the abominable malice of these husbandmen against Almighty God, treading them all under their feet, keeping in mind that the time of fruit is only during the course of this mortal life; for, after the end of this world, and the death of every one, there is no time to fructify more. For which reason St. Paul says, "whilst we have time let us work good to all men," (8) and that which is good for our own souls, and for our neighbours, because, if the time once be passed, we shall remain without remedy.

This presupposed, I will consider the *infinite charity of this our Father of the family,* who is God, who at all times is careful to *send patriarchs, and prophets, and preachers,* to exhort the husbandmen to labour for the good of their souls. And although these men were so rebellious, and so treacherous, as wickedly to illtreat and kill these prophets and preachers, yet He, out of His infinite bounty, instead of punishing these murderers, gave them His only begotten Son, made man, that He might come in person to preach to them, and exhort them: but so much did the malice of the husbandmen of that time increase, that they attempted to kill the Only-begotten Son, and to cast Him out of that vineyard which was His own, delivering Him to the Gentiles, by whom He suffered Himself like a most meek lamb to be taken, scourged and crucified, without the city of Jerusalem, and with His most precious blood

(7) Mat. xxi. 34.   (8) Gal. vi. 9.

He would water this vineyard, that it might bring forth fruit in greater abundance.

Colloquy.—O eternal Father, what profit dost Thou receive from the fruits of this vineyard, that Thou so sendest Thy Son to solicit the "husbandmen," knowing how ill they would entreat Him? O Son of the living God, wherefore dost Thou love this vineyard so much, as that Thou seekest to die for it? O excessive love of the Son of God! Now I see, O my Lord, how truly Thou saidst,—" What is there that I ought to do more to my vineyard that I have not done to it?"(9) Verily, Thou didst all that Thou couldst in making Thyself man, and dying for man; but man, ungrateful and rebellious, could not do greater evil than what he did, destroying Thy life, resisting Thy preaching, and revolting with the goods which Thou hast given him. But all this invites me to love Thee so much the more, and to labour to render Thee the fruit I owe Thee, doing all that I am able in Thy service, as Thou hast done for my profit.

3. Consider the *daily care which God our Lord has to admonish me*, to be solicitous of "the vineyard" of my soul, sometimes by the means of preachers, and spiritual masters, and sometimes by His invisible servants, which are His inspirations; although I am so wicked that oftentimes I illtreat and choke the spirit which incited me to good, and smother the remorse of conscience which reprehended me, and crucify within me the Son of God, (10) casting Him out of my heart to give entrance to sin. And though the bounty of the eternal Father has been such, that He would have His own Son to remain in the midst of "the vineyard" of His Church, in the Holy Sacrament of the Altar, that respecting His presence, I may animate myself to dress and cultivate my soul, yet this has not been sufficient to make me do it.

(9) Is. v. 4.   (10) Hebr. vi. 6.

Colloquy.—O rebellious hardness, O ungrateful rebellion, O abominable ingratitude of my heart, why dost thou not become mollified with so many favours to serve our Lord as thou oughtest, of whom thou receivest so many good things? Assist me, O my Saviour, with Thy holy grace, to begin from this moment a new life. Amen.

POINT III.

The parable being proposed, Jesus demanded of the Jews:—When "the Lord of the vineyard shall come, what will he do to those husbandmen? They say to him, He will bring those evil men to an evil end:" that is to say, *will punish them rigorously*, and *will let out his vineyard to other husbandmen* that shall render him the fruit in due season. " Therefore I say to you," replied Jesus Christ, " *that the Kingdom of God shall be taken from you*, and shall be given to a nation yielding the fruits thereof." (11)

1. Almighty God is just in His judgments, since even His enemies *pronounce that sentence against themselves which He was to pronounce;* and how abominable the malice of man is against Almighty God, since even he who commits it reproves and condemns the same in a third person, pro. nouncing against himself the same judgment which God was justly to pronounce against him, to chastise him as he deserved.

Colloquy.—O Father of mercy, and just judge, temper Thy just anger with Thy great mercy, and if Thou wilt convince us with such parables, let it not be to condemn us, like these Pharisees, but that, knowing our faults like David, we may do penance for them.(12)

2. Reflect on the *terrible but just chastisement* with which *Christ* threatened the Jews, saying, that He would take the Kingdom of God from them, which is the same

(11) Mat. xxi. 40.　　　　(12) 2 Reg. xii. 17.

vineyard, together with its "hedge," "press," and "tower," abandoning them for their perverseness to utter destruction. He took from them the right which they had to the sacraments and sacrifices, to the sacred books and laws of the Kingdom of the Messiah, transferring all to the Gentiles, out of whom He has gathered together His Church.

Colloquy.—Wherefore, O my soul, take thou heed by other men's harms, before the punishment come upon thee. Behold how Almighty God abandons those who abandon Him, and knows how to transfer His faith from one kingdom to another; and kingdoms and dignities from one person to another, taking them away from those that possess them, and putting others in their place. And if one fail in the faith and Religion which he professes, He calls innumerable others, (13) who preserve it and bring forth fruits thereof: hold fast that which thou hast, " that no man take thy crown."(14)

MEDITATION LVI.

ON THE PARABLE OF THOSE WHO WERE INVITED TO THE MARRIAGE AND TO THE SUPPER.

These two parables may be meditated together, on account of the great similitude they have betwixt them, and because they may be addressed to one and the same end.

POINT I.

" The Kingdom of heaven is likened to a *king who made a marriage for his son*, and sent to call them that were invited to the marriage." (1)

1. The eternal Father, King of heaven and earth, of His mere bounty and mercy, *would that His On'y-begotten Son*

(13) Job xxxiv. 24. (14)Apoc. iii. 11. (1) Mat. xxii. 1; Luc. xiv. 16.

should espouse human nature, uniting it with Himself in unity of person, endowing it with great jewels of grace and virtue, such as beseemed the spouse of a Son, who in all things was equal to His Father.

Colloquy.—O Sovereign Father, what moved Thee to will that Thy Son should espouse Himself to a spouse so vile and deformed ?   Was not the nature of angels far more noble and more beautiful ?   Wherefore then didst Thou, O Lord, leave this, and match with that ?   If it were because it was more vile, more deformed, and in more necessity, as indeed it was, then art Thou not deceived : but then in this I see the excess of Thy charity, which inclines itself more to honour, and remedy those who were most despised, and in most necessity.   Let all Thy creatures praise Thee for this, and let my soul dissolve itself in Thy praises.

2. But the bounty of this our celestial Father passed yet much further, forasmuch as He likewise would, that His Son, true God and true Man, should *espouse* (2) *and celebrate a marriage with the Church,* (3) which is the company of the faithful, joining to Him the souls of the just, by the union of charity, and adorning them with such virtues as were suitable to the spouse of so sovereign a King.

Colloquy.—Acknowledge, O my soul, the dignity to which God Almighty will exalt thee : wash thyself with penance, anoint thyself with devotion, adorn thyself with celestial virtues, that thou mayest be received for the spouse of this heavenly husband.

3. But the bounty of our God stays not here:—for if this favour had been offered only to a few souls, and those of persons very noble, very learned, or of great expectation, it would be without doubt a singular benefit; but yet it is

(2) Osee ii. 19; 2 Cor. xi. 2.   (3) Eph. v. 23—25, &c.

much greater, but He calls many to have part in this marriage, without excluding any man, although he be vile, ignorant, or a great sinner, even although he have oftimes broke the fidelity of this divine marriage.

Colloquy.—O immense ocean of the charity of God, how do I not go forth of myself, considering the depth of this charity? O my soul, animate myself to accept this divine marriage, which is offered to thee, which will change thee from foul to fair, from vile to noble, from poor to rich, and from earthly to heavenly.

POINT II.

To solemnize these espousals, as well the King of heaven as Jesus Christ Himself, made a solemn banquet, and a great supper, which being prepared, He sent His servants to call them that were invited to the marriage.

1. Consider the *greatness of this banquet*, and of this *supper*, which Almighty God prepared for men, in which three dishes, or three sorts of meat, very precious, are served up.

i. The first is, *celestial and divine doctrine* for the sustenance of the *understanding*, illuminated with faith, which feeds itself with this food, when it hears the word of God, or reads devout and sacred books, or when it meditates them by itself alone, Almighty God communicating to it great light and taste.

ii. A dish of *admirable precepts and counsels*, and of great perfection for the sustenance of the will, desirous of salvation, which incorporates this meat, when it accomplishes the will of God in all the things which He commands and counsels, infusing an exceeding joy into this generous obedience.

iii. *Sacraments, full of great efficacy*, to communicate His grace, His celestial gifts and virtues, which quicken, sustain, and perfect souls, amongst which the principal is, the most Holy Sacrament of the Altar, in which the same spouse, Jesus Christ, true God and true man, gives His body really and truly for meat under the species of bread, and His blood for drink, veiled under the species of wine, for the nourishment and support of souls that receive it, and to unite them with Himself as spouses, with the union of perfect love.

Colloquy.—O sovereign banquet, O great supper, far excelling all those which have been, or ever will be ! Oh how " blessed are they that are called to the marriage supper of the Lamb,"(4) where the Lamb of God, " who taketh away the sins of the world," is He that invites, is the banquet, is He that gives to eat, and He that is eaten, purifying with this meat him that eats it, and filling him with the delight of heaven. Open then thine eyes, O my soul, and consider that thou art called, not to tears, but to weddings and banquets. And if thou wert called to tears, it is that thou shouldst bewail thy sins, and the little preparation which thou hast for such a banquet, and by this means thou shalt make thyself worthy to be present at it.

2. *All the men in the world are invited to eat of these three dishes*, and are called to it by means of the preachers, which are the "servants" of "the King," and of the spouse, and by secret inspirations, to the end that they may come to the banquet. And so when I shall feel an interior touch within my heart, which may move me to the exercise of the three things before mentioned, I am to understand that Almighty God calls me, in order that I may be present at His banquet, and rejoice me in His delights.

POINT III.

Many of the "invited," would not come to the banquet,

(4) Apoc. xix. 9.

but "went their ways, one to his farm, and another to his merchandise, and the rest laid hands on His servants, and having treated them contumeliously, put them to death." (5)

1. Consider here, how *those who excused themselves* from going to the supper, were *three*, each taking for his excuse, *the vices to which they were addicted*, which are those which St. John, in his first canonical epistle, calls "the concupiscence of the flesh, and the concupiscence of the eyes, and the pride of life." (6)

"The first said to him, I have *bought a farm*, and I must needs go out and see it, I pray thee hold me excused. And another said, I have *bought five yoke of oxen*, and I go to try them, I pray thee, hold me excused. And another said, *I have married a wife*, and therefore I cannot come." He said not "hold me excused :" to signify, that the delight of marriage, had made him drunk, and out of himself. Now, if that delight of the flesh, which is lawful of itself, be an hindrance to a man if he be too much addicted to it, how much more does that hinder, which is unlawful and forbidden by the law of God?

2. Hence I may understand, which of these vices so detains me, that I go not to this banquet, nor delight to hear the doctrine of Jesus Christ, nor to read or meditate, nor to put it in practice, nor to receive His sacraments: and knowing the same, I will endeavour to take away the impediment, answering to the divine vocation, for fear of falling in the sentence of the same Lord, against those rebels, when He says: "none of those men that were invited, shall taste of my supper," who by the just judgment of Almighty God, which He permits in chastisement of their rebellions, die without the sacraments, or without profit from them, and come to be excluded from the supper, (7)

(5) Luc. xiv. 18; Matt. xxii. 5, 6. (6) 1 Joan. ii. 16. (7) Mat. xxii. 5.

and banquet, which Almighty God has prepared in heaven, for those that obey Him here on earth.

Colloquy.—Tremble, then, O my soul, at this sentence, and if love incite thee not to go to this supper, let fear terrify thee, lest thou be for ever excluded.

3. Lastly, *those who most shamefully killed the servants* who called them, are those *who abhor preachers and confessors,* and those which reprehend their vices, and counsel them what they ought to do; from whom with the sword of their tongue, they take away their honour and good name, and as much as is in them, their life of body and of soul. Against these the King of heaven, "was angry" vehemently, because to the sin of not coming to the banquet, they added another, to abuse His messengers: and so their punishment will be, not only to be excluded from the supper, but to be massacred and consumed with all that they have, the pain increasing, as the fault increases.

Colloquy.—O eternal King, mollify the hardness of rebellious Jews, of heretics, and infidels, who resist Thy inspirations, and kill Thy servants, who call them to Thy weddings and banquets; bridle, Lord, their anger, and have mercy on them.   Amen.

POINT IV.

"Then He saith to His servants, The marriage, indeed is ready, but they that were invited, were not worthy: Go ye therefore into the high ways, and *as many as you shall find, call to the marriage.* And His servants going into the ways, gathered together all that they found, both *good and bad,* and the marriage was filled with guests." (8)

1. Ponder here, the *liberality and charity of Almighty God,* who forsakes not mankind, although many contemn His banquets, and His favours, and even the principal of

(8) Mat. xxii. 9.

the world, most learned, and most advanced, who ought to be more respectful : but seeing that these are unworthy of His benefits, by reason of their sins, He will call with a most effectual vocation, *the vile* and contemned of the world, and such who have nothing in the world which possesses their heart.

2. *He admits "both good and bad,"* that is to say, such as are of good or evil nature, good or evil inclination, to the end that all may become good and holy, rejoicing in His banquet, although afterwards, some of them become evil; and which is more to be wondered at, in particular, He commanded to be called, "the poor, and the feeble, and the blind, and the lame," and if these were not sufficient, He was willing to call others forth, of "the highways, and hedges, and compel them to come in :" (9) not by force of arms, but by the force of miracles and reasons, and by the force which the good and holy life of the preacher works. And the same Lord Himself interiorly, with the light of His divine and effectual inspirations, compels them to come, with great delight and will, submitting themselves to that which He desires.

Colloquy.—O Father of mercy, who will force no man to serve Thee against his will, force me, O Lord, by this interior force, which may change my rebellious will, and with great delight make it obedient to Thine. Thou seest, O sovereign Father, that this world is full of " blind," " lame," " feeble," and miserable sinners, who see not by what way they are to walk to the marriage, and have not feet to go, nor forces either to begin, nor sufficiency to continue. O my God, I know right well that Thou art ready to give them whatsoever they stand in need of: but yet I beseech Thy bounty, that Thou wilt indeed give the light of faith to " the blind," feet of right intention to " the lame,"

(9) Luc. xiv. 21—23.

force to " the feeble," and sufficiency of grace, to such as be beggars, compelling them with the sweet force of Thy inspiration, to obey Thy holy vocation.

3. The house and table of Almighty God *is filled with such as "were invited,"* for He never wants means to accomplish His designs, and to fill up the number of the elect:—because if some resist, He knows, He can, and He will call others, in such a manner, as they will not resist. So that I have no cause to fear that the house and dwelling of Almighty God will remain unpeopled, when God will people it, nor the houses of Religion want people to be called to them, since it is Almighty God who founded them, and who is to call those who are to enter into them.   Hence I will draw motives of comfort, to behold such miserable falls as I see in the world, trusting in the providence of our celestial Father, that He will repair the same, by the means best known to His wisdom, although I cannot comprehend them.

POINT V.

"And the King went in to see the guests," that were sat at the table, "and He saw there *a man who had not on a wedding garment,* and he saith to him, Friend, how camest thou in hither, not having on a wedding garment? *But he was silent.*" (10)

1. *It suffices not to consent to the divine calling,* and to come to the banquet and supper, with the virtue of faith only, but that it is *also necessary* to come with the "wedding garment," which is *charity and purity of life,* which make a man "worthy" to be present at this banquet, and to be agreeable to Almighty God, who invited him. With this "garment," must he be attired who is to take the food of doctrine, of obedience to the law, and of the sacra-

(10) Mat. xxii. 11.

ments, especially of the body and blood of Jesus Christ our Lord, and he that has it not, ought to go to the sacraments so disposed, that by means of them he may receive it.

2. The *King of heaven* at the end of the marriage and banquet, that is to say, at the end of the world, or else at the end of each one's life, *will come to see all the guests, and to judge their works and life*, beholding if there be amongst them any one, who has not been present with that dignity and decency which was convenient, that we may chastise him severely, as he chastised those who would not come to the banquet: for as they offend Him who refuse to come, even so *they* offend Him who come, and have not on "them" the "garment" of charity, and of purity of life, but are present with an old garment, patched and polluted with many sins.

3. *From this judgment none can escape*, and this is the cause, that although there are many evil, who damn themselves, yet Christ our Lord only says, that He saw *one* without the nuptial garment;—to give us to understand, that although among all the Christians of the world, there were but one only evil, and who communicated sinfully, or kept not the law of Almighty God, even this one could not be hid, because the eyes of Almighty God would discover him, and condemn him. To give us moreover to understand, that condemnation is so terrible an evil, that although amongst all the Christians, one only were to be condemned, this were sufficient that all should fear and tremble with dread, not knowing whether himself should be that one; how much more, seeing they are *many*, because our Lord immediately added:—"Many are called, but few are chosen."(11) For they that come to the banquet, are "few," and those who are found there, with

(11) Mat. xxii. 14.

their "wedding garment," are "few," in respect of innumerable others, who resist the divine vocation.

4. Ponder, *the terribleness of the reprehension given by Jesus Christ*, not in hatred of the person, but *for the zeal of justice*, against sin, and the obstinate sinner: and for this cause, He calls him, "Friend," saying to him, "Friend, how camest thou in hither?" Who made thee so bold as to enter in, with a garment so torn and filthy? O what great confusion shall the accursed sinner suffer, seeing himself reprehended by Christ, in the presence of His angels, and remain so convinced that he become dumb, not knowing what to answer.

Colloquy.—O good Jesus, reprehend me in this life with mercy, so that I may hold my peace with humility, and receive Thy correction for my amendment, and may obtain the life eternal.   Amen.

POINT VI.

" Then the King said to the waiters, *Bind his hands and feet, and cast him into exterior darkness*, where shall be weeping and gnashing of teeth.   For many are called, but few are chosen."(12)

1. Ponder here the *terribleness of the sentence*, and the pains which it contains, which are four.

i. The first is, *the perpetual prison*, without any hope or means to issue forth.   This, the binding of "hands and feet," denotes in such a manner that he cannot undo them, in chastisement of the dissoluteness with which he lived in this life.

ii. The second is, *obstinacy in evil*, without having any more the liberty to do good works, signified by the "hands," nor of good affections, signified by the "feet," in punishment, because in this life he had both "hands and feet"

(12) Mat. xxii. 13.

bound with the chains of his passions and disordered affections.

iii. The third is, "*exterior*" *and terrible darkness* as well of the soul by the privation of the sight of Almighty God, and obscurity of judgment, darkened with its own misery, as also with the exterior darkness of the fire of hell, which fire will burn and not give light, as has been said in its place.

iv. The fourth is, *perpetual "weeping and gnashing of teeth :"* because he will weep, remembering the banquet, at which he was, and the helps and conveniences which he had to save himself, which he of his carelessness neglected, and made no use of so good an occasion. He will likewise weep for the misery which he now endures, and this "weeping" will be accompanied with "gnashing of teeth," for the rage and impatience which he will have in his torments, seeing himself without any hope of ever escaping from them.

2. All this the Lord will command the ministers, and executioners of His justice, which are the devils, who laying hold on this wretched guest, will pluck him out of the banqueting house, which is the Church, and will throw him into the prison of hell, which is his dwelling.

Colloquy.—O eternal King, and most just judge, whose judgments are right, although most terrible to the wicked; I present myself before Thy majesty with my "hands and feet" bound, not with the chains of obstinacy, but with the chains of obedience, resolved not to resist what so Thou commandest; confirm, Lord, this will with the chains and bonds of charity, that being constant in loving and obeying Thee, I may come to see Thee, and to enjoy Thee world without end. Amen.

MEDITATION LVII.

ON THE TEN VIRGINS.

POINT I.

"Then shall the Kingdom of heaven be *likened to ten virgins*, who, taking their lamps, went out to meet the bridegroom and the bride: and *five of them were foolish, and five wise*. But the five foolish having taken their lamps, did not take oil with them. But the wise took oil in their vessels, with their lamps."(1)

1. *In the Church, there are both just and sinners*, figured by these "ten virgins," and the one and the other, expect the coming of Christ our Lord, to judge them, and to celebrate "the marriage" with His spouse, the Church triumphant. All these furnish themselves, both with faith and works, common to Christians, as touching that which appertains to a Christian exteriorly, but yet in a different manner; for some are "wise," and furnish themselves of all that is necessary for the coming of "the bridegroom:" others are "foolish," who, providing themselves with some things, omit other things more necessary.

2. *"The foolish," are like the five unwise virgins*, who have "lamps," but with little oil in them, neither have they in vessels, with which to fill them: that is to say, they have faith, and not charity; they have the light of truth, and not the "oil" of virtues;—they have "lamps," which shine with exterior works, and not the fervent affections of interior works;—have sometimes sensible devotion, and tears which endure for a little while, but not interior and substantial devotion, which lasts long;—have virginity and integrity of body, but not purity and

(1) Mat. xxv. 1.

integrity of spirit;—make profession of perfection, and have many imperfections, with sinister and earthly intentions. Finally, they content themselves, to enjoy the good which lasts no longer than this present life, and leave that which is to last for the life to come in all eternity; and consequently when death comes, find themselves unprovided, of what were necessary for receiving "the bridegroom." Now what greater folly can there be, than to expect, with so little preparation the coming of a judge so rigorous, and of a "bridegroom," who has so sharp an eye, that pierces into both the interior and exterior, and is not content with exterior things, if they want the interior virtue.

Colloquy.—O sovereign judge and amiable bridegroom of my soul, deliver me, I beseech Thee, from this foolishness, and suffer not that I content myself to do the half of that which Thou commandest me, but to fulfil it entirely. Amen.

3. *The prudent are like "the wise" virgins* which have their lamps full of oil, and their vessels well provided for to fill them, being empty: because they have faith and charity, the light of verities and virtues, exterior and interior works, purity of body and of soul, and finally, all that good which endures to everlasting life. They content themselves not with "faith" alone, which is to "cease," nor with that which is pleasing and agreeable to men, which ends in death, but study to have the wisdom of spirit, and piety, which is profitable to all things, and "charity, which never falls away,"(2) and the nuptial robe,(3) which is so pleasing to the spouse.(4)

Colloquy.—O prudence and discretion worthy of Christian men, who work as they believe, and prepare

(2) 1 Tim. iv. 6; 1 Cor. xiii. 8.   (3) Mat. xxii. 11.
(4) Ephes. v. 29.

themselves, so that they may receive what they hope for. O God of my soul, give me this prudence and discretion, that I may in such a manner prepare and dispose the "lamp" of my heart with the light of verities, and "oil" of heroic virtues, that I may have what is necessary and sufficient to expect Thy coming, and to appear in Thy presence without confusion.

POINT II.

"And the bridegroom, tarrying," all the ten virgins "slumbered and slept, and *at midnight there was a cry made: Behold the bridegroom cometh*, go ye forth to meet Him."(5)   (He calls sleep a light slumber, which by and by passes; and in this sense will we use this word.)

1. *The coming of the bridegroom, as it seemed to all men, was very long*, because all imagine that their life will be long, and that it is far from hence to death, and to the judgment that is to be made then: whence it proceeds that the good sleep the sleep of slumbering, suffering their heads to incline to venial sins; and the evil sleep the sleep of mortal sin, utterly careless of the coming of the judge.

Colloquy.—O sovereign judge, deliver me from this sinful sleep, suffer not my soul to slumber, for fear that she fall into a deadly sleep. Grant that she do not neglect many light sins, for fear lest she fall into those that are great. Awake thee, O my soul, who sleepest, and cry to Jesus Christ, that He raise thee up, and quicken thee with His copious grace, by which thou mayest live everlastingly. Amen.

2. "They all *slumbered and slept*," because all men fall into sicknesses, age, feebleness, or some other like cause, which disposes them to the sleep of death; and finally, all come to sleep this last sleep, nor can any person escape the same. And death is called sleep, because as heavy

(5) Mat. xxv. 5, 6.

sleep oppresses and overcomes us, whether we will or no, and for the time deprives us of the use of our senses, and of all delectable things of this life: so also does death. And as seeing a picture I remember me of the thing it represents;—even so, as often as sleep seizes upon me, or that I go to lie down, I will endeavour to remember me of my death, which I will, as often as I can, set before my eyes; and then, seeing the bed in which the body sleeps is covered, I will remember me of the grave in which the dead body will be covered.

3. At midnight this clamorous voice sounded: "*Behold the bridegroom cometh, go ye forth to meet him.*" For on the sudden, and when we least think of it, we shall be called to judgment, which is made at the end of the life of every one, as to the universal, which is to be made at the end of the world. And notwithstanding that He who " comes," is the spouse of just souls, yet is He also judge, and so presents Himself adorned like a bridegroom to the good, and with the rigour of a judge to the wicked; He comes like a " bridegroom," to cherish and enrich those whom He shall find well disposed and prepared, and to exclude and drive forth those whom He shall find ill prepared.

Colloquy.—O my soul, let this dreadful voice, at the least, sound in thy ears, and endeavour to be ready, since thou knowest "not the day nor the hour" in which it will sound. When sickness shall touch thee, imagine it to be the sound of His voice, in order that thou mayest prepare thee, since thou knowest not what will happen to thee ; and to hear it then with security, hear it also when thou goest to communicate, imagining that it says to thee : " Behold," thy spouse " cometh, go forth to meet Him" with due preparation, since He comes to espouse thee to Him, in mercy and charity.

POINT III.

" Then all those virgins," hearing the voice, "arose and trimmed their lamps; and *the foolish* said to the wise, *Give us of your oil*, for our lamps are gone out. The wise answered, saying, *Lest perhaps there be not enough for us and for you*, go ye rather to them that sell and buy for yourselves. Now, whilst they went to buy, the bridegroom came, and they that were ready, went in with him to the marriage."(6)

1. *Both the good and evil must rise again*, and *appear at the general judgment:* and before this also, as soon as they are dead, they will open their eyes, as if they awaked from the sleep of this mortal life, and will find themselves presented to their particular judgment;—and every one will carry with him his lamp, according as he had prepared it in this life, either with oil or without oil, with little, or with much; because his works, whether good or evil, are to follow him, even such as they were in this world, and according to them will he be judged.(7)

2. It is certain that the *evil and foolish in that hour will find themselves deceived,* and acknowledge their folly, seeing their lamps out for lack of oil; and although they have recourse to the good to crave mercy and intercession, there will be none who will intercede and speak for them, as every one has enough to do for himself, and because the time of intercession for others is expired, they will even say to them by way of scorn; " Go and buy" of those that sell: which is to say,—" You have thought too late of making your provision, for now you find none that can give or sell to you; nor can you buy, because the hour of buying is wholly past."

Colloquy.—O my soul, be wise buying in time this

(6) Mat. xxv. 7.   (7) Apoc. xiv.

oil, forasmuch as Almighty God is ready to sell it thee, and He Himself will give to thee wherewith to buy it, which is so to give to thee, that it shall cost thee nothing.(8)　He invites thee with His grace and charity, with His virtues and celestial gifts, and He will give thee disposition meet to obtain them, preventing thee with His divine inspirations.　Hear then betimes what He inspires into thee, and do what He commands thee :—now thou hast intercessors who will pray for thee, and their prayers will be admitted, the sacred Virgin our Blessed Lady, the Apostles, the Martyrs, and the saints of heaven, with all the angelical choirs, will be thy advocates: have then now recourse to this multitude of prudent spirits, which all will favour thee during this life, for after this life, neither will they, nor can they.

3. The spouse coming to judgment, *all the pure and prudent souls* which are prepared, with the preparation which they have gained in this life, *will be admitted to the celestial wedding*, in the company of their sweet spouse.

Colloquy.—Oh, what contentments will they find for having prepared themselves in time ! Oh, what joyfulness to see themselves with Him whom they have so greatly loved ! Oh, what sweetness, and what comfort will they receive to see their celestial spouse face to face, and to embrace Him with beatifying love, and to eat with Him at His table, the meat of the divinity, and to drink of the river of His delights ! Oh, how resplendent will the lamp of their soul be with the light of His glory ! How ardent with the fire of His charity ! How devout and joyful with the " oil " of divine consolation ! How secure, no more to want the protection of God ! Oh, happy labours, which conduct to so precious a repose.

(8) Is. li. 1 et seq.

POINT IV.

The bridegroom entering with the wise virgins, "the door was shut : But at last came also the other virgins, saying : Lord, Lord open to us. But *He answering, said, Amen I say to you, I know you not.*"(9)

1. *At the day of the universal judgment, "the door" of heaven "is shut,"* in such manner that it will *never more be opened,* to cast him forth who once is entered, because his glory will be perpetual, so long as God shall be God, rejoicing everlastingly in His company, without fear or doubt of losing the same. Sometimes in this life, Almighty God brings us "into the cellar of" His "wine,"(10) or into His closet and retreat, and visits and comforts us with His inspirations, but always leaves the "door" open, and when we least think of it, either He turns us out, or we go out of ourselves; but entering into heaven, the "door" is "shut," in such a manner, that neither God will cast me forth, nor shall I myself go forth.

Colloquy.—O happy and blessed entrance! O secure place! Grant, O my God, that I may enter into this celestial " cellar," and into this cabinet of the Blessed, to be always with Thee, rejoicing with them. Amen.

2. This "door" is "shut" *against all those who are not ready at the hour of death to enter;* and if they be once excluded, it will never be opened again to them. And although they lament and cry, craving of God to "open" it to them, they will not be heard, but He will say to them: "I know you not," nor approve your lives, I know not these voices, nor will admit them. "Depart from me you that work iniquity,"(11) condemned to eternal fire.

(9) Mat. xxv. 10—12.　　(10) Cant. ii. 4.　　(11) Mat. 7; Luc. 13.

Colloquy.—O my soul, what dost thou hearing this! How dost thou not tremble for fear! Is it possible that if once in the judgment of death, thou be excluded from heaven, thou wilt remain for ever banished from thence!—That thou wilt never enter to see God!—That thy Creator will not acknowledge thee, but treat thee as a stranger and His enemy!—That thou art for ever to be inclosed in the obscure and dark dungeon of hell! O merciful God, spouse of souls, moderate the just indignation which Thou hast against me, acknowledge me, since I am Thy creature, made according to Thy image and likeness, and Thy slave, bought with the price of Thy precious blood. I confess, O Lord, that it is no wonder if Thou acknowledge me not, since by my innumerable sins I have blotted out that which Thou hast imprinted in me; and since I have not known Thee, nor acknowledged by my life Thy holy commandments, I have well deserved that Thou neither acknowledge nor approve me for Thy Paradise; I deserve not that Thou hear my cries, with which I beseech Thee to "open to" me the gates of heaven, since I would not hearken to Thine, with which Thou criedst to me, to open to Thee the gate of my heart. Notwithstanding, since all our life is a time of mercy, behold here the gates of my heart set wide open to receive Thee; open to me those of heaven, to receive me there, where I may see Thee and enjoy Thee, world without end. Amen.

3. Ponder finally, the conclusion of this parable, which is its end and intent, in these words:—"*Watch ye therefore, because you know not the day nor the hour;*(12) This I should hold imprinted in my memory, since, as St. Mark the Evangelist relates: "they are spoken to all, and every one in particular."(13) I will therefore stir up and awake myself with them, saying:—

(12) Mat. xxv. 13.　　　(13) Mar. xiii.

Colloquy.—O my soul, "watch" in prayer and penance, and in the continual exercise of good works ; and if thou "sleep" by lukewarmness, awake thyself by and by with diligence, because thou knowest not if this present hour shall be the last of thy watching, in which thou wilt be called to the wedding ;—and if thou be unprovided, thou wilt for ever be excluded ;— and if provided, thou wilt for ever be admitted, that so thou mayest rejoice with thy spouse, Christ Jesus, for ever and ever.   Amen.

MEDITATION LVIII.

ON THE TALENTS, AND THE POUNDS.

POINT I.

The Kingdom of heaven is "even as *a man going into a strange country*, who called his servants, and *delivered them his goods;* and to one he gave five talents, and to another two, and to another one, and to every one according to his proper ability."(1)

Consider here,—1. *what talents* these are ;—2. *who delivers* them ;—3. *to whom* they are delivered ;—4. *in what manner ;*—5. and *to what end.*

1. The first talent is, *necessary and convenient knowledge to purchase our own salvation,* and our neighbours', with all that which may serve to this end, and may be divided into five sorts of things.

i. The first comprehends *the gifts and natural parts,* as well of body as of soul : as health, bodily strength, ability, wit, liveliness of senses, and above all, natural light of reason, which is common, as well to Infidels as to the Faithful, and discovers to us good and evil, inclining itself to follow the good, and to fly the evil.

(1) Mat. xxv. 14.

ii. The second, comprehends those gifts and *parts which are got by human industry*, as riches, honours, dignities, sciences, liberal arts, moral and political virtues : all which are also gifts of our Lord, and may assist to our salvation.

iii. The third, comprehends the *supernatural virtues*, common to the faithful, as well good as evil: as the light of faith, and the virtue of hope, and the right to frequent the sacraments of the Church, by which they obtain grace and everlasting salvation.

iv. The fourth, comprehends the *same grace and charity*, with the virtues and gifts which accompany the same, with which we procure the increase of merits, and of everlasting rewards.

v. The fifth, comprehends all *the graces given gratis*, which are *ordained for the edification of the Church*, and for the salvation of our neighbour, as the grace to understand the sacred Scriptures, to preach and to teach; the gift to give counsel, to convert souls, with other offices of the Church ordained for this end; of all which things are composed divers and sundry talents, which are delivered to men.

2. *He who distributes them is God* our Lord, because they are all His goods, and proceed from His liberal hand. He gives the goods of nature, the goods of fortune, the goods of grace, and to Him they are all due; and whosoever will attribute these goods to himself, excluding God, is both proud and unworthy of them, and God will chastise him, by taking them from him, as ungrateful. It is, therefore, just that we give Him thanks for all, praising Him for the liberality with which He imparts to His slaves the goods He has, only to do them good, and because He is good, and loves to impart what He has to others.

3. *These talents are given to men in three degrees*, signified by the three servants.—To the one, Almighty God gives

talents in great abundance, signified by the number of *five*. —To others, He gives *in a mean degree*, signified by the number of *two*.—To others, He gives *the least degree*, signified by the number of *one:* in this He does not wrong to any person, for He owes nothing to any, and to whom nothing is due, honour is done him if *anything* be given him. Besides, it ought to suffice, that God will have it so, and so ordains by His providence : and for this respect alone I should hold it for good, and content me with it.

4. These talents are given to every one, *according to his proper ability*, that is to say,—according to the capacity and possibility which they have, in order to the end for which the talents are ordained and delivered, so that God our Lord overcharges no man with a greater burden than He sees he is able to bear, nor obliges him to more than he is able to do. And so in the distribution and delivery of the talents, He considers the natural forces and disposition of the party, as well that which he has of his own complexion, as that which he has gotten by industry, by the means of divine inspiration, which always prevents us, and assists with sweetness, to dispose us to receive those supernatural talents, and to the good employment of them.

5. *The end of these talents, is to procure with them our salvation*, and that of *our neighbours*, conformable to our capacity. This is that which He said more clearly in the Gospel of St. Luke, to the servants, to whom He delivered the ten pounds. :—"Trade till I come;" (2) as if He had said :—"consider that I give not to you this money, in order to be idle, nor that you should prodigally spend it, but that you should trade with it, and draw gain." So that He prohibited two vices in the use of the talents,—one, of idleness and laziness, not using them because of neg-

<hr>

(2) Luc. **xix.**

ligence;—another, of prodigality, dissipating them without discretion, and with danger of losing them.

And that they might be industrious, He adds: "*till I come*," assuring them that He would come to take an account; but would not tell them *what time* He would come, that they might traffic all that time, till He came.

Colloquy.—O Redeemer of the world, who, " ascending on high," hast given " gifts to men,"(3) distributing amongst Thy disciples sundry talents and graces for their good, and for the good of the Church, give me that " Spirit" which proceeds from Thee, whereby I may know those things(4) which Thou hast given me ; for unless I know Thy talents, I can neither be thankful to Thee for them, nor " trade" with them ; wherefore, make me to know them with humility, so that I deceive not myself, supposing they be more or greater, than indeed they are. Grant me likewise, O Lord, to be content with those which Thou hast given me ; in such manner, that I neither despise through pride those who have less, nor envy those who have more, aiming only to give Thee contentment, with that much or little which Thou hast given me. Grant me, also, that I always be mindful of Thy coming to take an account, to the end I may incessantly procure that which I would have wished to have procured. Let no day pass without my doing somewhat, since it displeases Thee if I remain any moment idle, so that death, finding me piously exercised, Thou mayest admit me into Thy holy Kingdom. Amen.

POINT II.

" And he that had received the *five* talents went away and traded with the same, and *gained other five.* And in like manner, he that had received the *two, gained other two.* But he that had received *one*, going his way, digged into the earth, and *hid his Lord's money.*" (5)

---

(3) Ephes. iv.   (4) 2 Cor. ii. 10.   (5) Mat. xxv, 16.

1. *Great or little spiritual merit consists* not so much in the talents received, as *in the great or little care* and diligence in *trafficing and negociating with them,* because he who received "five talents," might as well have hid them in the earth by slothfulness, as "he that had received the one;" and "he that had the one" might "trade" and double his as soon as those who received more. So that the slothful, through his own default, does not "trade," but the fervent profits by his diligence, cooperating with the grace of Almighty God, which prevents and assists his free will. And to declare this more evidently, the parable of St. Luke the Evangelist says, that with one pound one gained ten, another five;—whereby is to be seen, that the profit proceeds from diligence, but yet assisted by grace. This they confessed, when they said:—"Lord, thy pound hath gained ten pounds;" (6) as if he had said, "Not I," (7) but I in virtue thereof, and more it than I.

Colloquy.—Wherefore, O my soul, consider well what thou dost set thy hand to work, because the hand of God our Lord will always go accompanying thine, and His "mercy" will prevent thee, and will assist thee, and "will follow thee all the days of" thy "life,"(8) if thou hinder it not through thy default.

2. Christ our Lord proposed this example of the *fervent and the diligent, in the person of him who "received the five talents,"* and in him who received *two;* forasmuch as ordinarily those who have received great sums, receive great spirit and confidence to labour: and like rich merchants, venture upon great employments and "gain" much, provided that it be with humility, attributing their fervour not to their free will, but principally to the grace of Almighty God, as did the apostle St. Paul, when he said:— "I have laboured more abundantly than they all, yet not

(6) Luc. xix. 17.   (7) 1 Cor. xv. 10; Psal. lviii.   (8) Psal. xxii.

I, but the grace of God with me." (9)   And on the other
hand, Christ our Lord put the example of the slothful in
him "that had received one talent;" because those who
have but small "ability," if they be not very humble, are
ordinarily complainers, envious, and pusillanimous, and so
render themselves to slothfulness.   These have other
talents of the world and of the flesh, and employ themselves in seeking for earthly goods, and bury under this
earth the talent which they have received, to procure the
gifts of heaven.

Colloquy.—O God of my soul, oh, that I had used
as much care in trading, according to my ability, for
the goods eternal, as worldly merchants use in manag-
ing their temporal affairs ! Suffer not, O Lord, that I
bury such precious talents under so vile a cover ; help
me to use them and to double and redouble them with
great gain, since Thou hast set no stint in them.

3. The industrious merchant is to "trade" and traffic
with all the talents he has, and with every one of them,
because of all and of every one of them he must render
account, and the more he has received, of so much more
must he render account, if he does not traffic with them,
because as St. Gregory says, (10) "As much as the gifts of
God increase, so much the obligation increases to give a
reckoning of them."

POINT III.

"But after a long time, the lord of those servants came
and reckoned with them. And he that had received the
five talents, coming, brought other five talents, saying:
Lord, thou didst deliver to me five talents, behold, I have
gained other five over and above. His lord said to him:
Well done, good and faithful servant; because thou hast

(9) 1 Cor. xv. 10.   (10) Hom. 9, in Evang.

been faithful over a few things, I will set thee over many things: *enter thou into the joy of thy Lord.*" (11) And the like passed with him that received " the two talents," who " gained other two."

1. *The coming of Christ our Lord to take a reckoning* of His servants, *was,* " *after a long time,*" both because the coming to the general judgment is deferred for many days, as also to signify that He gives to every servant leisure and time enough to procure what is necessary for his salvation, in such a manner that no man can complain that he wants time to convert himself to God, if himself will; and if when he has will to be converted life fails him, the fault is his own, because he had time enough before to purchase the eternal.

2. Consider the great *confidence and security* which the *fervent* have at the hour of death and final reckoning, which they render well, because they see what they have " received," and what they " have gained," and to say confidently:—" Thou didst deliver to me five talents, behold I have gained other five over and above," augmenting the gifts which I have received of Thy grace, and gaining with them other new gifts. O fortunate fervour, which causes such assurance in time of so great fear.

3. Consider the *reward which Christ our Redeemer gives to him,* qualifying him for a good and faithful servant;— " good," because he lived holy, keeping the law of Almighty God,—" faithful," because he used faithfully the gifts and graces which he had received, which, although great in themselves, yet were but little in respect of the eternal, and for this cause said :—" Because thou hast been faithful over a few things," as that is which passes in this mortal life, " I will place thee over many things" in the Kingdom of heaven, and will do thee many and great

(11) Mat. xxv. 21.

favours, "enter thou into the joy of thy Lord," engulf thyself into the abyss of His celestial delights, that thou mayest be full within and without, and replenished with joy, drinking of the copious torrent of "His pleasure," (12) until thou hast drunk thy full satiety.

Colloquy.—O joy immense! joy eternal! joy worthy of Almighty God! O blessed purchase, in which is the joy of heaven, which no man can take from us!(13)

4. He used the *same words to him who with " two talents" had gained " other two,"*—to give us to understand that in the payment of heaven, the diligence of the work is more respected than the number of talents; and if he who receives "two" labour so much as to make his of equal value with him "that receiveth five," he will receive equal reward; notwitstanding this, he who travails most, and most augments the talents received, shall be most rewarded. This Christ our Lord declared more plainly in the parable of the pounds; for to him who with "one" alone gained " ten," because his diligence was the greater, He gave " ten cities." And to him who with "one" gained " five," because he had used less diligence, He gave only " five."

Colloquy.—Wherefore, O my soul, labour at all times with all possible fervour, for God has " many mansions" in the Kingdom of heaven, and if with one pound or talent thou canst deserve " ten cities," that is to say, ten most excellent degrees of glory, do not content thyself with " five ;" not so much for thine own interest, as to love Him so much the more, who is worthy to be beloved with an infinite love for ever and ever. Amen.

POINT IV.

"But he that *received the one talent*, came and said,

(12) Psal. xxxv. 9.   (13) Joan. xvi. 22.

Lord, I know that thou art a hard man, thou reapest where thou hast not sown, and gatherest where thou hast not strewed, and being afraid, I went and hid thy talent in the earth. *Behold, here thou hast that which is thine.*" (14)

1. In this discourse is represented to us *the malice of the slothful servant*, who, to cover his slothfulness feigned difficulties and terrible dangers, and feared where there was no cause to fear, as many do now-a-days. Some bury in the the earth " the talent" of prayer and contemplation, and leave it off for fear of being deceived;—others " hide the talent" of preaching and converting souls, fearing lest they should lose their own;—others, worse, cease to keep the commandments of the law, feigning them to be very severe, and that they have not forces for them, taxing God with hardness towards them, because He will gather fruit where He hath not sowed, and without affording them sufficient force, will that they fructify in good works. O abominable blindness ! O cursed slothfulness, which to excuse thyself darest to blame Almighty God !

Colloquy.—O my Redeemer, quite contrary to this " wicked servant" do I say, that I know Thee right well to be a man, not " hard," but soft, not cruel, but merciful, not seeking to reap " where Thou hast not sown," for unless Thou first sowedst the seeds of Thy talents, it were impossible to gather any fruits ; and Thou art so far from seeking to gather where Thou didst not sow, that many times Thou sowest much, and gatherest little, and Thy gentleness is such, that Thou contentest Thyself with very little gain.

2. To this saying our Lord replied:—" Wicked and slothful servant, thou knewest that I reap where I sow not, and gather where I have not strewed, thou oughtest

therefore to have committed my money to the bankers, and at my coming I should have received my own with usury. Take ye away therefore the talent from him, and give it him that hath ten talents. For to every one that hath shall be given, and he shall abound: but from him that hath not, that also which he seemeth to have shall be taken away. And the unprofitable servant cast ye out into the exterior darkness, there shall be weeping and gnashing of teeth." (15)

3. In this sentence there'are three terrible things to be considered.

i. The first is, the *severe reprehension of our Lord*, to the great confusion of the evil servant. For what confusion can be greater than to be termed by Almighty God, and before His angels, for a " wicked," "slothful," " uupro- fitable," and unfaithful "servant?" And what disgrace greater than to be convinced by his own reasons. " Ex ore tuo, te judica serve nequam." "Out of thy own mouth I judge thee, wicked servant."(16) "If thou knewest that I gather fruit where I sow not, how much more oughtest thou to know that I will gather fruit of the talent which I gave thee?"

ii. The second was, to " *take from him*" *the talents which he had*, and to despoil him of all the gifts of grace, and of all other supernatural qualities bestowed on him, in chas- tisement of his slothfulness, which Almighty God some- times does even in this life, chastising those who use not well the talents they have received, by taking them from them, in the same manner as He suffers him sometimes to lose his faith who used it evilly; but in the other life they are deprived of it without any remedy, as has been con- sidered in the first part, and ninth meditation. And to say that it is given to him who had "gained five talents,"

(15) Mat. xxv. 26.   (16) Luc. xix.

is to say that the saints receive an accidental glory from all things, as well from the use of their own talents, as from the joy which they have of those which God imparts liberally to others, as also for those which he justly takes away.

iii. The third was, to " *cast*" *him* " *out into the exterior darkness*" *of hell*, where he will deplore and rage for his unprofitable sloth. And if such chastisement will be given to him who, for slothfulness, used not the talent he had received, what chastisement shall be given to him that uses it to offend Almighty God, and scandalise or damage his neighbour?

Colloquy.—O eternal God, just and holy judge, " enter not into" rigorous "judgment with" me, because I know that upon my own words Thou mayest justly condemn me. I have deserved that Thou shouldst take from me the talents which Thou gavest me for having hidden them in the ground, but since of Thy mercy Thou hast suffered me till now, help me to dig them out of the ground, that since with them, as Thou desirest, I may obtain what Thou promisest, and reign with Thee, world without end. Amen.

END OF VOL. III.

RICHARDSON AND SON, DERBY.